PEARS
BOOK OF
WINNERS
AND
CHAMPIONS

PEARS

BOOK OF

WINNERS

AND

CHAMPIONS

Edited by Dr Chris Cook

Sports Editor: Tony Johnson

Pelham Books
London

PELHAM BOOKS

Published by the Penguin Group
27 Wrights Lane, London W8 5TZ
Viking Penguin Inc., 375 Hudson Street, New York, New York 10014, USA
Penguin Books Australia Ltd, Ringwood, Victoria, Australia
Penguin Books Canada Ltd, 10 Alcorn Avenue, Toronto, Ontario, Canada M4V 3B2
Penguin Books (NZ) Ltd, 182–190 Wairau Road, Auckland 10, New Zealand
Penguin Books Ltd, Registered Offices: Harmondsworth, Middlesex, England

First published in 1994

Filmset by Datix International Limited, Bungay, Suffolk
Printed in England by Clays Ltd, St Ives plc
Set in Plantin Light and Helvetica

A CIP catalogue record for this book is available from the British Library

ISBN 0 7207 2038 9

The moral right of the author has been asserted

CONTENTS

LIST OF ILLUSTRATIONS

PREFACE

This first edition of the *Pears Book of Winners and Champions* aims to provide an informative and fact-packed compendium, a wide-ranging, authoritative and yet often amusing book of equal value for reference and for pleasure. In compiling this book, the aim has been to span the whole range of human activities, from the glamorous worlds of sport and show business through literature and music to subjects as varied as cars and cameras, food and wine, the Magic Circle and tiddlywinks.

The entries range from such internationally-renowned prizes as the Oscars and Nobels to the Eurovision Song Contest and the CAMRA Beer of the Year; sports enthusiasts will find a wealth of results, Olympic and international, as well as purely British; pop music fans will find the latest rock and pop awards – to name just a few of the categories included.

Each competition is arranged under a main heading (e.g. all the film awards are under Cinema) but the comprehensive index at the end of the book should be consulted if in any doubt. Nationalities of individuals are included, where appropriate, in brackets after the name (see list of abbreviations of countries, p. 11). Joint winners are indicated by a bracket.

Inevitably, no book of this kind can be comprehensive. Indeed, in some subjects such as literature, cinema and television, or the world of music, a whole book could be filled with their numerous awards. Hence, given so much material available and in attempting to give a wide-ranging book that will appeal to all members of the family, the editor has had to be selective. There has not always been enough space to list winners from every year that the competition has been running, in which cases the editor has selected recent years. The editor has attempted to give the latest available results at the time of going to press but in some cases minor gaps inevitably occur when reliable information is not always to hand. It is hoped that the overall contents of the volume are representative as well as informative. The editor would welcome suggestions for additional entries and would be grateful for any information concerning updated entries to include in the next edition of this book.

ACKNOWLEDGEMENTS

The appearance of this book owes a great debt to a very large number of people. Countless information officers and secretaries of a host of organizations, many of them replying voluntarily in their spare time, supplied much of the information that provided the basis of entries contained in this book.

I have received tremendous help in compiling this book from specialists in particular areas. Tony Johnson provided all the material for the sports sections. Don Hawes undertook a similar task for literature and the arts. Neil Sinyard gave great assistance on cinema and television. Michel Petheram and Pat Smith helped enormously with the media entries and music. David Cook in Blaby helped monitor the press for announcements of winners and competitions. Vange Bute masterminded the vast numbers of enquiries sent out to sponsors and event organizers. Others I must thank include Harry Harmer, Jane Leonard and John Stevenson. For their help in compiling the sports sections particular mention should be made of Barry Hugman, editor of the British Boxing Board of Control Yearbook, Matthew Engel, editor of *Wisden Cricketer's Almanac* and Jeff Fletcher of the Press Connection.

For their secretarial help I am very grateful to Pamela Beattie, Linda Hollingworth and Michele Regan. A special debt is due to my colleagues at Pelham Books, in particular to Anne Askwith and Chris Beith. Finally, James Robinson helped in innumerable ways to preserve something of my sanity whilst this book was being produced.

Chris Cook
London
8 August 1994

ABBREVIATIONS OF COUNTRIES

Alb	Albania	Gua	Guatemala	Phi	Philippines
Alg	Algeria	Guy	Guyana	PNG	Papua New Guinea
Ant	Antigua				
Arg	Argentina	Haw	Hawaii	Pol	Poland
Aus	Australia	HK	Hong Kong	Por	Portugal
Aut	Austria	Hol	Holland	PuR	Puerto Rico
		Hun	Hungary		
Bah	Bahamas			Rom	Romania
Bar	Barbados	Ice	Iceland	Rus	Russia
Bel	Belgium	Ina	Indonesia		
Bls	Belarus	Ind	India	SAf	South Africa
Bra	Brazil	Ira	Iran	Sco	Scotland
Bul	Bulgaria	Ire	Ireland	Sen	Senegal
		Isr	Israel	SKo	South Korea
Can	Canada	Ita	Italy	Som	Somalia
Chi	Chile			Spa	Spain
Chn	China	Jam	Jamaica	SRho	Southern Rhodesia
CIS	Commonwealth of Independent States	Jap	Japan	StL	St Lucia
		Kaz	Kazakhstan	Sur	Suriname
Col	Colombia	Ken	Kenya	Swe	Sweden
CoR	Costa Rica	Kor	Korea	Swi	Switzerland
Cub	Cuba				
Cze	Czechoslovakia	Lat	Latvia	Tai	Taiwan
		Lie	Liechtenstein	Tha	Thailand
		Lit	Lithuania	Tib	Tibet
Den	Denmark	Lux	Luxembourg	Tjk	Tajikistan
DoR	Dominican Republic			Tri	Trinidad
		Mex	Mexico	Tun	Tunisia
Ecu	Ecuador	Mor	Morocco	Tur	Turkey
Egy	Egypt	Moz	Mozambique		
Eng	England	Mya	Myanmar	Uga	Uganda
Est	Estonia			UK	United Kingdom
Eth	Ethiopia	Nam	Namibia	Ukr	Ukraine
		Nic	Nicaragua	Uru	Uruguay
Fin	Finland	Nig	Nigeria	USA	United States of America
Fra	France	NIre	Northern Ireland		
FRG	Federal Republic of Germany	NKo	North Korea	VirI	Virgin Islands
		Nor	Norway		
		NViet	North Vietnam	Wal	Wales
GB	Great Britain	NZ	New Zealand		
GDR	German Democratic Republic			Yug	Yugoslavia
		Pak	Pakistan		
		Pan	Panama	Zai	Zaire
Gha	Ghana	Par	Paraguay	Zam	Zambia
Gre	Greece	Per	Peru	Z	Zimbabwe

PEARS
BOOK OF
WINNERS
AND
CHAMPIONS

AGEING

THE 'OLDIE' AWARDS

The last of these entertaining and often highly humorous satirical awards was made on 20 January 1994 at the 'Oldie of the Year' lunch in London. Among the awards, dreamed up by Richard Ingrams, editor of *The Oldie*, were:

Oldie of the Year
Judge Stephen Tumim, sixty-three, for his prison report calling for an end to 'slopping out'

Wannabee Oldie of the Year
Jeremy Paxman, forty-three, presenter of *Newsnight*, for the failure of his attempt to join the Garrick Club

Letting the Side Down (Special Award)
Joan Collins, sixty(ish), who walked out of an interview when asked her age. Author of *How to Stay Young*

Oldie 'Back to Basics' Award
Francis Urquhart, the duplicitous Prime Minister played by Ian Richardson in the BBC TV series *House of Cards*

Oldie Prince Consort Award
Sir Denis Thatcher for 'services to Maggie', notably his role in escorting Lady Thatcher during thousands of engagements without saying anything

AMERICAN FOOTBALL

SUPERBOWL

The SuperBowl is awarded to the winner of the game between the Champions of the American Football Conference and the National Football Conference, the two bodies that make up the Professional game in the USA.

1967	Green Bay Packers	1981	Oakland Raiders
1968	Green Bay Packers	1982	San Francisco 49ers
1969	New York Jets	1983	Washington Redskins
1970	Kansas City Chiefs	1984	Los Angeles Raiders
1971	Baltimore Colts	1985	San Francisco 49ers
1972	Dallas Cowboys	1986	Chicago Bears
1973	Miami Dolphins	1987	New York Giants
1974	Miami Dolphins	1988	Washington Redskins
1975	Pittsburgh Steelers	1989	San Francisco 49ers
1976	Pittsburgh Steelers	1990	San Francisco 49ers
1977	Oakland Raiders	1991	New York Giants
1978	Dallas Cowboys	1992	Washington Redskins
1979	Pittsburgh Steelers	1993	Dallas Cowboys
1980	Pittsburgh Steelers	1994	Dallas Cowboys

SuperBowl MVPs

The MVP is the Most Valuable Player in the SuperBowl as chosen by the press on the day of the game.

1967	Bart Starr (QB), Green Bay Packers	1981	Jim Plunkett (QB), Oakland Raiders
1968	Bart Starr (QB), Green Bay Packers	1982	Joe Montana (QB), San Francisco 49ers
1969	Joe Namath (QB), New York Jets	1983	Joe Riggins (RB), Washington Redskins
1970	Len Dawson (QB), Kansas City Chiefs	1984	Marcus Allen (RB), Los Angeles Raiders
1971	Chuck Howley (LB), Dallas Cowboys	1985	Joe Montana (QB), San Francisco 49ers
1972	Roger Staubach (QB), Dallas Cowboys	1986	Richard Dent (DE), Chicago Bears
1973	Jake Scott (S), Miami Dolphins	1987	Phil Simms (QB), New York Giants
1974	Larry Csonka (RB), Miami Dolphins	1988	Doug Williams (QB), Washington Redskins
1975	Franco Harris (RB), Pittsburgh Steelers	1989	Jerry Rice (WR), San Francisco 49ers
1976	Lynn Swann (WR), Pittsburgh Steelers	1990	Joe Montana (QB), San Francisco 49ers
1977	Fred Biletnikoff (WR), Oakland Raiders	1991	Ottis Anderson (RB), New York Giants
1978	Randy White (DT) & Harvey Martin (DE), Dallas Cowboys	1992	Mark Rypien (QB), Washington Redskins
1979	Terry Bradshaw (QB), Pittsburgh Steelers	1993	Troy Aikman (QB), Dallas Cowboys
1980	Terry Bradshaw (QB), Pittsburgh Steelers	1994	EmmittSmith(RB),DallasCowboys

HEISMAN TROPHY

The Heisman Trophy is awarded by the press to the most promising player on the US College Football circuit.

1935	Jay Berwanger (Chicago)	1949	Leon Hart (Notre Dame)
1936	Larry Kelley (Yale)	1950	Vic Janowicz (Ohio State)
1937	Clint Frank (Yale)	1951	Dick Kazmaier (Princeton)
1938	Davey O'Brien (Texas Christian)	1952	Billy Vessels (Oklahoma)
1939	Nile Kinnick (Iowa)	1953	John Lattner (Notre Dame)
1940	Tom Harmon (Michigan)	1954	Alan Ameche (Wisconsin)
1941	Bruce Smith (Minnesota)	1955	Howard Cassady (Ohio State)
1942	Frank Sinkwich (Georgia)	1956	Paul Hornung (Notre Dame)
1943	Angelo Bertelli (Notre Dame)	1957	John Crow (Texas A & M)
1944	Les Horvath (Ohio State)	1958	Pete Dawkins (Army)
1945	Doc Blanchard (Army)	1959	Billy Cannon (Louisiana State)
1946	Glenn Davis (Army)	1960	Joe Bellino (Navy)
1947	John Lujack (Notre Dame)	1961	Ernie Davis (Syracuse)
1948	Doak Walker (Southern Methodist)	1962	Terry Baker (Oregon State)
		1963	Roger Staubach (Navy)

1964	John Huarte (Notre Dame)	1979	Charles White (USC)
1965	Mike Garrett (USC)	1980	George Rogers (South Carolina)
1966	Steve Spurrier (Florida)	1981	Marcus Allen (USC)
1967	Gary Beban (UCLA)	1982	Herschel Walker (Georgia)
1968	O.J. Simpson (USC)	1983	Mike Rozier (Nebraska)
1969	Steve Owens (Oklahoma)	1984	Doug Flutie (Boston College)
1970	Jim Plunkett (Stanford)	1985	Bo Jackson (Auburn)
1971	Pat Sullivan (Auburn)	1986	Vinny Testaverde (Miami)
1972	Johnny Rogers (Nebraska)	1987	Tim Brown (Notre Dame)
1973	John Cappelletti (Penn State)	1988	Barry Sanders (Oklahoma)
1974	Archie Griffin (Ohio State)	1989	Andre Ware (Houston)
1975	Archie Griffin (Ohio State)	1990	Ty Detmer (Brigham Young)
1976	Tony Dorsett (Pittsburgh)	1991	Desmond Howard (Michigan)
1977	Earl Campbell (Texas)	1992	Gino Toretta (Miami)
1978	Billy Sims (Oklahoma)	1993	Charlie Ward (Florida State)

ANGLING

WORLD FRESHWATER CHAMPIONSHIPS

Individual

		1975	Ian Heaps (Eng)
1957	Mandeli (Ita)	1976	Dino Bassi (Ita)
1958	Garroit (Bel)	1977	Jean Mainil (Bel)
1959	Robert Tesse (Fra)	1978	Jean-Pierre Fourgeat (Fra)
1960	Robert Tesse (Fra)	1979	Gérard Heulard (Fra)
1961	Ramon Legogue (Fra)	1980	Wolf-Rüdiger Kremkus (FRG)
1962	Raimondo Tedasco (Ita)	1981	Dave Thomas (Eng)
1963	William Lane (Eng)	1982	Kevin Ashurst (Eng)
1964	Joseph Fontanet (Fra)	1983	Wolf-Rüdiger Kremkus (FRG)
1965	Robert Tesse (Fra)	1984	Bobby Smithers (Ire)
1966	Henri Guiheneuf (Fra)	1985	Dave Roper (Eng)
1967	Jacques Isenbaert (Bel)	1986	Lud Wever (Hol)
1968	Günter Grebenstein (FRG)	1987	Clive Branson (Wal)
1969	Robin Harris (Eng)	1988	Jean-Pierre Fourgeat (Fra)
1970	Marcel Van den Eynde (Bel)	1989	Tom Pickering (Eng)
1971	Dino Bassi (Ita)	1990	Bob Nudd (Eng)
1972	Hubert Levels (Hol)	1991	Bob Nudd (Eng)
1973	Pierre Michiels (Bel)	1992	David Wesson (Aus)
1974	Aribert Richter (FRG)	1993	Mario Barros (Por)

Team

1957	Italy	1965	Romania	1973	Belgium
1958	Belgium	1966	France	1974	France
1959	France	1967	Belgium	1975	France
1960	Belgium	1968	France	1976	Italy
1961	East Germany	1969	Holland	1977	Luxembourg
1962	Italy	1970	Belgium	1978	France
1963	France	1971	Italy	1979	France
1964	France	1972	France	1980	West Germany

1981	France	1986	Italy	1991	England
1982	Holland	1987	England	1992	Italy
1983	Belgium	1988	England	1993	Italy
1984	Luxembourg	1989	Wales		
1985	England	1990	France		

ARCHERY

WORLD CHAMPIONSHIPS

Men's Team

1931	France
1932	Poland
1933	Belgium
1934	Sweden
1935	Belgium
1936	Czechoslovakia
1937	Poland
1938	Czechoslovakia
1939	France
1946	Denmark
1947	Czechoslovakia
1948	Sweden
1949	Czechoslovakia
1950	Denmark
1952	Sweden
1953	Sweden
1955	Sweden
1957	USA
1958	Finland
1959	USA
1961	USA
1963	USA
1965	USA
1967	USA
1969	USA
1971	USA
1973	USA
1975	USA
1977	USA
1979	USA
1981	USA
1983	USA
1985	South Korea
1987	West Germany
1989	USSR
1991	South Korea
1993	France

Men's Individual

1931	Michal Sawicki (Pol)
1932	Laurent Reith (Bel)
1933	Donald Mackenzie (USA)
1934	Henry Kjellson (Swe)
1935	Adriaan van Kohlen (Bel)
1936	Emil Heilborn (Swe)
1937	George De Rons (Bel)
1938	Frantisek Hadas (Cze)
1939	Roger Beday (Fra)
1946	Einar Tang Holbek (Den)
1947	Hans Deutgen (Swe)
1948	Hans Deutgen (Swe)
1949	Hans Deutgen (Swe)
1950	Hans Deutgen (Swe)
1952	Stellan Andersson (Swe)
1953	Bror Lundgren (Swe)
1955	Nils Andersson (Swe)
1957	Ozziek Smathers (USA)
1958	Stig Thysell (Swe)
1959	James Caspers (USA)
1961	Joseph Thornton (USA)
1963	Charles Sandlin (USA)
1965	Matti Haikonen (Fin)
1967	Ray Rogers (USA)
1969	Hardy Ward (USA)
1971	John Williams (USA)
1973	Viktor Sidóruk (USSR)
1975	Darrell Pace (USA)
1977	Richard McKinney (USA)
1979	Darrell Pace (USA)
1981	Kyösti Laasonen (Fin)
1983	Richard McKinney (USA)
1985	Richard McKinney (USA)
1987	Vladimir Yesheyev (USSR)
1989	Stanislav Zabrodskiy (USSR)
1991	Simon Fairweather (Aus)
1993	Kyung Mo Park (SKo)

Women's Team

1933	Poland
1934	Poland
1935	United Kingdom
1936	Poland
1937	United Kingdom
1938	Poland
1939	Poland
1946	United Kingdom
1947	Denmark
1948	Czechoslovakia
1949	United Kingdom
1950	Finland
1952	USA
1953	Finland
1955	United Kingdom
1957	USA
1958	USA
1959	USA
1961	USA
1963	USA
1965	USA
1967	Poland
1969	USSR
1971	Poland
1973	USSR
1975	USSR
1977	USA
1979	South Korea
1981	USSR
1983	South Korea
1985	USSR
1987	USSR
1989	South Korea
1991	South Korea
1993	South Korea

Women's Individual

1931	Janina Kurkowska (Pol)
1932	Janina Kurkowska (Pol)
1933	Janina Kurkowska (Pol)
1934	Janina Kurkowska (Pol)
1935	Ina Catani (Swe)
1936	Janina Kurkowska (Pol)
1937	Ingo Simon (UK)
1938	Nora Weston Martyr (UK)
1939	Janina Kurkowska (Pol)
1946	Nilla de Wharton Burr (UK)
1947	Janina Kurkowska (Pol)
1948	Nilla de Wharton Burr (UK)
1949	Barbara Waterhouse (UK)
1950	Jean Lee (USA)
1952	Jean Lee (USA)
1953	Jean Richards (USA)
1955	Katarzyna Wisniowska (Pol)
1957	Carole Meinhart (USA)
1958	Sigrid Johansson (Swe)
1959	Ann Corby (née Weber) (USA)
1961	Nancy Vanderheide (USA)
1963	Victoria Cook (USA)
1965	Maire Lindholm (Fin)
1967	Maria Maczynska (Pol)
1969	Dorothy Lidstone (Can)
1971	Emma Gapchenko (USSR)
1973	Linda Myers (USA)
1975	Zebiniso Rustamova (USSR)
1977	Luann Ryon (USA)
1979	Kim Jin-ho (SKo)
1981	Natalya Butuzova (USSR)
1983	Kim Jin-ho (SKo)
1985	Irina Soldatova (USSR)
1987	Ma Xiaojun (Chn)
1989	Kim Soo-nyung (SKo)
1991	Kim Soo-nyung (SKo)
1993	Hyo Jung Kim (SKo)

OLYMPIC GAMES

Men's Team

1988	South Korea
1992	Spain

Women's Team

1988	South Korea
1992	South Korea

Men's Individual

1972	John Williams (USA)
1976	Darrell Pace (USA)
1980	Tomi Poikolainen (Fin)
1984	Darrell Pace (USA)
1988	Jay Barrs (USA)
1992	Sebastian Flute (Fra)

Women's Individual

1972	Doreen Wilber (USA)
1976	Luann Ryan (USA)
1980	Keto Lossaberidze (USSR)
1984	Seo Hyang-Soon (SKo)
1988	Soo Nyang-Kim (SKo)
1992	Cho Youn-Jeong (SKo)

ARCHITECTURE

RIBA ARCHITECTURE AWARDS

The Royal Institution of British Architects has operated the annual RIBA Architecture Awards since 1966. The purpose of the awards is to give public recognition to outstanding examples of current architecture, and thereby to achieve greater public appreciation of good architectural design. Juries are asked to judge a building in its setting, the fitness for purpose, the consistency of design, the appropriate use of materials and whether it is likely to remain a fine example of architecture throughout its full working life. The Building of the Year was introduced in 1988 – the personal choice of the president from the year's National Awards.

Building of the Year

1988	St Oswald's Hospice, Newcastle-upon-Tyne (Jane and David Darbyshire)	1991	Broadgate Centre, London (Arup Associates)
1989	Nelson Mandela School, Birmingham (City of Birmingham Architect's Department)	1992	Sackler Gallery, Royal Academy of Arts, London (Sir Norman Foster & Partners)
1990	Queen's Inclosure, Hants (Hampshire County Council Architect's Department)	1993	Woodlea Primary School, Bordon, Hants (Hampshire County Council Architect's Department)

THE *FINANCIAL TIMES* ARCHITECTURE AWARD

Since 1967, the *Financial Times* has sponsored an award to encourage higher standards of architectural and environmental design for industrial and commercial buildings. The *Financial Times* Architecture Award (formerly the *Financial Times* Architecture at Work Award and the *Financial Times* Industrial Architecture Award) is recognized as one of the leading awards of its kind in the UK. It is for major new buildings that enhance both the urban or rural landscape of Britain and the lives of the people who work in them. Winners (over the last decade) have included:

1983	Gateway House, Basingstoke, Hants (Arup Associates)	1986	Control Building, Megget Reservoir, Selkirk, Scotland (W. J. Cairns & Partners and R. H. Cuthbertson & Partners (Engineers))
1984	Renault Centre, Swindon, Wilts (Foster Associates)		
1985	1 Finsbury Avenue, London (Arup Associates) Schlumberger Research Centre, Cambridge (Michael Hopkins & Partners)	1987	Lloyd's of London, Lime Street, London (Richard Rogers Partnership)
		1989	Courts of Justice, Truro, Cornwall (Evans & Shalev)

1991	RMC House, Egham, Surrey (Edward Cullinan Architects Ltd)	1993	Queen's Stand, Epsom Racecourse (Richard Horden of Richard Horden Associates for United Racecourses Ltd)

The Queen's Stand won the award for its 'stunning geometry and its pure, simple and disciplined design'. The judges were particularly impressed by the accommodation provided for the jockeys as well as the private boxes.

The design team included engineers Ove Arup & Partners, quantity surveyors Davis Langdon & Everest and contractors Willett Ltd (Trafalgar House).

National Awards

1991   Sterling Hotel, Heathrow, Terminal 4, Snowdon Road West, Heathrow Airport, Hounslow, Middx
(Manser Associates)
London Region

Charing Cross, 1 Embankment Place, London
(Terry Farrell & Co)
London Region

The Deckhouse, 9 Thames Reach, Rainville Road, London
(John Young)
London Region

Broadgate, Phase 1 – 4, Broadgate, London
(Arup Associates)
London Region

Cardiff Bay Visitors Centre, East of Pierhead Building, Bute Docks, Cardiff Bay
(Alsop Lyall & Stormer)
Wales Region

Imperium, Reading, Worton Drive, Worton Grange, Reading, Berks
(Bennetts Associates)
Southern Region

1992   Stansted Airport Terminal, Stansted Airport, Essex
(Sir Norman Foster & Partners)
Eastern Region

Bracken House, 1 Friday Street, London
(Michael Hopkins & Partners)
London Region

Blackwall Yard Phase One, Blackwall Way, London
(Richard Rogers Partnership)
London Region

Sackler Galleries, Royal Academy of Arts, Piccadilly, London
(Sir Norman Foster & Partners)
London Region

1993   Woodlea Primary School, Bordon, Hants
(Hampshire County Council Architect's Department)
Southern Region

Queen's Stand, Epsom Racecourse, Surrey
(Richard Horden Associates)
South East Region

The Fountains Abbey Visitor Centre, Ripon, N. Yorks
(Edward Cullinan Architects)
Yorkshire & Humberside Region

ART

THE ADAM & COMPANY/*SPECTATOR* ART AWARD

The first prize is £2000 and the winning work is purchased by Adam & Company (a private bank in Edinburgh, Glasgow and London) or a commission is given to the artist. The second prize is £1000 and the third prize is £500. The award began in 1988.

1988	Robert Morgan	1991	Richard Winkworth
1989	Hilary Daltry	1992	Paul Handley
1990	Kate Downie	1993	Douglas Hunter

BP PORTRAIT AWARD

There is a first prize of £10,000 with (at the judges' discretion) a commission worth £2,000 to be agreed between the National Portrait Gallery, London and the winning artist. There are second and third prizes of £4,000 and £2,000 respectively. All the shortlisted entries are annually exhibited at the gallery.

1980	Margaret Foreman	1988	Allan Ramsay
1981	Emma Sergeant	1989	Paula MacArthur
1982	Humphrey Ocean		Tai Shan Schierenberg
1983	Michael Taylor	1990	Annabel Cullen
1984	Rosemary Beaton	1991	Justin Mortimer
1985	Jeff Stultiens	1992	Lucy Willis
1986	Ivy Smith	1993	Philip Harris
1987	Alison Watt	1994	Peter Edwards

THE TURNER PRIZE

£20,000 is awarded to a British artist under the age of fifty for an outstanding exhibition or other presentation of his or her work in the preceding twelve months. It is intended to promote public discussion of new developments in contemporary British art. The prize is named after one of the most celebrated British artists, J. M. W. Turner (1775–1851). Originally sponsored by an individual, it is now sponsored by Channel 4, which annually televises the award. It is therefore highly publicized but is also much criticized for not celebrating what is usually considered to be traditional art.

1984	Malcolm Morley	1989	Richard Long
1985	Howard Hodgkin	1990	*prize suspended*
1986	Gilbert and George	1991	Anish Kapoor
1987	Richard Deacon	1992	Grenville Davey
1988	Tony Cragg	1993	Rachel Whiteread

Rachel Whiteread is a sculptor who makes concrete and plaster casts of the interiors of objects and buildings. Her cast of the interior of a small house stood for some time in the East End of London. The K Foundation, funded from the proceeds of a pop group, also awarded her a prize of £40,000, for 'producing the worst body of work in the preceding 12 months'.

ROYAL ACADEMY OF ARTS: SUMMER EXHIBITION PRIZES

A number of awards and prizes are given at the annual Summer Exhibitions. The Charles Wollaston Award, currently worth £10,000, is given by the President and Council for the most distinguished work in the exhibition. Charles Wollaston (1914–92), who established the fund for the award, was a painter, potter, teacher and collector of art.

Charles Wollaston Award

1980	Anthony Gross ARA, *Les Causses* (oil)	1988	Carel Weight RA, *The Invasion* (oil)
1981	Anthony Eyton ARA, *A Fireplace* (oil)	1989	Gillian Ayres ARA, *Full Fathom Five* (oil)
1982	Robert Buhler RA, *Water Meadow, Dusk* (oil)	1990	Patrick Symons ARA, *Mary Iliff's Viola, Played by Electric Light and Drawn by Gaslight* (oil)
1983	Victor Pasmore RA, *The Man Between* (oil)	1991	Neil Jeffries, *Piltdown Poetry* (mixed media)
1984	Norman Blamey RA, *Ruth* (oil)		
1985	Carel Weight RA, *Day of Doom* (oil)	1992	Sandra Blow RA, *Whisperings* (acrylic)
1986	Jeffery Camp RA, *Thames, 1986* (oil)	1993	Sir Eduardo Paolozzi RA, *The Road to the Isles* (bronze)
1987	John Bellany ARA, *Janus Concerto* (oil)	1994	Robert Medley RA *Preparing for the Execution*

PRUDENTIAL AWARD FOR THE ARTS

£75,000 is awarded to the overall winner from winners in five categories: music, theatre, dance, opera and visual arts. The competition is open to all professional arts organizations in the UK.

1989	Rambert Dance Company (dance)	1992	Dance Umbrella (dance)
1990	The Grizedale Society (visual arts)	1993	Shobana Jeyasingh Dance Company (dance)
1991	Scottish Chamber Orchestra (music)		

THE PAUL HAMLYN FOUNDATION AWARDS FOR ARTISTS

The Paul Hamlyn Foundation was created by the publisher, Paul Hamlyn, in 1972 and funds many projects in education, the arts and book publishing. It launched its Awards for Artists in 1993. Each year a different art form will be chosen, with cash awards of £12,000 to five individual artists. In 1993, the following five composers received the awards:

Sally Beamish	b. 1956. A violin concerto is among her forthcoming compositions
Simon Holt	b. 1958. His *Minotaur Games*, written for the Scottish Chamber Orchestra, has recently been premièred
Paul Newland	b. 1966. He writes mainly for traditional acoustic instruments
David Sawer	b. 1961. His works were performed at the 1991 and 1992 Proms
Andrew Simpson	b. 1968. His *Montage* was recorded in January 1993 for a broadcast by the BBC Symphony Orchestra

ASSOCIATION FOOTBALL

WORLD CUP

1930	Uruguay		1970	Brazil
1934	Italy		1974	West Germany
1938	Italy		1978	Argentina
1950	Uruguay		1982	Italy
1954	West Germany		1986	Argentina
1958	Brazil		1990	West Germany
1962	Brazil		1994	Brazil
1966	England			

OLYMPIC CHAMPIONSHIPS

1896	Denmark*		1956	USSR
1900	Great Britain*		1960	Yugoslavia
1904	Canada*		1964	Hungary
1908	Great Britain		1968	Hungary
1912	England		1972	Poland
1920	Belgium		1976	East Germany
1924	Uruguay		1980	Czechoslovakia
1928	Uruguay		1984	France
1936	Italy		1988	USSR
1948	Sweden		1992	Spain
1952	Hungary			

* Unofficial

EUROPEAN CHAMPIONS CUP

1955/6	Real Madrid		1975/6	Bayern Munich
1956/7	Real Madrid		1976/7	Liverpool
1957/8	Real Madrid		1977/8	Liverpool
1958/9	Real Madrid		1978/9	Nottingham Forest
1959/60	Real Madrid		1979/80	Nottingham Forest
1960/1	Benfica		1980/1	Liverpool
1961/2	Benfica		1981/2	Aston Villa
1962/3	A C Milan		1982/3	SV Hamburg
1963/4	Inter-Milan		1983/4	Liverpool
1964/5	Inter-Milan		1984/5	Juventus
1965/6	Real Madrid		1985/6	Steaua Bucharest
1966/7	Glasgow Celtic		1986/7	FC Porto
1967/8	Manchester United		1987/8	PSV Eindhoven
1968/9	A C Milan		1988/9	A C Milan
1969/70	Feyenoord		1989/90	A C Milan
1970/1	Ajax Amsterdam		1990/1	Red Star Belgrade
1971/2	Ajax Amsterdam		1991/2	Barcelona
1972/3	Ajax Amsterdam		1992/3	Marseille
1973/4	Bayern Munich		1993/4	A C Milan
1974/5	Bayern Munich			

EUROPEAN CUP-WINNERS CUP

1960/1	Fiorentina
1961/2	Atletico Madrid
1962/3	Tottenham Hotspur
1963/4	Sporting Lisbon
1964/5	West Ham United
1965/6	Borussia Dortmund
1966/7	Bayern Munich
1967/8	A C Milan
1968/9	Slovan Bratislava
1969/70	Manchester City
1970/1	Chelsea
1971/2	Glasgow Rangers
1972/3	A C Milan
1973/4	FC Magdeburg
1974/5	Dynamo Kiev
1975/6	Anderlecht
1976/7	Hamburg SV
1977/8	Anderlecht
1978/9	Barcelona
1979/80	Valencia
1980/1	Dynamo Tbilisi
1981/2	Barcelona
1982/3	Aberdeen
1983/4	Juventus
1984/5	Everton
1985/6	Dynamo Kiev
1986/7	Ajax Amsterdam
1987/8	Mechelen
1988/9	Barcelona
1989/90	Sampdoria
1990/1	Manchester United
1991/2	Werder Bremen
1992/3	Parma
1993/4	Arsenal

UEFA CUP

1957/8	Barcelona
1959/60	Barcelona
1960/1	A S Roma
1961/2	Valencia
1962/3	Valencia
1963/4	Real Zaragoza
1964/5	Ferencvaros
1965/6	Barcelona
1966/7	Dynamo Zagreb
1967/8	Leeds United
1968/9	Newcastle United
1969/70	Arsenal
1970/1	Leeds United
1971/2	Tottenham Hotspur
1972/3	Liverpool
1973/4	Feyenoord
1974/5	Borussia Moenchengladbach
1975/6	Liverpool
1976/7	Juventus
1977/8	PSV Eindhoven
1978/9	Borussia Moenchengladbach
1979/80	Eintracht Frankfurt
1980/1	Ipswich Town
1981/2	IFK Gothenburg
1982/3	Anderlecht
1983/4	Tottenham Hotspur
1984/5	Real Madrid
1985/6	Real Madrid
1986/7	IFK Gothenburg
1987/8	Bayer Leverkusen
1988/9	Napoli
1989/90	Juventus
1990/1	Inter-Milan
1991/2	Ajax Amsterdam
1992/3	Juventus
1993/4	Inter-Milan

EUROPEAN CHAMPIONSHIPS

1960	USSR
1964	Spain
1968	Italy
1972	West Germany
1976	Czechoslovakia
1980	West Germany
1984	France
1988	Holland
1992	Denmark

AFRICAN NATIONS CUP

1957	Egypt	1976	Morocco
1959	Egypt	1978	Ghana
1962	Ethiopia	1980	Nigeria
1963	Ghana	1982	Ghana
1965	Ghana	1984	Cameroon
1968	Zaïre	1986	Egypt
1970	Sudan	1988	Cameroon
1972	Congo	1990	Algeria
1974	Zaïre	1992	Ivory Coast

SOUTH AMERICAN CHAMPIONSHIPS

1916	Uruguay	1935	Uruguay	1957	Argentina
1917	Uruguay	1937	Argentina	1959	Argentina
1919	Brazil	1939	Peru	1963	Bolivia
1920	Uruguay	1941	Argentina	1967	Uruguay
1921	Argentina	1942	Uruguay	1975	Peru
1922	Brazil	1945	Argentina	1979	Paraguay
1923	Uruguay	1946	Argentina	1983	Uruguay
1924	Uruguay	1947	Argentina	1987	Uruguay
1925	Argentina	1949	Brazil	1989	Brazil
1926	Uruguay	1953	Paraguay	1991	Argentina
1927	Argentina	1955	Argentina	1993	Argentina
1929	Argentina	1956	Uruguay		

SOUTH AMERICAN CLUB CUP (*COPA LIBERRA DORES*)

1960	Peñarol (Uru)	1977	Boca Juniors (Arg)
1961	Peñarol (Uru)	1978	Boca Juniors (Arg)
1962	Santos (Bra)	1979	Olimpia (Par)
1963	Santos (Bra)	1980	Nacional Montevideo (Uru)
1964	Independiente (Arg)	1981	Flamengo (Bra)
1965	Independiente (Arg)	1982	Peñarol (Uru)
1966	Peñarol (Uru)	1983	Gremio (Bra)
1967	Racing Club (Arg)	1984	Independiente (Arg)
1968	Estudiantes (Arg)	1985	Argentinos Juniors (Arg)
1969	Estudiantes (Arg)	1986	River Plate (Arg)
1970	Estudiantes (Arg)	1987	Peñarol (Uru)
1971	Nacional Montevideo (Uru)	1988	Nacional Montevideo (Uru)
1972	Independiente (Arg)	1989	Nacional Medellin (Col)
1973	Independiente (Arg)	1990	Olimpia (Par)
1974	Independiente (Arg)	1991	Colo Colo (Chi)
1975	Independiente (Arg)	1992	São Paulo (Bra)
1976	Cruzeiro (Bra)	1993	Universitario Catolica (Chi)

ENGLISH LEAGUE

1888/9	Preston North End
1889/90	Preston North End
1890/1	Everton
1891/2	Sunderland
1892/3	Sunderland
1893/4	Aston Villa
1894/5	Sunderland
1895/6	Aston Villa
1896/7	Aston Villa
1897/8	Sheffield United
1898/9	Aston Villa
1899/1900	Aston Villa
1900/1	Liverpool
1901/2	Sunderland
1902/3	Sheffield Wednesday
1903/4	Sheffield Wednesday
1904/5	Newcastle United
1905/6	Liverpool
1906/7	Newcastle United
1907/8	Manchester United
1908/9	Newcastle United
1909/10	Aston Villa
1910/1	Manchester United
1911/2	Blackburn Rovers
1912/3	Sunderland
1913/4	Blackburn Rovers
1914/5	Everton
1919/20	West Bromwich Albion
1920/1	Burnley
1921/2	Liverpool
1922/3	Liverpool
1923/4	Huddersfield Town
1924/5	Huddersfield Town
1925/6	Huddersfield Town
1926/7	Newcastle United
1927/8	Everton
1928/9	Sheffield Wednesday
1929/30	Sheffield Wednesday
1930/1	Arsenal
1931/2	Everton
1932/3	Arsenal
1933/4	Arsenal
1934/5	Arsenal
1935/6	Sunderland
1936/7	Manchester City
1937/8	Arsenal
1938/9	Everton
1946/7	Liverpool
1947/8	Arsenal
1948/9	Portsmouth
1949/50	Portsmouth
1950/1	Tottenham Hotspur
1951/2	Manchester United
1952/3	Arsenal
1953/4	Wolverhampton Wanderers
1954/5	Chelsea
1955/6	Manchester United
1956/7	Manchester United
1957/8	Wolverhampton Wanderers
1958/9	Wolverhampton Wanderers
1959/60	Burnley
1960/1	Tottenham Hotspur
1961/2	Ipswich Town
1962/3	Everton
1963/4	Liverpool
1964/5	Manchester United
1965/6	Liverpool
1966/7	Manchester United
1967/8	Manchester City
1968/9	Leeds United
1969/70	Everton
1970/1	Arsenal
1971/2	Derby County
1972/3	Liverpool
1973/4	Leeds United
1974/5	Derby County
1975/6	Liverpool
1976/7	Liverpool
1977/8	Nottingham Forest
1978/9	Liverpool
1979/80	Liverpool
1980/1	Aston Villa
1981/2	Liverpool
1982/3	Liverpool
1983/4	Liverpool
1984/5	Everton
1985/6	Liverpool
1986/7	Everton
1987/8	Liverpool
1988/9	Arsenal
1989/90	Liverpool
1990/1	Arsenal
1991/2	Leeds United
1992/3	Manchester United
1993/4	Manchester United

FA CUP

1871/2	Wanderers
1872/3	Wanderers
1873/4	Oxford University
1874/5	Royal Engineers
1875/6	Wanderers
1876/7	Wanderers
1877/8	Wanderers
1878/9	Old Etonians
1879/80	Clapham Rovers
1880/1	Old Carthusians
1881/2	Old Etonians
1882/3	Blackburn Olympic
1883/4	Blackburn Rovers
1884/5	Blackburn Rovers
1885/6	Blackburn Rovers
1886/7	Aston Villa
1887/8	West Bromwich Albion
1888/9	Preston North End
1889/90	Blackburn Rovers
1890/1	Blackburn Rovers
1891/2	West Bromwich Albion
1892/3	Wolverhampton Wanderers
1893/4	Notts County
1894/5	Aston Villa
1895/6	Sheffield Wednesday
1896/7	Aston Villa
1897/8	Nottingham Forest
1898/9	Sheffield United
1899/1900	Bury
1900/1	Tottenham Hotspur
1901/2	Sheffield United
1902/3	Bury
1903/4	Manchester City
1904/5	Aston Villa
1905/6	Everton
1906/7	Sheffield Wednesday
1907/8	Wolverhampton Wanderers
1908/9	Manchester United
1909/10	Newcastle United
1910/1	Bradford City
1911/2	Barnsley
1912/3	Aston Villa
1913/4	Burnley
1914/5	Sheffield United
1919/20	Aston Villa
1920/1	Tottenham Hotspur
1921/2	Huddersfield Town
1922/3	Bolton Wanderers
1923/4	Newcastle United
1924/5	Sheffield United
1925/6	Bolton Wanderers
1926/7	Cardiff City
1927/8	Blackburn Rovers
1928/9	Bolton Wanderers
1929/30	Arsenal
1930/1	West Bromwich Albion
1931/2	Newcastle United
1932/3	Everton
1933/4	Manchester City
1934/5	Sheffield Wednesday
1935/6	Arsenal
1936/7	Sunderland
1937/8	Preston North End
1938/9	Portsmouth
1945/6	Derby County
1946/7	Charlton Athletic
1947/8	Manchester United
1948/9	Wolverhampton
1949/50	Arsenal
1950/1	Newcastle United
1951/2	Newcastle United
1952/3	Blackpool
1953/4	West Bromwich Albion
1954/5	Newcastle United
1955/6	Manchester City
1956/7	Aston Villa
1957/8	Bolton Wanderers
1958/9	Nottingham Forest
1959/60	Wolverhampton
1960/1	Tottenham Hotspur
1961/2	Tottenham Hotspur
1962/3	Manchester United
1963/4	West Ham United
1964/5	Liverpool
1965/6	Everton
1966/7	Tottenham Hotspur
1967/8	West Bromwich Albion
1968/9	Manchester City
1969/70	Chelsea
1970/1	Arsenal
1971/2	Leeds United
1972/3	Sunderland
1973/4	Liverpool
1974/5	West Ham United
1975/6	Southampton
1976/7	Manchester United
1977/8	Ipswich Town
1978/9	Arsenal

1979/80	West Ham United
1980/1	Tottenham Hotspur
1981/2	Tottenham Hotspur
1982/3	Manchester United
1983/4	Everton
1984/5	Manchester United
1985/6	Liverpool
1986/7	Coventry City
1987/8	Wimbledon
1988/9	Liverpool
1989/90	Manchester United
1990/1	Tottenham Hotspur
1991/2	Liverpool
1992/3	Arsenal
1993/4	Manchester United

FOOTBALL LEAGUE CUP

1960/1	Aston Villa
1961/2	Norwich City
1962/3	Birmingham City
1963/4	Leicester City
1964/5	Chelsea
1965/6	West Bromwich Albion
1966/7	Queen's Park Rangers
1967/8	Leeds United
1968/9	Swindon Town
1969/70	Manchester City
1970/1	Tottenham Hotspur
1971/2	Stoke City
1972/3	Tottenham Hotspur
1973/4	Wolverhampton Wanderers
1974/5	Aston Villa
1975/6	Manchester City
1976/7	Aston Villa
1977/8	Nottingham Forest
1978/9	Nottingham Forest
1979/80	Wolverhampton Wanderers
1980/1	Liverpool
1981/2	Liverpool
1982/3	Liverpool
1983/4	Liverpool
1984/5	Norwich City
1985/6	Oxford United
1986/7	Arsenal
1987/8	Luton Town
1988/9	Nottingham Forest
1989/90	Nottingham Forest
1990/1	Sheffield Wednesday
1991/2	Manchester United
1992/3	Arsenal
1993/4	Aston Villa

SCOTTISH LEAGUE

1890/1	Dumbarton/ Rangers	1910/1	Rangers	1931/2	Motherwell
1891/2	Dumbarton	1911/2	Rangers	1932/3	Rangers
1892/3	Celtic	1912/3	Rangers	1933/4	Rangers
1893/4	Celtic	1913/4	Celtic	1934/5	Rangers
1894/5	Hearts	1914/5	Celtic	1935/6	Celtic
1895/6	Celtic	1915/6	Celtic	1936/7	Rangers
1896/7	Hearts	1916/7	Celtic	1937/8	Celtic
1897/8	Celtic	1917/8	Rangers	1938/9	Rangers
1898/9	Rangers	1918/9	Celtic	1946/7	Rangers
1899/1900	Rangers	1919/20	Rangers	1947/8	Hibernian
1900/1	Rangers	1920/1	Rangers	1948/9	Rangers
1901/2	Rangers	1921/2	Celtic	1949/50	Rangers
1902/3	Hibernian	1922/3	Rangers	1950/1	Hibernian
1903/4	Third Lanark	1923/4	Rangers	1951/2	Hibernian
1904/5	Celtic	1924/5	Rangers	1952/3	Rangers
1905/6	Celtic	1925/6	Celtic	1953/4	Celtic
1906/7	Celtic	1926/7	Rangers	1954/5	Aberdeen
1907/8	Celtic	1927/8	Rangers	1955/6	Rangers
1908/9	Celtic	1928/9	Rangers	1956/7	Rangers
1909/10	Celtic	1929/30	Rangers	1957/8	Hearts
		1930/1	Rangers	1958/9	Rangers

1959/60	Hearts	1971/2	Celtic	1983/4	Aberdeen
1960/1	Rangers	1972/3	Celtic	1984/5	Aberdeen
1961/2	Dundee	1973/4	Celtic	1985/6	Celtic
1962/3	Rangers	1974/5	Rangers	1986/7	Rangers
1963/4	Rangers	1975/6	Rangers	1987/8	Celtic
1964/5	Kilmarnock	1976/7	Celtic	1988/9	Rangers
1965/6	Celtic	1977/8	Rangers	1989/90	Rangers
1966/7	Celtic	1978/9	Celtic	1990/1	Rangers
1967/8	Celtic	1979/80	Aberdeen	1991/2	Rangers
1968/9	Celtic	1980/1	Celtic	1992/3	Rangers
1969/70	Celtic	1981/2	Celtic	1993/4	Rangers
1970/1	Celtic	1982/3	Dundee United		

SCOTTISH FA CUP

1874	Queen's Park	1911	Celtic	1960	Rangers
1875	Queen's Park	1912	Celtic	1961	Dunfermline
1876	Queen's Park	1913	Falkirk		Athletic
1877	Vale of Leven	1914	Celtic	1962	Rangers
1878	Vale of Leven	1920	Kilmarnock	1963	Rangers
1879	Vale of Leven	1921	Partick Thistle	1964	Rangers
1880	Queen's Park	1922	Morton	1965	Celtic
1881	Queen's Park	1923	Celtic	1966	Rangers
1882	Queen's Park	1924	Airdrieonians	1967	Celtic
1883	Dumbarton	1925	Celtic	1968	Dunfermline
1884	Queen's Park	1926	St Mirren		Athletic
1885	Renton	1927	Celtic	1969	Celtic
1886	Queen's Park	1928	Rangers	1970	Aberdeen
1887	Hibernian	1929	Kilmarnock	1971	Celtic
1888	Renton	1930	Rangers	1972	Celtic
1889	Third Lanark	1931	Celtic	1973	Rangers
1890	Queen's Park	1932	Rangers	1974	Celtic
1891	Hearts	1933	Celtic	1975	Celtic
1892	Celtic	1934	Rangers	1976	Rangers
1893	Queen's Park	1935	Rangers	1977	Celtic
1894	Rangers	1936	Rangers	1978	Rangers
1895	St Bernard's	1937	Celtic	1979	Rangers
1896	Hearts	1938	East Fife	1980	Celtic
1897	Rangers	1939	Clyde	1981	Rangers
1898	Rangers	1947	Aberdeen	1982	Aberdeen
1899	Celtic	1948	Rangers	1983	Aberdeen
1900	Celtic	1949	Rangers	1984	Aberdeen
1901	Hearts	1950	Rangers	1985	Celtic
1902	Hibernian	1951	Celtic	1986	Aberdeen
1903	Rangers	1952	Motherwell	1987	St Mirren
1904	Celtic	1953	Rangers	1988	Celtic
1905	Third Lanark	1954	Celtic	1989	Celtic
1906	Hearts	1955	Clyde	1990	Aberdeen
1907	Celtic	1956	Hearts	1991	Motherwell
1908	Celtic	1957	Falkirk	1992	Rangers
1909	*not awarded*	1958	Clyde	1993	Rangers
1910	Dundee	1959	St Mirren	1994	Dundee United

SCOTTISH LEAGUE CUP

1946/7	Rangers	1962/3	Hearts	1978/9	Rangers
1947/8	East Fife	1963/4	Rangers	1979/80	Dundee United
1948/9	Rangers	1964/5	Rangers	1980/1	Dundee United
1949/50	East Fife	1965/6	Celtic	1981/2	Rangers
1950/1	Motherwell	1966/7	Celtic	1982/3	Celtic
1951/2	Dundee	1967/8	Celtic	1983/4	Rangers
1952/3	Dundee	1968/9	Celtic	1984/5	Rangers
1953/4	East Fife	1969/70	Celtic	1985/6	Aberdeen
1954/5	Hearts	1970/1	Rangers	1986/7	Rangers
1955/6	Aberdeen	1971/2	Partick Thistle	1987/8	Rangers
1956/7	Celtic	1972/3	Hibernian	1988/9	Rangers
1957/8	Celtic	1973/4	Dundee United	1989/90	Aberdeen
1958/9	Hearts	1974/5	Celtic	1990/1	Rangers
1959/60	Hearts	1975/6	Rangers	1991/2	Hibernian
1960/1	Rangers	1976/7	Aberdeen	1992/3	Rangers
1961/2	Rangers	1977/8	Rangers	1993/4	Rangers

WORLD FOOTBALLER OF THE YEAR

1982	Paolo Rossi (Juventus)	1989	Ruud Gullit (AC Milan)
1983	Zico (Udinese)	1990	Lothar Matthäus (Internazionale Milan)
1984	Michel Platini (Juventus)		
1985	Michel Platini (Juventus)	1991	Jean-Pierre Papin (Marseille)
1986	Diego Maradona (Napoli)	1992	Marco Van Basten (AC Milan)
1987	Ruud Gullit (AC Milan)	1993	Roberto Baggio (Juventus)
1988	Marco Van Basten (AC Milan)		

EUROPEAN FOOTBALLER OF THE YEAR

1956	Stanley Matthews (Blackpool)	1976	Franz Beckenbauer (Bayern Munich)
1957	Alfredo Di Stefano (Real Madrid)		
1958	Raymond Kopa (Real Madrid)	1977	Allan Simonsen (Borussia Moenchengladbach)
1959	Alfredo Di Stefano (Real Madrid)		
1960	Luis Suarez (Barcelona)	1978	Kevin Keegan (SV Hamburg)
1961	Omar Sivori (Juventus)	1979	Kevin Keegan (SV Hamburg)
1962	Josef Masopust (Dukla Prague)	1980	Karl-Heinz Rummenigge (Bayern Munich)
1963	Lev Yashin (Moscow Dynamo)		
1964	Denis Law (Manchester United)	1981	Karl-Heinz Rummenigge (Bayern Munich)
1965	Eusebio (Benfica)		
1966	Bobby Charlton (Manchester United)	1982	Paolo Rossi (Juventus)
		1983	Michel Platini (Juventus)
1967	Florian Albert (Ferencvaros)	1984	Michel Platini (Juventus)
1968	George Best (Manchester United)	1985	Michel Platini (Juventus)
1969	Gianni Rivera (AC Milan)	1986	Igor Belanov (Dynamo Kiev)
1970	Gerd Müller (Bayern Munich)	1987	Ruud Gullit (AC Milan)
1971	Johan Cruyff (Ajax)	1988	Marco Van Basten (AC Milan)
1972	Franz Beckenbauer (Bayern Munich)	1989	Marco Van Basten (AC Milan)
		1990	Lothar Matthäus (Inter-Milan)
1973	Johan Cruyff (Barcelona)	1991	Jean-Pierre Papin (Marseille)
1974	Johan Cruyff (Barcelona)	1992	Marco Van Basten (AC Milan)
1975	Oleg Blokhin (Dynamo Kiev)	1993	Roberto Baggio (Juventus)

ADIDAS 'GOLDEN BOOT' AWARD

1968	Eusebio (Benfica)	1981	Georgi Slavkov (Trakia)
1969	Petar Jekov (CSKA Sofia)	1982	Wim Kieft (Ajax)
1970	Gerd Müller (Bayern Munich)	1983	Fernando Gomes (FC Porto)
1971	Josip Skoblar (Marseille)	1984	Ian Rush (Liverpool)
1972	Gerd Müller (Bayern Munich)	1985	Fernando Gomes (FC Porto)
1973	Eusebio (Benfica)	1986	Marco Van Basten (Ajax)
1974	Hector Yazalde (Sporting Lisbon)	1987	Rodion Camataru (Dinamo Bucuresti)
1975	Dudu Georgescu (Dinamo Bucuresti)	1988	Tanjn Colak (Galatasaray)
		1989	Dorin Mateut (Dinamo Bucuresti)
1976	Sotiris Kaiafas (Omonia Nicosia)	1990	Hugo Sánchez (Real Madrid) / Khristo Stoichkov (CSKA Sofia)
1977	Dudu Georgescu (Dinamo Bucuresti)	1991	Darko Pancev (Crvena Zvezda Beograd)
1978	Hans Krankl (Rapid Vienna)	1992	Ally McCoist (Rangers)
1979	Kees Kist (AZ 67 Alkmaar)	1993	David Taylor (Porthmadog FC)
1980	Erwin van den Bergh (Lierse)		

ENGLISH PROFESSIONAL FOOTBALLERS ASSOCIATION (PFA) FOOTBALLER OF THE YEAR

1974	Norman Hunter (Leeds United)	1986	Gary Lineker (Everton)
1975	Colin Todd (Derby County)	1987	Clive Allen (Tottenham Hotspur)
1976	Pat Jennings (Tottenham Hotspur)	1988	John Barnes (Liverpool)
1977	Andy Gray (Aston Villa)	1989	Mark Hughes (Manchester United)
1978	Peter Shilton (Nottingham Forest)	1990	David Platt (Aston Villa)
1979	Liam Brady (Arsenal)	1991	Mark Hughes (Manchester United)
1980	Terry McDermott (Liverpool)		
1981	John Wark (Ipswich Town)	1992	Gary Pallister (Manchester United)
1982	Kevin Keegan (Southampton)		
1983	Kenny Dalglish (Liverpool)	1993	Chris Waddle (Sheffield Wednesday)
1984	Ian Rush (Liverpool)		
1985	Peter Reid (Everton)	1994	Eric Cantona (Manchester United)

ENGLISH PFA YOUNG FOOTBALLER OF THE YEAR

1974	Kevin Beattie (Ipswich Town)	1984	Paul Walsh (Luton Town)
1975	Mervyn Day (West Ham United)	1985	Mark Hughes (Manchester United)
1976	Peter Barnes (Manchester City)	1986	Tony Cottee (West Ham United)
1977	Andy Gray (Aston Villa)	1987	Tony Adams (Arsenal)
1978	Tony Woodcock (Nottingham Forest)	1988	Paul Gascoigne (Newcastle United)
1979	Cyrille Regis (West Bromwich Albion)	1989	Paul Merson (Arsenal)
		1990	Matthew Le Tissier (Southampton)
1980	Glenn Hoddle (Tottenham Hotspur)	1991	Lee Sharpe (Manchester United)
1981	Gary Shaw (Aston Villa)	1992	Ryan Giggs (Manchester United)
1982	Steve Moran (Southampton)	1993	Ryan Giggs (Manchester United)
1983	Ian Rush (Liverpool)	1994	Andy Cole (Newcastle United)

ATHLETICS

WORLD CHAMPIONSHIPS

Men's 100m

1983	Carl Lewis (USA)
1987	Carl Lewis (USA)
1991	Carl Lewis (USA)
1993	Linford Christie (GB)

Men's 200m

1983	Calvin Smith (USA)
1987	Calvin Smith (USA)
1991	Michael Johnson (USA)
1993	Frankie Fredericks (Nam)

Men's 400m

1983	Bert Cameron (Jam)
1987	Thomas Schönlebe (GDR)
1991	Antonio Pettigrew (USA)
1993	Michael Johnson (USA)

Men's 800m

1983	Willi Wülbeck (FRG)
1987	Billy Konchellah (Ken)
1991	Billy Konchellah (Ken)
1993	Paul Ruto (Ken)

Men's 1500m

1983	Steve Cram (UK)
1987	Abdi Bile (Som)
1991	Noureddine Morceli (Alg)
1993	Noureddine Morceli (Alg)

Men's 5000m

1983	Eamonn Coghlan (Ire)
1987	Saïd Aouita (Mor)
1991	Yobes Ondieki (Ken)
1993	Ismael Kirui (Ken)

Men's 10,000m

1983	Alberto Cova (Ita)
1987	Paul Kipkoech (Ken)
1991	Moses Tanui (Ken)
1993	Haile Gebresilasie (Eth)

Men's Marathon

1983	Rob de Castella (Aus)
1987	Douglas Wakiihuri (Ken)
1991	Hiromi Taniguchi (Jap)
1993	Mark Plaatjes (USA)

Men's 3000m Steeplechase

1983	Patriz Ilg (FRG)
1987	Francesco Panetta (Ita)
1991	Moses Kiptanui (Ken)
1993	Patrick Sang (Ken)

Men's 110m Hurdles

1983	Greg Foster (USA)
1987	Greg Foster (USA)
1991	Greg Foster (USA)
1993	Colin Jackson (GB)

Men's 400m Hurdles

1983	Edwin Moses (USA)
1987	Edwin Moses (USA)
1991	Samuel Matete (Zam)
1993	Kevin Young (USA)

Men's High Jump

1983	Gennadiy Avdeyenko (USSR)
1987	Patrik Sjöberg (Swe)
1991	Charles Austin (USA)
1993	Javier Sotomayor (Cub)

Men's Pole Vault

1983	Sergey Bubka (USSR)
1987	Sergey Bubka (USSR)
1991	Sergey Bubka (USSR)
1993	Sergey Bubka (Rus)

Men's Long Jump

1983	Carl Lewis (USA)
1987	Carl Lewis (USA)
1991	Mike Powell (USA)
1993	Mike Powell (USA)

Men's Triple Jump

1983	Zdzislaw Hoffmann (Pol)
1987	Khristo Markov (Bul)
1991	Kenny Harrison (USA)
1993	Mike Conley (USA)

Men's Shot

1983	Edward Sarul (Pol)
1987	Werner Günthör (Swi)
1991	Werner Günthör (Swi)
1993	Werner Günthör (Swi)

Men's Discus

1983	Imrich Bugár (Cze)
1987	Jürgen Schult (GDR)
1991	Lars Riedel (Ger)
1993	Lars Riedel (Ger)

Men's Hammer

1983	Sergey Litvinov (USSR)
1987	Sergey Litvinov (USSR)
1991	Yuriy Sedykh (USSR)
1993	Andrey Abduvaliyev (Tjk)

Men's Javelin

1983	Detlef Michel (GDR)
1987	Seppo Räty (Fin)
1991	Kimmo Kinnunen (Fin)
1993	Jan Zelezny (Cze)

Men's Decathlon

1983	Daley Thompson (UK)
1987	Torsten Voss (GDR)
1991	Dan O'Brien (USA)
1993	Dan O'Brien (USA)

Men's 4 × 100m Relay

1983	USA
1987	USA
1991	USA
1993	USA

Men's 4 × 400m Relay

1983	USSR
1987	USA
1991	Great Britain
1993	USA

Men's 20km Walk

1983	Ernesto Canto (Mex)
1987	Maurizio Damilano (Ita)
1991	Maurizio Damilano (Ita)
1993	Valentin Massana (Spa)

Men's 50km Walk

1983	Ronald Weigel (GDR)
1987	Hartwig Gauder (GDR)
1991	Aleksandr Potashov (USSR)
1993	José Garcia (Spa)

Women's 100m

1983	Marlies Göhr (GDR)
1987	Silke Gladisch (GDR)
1991	Katrin Krabbe (Ger)
1993	Gail Devers (USA)

Women's 200m

1983	Marita Koch (GDR)
1987	Silke Gladisch (GDR)
1991	Katrin Krabbe (Ger)
1993	Merlene Ottey (Jam)

Women's 400m

1983	Jarmila Kratochvílová (Cze)
1987	Olga Bryzgina (USSR)
1991	Marie-José Pérec (Fra)
1993	Jearl Miles (USA)

Women's 800m

1983	Jarmila Kratochvílová (Cze)
1987	Sigrun Wodars (GDR)
1991	Lilia Nurutdinova (USSR)
1993	Maria Mutola (Moz)

Women's 1500m

1983	Mary Decker (USA)
1987	Tatyana Samolenko (USSR)
1991	Hassiba Boulmerka (Alg)
1993	Dong Liu (Chn)

Women's 3000m

1983	Mary Decker (USA)
1987	Tatyana Samolenko (USSR)
1991	Tatyana Dorovskikh (USSR)
1993	Yungxia Qu (Chn)

Women's 10,000m

1983	*not held*
1987	Ingrid Kristiansen (Nor)
1991	Liz McColgan (UK)
1993	Junxia Wang (Chn)

Women's Marathon

1983	Grete Waitz (Nor)
1987	Rosa Mota (Por)
1991	Wanda Panfil (Pol)
1993	Junko Asari (Jap)

Women's 100m Hurdles

1983	Bettine Jahn (GDR)
1987	Ginka Zagorcheva (Bul)
1991	Lyudmila Narozhilenko (USSR)
1993	Gail Devers (USA)

Women's 400m Hurdles

1983	Yekaterina Fesenko (USSR)
1987	Sabine Busch (GDR)
1991	Tatyana Ledovskaya (USSR)
1993	Sally Gunnell (GB)

Women's High Jump

1983	Tamara Bykova (USSR)
1987	Stefka Kostadinova (Bul)
1991	Heike Henkel (Ger)
1993	Ioamnet Quintero (Cub)

Women's Long Jump

1983	Heike Daute (GDR)
1987	Jackie Joyner-Kersee (USA)
1991	Jackie Joyner-Kersee (USA)
1993	Heike Drechsler (Ger)

Women's Shot

1983	Helena Fibingerová (Cze)
1987	Natalya Lisovskaya (USSR)
1991	Huang Zhihong (Chn)
1993	Huang Zhihong (Chn)

Women's Discus

1983	Martina Opitz (GDR)
1987	Martina Hellman (née Opitz) (GDR)
1991	Tsvetanka Khristova (Bul)
1993	Olga Burova (Rus)

Women's Javelin

1983	Tiina Lillak (Fin)
1987	Fatima Whitbread (GB)

1991	Xu Demei (Chn)
1993	Trine Hattesvad (Nor)

Women's Heptathlon

1983	Ramona Neubert (GDR)
1987	Jackie Joyner-Kersee (USA)
1991	Sabine Braun (Ger)
1993	Jackie Joyner-Kersee (USA)

Women's 4 × 100m Relay

1983	East Germany
1987	USA
1991	Jamaica
1993	Russia

Women's 4 × 400m Relay

1983	East Germany
1987	East Germany
1991	USSR
1993	USA

Women's 10km Walk

1983	*not held*
1987	Irina Strakhova (USSR)
1991	Alina Ivanova (USSR)
1993	Sari Essayah (Fin)

OLYMPIC GAMES

Men's 100m

1896	Thomas Burke (USA)
1900	Francis Jarvis (USA)
1904	Archie Hahn (USA)
1906	Archie Hahn (USA)
1908	Reginald Walker (SAf)
1912	Ralph Craig (USA)
1920	Charles Paddock (USA)
1924	Harold Abrahams (UK)
1928	Percy Williams (Can)
1932	Eddie Tolan (USA)
1936	Jesse Owens (USA)
1948	Harrison Dillard (USA)
1952	Lindy Remigino (USA)
1956	Bobby Morrow (USA)
1960	Armin Hary (FRG)
1964	Robert Hayes (USA)
1968	James Hines (USA)
1972	Valeriy Borzov (USSR)
1976	Hasely Crawford (Tri)

1980	Allan Wells (UK)
1984	Carl Lewis (USA)
1988	Carl Lewis (USA)
1992	Linford Christie (UK)

Men's 200m

1900	Walter Tewksbury (USA)
1904	Archie Hahn (USA)
1908	Robert Kerr (Can)
1912	Ralph Craig (USA)
1920	Allen Woodring (USA)
1924	Jackson Scholz (USA)
1928	Percy Williams (Can)
1932	Eddie Tolan (USA)
1936	Jesse Owens (USA)
1948	Melvin Patton (USA)
1952	Andrew Stanfield (USA)
1956	Bobby Morrow (USA)
1960	Livio Berruti (Ita)

1964	Henry Carr (USA)
1968	Tommie Smith (USA)
1972	Valeriy Borzov (USSR)
1976	Donald Quarrie (Jam)
1980	Pietro Mennea (Ita)
1984	Carl Lewis (USA)
1988	Joe DeLoach (USA)
1992	Michael Marsh (USA)

Men's 400m

1896	Thomas Burke (USA)
1900	Maxie Long (USA)
1904	Harry Hillman (USA)
1906	Paul Pilgrim (USA)
1908	Wyndham Halswelle (UK)
1912	Charles Reidpath (USA)
1920	Bevil Rudd (SAf)
1924	Eric Liddell (UK)
1928	Ray Barbuti (USA)
1932	Bill Carr (USA)
1936	Archie Williams (USA)
1948	Arthur Wint (Jam)
1952	George Rhoden (Jam)
1956	Charles Jenkins (USA)
1960	Otis Davis (USA)
1964	Michael Larrabee (USA)
1968	Lee Evans (USA)
1972	Vincent Matthews (USA)
1976	Alberto Juantorena (Cub)
1980	Viktor Markin (USSR)
1984	Alonzo Babers (USA)
1988	Steve Lewis (USA)
1992	Quincy Watts (USA)

Men's 800m

1896	Edwin Flack (Aus)
1900	Alfred Tysoe (UK)
1904	James Lightbody (USA)
1906	Paul Pilgrim (USA)
1908	Mel Sheppard (USA)
1912	James Meredith (USA)
1920	Albert Hill (UK)
1924	Douglas Lowe (UK)
1928	Douglas Lowe (UK)
1932	Tom Hampson (UK)
1936	John Woodruff (USA)
1948	Malvin Whitfield (USA)
1952	Malvin Whitfield (USA)
1956	Thomas Courtney (USA)
1960	Peter Snell (NZ)
1964	Peter Snell (NZ)
1968	Ralph Doubell (Aus)

1972	David Wottle (USA)
1976	Alberto Juantorena (Cub)
1980	Steven Ovett (UK)
1984	Joaquim Cruz (Bra)
1988	Paul Ereng (Ken)
1992	William Tanui (Ken)

Men's 1500m

1896	Edwin Flack (Aus)
1900	Charles Bennett (UK)
1904	James Lightbody (USA)
1906	James Lightbody (USA)
1908	Mel Sheppard (USA)
1912	Arnold Jackson (UK)
1920	Albert Hill (UK)
1924	Paavo Nurmi (Fin)
1928	Harri Larva (Fin)
1932	Luigi Beccali (Ita)
1936	Jack Lovelock (NZ)
1948	Henry Eriksson (Swe)
1952	Josef Barthel (Lux)
1956	Ron Delany (Ire)
1960	Herbert Elliott (Aus)
1964	Peter Snell (NZ)
1968	Kipchoge Keino (Ken)
1972	Pekka Vasala (Fin)
1976	John Walker (NZ)
1980	Sebastian Coe (UK)
1984	Sebastian Coe (UK)
1988	Peter Rono (Ken)
1992	Fermin Cacho (Spa)

Men's 5000m

1912	Hannes Kolehmainen (Fin)
1920	Joseph Guillemot (Fra)
1924	Paavo Nurmi (Fin)
1928	Ville Ritola (Fin)
1932	Lauri Lehtinen (Fin)
1936	Gunnar Höckert (Fin)
1948	Gaston Reiff (Bel)
1952	Emil Zátopek (Cze)
1956	Vladimir Kuts (USSR)
1960	Murray Halberg (NZ)
1964	Robert Schul (USA)
1968	Mohamed Gammoudi (Tun)
1972	Lasse Viren (Fin)
1976	Lasse Viren (Fin)
1980	Miruts Yifter (Eth)
1984	Saïd Aouita (Mor)
1988	John Ngugi (Ken)
1992	Dieter Baumann (Ger)

Men's 10,000m

1912	Hannes Kolehmainen (Fin)
1920	Paavo Nurmi (Fin)
1924	Ville Ritola (Fin)
1928	Paavo Nurmi (Fin)
1932	Janusz Kusocinski (Pol)
1936	Ilmari Salminen (Fin)
1948	Emil Zátopek (Cze)
1952	Emil Zátopek (Cze)
1956	Vladimir Kuts (USSR)
1960	Pyotr Bolotnikov (USSR)
1964	William Mills (USA)
1968	Naftali Temu (Ken)
1972	Lasse Viren (Fin)
1976	Lasse Viren (Fin)
1980	Miruts Yifter (Eth)
1984	Alberto Cova (Ita)
1988	Brahim Boutayeb (Mor)
1992	Khalid Skah (Mor)

Men's Marathon

1896	Spyridon Louis (Gre)
1900	Michel Théato (Fra)
1904	Thomas Hicks (USA)
1906	William Sherring (Can)
1908	John Hayes (USA)
1912	Kenneth McArthur (SAf)
1920	Hannes Kolehmainen (Fin)
1924	Albin Stenroos (Fin)
1928	Mohamed Boughéra El Ouafi (Fra)
1932	Juan Carlos Zabala (Arg)
1936	Kitei Son (Jap)
1948	Delfo Cabrera (Arg)
1952	Emil Zátopek (Cze)
1956	Alain Mimoun (Fra)
1960	Abebe Bikila (Eth)
1964	Abebe Bikila (Eth)
1968	Mamo Wolde (Eth)
1972	Frank Shorter (USA)
1976	Waldemar Cierpinski (GDR)
1980	Waldemar Cierpinski (GDR)
1984	Carlos Lopes (Por)
1988	Gelindo Bordin (Ita)
1992	Hwang Young-jo (SKo)

Men's Steeplechase

1896	George Orton (Can)
1900	John Rimmer (UK)
1904	James Lightbody (USA)
1908	Arthur Russell (UK)
1920	Percy Hodge (UK)
1924	Ville Ritola (Fin)
1928	Toivo Loukola (Fin)
1932	Volmari Iso-Hollo (Fin)
1936	Volmari Iso-Hollo (Fin)
1948	Tore Sjöstrand (Swe)
1952	Horace Ashenfelter (USA)
1956	Christopher Brasher (UK)
1960	Zdzislaw Kryszkowiak (Pol)
1964	Gaston Roelants (Bel)
1968	Amos Biwott (Ken)
1972	Kipchoge Keino (Ken)
1976	Anders Gärderud (Swe)
1980	Bronislaw Malinowski (Pol)
1984	Julius Korir (Ken)
1988	Julius Kariuki (Ken)
1992	Matthew Birir (Ken)

Men's 110m Hurdles

1896	Thomas Curtis (USA)
1900	Alvin Kraenzlein (USA)
1904	Fred Schule (USA)
1906	Robert Leavitt (USA)
1908	Forrest Smithson (USA)
1912	Fred Kelly (USA)
1920	Earl Thomson (Can)
1924	Daniel Kinsey (USA)
1928	Sydney Atkinson (SAf)
1932	George Saling (USA)
1936	Forrest Towns (USA)
1948	William Porter (USA)
1952	Harrison Dillard (USA)
1956	Lee Calhoun (USA)
1960	Lee Calhoun (USA)
1964	Hayes Jones (USA)
1968	Willie Davenport (USA)
1972	Rodney Milburn (USA)
1976	Guy Drut (Fra)
1980	Thomas Munkelt (GDR)
1984	Roger Kingdom (USA)
1988	Roger Kingdom (USA)
1992	Mark McKoy (Can)

Men's 400m Hurdles

1900	Walter Tewksbury (USA)
1904	Harry Hillman (USA)
1908	Charles Bacon (USA)
1920	Frank Loomis (USA)
1924	Morgan Taylor (USA)
1928	Lord Burghley (UK)
1932	Robert Tisdall (Ire)
1936	Glenn Hardin (USA)
1948	Roy Cochran (USA)

1952	Charles Moore (USA)
1956	Glenn Davis (USA)
1960	Glenn Davis (USA)
1964	Rex Cawley (USA)
1968	David Hemery (UK)
1972	John Akii-Bua (Uga)
1976	Edwin Moses (USA)
1980	Volker Beck (GDR)
1984	Edwin Moses (USA)
1988	Andre Phillips (USA)
1992	Kevin Young (USA)

Men's High Jump

1896	Ellery Clark (USA)
1900	Irving Baxter (USA)
1904	Samuel Jones (USA)
1906	Con Leahy (UK/Ire)
1908	Harry Porter (USA)
1912	Alma Richards (USA)
1920	Richard Landon (USA)
1924	Harold Osborn (USA)
1928	Robert King (USA)
1932	Duncan McNaughton (Can)
1936	Cornelius Johnson (USA)
1948	John Winter (Aus)
1952	Walter Davis (USA)
1956	Charles Dumas (USA)
1960	Robert Shavlakadze (USSR)
1964	Valeriy Brumel (USSR)
1968	Dick Fosbury (USA)
1972	Jüri Tarmak (USSR)
1976	Jacek Wszola (Pol)
1980	Gerd Wessig (GDR)
1984	Dietmar Mögenburg (FRG)
1988	Gennadiy Avdeyenko (USSR)
1992	Javier Sotomayor (Cub)

Men's Pole Vault

1896	William Hoyt (USA)
1900	Irving Baxter (USA)
1904	Charles Dvorak (USA)
1906	Fernand Gonder (Fra)
1908	Edward Cooke (USA) / Alfred Gilbert (USA)
1912	Harry Babcock (USA)
1920	Frank Foss (USA)
1924	Lee Barnes (USA)
1928	Sabin Carr (USA)
1932	Bill Miller (USA)
1936	Earle Meadows (USA)
1948	Guinn Smith (USA)
1952	Robert Richards (USA)

1956	Robert Richards (USA)
1960	Donald Bragg (USA)
1964	Frederick Hansen (USA)
1968	Bob Seagren (USA)
1972	Wolfgang Nordwig (GDR)
1976	Tadeusz Slusarski (Pol)
1980	Wladyslaw Kozakiewicz (Pol)
1984	Pierre Quinon (Fra)
1988	Sergey Bubka (USSR)
1992	Maksim Tarasov (CIS/Rus)

Men's Triple Jump

1896	James Connolly (USA)
1900	Myer Prinstein (USA)
1904	Myer Prinstein (USA)
1906	Peter O'Connor (UK/Ire)
1908	Tim Ahearne (UK/Ire)
1912	Gustaf Lindblom (Swe)
1920	Vilho Tuulos (Fin)
1924	Anthony Winter (Aus)
1928	Mikio Oda (Jap)
1932	Chuhei Nambu (Jap)
1936	Naoto Tajima (Jap)
1948	Arne Åhman (Swe)
1952	Adhemar Ferreira da Silva (Bra)
1956	Adhemar Ferreira da Silva (Bra)
1960	Jozef Schmidt (Pol)
1964	Jozef Schmidt (Pol)
1968	Viktor Saneyev (USSR)
1972	Viktor Saneyev (USSR)
1976	Viktor Saneyev (USSR)
1980	Jaak Uudmäe (USSR)
1984	Al Joyner (USA)
1988	Khristo Markov (Bul)
1992	Mike Conley (USA)

Men's Long Jump

1896	Ellery Clark (USA)
1900	Alvin Kraenzlein (USA)
1904	Myer Prinstein (USA)
1906	Myer Prinstein (USA)
1908	Francis Irons (USA)
1912	Albert Gutterson (USA)
1920	William Pettersson (Swe)
1924	William De Hart Hubbard (USA)
1928	Edward Hamm (USA)
1932	Edward Gordon (USA)
1936	Jesse Owens (USA)
1948	William Steele (USA)
1952	Jerome Biffle (USA)
1956	Gregory Bell (USA)
1960	Ralph Boston (USA)

1964	Lynn Davies (UK)	1972	Ludvik Danek (Cze)
1968	Bob Beamon (USA)	1976	Mac Wilkins (USA)
1972	Randy Williams (USA)	1980	Viktor Rashchupkin (USSR)
1976	Arnie Robinson (USA)	1984	Rolf Danneberg (FRG)
1980	Lutz Dombrowski (GDR)	1988	Jürgen Schult (GDR)
1984	Carl Lewis (USA)	1992	Romas Ubartas (Lit)
1988	Carl Lewis (USA)		
1992	Carl Lewis (USA)		

Men's Shot

Men's Javelin

1896	Robert Garrett (USA)	1906	Erik Lemming (Swe)
1900	Richard Sheldon (USA)	1908	Erik Lemming (Swe)
1904	Ralph Rose (USA)	1912	Erik Lemming (Swe)
1906	Martin Sheridan (USA)	1920	Jonni Myyrä (Fin)
1908	Ralph Rose (USA)	1924	Jonni Myyrä (Fin)
1912	Patrick McDonald (USA)	1928	Erik Lundkvist (Swe)
1920	Ville Pörhölä (Fin)	1932	Matti Järvinen (Fin)
1924	Clarence Houser (USA)	1936	Gerhard Stöck (Ger)
1928	John Kuck (USA)	1948	Tapio Rautavaara (Fin)
1932	Leo Sexton (USA)	1952	Cyrus Young (USA)
1936	Hans Woellke (Ger)	1956	Egil Danielsen (Nor)
1948	Wilbur Thompson (USA)	1960	Viktor Tsibulenko (USSR)
1952	Parry O'Brien (USA)	1964	Pauli Nevala (Fin)
1956	Parry O'Brien (USA)	1968	Janis Lusis (USSR)
1960	William Nieder (USA)	1972	Klaus Wolfermann (FRG)
1964	Dallas Long (USA)	1976	Miklós Németh (Hun)
1968	Randy Matson (USA)	1980	Dainis Kula (USSR)
1972	Wladyslaw Komar (Pol)	1984	Arto Härkönen (Fin)
1976	Udo Beyer (GDR)	1988	Tapio Korjus (Fin)
1980	Vladimir Kiselyov (USSR)	1992	Jan Zelezny (Cze)
1984	Alessandro Andrei (Ita)		
1988	Ulf Timmermann (GDR)		
1992	Mike Stulce (USA)		

Men's Discus

Men's Hammer

1896	Robert Garrett (USA)	1900	John Flanagan (USA)
1900	Rudolf Bauer (Hun)	1904	John Flanagan (USA)
1904	Martin Sheridan (USA)	1908	John Flanagan (USA)
1906	Martin Sheridan (USA)	1912	Matt McGrath (USA)
1908	Martin Sheridan (USA)	1920	Patrick Ryan (USA)
1912	Armas Taipale (Fin)	1924	Fred Tootell (USA)
1920	Elmer Niklander (Fin)	1928	Patrick O'Callaghan (Ire)
1924	Clarence Houser (USA)	1932	Patrick O'Callaghan (Ire)
1928	Clarence Houser (USA)	1936	Karl Hein (Ger)
1932	John Anderson (USA)	1948	Imre Németh (Hun)
1936	Ken Carpenter (USA)	1952	József Csermak (Hun)
1948	Adolfo Consolini (Ita)	1956	Harold Connolly (USA)
1952	Sim Iness (USA)	1960	Vasiliy Rudenkov (USSR)
1956	Al Oerter (USA)	1964	Romuald Klim (USSR)
1960	Al Oerter (USA)	1968	Gyula Zsivótzky (Hun)
1964	Al Oerter (USA)	1972	Anatoliy Bondarchuk (USSR)
1968	Al Oerter (USA)	1976	Yuriy Sedykh (USSR)
		1980	Yuriy Sedykh (USSR)
		1984	Juha Tiainen (Fin)
		1988	Sergey Litvinov (USSR)
		1992	Andrey Abduvaliyev (CIS/Tjk)

Men's Decathlon
1904	Thomas Kiely (UK/Ire)
1912	Jim Thorpe (USA)
1920	Helge Lövland (Nor)
1924	Harold Osborn (USA)
1928	Paavo Yrjölä (Fin)
1932	James Bausch (USA)
1936	Glenn Morris (USA)
1948	Robert Mathias (USA)
1952	Robert Mathias (USA)
1956	Milton Campbell (USA)
1960	Rafer Johnson (USA)
1964	Willi Holdorf (FRG)
1968	Bill Toomey (USA)
1972	Nikolay Avilov (USSR)
1976	Bruce Jenner (USA)
1980	Daley Thompson (UK)
1984	Daley Thompson (UK)
1988	Christian Schenk (GDR)
1992	Robert Zmelik (Cze)

Men's 20km Walk
1956	Leonid Spirin (USSR)
1960	Vladimir Golubnichiy (USSR)
1964	Kenneth Matthews (UK)
1968	Vladimir Golubnichiy (USSR)
1972	Peter Frenkel (GDR)
1976	Daniel Bautista (Mex)
1980	Maurizio Damilano (Ita)
1984	Ernesto Canto (Mex)
1988	Jozef Pribilinec (Cze)
1992	Daniel Plaza (Spa)

Men's 50km Walk
1932	Thomas Green (UK)
1936	Harold Whitlock (UK)
1948	John Ljunggren (Swe)
1952	Giuseppe Dordoni (Ita)
1956	Norman Read (NZ)
1960	Don Thompson (UK)
1964	Abdon Pamich (Ita)
1968	Christophe Höhne (GDR)
1972	Bernd Kannenberg (GDR)
1980	Hartwig Gauder (GDR)
1984	Raúl Gonzales (Mex)
1988	Vyacheslav Ivanenko (USSR)
1992	Andrey Perlov (CIS/Rus)

Men's 4 × 100m Relay
1912	UK
1920	USA
1924	USA

1928	USA
1932	USA
1936	USA
1948	USA
1952	USA
1956	USA
1960	West Germany
1964	USA
1968	USA
1972	USA
1976	USA
1980	USSR
1984	USA
1988	USSR
1992	USA

Men's 4 × 400m Relay
1912	USA
1920	UK
1924	USA
1928	USA
1932	USA
1936	UK
1948	USA
1952	Jamaica
1956	USA
1960	USA
1964	USA
1968	USA
1972	Kenya
1976	USA
1980	USSR
1984	USA
1988	USA
1992	USA

Women's 100m
1928	Elizabeth Robinson (USA)
1932	Stanislawa Walasiewicz (Pol)
1936	Helen Stephens (USA)
1948	Fanny Blankers-Koen (Hol)
1952	Marjorie Jackson (Aus)
1956	Betty Cuthbert (Aus)
1960	Wilma Rudolph (USA)
1964	Wyomia Tyus (USA)
1968	Wyomia Tyus (USA)
1972	Renate Stecher (GDR)
1976	Annegret Richter (FRG)
1980	Lyudmila Kondratyeva (USSR)
1984	Evelyn Ashford (USA)
1988	Florence Griffith-Joyner (USA)
1992	Gail Devers (USA)

Women's 200m

1948	Fanny Blankers-Koen (Hol)
1952	Marjorie Jackson (Aus)
1956	Betty Cuthbert (Aus)
1960	Wilma Rudolph (USA)
1964	Edith Maguire (USA)
1968	Irena Szewinska (Pol)
1972	Renate Stecher (GDR)
1976	Bärbel Eckert (GDR)
1980	Bärbel Wöckel (née Eckert) (GDR)
1984	Valerie Brisco-Hooks (USA)
1988	Florence Griffith-Joyner (USA)
1992	Gwen Torrence (USA)

Women's 400m

1964	Betty Cuthbert (Aus)
1968	Colette Besson (Fra)
1972	Monika Zehrt (GDR)
1976	Irena Szewinska (Pol)
1980	Marita Koch (GDR)
1984	Valerie Brisco-Hooks (USA)
1988	Olga Bryzgina (USSR)
1992	Marie-José Pérec (Fra)

Women's 800m

1928	Lina Radke (Ger)
1960	Lyudmila Shevtsova (USSR)
1964	Ann Packer (UK)
1968	Madeline Manning (USA)
1972	Hildegard Falck (FRG)
1976	Tatyana Kazankina (USSR)
1980	Nadezhda Olizarenko (USSR)
1984	Doina Melinte (Rom)
1988	Sigrun Wodars (GDR)
1992	Ellen van Langen (Hol)

Women's 1500m

1972	Lyudmila Bragina (USSR)
1976	Tatyana Kazankina (USSR)
1980	Tatyana Kazankina (USSR)
1984	Gabriella Doria (Ita)
1988	Paula Ivan (Rom)
1992	Hassiba Boulmerka (Alg)

Women's 3000m

1984	Maricica Puica (Rom)
1988	Tatyana Samolenko (USSR)
1992	Yelena Romanova (CIS/Rus)

Women's 10,000m

1988	Olga Bondarenko (USSR)
1992	Derartu Tulu (Eth)

Women's Marathon

1984	Joan Benoit (USA)
1988	Rosa Mota (Por)
1992	Valentina Yegorova (CIS/Rus)

Women's 80m Hurdles

1932	Mildred Didrikson (USA)
1936	Trebisonda Valla (Ita)
1948	Fanny Blankers-Koen (Hol)
1952	Shirley Strickland (Aus)
1956	Shirley Strickland (Aus)
1960	Irina Press (USSR)
1964	Karin Balzer (GDR)
1968	Maureen Caird (Aus)

Women's 100m Hurdles

1972	Annelie Ehrhardt (GDR)
1976	Johanna Schaller (GDR)
1980	Vera Komisova (USSR)
1984	Benita Fitzgerald-Brown (USA)
1988	Yordanka Donkova (Bul)
1992	Paraskevi Patoulidou (Gre)

Women's 400m Hurdles

1984	Newal El Moutawakil (Mor)
1988	Debbie Flintoff-King (Aus)
1992	Sally Gunnell (UK)

Women's High Jump

1928	Ethel Catherwood (Can)
1932	Jean Shiley (USA)
1936	Ibolya Csák (Hun)
1948	Alice Coachman (USA)
1952	Esther Brand (SAf)
1956	Mildred McDaniel (USA)
1960	Iolanda Balas (Rom)
1964	Iolanda Balas (Rom)
1968	Miloslava Rezková (Cze)
1972	Ulrike Meyfarth (FRG)
1976	Rosemarie Ackermann (GDR)
1980	Sara Simeoni (Ita)
1984	Ulrike Meyfarth (FRG)
1988	Louise Ritter (USA)
1992	Heike Henkel (Ger)

Women's Long Jump

1948	Olga Gyarmati (Hun)
1952	Yvette Williams (NZ)
1956	Elzbieta Krzesinska (Pol)
1960	Vyera Krepkina (USSR)
1964	Mary Rand (UK)
1968	Viorica Viscopoleanu (Rom)
1972	Heide Rosendahl (FRG)

1976	Angela Voigt (GDR)
1980	Tatyana Kolpakova (USSR)
1984	Anisoara Stanciu (Rom)
1988	Jackie Joyner-Kersee (USA)
1992	Heike Drechsler (Ger)

Women's Shot

1948	Micheline Ostermeyer (Fra)
1952	Galina Zybina (USSR)
1956	Tamara Tishkyevich (USSR)
1960	Tamara Press (USSR)
1964	Tamara Press (USSR)
1968	Margitta Gummel (GDR)
1972	Nadezhda Chizhova (USSR)
1976	Ivanka Khristova (Bul)
1980	Ilona Slupianek (GDR)
1984	Claudia Losch (FRG)
1988	Natalya Lisovskaya (USSR)
1992	Svetlana Krivelyova (CIS/Rus)

Women's Discus

1928	Helena Konopacka (Pol)
1932	Lillian Copeland (USA)
1936	Gisela Mauermayer (Ger)
1948	Micheline Ostermeyer (Fra)
1952	Nina Ponomaryeva (USSR)
1956	Olga Fikotová (Cze)
1960	Nina Ponomaryeva (USSR)
1964	Tamara Press (USSR)
1968	Lia Manoliu (Rom)
1972	Faina Melnik (USSR)
1976	Evelin Schlaak (GDR)
1980	Evelin Jahl (née Schlaak) (GDR)
1984	Ria Stalmach (Hol)
1988	Martina Hellmann (GDR)
1992	Maritza Marten (Cub)

Women's Javelin

1932	Mildred Didrikson (USA)
1936	Tilly Fleischer (Ger)
1948	Herma Bauma (Aut)
1952	Dana Zátopková (Cze)
1956	Inese Jaunzeme (USSR)
1960	Elvira Ozolina (USSR)
1964	Mihaela Penes (Rom)
1968	Angéla Németh (Hun)
1972	Ruth Fuchs (GDR)
1976	Ruth Fuchs (GDR)
1980	Maria C. Colón (Cub)
1984	Tessa Sanderson (UK)
1988	Petra Felke (GDR)
1992	Silke Renk (Ger)

Women's Heptathlon

1984	Glynis Nunn (Aus)
1988	Jackie Joyner-Kersee (USA)
1992	Jackie Joyner-Kersee (USA)

Women's 10km Walk

| 1992 | Chen Yueling (Chn) |

Women's 4 × 100m Relay

1928	Canada
1932	USA
1936	USA
1948	Holland
1952	USA
1956	Australia
1960	USA
1964	Poland
1968	USA
1972	West Germany
1976	East Germany
1980	East Germany
1984	USA
1988	USA
1992	USA

Women's 4 × 400m Relay

1972	East Germany
1976	East Germany
1980	USSR
1984	USA
1988	USSR
1992	CIS (united team)

LONDON MARATHON

Men

1981	{ Dick Beardsley (USA) Inge Simonsen (Nor)
1982	Hugh Jones (UK)
1983	Mike Gratton (UK)
1984	Charlie Spedding (UK)
1985	Steve Jones (UK)
1986	Toshihiko Seko (Jap)
1987	Hiromi Taniguchi (Jap)
1988	Henrik Jørgensen (Den)
1989	Douglas Wakiihuri (Ken)
1990	Allister Hutton (UK)

1991	Yakov Tolstikov (USSR)	1985	Ingrid Kristiansen (Nor)
1992	António Pinto (Por)	1986	Grete Waitz (Nor)
1993	Eamon Martin (Ire)	1987	Ingrid Kristiansen (Nor)
1994	Dionicio Ceron (Mex)	1988	Ingrid Kristiansen (Nor)
		1989	Véronique Marot (UK)
Women		1990	Wanda Panfil (Pol)
1981	Joyce Smith (UK)	1991	Rosa Mota (Por)
1982	Joyce Smith (UK)	1992	Katrin Dörre (Ger)
1983	Grete Waitz (Nor)	1993	Katrin Dörre (Ger)
1984	Ingrid Kristiansen (Nor)	1994	Katrin Dörre (Ger)

AUSTRALIAN FOOTBALL

GRAND FINAL

1897	Essendon	1930	Collingwood	1963	Geelong
1898	Fitzroy	1931	Geelong	1964	Melbourne
1899	Fitzroy	1932	Richmond	1965	Essendon
1900	Melbourne	1933	South Melbourne	1966	St Kilda
1901	Essendon	1934	Richmond	1967	Richmond
1902	Collingwood	1935	Collingwood	1968	Carlton
1903	Collingwood	1936	Collingwood	1969	Richmond
1904	Fitzroy	1937	Geelong	1970	Carlton
1905	Fitzroy	1938	Carlton	1971	Hawthorn
1906	Carlton	1939	Melbourne	1972	Carlton
1907	Carlton	1940	Melbourne	1973	Richmond
1908	Carlton	1941	Melbourne	1974	Richmond
1909	South Melbourne	1942	Essendon	1975	North Melbourne
1910	Collingwood	1943	Richmond	1976	Hawthorn
1911	Essendon	1944	Fitzroy	1977	North Melbourne
1912	Essendon	1945	Carlton	1978	Hawthorn
1913	Fitzroy	1946	Essendon	1979	Carlton
1914	Carlton	1947	Carlton	1980	Richmond
1915	Carlton	1948	Melbourne	1981	Carlton
1916	Fitzroy	1949	Essendon	1982	Carlton
1917	Collingwood	1950	Essendon	1983	Hawthorn
1918	South Melbourne	1951	Geelong	1984	Essendon
1919	Collingwood	1952	Geelong	1985	Essendon
1920	Richmond	1953	Collingwood	1986	Hawthorn
1921	Richmond	1954	Footscray	1987	Carlton
1922	Fitzroy	1955	Melbourne	1988	Hawthorn
1923	Essendon	1956	Melbourne	1989	Hawthorn
1924	Essendon	1957	Melbourne	1990	Collingwood
1925	Geelong	1958	Collingwood	1991	Hawthorn
1926	Melbourne	1959	Melbourne	1992	West Coast
1927	Collingwood	1960	Melbourne	1993	Essendon
1928	Collingwood	1961	Hawthorn		
1929	Collingwood	1962	Essendon		

BABIES

FARLEY'S FIRST BABY AWARD

Baby competitions are a feature of almost every annual village or community show. But there is one baby contest about which there can be no dispute – the annual Farley's award to the first baby born each year. In 1993, eleven babies were born at eleven hospitals within the first minute of the New Year. To win the contest, the delivery time of the baby's birth is taken as the complete delivery of the baby, *i.e.* down to its last little toe, when the time is recorded by the attendant midwife. In the event of more than one baby claiming first place, a draw is held and the prize is awarded to the first baby out of the draw.

The overall winner receives £1,500 and a bumper pack of Farley's weaning products (Farley's Farex, Farley's Follow-On Milk, Farley's Rusks and Farley's Meal Timers). £500 of babycare equipment also goes to the maternity unit responsible for delivering the first baby.

Recent winners were:

1993	Laura Kennea, born to Jane Kennea at the Birmingham Maternity Hospital on the first stroke of midnight	1994	Erin Reid, born to Amanda and Marcus Reid in Scotland, at precisely one second past midnight

BADMINTON

WORLD CHAMPIONSHIPS

Men's Team

1949	Malaya
1952	Malaya
1955	Malaya
1958	Indonesia
1961	Indonesia
1964	Indonesia
1967	Malaysia
1970	Indonesia
1973	Indonesia
1976	Indonesia
1979	Indonesia
1982	China
1984	Indonesia
1986	China
1988	China
1990	China
1992	Malaysia

Men's Singles

1977	Flemming Delfs (Den)
1980	Rudy Hartono (Ina)
1983	Icuk Sugiarto (Ina)
1985	Han Jian (Chn)
1987	Yang Yang (Chn)
1989	Yang Yang (Chn)
1991	Zhao Jianhua (Chn)
1993	Joko Suprianto (Ina)

Women's Team

1957	USA
1960	USA
1963	USA
1966	Japan
1969	Japan
1972	Japan
1975	Indonesia

1978	Japan
1981	Japan
1984	China
1986	China
1988	China
1990	China
1992	China

Women's Singles

1977	Lene Köppen (Den)
1980	Wiharjo Verawaty (Ina)
1983	Li Lingwei (Chn)
1985	Han Aiping (Chn)
1987	Han Aiping (Chn)
1989	Li Lingwei (Chn)
1991	Tang Jiuhong (Chn)
1993	Susi Susanti (Ina)

OLYMPIC GAMES

Men's Singles

| 1992 | Allan Kusuma (Ina) |

Women's Singles

| 1992 | Susi Susanti (Ina) |

Men's Doubles

| 1992 | Kim Moon-soo and Park Joo Bong (SKo) |

Women's Doubles

| 1992 | Hwang Hye-young and Chung So-young (SKo) |

BALLET

THE *EVENING STANDARD* BALLET, OPERA AND CLASSICAL MUSIC AWARDS

These awards extended the old *Standard* Ballet and Opera Awards, begun in the 1970s. It was decided to expand the awards and to institute an annual presentation lunch in the same style as the Drama and Film Awards occasions, both recognized as the outstanding ceremonies of their kind in the British arts and entertainment field. These new awards first made their appearance in March 1994, when the following winners (for 1993) were announced:

Ballet Awards

Outstanding performance Thomas Edur of the English National Ballet

Artistic achievement Barry Wordsworth, musical director of the Royal Ballet

Opera Awards

Outstanding performance Anne Evans of the Welsh National Opera

Outstanding production Bernard Haitink, for *Die Meistersinger von Nürnberg*

Artistic achievement Sir Colin Davis

Dame Kiri Te Kanawa received a special award for her services to classical music.

BASEBALL

WORLD SERIES

1903	Boston Red Sox
1904	*not held*
1905	New York Giants
1906	Chicago White Sox
1907	Chicago Cubs
1908	Chicago Cubs
1909	Pittsburg Pirates
1910	Philadelphia Athletics
1911	Philadelphia Athletics
1912	Boston Red Sox
1913	Philadelphia Athletics
1914	Boston Braves
1915	Boston Red Sox
1916	Boston Red Sox
1917	Chicago White Sox
1918	Boston Red Sox
1919	Cincinnati Reds
1920	Cleveland Indians
1921	New York Giants
1922	New York Giants
1923	New York Yankees
1924	Washington Senators
1925	Pittsburg Pirates
1926	St Louis Cardinals
1927	New York Yankees
1928	New York Yankees
1929	Philadelphia Athletics
1930	Philadelphia Athletics
1931	St Louis Cardinals
1932	New York Yankees
1933	New York Giants
1934	St Louis Cardinals
1935	Detroit Tigers
1936	New York Yankees
1937	New York Yankees
1938	New York Yankees
1939	New York Yankees
1940	Cincinnati Reds
1941	New York Yankees
1942	St Louis Cardinals
1943	New York Yankees
1944	St Louis Cardinals
1945	Detroit Tigers
1946	St Louis Cardinals
1947	New York Yankees
1948	Cleveland Indians
1949	New York Yankees
1950	New York Yankees
1951	New York Yankees
1952	New York Yankees
1953	New York Yankees
1954	New York Giants
1955	Brooklyn Dodgers
1956	New York Yankees
1957	Milwaukee Braves
1958	New York Yankees
1959	Los Angeles Dodgers
1960	Pittsburgh Pirates
1961	New York Yankees
1962	New York Yankees
1963	Los Angeles Dodgers
1964	St Louis Cardinals
1965	Los Angeles Dodgers
1966	Baltimore Orioles
1967	St Louis Cardinals
1968	Detroit Tigers
1969	New York Mets
1970	Baltimore Orioles
1971	Pittsburgh Pirates
1972	Oakland Athletics
1973	Oakland Athletics
1974	Oakland Athletics
1975	Cincinnati Reds
1976	Cincinnati Reds
1977	New York Yankees
1978	New York Yankees
1979	Pittsburgh Pirates
1980	Philadelphia Phillies
1981	Los Angeles Dodgers
1982	St Louis Cardinals
1983	Baltimore Orioles
1984	Detroit Tigers
1985	Kansas City Royals
1986	New York Mets
1987	Minnesota Twins
1988	Los Angeles Dodgers
1989	Oakland Athletics
1990	Cincinnati Reds
1991	Minnesota Twins
1992	Toronto Blue Jays
1993	Toronto Blue Jays

BASKETBALL

WORLD CHAMPIONSHIPS

Men		Women	
1950	Argentina	1953	USA
1954	USA	1957	USA
1959	Brazil	1959	USSR
1963	Brazil	1964	USSR
1967	USSR	1967	USSR
1970	Yugoslavia	1971	USSR
1974	USSR	1975	USSR
1978	Yugoslavia	1979	USA
1982	USSR	1983	USSR
1986	USA	1986	USA
1990	Yugoslavia	1990	USA

OLYMPIC GAMES

Men				Women	
1936	USA	1968	USA	1976	USSR
1948	USA	1972	USSR	1980	USSR
1952	USA	1976	USA	1984	USA
1956	USA	1980	Yugoslavia	1988	USA
1960	USA	1984	USA	1992	CIS
1964	USA	1988	USSR		
		1992	USA		

EUROPEAN CHAMPIONSHIPS

Men					
1935	Latvia	1975	Yugoslavia	1962	USSR
1937	Lithuania	1977	Yugoslavia	1964	USSR
1939	Lithuania	1979	USSR	1966	USSR
1946	Czechoslovakia	1981	USSR	1968	USSR
1947	USSR	1983	Italy	1970	USSR
1949	Egypt	1985	USSR	1972	USSR
1951	USSR	1987	Greece	1974	USSR
1953	USSR	1989	Yugoslavia	1976	USSR
1955	Hungary	1991	Yugoslavia	1978	USSR
1957	USSR	1993	Germany	1980	USSR
1959	USSR			1981	USSR
1961	USSR	**Women**		1983	USSR
1963	USSR	1938	Italy	1985	USSR
1965	USSR	1950	USSR	1987	USSR
1967	USSR	1952	USSR	1989	USSR
1969	USSR	1954	USSR	1991	USSR
1971	USSR	1956	USSR	1993	Spain
1973	Yugoslavia	1958	Bulgaria		
		1960	USSR		

EUROPEAN CHAMPIONSHIP FOR CLUBS

Men		Women	
1958	ASK Riga (USSR)	1959	Slavia Sofia (Bul)
1959	ASK Riga (USSR)	1960	Daugawa Riga (USSR)
1960	ASK Riga (USSR)	1961	Daugawa Riga (USSR)
1961	CSKA Moscow (USSR)	1962	Daugawa Riga (USSR)
1962	Dynamo Tbilisi (USSR)	1963	Slavia Sofia (Bul)
1963	CSKA Moscow (USSR)	1964	Daugawa Riga (USSR)
1964	Real Madrid (Spa)	1965	Daugawa Riga (USSR)
1965	Real Madrid (Spa)	1966	Daugawa Riga (USSR)
1966	Milan (Ita)	1967	Daugawa Riga (USSR)
1967	Real Madrid (Spa)	1968	Daugawa Riga (USSR)
1968	Real Madrid (Spa)	1969	Daugawa Riga (USSR)
1969	CSKA Moscow (USSR)	1970	Daugawa Riga (USSR)
1970	Varese (Ita)	1971	Daugawa Riga (USSR)
1971	CSKA Moscow (USSR)	1972	Daugawa Riga (USSR)
1972	Varese (Ita)	1973	Daugawa Riga (USSR)
1973	Varese (Ita)	1974	Daugawa Riga (USSR)
1974	Real Madrid (Spa)	1975	Daugawa Riga (USSR)
1975	Varese (Ita)	1976	CKD Praha (Cze)
1976	Varese (Ita)	1977	Daugawa Riga (USSR)
1977	Maccabi Tel Aviv (Isr)	1978	Sesto San Giovanni (Ita)
1978	Real Madrid (Spa)	1979	Red Star Belgrade (Yug)
1979	Bosna Sarajevo (Yug)	1980	Turin (Ita)
1980	Real Madrid (Spa)	1981	Daugawa Riga (USSR)
1981	Maccabi Tel Aviv (Isr)	1982	Daugawa Riga (USSR)
1982	Cantu (Ita)	1983	AS Vicenza (Ita)
1983	Cantu (Ita)	1984	Levski Spartak Sofia (Bul)
1984	Banco di Roma (Ita)	1985	AS Vicenza (Ita)
1985	Cibona Zagreb (Yug)	1986	AS Vicenza (Ita)
1986	Cibona Zagreb (Yug)	1987	AS Vicenza (Ita)
1987	Milan (Ita)	1988	AS Vicenza (Ita)
1988	Milan (Ita)	1989	Jedinsto Aida Tuzia (Yug)
1989	Jugoplastica Split (Yug)	1990	Enimont Priolo (Ita)
1990	Jugoplastica Split (Yug)	1991	Cesena (Ita)
1991	Pop 84 Split (Yug)	1992	Valencia (Spa)
1992	Partizan Belgrade (Yug)	1993	Valencia (Spa)
1993	Limoges (Fra)		

USA NATIONAL BASKETBALL ASSOCIATION CHAMPIONSHIPS

1947	Philadelphia Warriors	1956	Philadelphia Warriors
1948	Baltimore Bullets	1957	Boston Celtics
1949	Minneapolis Lakers	1958	St Louis Hawks
1950	Minneapolis Lakers	1959	Boston Celtics
1951	Rochester Royals	1960	Boston Celtics
1952	Minneapolis Lakers	1961	Boston Celtics
1953	Minneapolis Lakers	1962	Boston Celtics
1954	Minneapolis Lakers	1963	Boston Celtics
1955	Syracuse Nationals	1964	Boston Celtics

1965	Boston Celtics	1980	Los Angeles Lakers
1966	Boston Celtics	1981	Boston Celtics
1967	Philadelphia 76ers	1982	Los Angeles Lakers
1968	Boston Celtics	1983	Philadelphia 76ers
1969	Boston Celtics	1984	Boston Celtics
1970	New York Knicks	1985	Los Angeles Lakers
1971	Milwaukee Bucks	1986	Boston Celtics
1972	Los Angeles Lakers	1987	Los Angeles Lakers
1973	New York Knicks	1988	Los Angeles Lakers
1974	Boston Celtics	1989	Detroit Pistons
1975	Golden State Warriors	1990	Detroit Pistons
1976	Boston Celtics	1991	Chicago Bulls
1977	Portland Trail Blazers	1992	Chicago Bulls
1978	Washington Bullets	1993	Chicago Bulls
1979	Seattle Supersonics		

BEACHES

EUROPEAN BLUE FLAG AWARD

The cleanliness of beaches has become a matter of increasing public concern. In 1991 thirty-five UK beaches were awarded European Blue Flags, the criteria for which include meeting EC water quality standards. Beaches had to have less than 2000 faecal bacteria per 100ml of water. In 1992, however, the Blue Flag judges made that target 100 bacteria per 100ml and only nineteen UK beaches qualified for Blue Flags.

In 1992 the nineteen awards of the European Blue Flag to the UK went to:

Tynemouth, Longsands South, Tyne and
    Wear
Hunstanton, Norfolk
Southwold, Suffolk
Sheerness, Kent
Hayling Island West, Hants
Colwell Bay, Isle of Wight
Bournemouth, Dorset
Poole Sandbanks, Dorset
Oddicombe, Devon
Meadfoot, Devon

Crinnis, Cornwall
Sennen Cove, Cornwall
Porthmeor, Cornwall
Woolacombe, Devon
Cefn Sidan Pembrey, Dyfed
Tenby North, Dyfed
Whitesands, St David's, Dyfed
West Bay, Strand/Portrush, Northern
    Ireland
Benone, Northern Ireland

In 1993 the European Union's Blue Flag was again awarded to the best of Britain's beaches. These were:

Southwold, Suffolk
Hayling Island West, Hants
Beach Street, Sheerness, Kent
Crinnis, Cornwall
Porthmeor, Cornwall
Sennen Cove, Cornwall
Broadsands, Devon
Torbay, Devon
Meadfoot, Devon
Torquay, Devon

Oddicombe, Devon
Woolacombe, Devon
Durley and Fisherman's Walk,
    Bournemouth, Dorset
Sandbanks, Poole, Dorset
Cefn Sidan, Pembrey Country Park, Dyfed
Whitesands, St Davids, Dyfed
West Bay Strand, Portrush, Northern
    Ireland
Benone, Northern Ireland

BEAUTY

NEW WOMAN BEAUTY AWARDS

In 1992 *New Woman* launched the first-ever beauty awards in this country. The aim was to provide consumers with a unique and authoritative guide to the very best beauty products on the market. The 1993 winning products (name of manufacturer in brackets) were:

Best

New Product Design After Hours Compact (Estée Lauder)

New Cosmetics Product Radiant Touch (Yves Saint Laurent)

Best New Product of the Year Radiant Touch (Yves Saint Laurent)

Established Cosmetics Product Blended Face Powder and Brush (Clinique)

New Haircare Product Pantene Pro-V Treatment Shampoo and Conditioner (Procter and Gamble)

Established Haircare Product Herbal Pack Conditioner (Estée Lauder)

New Women's Fragrance Wings (Giorgio Beverly Hills)

Established Women's Fragrance Coco (Chanel)

New Men's Fragrance Safari for Men (Parfums Ralph Lauren)

Established Men's Fragrance Eternity for Men (Calvin Klein)

New Skincare Product Ceramide Time Complex Moisture Cream (Elizabeth Arden)

Established Skincare Product Capture (Christian Dior)

New Suncare Product/Product Range Ambre Solaire UV Sport (Garnier)

Consumer Initiative Vichy News (Vichy)

Established Suncare Range Nivea Sun (Beiersdorf)

Beauty Gadget No overall winner

Consumer Service Clarins

Favourite

Make-up Range Estée Lauder

Skincare Range Clinique

BEAUTY CONTESTS

MISS WORLD

The original Miss World contest was organized in 1951 by Eric Morley, Publicity Officer of Mecca Ltd, in response to a request by his management to devise an event of international interest to coincide with the Festival of Britain celebrations. For the initial contest, held at the Lyceum Ballroom in London on 19 April, there were thirty contestants – all parading in bikinis (an innovation in Britain). The winner of the title and the £1,000 prize that accompanied it was Miss Sweden, 21-year-old Kiki Haakonson. The first UK winner of the title was Rosemarie Frankland in 1961 – followed by Ann Sidney in 1964 and Lesley Langley the next year.

The 1993 winner was Lisa Hanna, 18, a television announcer of Jamaica. Runners-up were the first black Miss South Africa, Jacqui Mofokeng, 21, and, in third place, Sharma Gutierrez of the Philippines. Miss World was crowned at South Africa's Sun City resort, west of Pretoria, in the Bophuthatswana homeland. Judges, including novelist Frederick Forsyth and actress Twiggy, chose Lisa Hanna to receive prizes totalling £125,000.

MISS UNITED KINGDOM

This competition has been held annually since 1958 in Blackpool, with the winner gaining automatic entry into the Miss World contest. The first winner was Eileen Sheridan of Walton-on-Thames. Recent winners were:

1992	Claire Smith
1993	Amanda Johnson, 19, of Nottingham

MISS GREAT BRITAIN

This was inaugurated in 1945 by the then Morecambe and Heysham Borough Council. After local government reorganization in 1974 Lancaster City Council promoted the contest in association with Pontin's Holidays. The first winner in 1945 was Lydia Reed of Morecambe and Heysham.

MISS AMERICA

According to the *Shell Book of Firsts* the original bathing beauty contest in which competitors were judged in swimsuits was held at Atlantic City, New Jersey, for the title of Miss America on 7 September 1921. The practice of naming beauty queens after their country originated with this. The first Miss America, Margaret Gorman, was only 15 years old when she was chosen to enter the contest as Miss Washington, DC and was still a pupil at Western High School in Georgetown.

In 1993, 18-year-old Kimberly Aiken, of South Carolina, was picked in Atlantic City from five finalists each of whom was required to explain her platform – the special cause she planned to promote if chosen as Miss America. As well as the title, Miss Aiken received a $35,000 (£22,800) college scholarship, a car and an estimated $200,000 (£130,000) in speaking fees.

BEER

CAMRA CHAMPION BEER OF BRITAIN

The Champion Beer of Britain awards are judged at CAMRA's Great British Beer Festival.

1978	Thwaites Mild/Fuller's ESB	1986	Bateman's XXXB
1979	Fuller's London Pride	1987	Pitfield Dark Star
1980	Thwaites Best Mild	1988	Ringwood Old Thumper
1981	Fuller's ESB	1989	Fuller's Chiswick Bitter
1982	Taylor Landlord	1990	Ind Coope Burton Ale
1983	Taylor Landlord	1991	Mauldon's Black Adder
1984	*not held*	1992	Woodforde's Norfolk Nog
1985	Fuller's ESB	1993	Adnam's Extra

In addition to the supreme champion, listed above, winners are also announced in eight classes. Category winners for 1993 were:

Milds Woodeforde's Mardler's Mild

Bitters Taylor's Best Bitter

Best Bitters Adnam's Extra

Strong Bitters Exe Valley Exeter Old Bitter

Old Ales Sarah Hughes Original Mild

Barley Wines Woodeforde's Headcracker

Porters and Stouts Coach House Blunderbus Porter

Bottle-conditioned beers Eldridge Pope's Thomas Hardy Ale

See also **Pubs**

BIATHLON

OLYMPIC GAMES

Men's 10km

1980	Frank Ullrich (GDR)
1984	Eirik Kvalfoss (Nor)
1988	Frank-Peter Rötsch (GDR)
1992	Mark Kirchner (Ger)
1994	Serguei Tchepikov (Rus)

Men's 20km

1960	Klas Lestander (Swe)
1964	Vladimir Melanin (USSR)
1968	Magnar Solberg (Nor)
1972	Magnar Solberg (Nor)
1976	Nikolai Kruglov (USSR)
1980	Anatoly Alyabyev (USSR)
1984	Peter Angerer (FRG)
1988	Frank-Peter Rötsch (GDR)
1992	Yevgeniy Redkine (CIS)
1994	Serguei Tarasov (Rus)

Men's 4 × 7.5km Relay

1968	USSR
1972	USSR
1976	USSR
1980	USSR
1984	USSR
1988	USSR
1992	Germany
1994	Germany

Women's 7.5km

1992	Anfissa Restzova (CIS)

Women's 15km

1992	Antje Misersky (Ger)
1994	

Women's 3 × 7.5km

1992	France

BIRDS

BIRD PHOTOGRAPH OF THE YEAR

An annual competition run by *British Birds* magazine and sponsored by publishers Christopher Helm and HarperCollins. Amateur and professional photographers are invited to submit up to three colour transparencies for consideration for the title 'Bird Photograph of the Year'. They are judged not only on technical excellence, but also on originality, scientific interest, aesthetic appeal and artistic composition.

1977	Michael C. Wilkes	1986	Alan Moffett
1978	Peter Lowes	1987	Dr Kevin Carlson
1979	Dr Edmund Fellowes	1988	Bob Glover
1980	Don Smith	1989	Hanne Eriksen
1981	Richard T. Mills	1990	Hanne Eriksen
1982	Dennis Coutts	1991	Philip Perry
1983	David M. Cottridge	1992	Bob Glover
1984	John Lawton Roberts	1993	Alan Williams
1985	C. R. Knights		

BIRD ILLUSTRATOR OF THE YEAR

An annual award run by *British Birds* magazine and sponsored by Kowa Telescopes. In 1994, amateur and professional artists were invited to submit four line-drawings suitable for publication (pen and ink or scraperboard, but not pencil or wash). The subjects should be birds recorded in the West Palearctic (Europe, North Africa and the Middle East).

1979	Crispin Fisher	1987	David Quinn
1980	Norman Arlott	1988	Martin Hallam
1981	Norman Arlott	1989	John Cox
1982	Alan Harris	1990	Gordon Trunkfield
1983	Martin Woodcock	1991	John Davis
1984	Bruce Pearson	1992	John Gale
1985	Ian Lewington	1993	Richard Allen
1986	Chris Rose		

RICHARD RICHARDSON AWARD

British Birds magazine also organizes the Richard Richardson Award, to encourage young, up-and-coming bird artists, in memory of the famous Norfolk ornithologist and bird-artist, the late R. A. Richardson. The rules for entry are exactly the same as for Bird Illustrator of the Year and entries by persons under 21 are automatically considered for both awards.

1979	Alan F. Johnston	1987	Andy Birch
1980	Andrew Stock	1988	John Cox
1981	Darren Rees	1989	Stephen Message
1982	Keith Colcombe	1990	Antony Disley
1983	Gary Wright	1991	{ Andrew Birch
1984	Keith Colcombe		Peter Leonard
1985	Ian Lewington	1992	Antony Disley
1986	Timothy Hinley	1993	Peter Leonard

BIRD BRAIN OF BRITAIN

Rather different from the above is *Birdkeeper* magazine's *Bird Brain of Britain* – awarded in 1993 to Penny, an Amazon parrot who renders impressions of a baby crying and a horse.

BOBSLEIGH

OLYMPIC GAMES

Two-man Bob

1932	Hubert Stevens and Curtis Stevens (USA)
1936	Ivan Brown and Alan Washbond (USA)
1948	Felix Endrich and Friedrich Waller (Swi)
1952	Andreas Ostler and Lorenz Nieberl (FRG)
1956	Lamberto Dalla Costa and Giacomo Conti (Ita)
1964	Tony Nash and Robin Dixon (UK)
1968	Eugenio Monti and Luciano de Paolis (Ita)
1972	Wolfgang Zimmerer and Peter Utzschneider (FRG)
1976	Meinhard Nehmer and Bernhard Germeshausen (GDR)
1980	Erich Schärer and Josef Benz (Swi)
1984	Wolfang Hoppe and Dietmar Schauerhammer (GDR)
1988	Janis Kipurs and Vladimir Kozlov (USSR)
1992	Gustav Weder and Donad Acklin (Swi)
1994	Switzerland

Four-man Bob

1924	Switzerland
1928	USA
1932	USA
1936	Switzerland
1948	USA
1952	West Germany
1956	Switzerland
1964	Canada
1968	Italy
1972	Switzerland
1976	East Germany
1980	East Germany
1984	East Germany
1988	Switzerland
1992	Austria
1994	Germany

Men's Luge Single-seater

1964	Thomas Köhler (GDR)
1968	Manfred Schmid (Aut)
1972	Wolfgang Scheidel (GDR)
1976	Detlef Günther (GDR)
1980	Bernhard Glass (GDR)
1984	Paul Hildgartner (Ita)
1988	Jens Müller (GDR)
1992	Georg Hackl (Ger)
1994	Georg Hackl (Ger)

Women's Luge Single-seater

1964	Ortrun Enderlein (GDR)
1968	Erica Lechner (Ita)
1972	Anna-Maria Müller (GDR)
1976	Margit Schumann (GDR)
1980	Vera Zozulya (USSR)
1984	Steffi Martin (GDR)
1988	Steffi Walter (née Martin) (GDR)
1992	Doris Neuner (Aut)
1994	Gerda Weissensteiner (Ita)

Luge Two-seater

1964	Josef Feistmantl and Manfred Stengl (Aut)
1968	Thomas Köhler and Klaus Bonsack (GDR)
1972	Paul Hildgartner and Walter Plaikner (Ita)
	Horst Hörnlein and Reinhard Bredow (GDR)
1976	Hans Rinn and Norbert Hahn (GDR)
1980	Hans Rinn and Norbert Hahn (GDR)
1984	Hans Stanggasinger and Franz Wembacher (FRG)
1988	Jörg Hoffman and Jochen Pietzsch (GDR)
1992	Stefan Krausse and Jan Behrendt (Ger)
1994	Italy

BOOKS

BRITISH BOOK AWARDS

These are awarded by various organizations and individuals in different categories to celebrate the previous year in the book trade. Categories may vary each year.

The KPMG Peat Marwick Publisher of the Year

1989	Faber and Faber
1990	Transworld Publishers
1991	Headline Books
1992	Dorling Kindersley
1993	Transworld

The David and Charles Independent Bookseller of the Year

1989	Alison's Bookshop, Bolton, Greater Manchester
1990	Pritchard's Bookshop, Crosby, Cumbria
1991	Kaydee Bookshop, Clitheroe, Lancs
1992	James Thin, Dundee
1993	The Pan Bookshop, Fulham Road, London

The Reader's Digest Chain Bookseller of the Year

1989	Waterstone's, Edinburgh
1990	Sherratt and Hughes, Manchester
1991	Waterstone's, Bournemouth
1992	Waterstone's, Nottingham
1993	Books etc, Charing Cross Road, London

The Securicor Omega Express Author of the Year

1989	HRH the Prince of Wales for *A Vision of Britain*
1990	Peter Ackroyd for *Dickens*
1991	Peter Mayle for *Toujours Provence*
1992	Andrew Morton for *Diana: Her True Story*
1993	Roddy Doyle for *Paddy Clarke Ha Ha Ha*

The Editor of the Year (sponsored by author Ken Follett)

1990	Dan Franklin
1991	Michael Fishwick
1992	Neil Belton
1993	Diane Pearson

The Vista Computer Services Distributor of the Year

1990	Grantham Book Services
1991	Penguin Distribution
1992	Tiptree Book Services
1993	Penguin Distribution

The Book Jacket of the Year

1989	Virago Crime Series (Virago)
1990	William Boyd, *Brazzaville Beach* (Sinclair-Stevenson)
1991	Roddy Doyle, *The Van* (Secker & Warburg)
1992	Donna Tartt, *The Secret History* (Viking)

The Book Promotion of the Year

1989	Debbie Wilkinson and Caroline Bishop for *Stark* by Ben Elton
1990	Louise Weir for *Joy* by Marsha Hunt
1991	Nick McDowell for *Scarlett* by Alexandra Ripley
1992	Briar Silich and Mary Harpley for *Sex* by Madonna / Alison Barrow for *Nobody Nowhere* by Donna Williams

ODDEST OF THE ODD BOOK TITLE AWARD

Much amusement is generated each year when *The Bookseller*, the established organ of the book trade, presents this annual award. The December 1993 award went to *Proceedings of the Second International Workshop on Nude Mice.* It was a narrow victory. Close challengers included *Big and Very Big Hole Drilling, Oral Sadism and the Vegetarian Personality* and *The Joy of Chickens. How to Avoid Huge Ships* came close, as did *Versailles: The View from Sweden.*

BESTSELLING TITLES

Bookwatch Ltd produce a weekly list of bestselling titles for *The Bookseller* magazine (excluding dictionaries and the *Highway Code*). Below is the list of annual bestsellers for 1993, based on the number of appearances in the weekly list (given in the right-hand column).

Hardbacks   *Number of appearances*

John McCarthy, Jill Morrell, *Some Other Rainbow*	36 weeks
Delia Smith, *Delia Smith's Summer Collection*	31 weeks
Roddy Doyle, *Paddy Clarke Ha Ha Ha*	23 weeks
Guinness Book of Records (two editions combined)	23 weeks
Michelin: Red Guide to France 1993	20 weeks

Hardback Fiction

Roddy Doyle, *Paddy Clarke Ha Ha Ha*	24 weeks
Wilbur Smith, *River God*	20 weeks

Vikram Seth, *A Suitable Boy*	18 weeks
Jilly Cooper, *The Man Who Made Husbands Jealous*	18 weeks
Sue Townsend, *Adrian Mole: The Wilderness Years*	16 weeks

Paperbacks

Jung Chang, *Wild Swans*	26 weeks
Joanna Trollope, *The Rector's Wife*	26 weeks
Joanna Trollope, *The Choir*	23 weeks
John Grisham, *The Pelican Brief*	21 weeks
Robert Harris, *Fatherland*	18 weeks
Joanna Trollope, *The Men and The Girls*	18 weeks

BOWLS

The major championship winners in this sport are:

WORLD OUTDOOR CHAMPIONSHIPS

Men's Singles

1966	David Bryant (Eng)
1972	Malwyn Evans (Wal)
1976	Doug Watson (SAf)
1980	David Bryant (Eng)
1984	Peter Belliss (NZ)
1988	David Bryant (Eng)
1992	Tony Allcock (Eng)

1980	Alf Sandercock & Peter Rheuben (Aus)
1984	George Adrain (Scott) & Skippy Arculli (USA)
1988	Rowan Brassey & Peter Belliss (NZ)
1992	Richard Corsie & Alex Marshall (Sco)

Men's Pairs

1966	Geoff Kelly & Bert Palm (Aus)
1972	Clementi Delgado & Eric Liddell (HK)
1976	Doug Watson & William Moseley (SAf)

Men's Triples

1966	Australia
1972	United States
1976	South Africa
1980	England
1984	Ireland

| 1988 | New Zealand |
| 1992 | Israel |

Men's Fours

1966	New Zealand
1972	England
1976	South Africa
1980	Hong Kong
1984	England
1988	Ireland
1992	Scotland

Leonard Trophy

1966	Australia
1972	Scotland
1976	South Africa
1980	England
1984	England
1988	England
1992	Scotland

Women's Singles

1969	Gladys Doyle (PNG)
1973	Elsie Wilke (NZ)
1977	Elsie Wilke (NZ)
1981	Norma Shaw (Eng)
1985	Merle Richardson (Aus)
1988	Janet Ackland (Wal)
1992	Margaret Johnston (Ire)

Women's Pairs

| 1969 | Elsie McDonald & May Cridian (SAf) |
| 1973 | Lorna Lucas & Dot Jenkinson (Aus) |

1977	Helen Wong & Elvie Chok (HK)
1981	Eileen Bell & Nan Allely (Ire)
1985	Merle Richardson & Fay Craig (Aus)
1988	Margaret Johnston & Phyliss Nolan (Ire)
1992	Margaret Johnston & Phyllis Nolan (Ire)

Women's Triples

1969	South Africa
1973	New Zealand
1977	Wales
1981	Hong Kong
1985	Australia
1988	Australia
1992	Scotland

Women's Fours

1969	South Africa
1973	New Zealand
1977	Australia
1981	England
1985	Scotland
1988	Australia
1992	Scotland

Women's Team

1969	South Africa
1973	New Zealand
1977	Australia
1981	England
1985	Australia
1988	England
1992	Scotland

WORLD INDOOR CHAMPIONSHIPS

Men's Singles

1979	David Bryant (Eng)
1980	David Bryant (Eng)
1981	David Bryant (Eng)
1982	John Watson (Sco)
1983	Bob Sutherland (Sco)
1984	Jim Baker (Ire)
1985	Terry Sullivan (Wal)
1986	Tony Allcock (Eng)
1987	Tony Allcock (Eng)
1988	Hugh Duff (Sco)
1989	Richard Corsie (Sco)
1990	John Price (Wal)
1991	Richard Corsie (Sco)

| 1992 | Ian Schuback (Aus) |
| 1993 | Richard Corsie (Sco) |

Men's Pairs

1986	David Bryant & Tony Allcock (Eng)
1987	David Bryant & Tony Allcock (Eng)
1988	Ian Schuback & Jim Yates (Aus)
1989	David Bryant & Tony Allcock (Eng)
1990	David Bryant & Tony Allcock (Eng)
1991	David Bryant & Tony Allcock (Eng)
1992	David Bryant & Tony Allcock (Eng)
1993	Andy Thomson & Gary Smith (Eng)

Women's Singles

1988	Margaret Johnston (Ire)
1989	Margaret Johnston (Ire)
1990	Fleur Bougourd (Eng)
1991	Mary Price (Eng)
1992	Sarah Gourlay (Sco)
1993	Kate Adams (Sco)

BOXING

WORLD CHAMPIONSHIPS

The status of world boxing champions is, as it always has been and probably always will be, very complicated. Rather than try to condense the results, the information given here includes every champion of each weight since the introduction of gloves. The current categories are: IBF (International Boxing Federation); WBA (World Boxing Association); WBC (World Boxing Council); and WBO (World Boxing Organization).

Heavyweight

1892/7	James J. Corbett (USA)
1897/9	Bob Fitzsimmons (Eng)
1899/1905	James J. Jeffries (USA)
1905/6	Marvin Hart (USA)
1906/8	Tommy Burns (Can)
1908/15	Jack Johnson (USA)
1915/9	Jess Willard (USA)
1919/26	Jack Dempsey (USA)
1926/8	Gene Tunney (USA)
1930/2	Max Schmeling (Ger)
1932/3	Jack Sharkey (USA)
1933/4	Primo Carnera (Ita)
1934/5	Max Baer (USA)
1935/7	James J. Braddock (USA)
1937/49	Joe Louis (USA)
1949/50	Ezzard Charles (USA) (NBA)
1950	Lee Savold (USA) (GB/EBU)
1950/1	Ezzard Charles (USA)
1951/2	Jersey Joe Walcott (USA)
1952/6	Rocky Marciano (USA)
1956/9	Floyd Patterson (USA)
1959/60	Ingemar Johansson (Swe)
1960/2	Floyd Patterson (USA)
1962/4	Sonny Liston (USA)
1964/5	Muhammad Ali (USA)
1965/7	Muhammad Ali (USA) (WBC)
1965/7	Ernie Terrell (USA) (WBA)
1967	Muhammad Ali (USA)
1968/70	Joe Frazier (USA) (WBC)
1968/70	Jimmy Ellis (USA) (WBA)
1970/3	Joe Frazier (USA)
1973/4	George Foreman (USA)
1974/8	Muhammad Ali (USA)
1978	Leon Spinks (USA)
1978	Leon Spinks (USA) (WBA)
1978/83	Larry Holmes (USA) (WBC)
1978/9	Muhammad Ali (USA) (WBA)
1979/80	John Tate (USA) (WBA)
1980/2	Mike Weaver (USA) (WBA)
1982/3	Michael Dokes (USA) (WBA)
1983/4	Gerrie Coetzee (SAf) (WBA)
1984	Tim Witherspoon (USA) (WBC)
1984/6	Pinklon Thomas (USA) (WBC)
1984/5	Larry Holmes (USA) (IBF)
1984/5	Greg Page (USA) (WBA)
1985/6	Tony Tubbs (USA) (WBA)
1985/7	Michael Spinks (USA) (IBF)
1986	Tim Witherspoon (USA) (WBA)
1986	Trevor Berbick (Jam) (WBC)
1986/7	Mike Tyson (USA) (WBC)
1986/7	James Smith (USA) (WBA)
1987	Mike Tyson (USA) (WBA/WBC)
1987	Tony Tucker (USA) (IBF)
1987/9	Mike Tyson (USA)
1989/90	Mike Tyson (USA) (IBF/WBA/WBC)
1989/91	Francesco Damiani (Ita) (WBO)
1990	James Douglas (USA) (IBF/WBA/WBC)
1990/2	Evander Holyfield (USA) (IBF/WBA/WBC)
1991/2	Ray Mercer (USA) (WBO)
1992/3	Michael Moorer (USA) (WBO)
1992	Riddick Bowe (USA) (IBF/WBA/WBC)
1992/3	Riddick Bowe (USA) (IBF/WBA)
1992–	Lennox Lewis (GB) (WBC)
1993	Tommy Morrison (USA) (WBO)

1993/4	Michael Bent (GB) (WBO)
1993/4	Evander Holyfield (USA) (IBF/WBA)
1994–	Michael Moorer (USA) (IBF/WBA)
1994–	Herbie Hyde (GB) (WBO)

Cruiserweight

1979/80	Marvin Camel (USA) (WBC)
1980/2	Carlos de Leon (PuR) (WBC)
1982/4	Ossie Ocasio (PuR) (WBA)
1982/3	S. T. Gordon (USA) (WBC)
1983/4	Marvin Camel (USA) (IBF)
1983/5	Carlos de Leon (PuR) (WBC)
1984/6	Lee Roy Murphy (USA) (IBF)
1984/5	Piet Crous (SAf) (WBA)
1985	Alfonso Ratliff (USA) (WBC)
1985/6	Dwight Muhammad Qawi (USA) (WBA)
1985/6	Bernard Benton (USA) (WBC)
1986/8	Carlos de Leon (PuR) (WBC)
1986/7	Rickey Parkey (USA) (IBF)
1986/7	Evander Holyfield (USA) (WBA)
1987/8	Evander Holyfield (USA) (WBA/IBF)
1988	Evander Holyfield (USA)
1989	Taoufik Belbouli (Fra) (WBA)
1989/90	Carlos de Leon (PuR) (WBC)
1989/90	Glenn McCrory (Eng) (IBF)
1989/91	Robert Daniels (USA) (WBA)
1989/90	Boone Pultz (USA) (WBO)
1990/1	Jeff Lampkin (USA) (IBF)
1990/2	Magne Havnaa (Nor) (WBO)
1990/1	Masimilliano Duran (Ita) (WBC)
1991/3	Bobby Czyz (USA) (WBA)
1991–	Anaclet Wamba (Fra) (WBC)
1991/2	James Warring (USA) (IBF)
1992/3	Tyrone Booze (USA) (WBO)
1992–	Al Cole (USA) (IBF)
1993	Markus Bott (Ger) (WBO)
1993–	Nestor Giovannini (Arg) (WBO)
1993–	Orlin Norris (USA) (WBA)

Light Heavyweight

1903	Jack Root (Aut) (USA)
1903	George Gardner (Ire) (USA)
1903/5	Bob Fitzsimmons (Eng)
1905/12	Jack O'Brien (USA)
1912/6	Jack Dillon (USA)
1916/20	Battling Levinsky (USA)
1920/2	Georges Carpentier (Fra)
1922/3	Battling Siki (Sen)
1923/5	Mike McTigue (Ire)

1925/6	Paul Berlenbach (USA)
1926/7	Jack Delaney (Can)
1927	Jimmy Slattery (USA) (NBA)
1927	Tommy Loughran (USA) (NY)
1927/9	Tommy Loughran (USA)
1930	Jimmy Slattery (USA) (NY)
1930/3	Maxie Rosenbloom (USA) (NY)
1932	George Nichols (USA) (NBA)
1933	Bob Godwin (USA) (NBA)
1933/4	Maxie Rosenbloom (USA)
1934/5	Bob Olin (USA)
1935/8	John Henry Lewis (USA)
1938/9	Tiger Jack Fox (USA) (NY)
1939	Melio Bettina (USA) (NY)
1939/42	Len Harvey (Eng) (GB)
1939/40	Billy Conn (USA) (NY/NBA)
1941	Anton Christoforidis (Gre) (NBA)
1941/6	Gus Lesnevich (USA) (NY/NBA)
1942/6	Freddie Mills (Eng) (GB)
1946/8	Gus Lesnevich (USA)
1948/50	Freddie Mills (Eng)
1950/2	Joey Maxim (USA)
1952/61	Archie Moore (USA)
1961/2	Archie Moore (USA) (NY/EBU)
1961/2	Harold Johnson (USA) (NBA)
1962/3	Harold Johnson (USA)
1963/5	Willie Pastrano (USA)
1965/6	Jose Torres (PuR)
1966/8	Dick Tiger (Nig)
1968/71	Bob Foster (USA)
1971/2	Bob Foster (USA) (WBC)
1971/2	Vicente Rondon (Ven) (WBA)
1972/4	Bob Foster (USA)
1974/7	John Conteh (Eng) (WBC)
1974/8	Victor Galindez (Arg) (WBA)
1977/8	Miguel Cuello (Arg) (WBC)
1978	Mate Parlov (Yug) (WBC)
1978/9	Mike Rossman (USA) (WBA)
1978/9	Marvin Johnson (USA) (WBC)
1979	Victor Galindez (Arg) (WBA)
1979/81	Matt Saad Muhammad (USA) (WBC)
1979/80	Marvin Johnson (USA) (WBA)
1980/1	Mustafa Muhammad (USA) (WBA)
1981/3	Michael Spinks (USA) (WBA)
1981/3	Dwight Muhammad Qawi (USA) (WBC)
1983/5	Michael Spinks (USA)
1985/6	J. B. Williamson (USA) (WBC)
1985/6	Slobodan Kacar (Yug) (IBF)

1986/7	Marvin Johnson (USA) (WBA)
1986/7	Dennis Andries (Guy) (WBC)
1986/7	Bobby Czyz (USA) (IBF)
1987	Thomas Hearns (USA) (WBC)
1987	Leslie Stewart (Tri) (WBA)
1987/91	Virgil Hill (USA) (WBA)
1987/93	Charles Williams (USA) (IBF)
1987/8	Don Lalonde (Can) (WBC)
1988	Sugar Ray Leonard (USA) (WBC)
1988/91	Michael Moorer (USA) (WBO)
1989	Dennis Andries (Guy) (WBC)
1989/90	Jeff Harding (Aus) (WBC)
1990/1	Dennis Andries (Eng) (WBC)
1991/2	Thomas Hearns (USA) (WBA)
1991–	Leonzer Barber (USA) (WBO)
1991–	Jeff Harding (Aus) (WBC)
1992	Iran Barkley (USA) (WBA)
1992–	Virgil Hill (USA) (WBA)
1993–	Henry Maske (Ger) (IBF)

Super-Middleweight

1984	Murray Sutherland (Sco) (IBF)
1984/7	Chong-Pal Park (SKo) (IBF)
1987/8	Chong-Pal Park (SKo) (WBA)
1988/9	Graciano Rocchigiani (Ger) (IBF)
1988/9	Fully Obelmejias (Ven) (WBA)
1988/90	Sugar Ray Leonard (USA) (WBC)
1988/91	Thomas Hearns (USA) (WBO)
1989/90	In-Chul Baek (SKo) (WBA)
1990/1	Lindell Holmes (USA) (IBF)
1990/1	Christophe Tiozzo (Fra) (WBA)
1990/2	Mauro Galvano (Ita) (WBC)
1991/2	Victor Cordoba (Pan) (WBA)
1991/2	Darrin van Horn (USA) (IBF)
1991–	Chris Eubank (Eng) (WBO)
1992/3	Iran Barkley (USA) (IBF)
1992/4	Michael Nunn (USA) (WBA)
1992–	Nigel Benn (Eng) (WBC)
1993–	James Toney (USA) (IBF)
1994–	Steve Little (USA) (WBA)

Middleweight

1890/1	Nonpareil Jack Dempsey (Ire)
1891/7	Bob Fitzsimmons (Eng)
1897/8	Kid McCoy (USA)
1898/1907	Tommy Ryan (USA)
1907/8	Stanley Ketchel (USA)
1908	Billy Papke (USA)
1908/10	Stanley Ketchel (USA)
1911/2	Billy Papke (USA) (GB)
1912/3	Frank Mantell (USA) (USA)
1912/3	Billy Papke (USA) (IBU)

1913	Frank Klaus (USA) (IBU)
1913/4	George Chip (USA) (USA)
1914	Eddie McGoorty (USA) (AUSTR)
1914	Jeff Smith (USA) (AUSTR)
1914/7	Al McCoy (USA) (USA)
1914	Mick King (Aus) (AUSTR)
1914/5	Jeff Smith (USA) (AUSTR)
1915/7	Les Darcy (Aus) (AUSTR)
1917/20	Mike O'Dowd (USA)
1920/3	Johnny Wilson (USA)
1922	Bryan Downey (USA) (OHIO)
1922	Dave Rosenberg (USA) (NY)
1922/3	Jock Malone (USA) (OHIO)
1922/3	Mike O'Dowd (USA) (NY)
1923	Lou Bogash (USA) (NY)
1923/6	Harry Greb (USA)
1926	Tiger Flowers (USA)
1926/31	Mickey Walker (USA)
1931/2	Gorilla Jones (USA) (NBA)
1932	Marcel Thil (Fra) (NBA/IBU)
1932/7	Marcel Thil (Fra) (IBU)
1933	Ben Jeby (USA) (NY)
1933	Gorilla Jones (USA) (NBA)
1933	Lou Brouillard (Can) (NY/NBA)
1933/4	Vince Dundee (USA) (NY/NBA)
1934/5	Teddy Yarosz (USA) (NY/NBA)
1935/6	Babe Risko (USA) (NY/NBA)
1936/7	Freddie Steele (USA) (NY/NBA)
1937/8	Freddie Steele (USA) (NBA)
1937/8	Fred Apostoli (USA) (IBU)
1937/9	Fred Apostoli (USA) (NY)
1938	Edouard Tenet (Fra) (IBU)
1938	Al Hostak (USA) (NBA)
1938/9	Solly Krieger (USA) (NBA)
1939/40	Al Hostak (USA) (NBA)
1939/40	Ceferino Garcia (Phi) (NY)
1940/1	Ken Overlin (USA) (NY)
1940/1	Tony Zale (USA) (NBA)
1941	Billy Soose (USA) (NY)
1941/7	Tony Zale (USA)
1947/8	Rocky Graziano (USA)
1948	Tony Zale (USA)
1948/9	Marcel Cerdan (Alg)
1949/50	Jake la Motta (USA)
1950/1	Jake la Motta (USA) (NY/NBA)
1950/1	Sugar Ray Robinson (USA) (PEN)
1951	Sugar Ray Robinson (USA)
1951	Randy Turpin (Eng)
1951/2	Sugar Ray Robinson (USA)
1953	Randy Turpin (Eng) (EBU)
1953/5	Carl Bobo Olsón (Haw)

1955/7	Sugar Ray Robinson (USA)
1957	Gene Fullmer (USA)
1957	Sugar Ray Robinson (USA)
1957/8	Carmen Basilio (USA)
1958/9	Sugar Ray Robinson (USA)
1959/60	Sugar Ray Robinson (USA) (NY/EBU)
1959/62	Gene Fullmer (USA) (NBA)
1960/1	Paul Pender (USA) (NY/EBU)
1961/2	Terry Downes (Eng) (NY/EBU)
1962/3	Paul Pender (USA) (NY/EBU)
1962/3	Dick Tiger (Nig) (NBA)
1963	Dick Tiger (Nig)
1963/5	Joey Giardello (USA)
1965/6	Dick Tiger (Nig)
1966/7	Emile Griffith (Virl)
1967	Nino Benvenuti (Ita)
1967/8	Emile Griffith (Virl)
1968/70	Nino Benvenuti (Ita)
1970/4	Carlos Monzon (Arg)
1974/6	Carlos Monzon (Arg) (WBA)
1974/6	Rodrigo Valdez (Col) (WBC)
1976/7	Carlos Monzon (Arg)
1977/8	Rodrigo Valdez (Col)
1978/9	Hugo Corro (Arg)
1979/80	Vito Antuofermo (Ita)
1980	Alan Minter (Eng)
1980/7	Marvin Hagler (USA)
1987	Marvin Hagler (USA) (WBC/IBF)
1987	Sugar Ray Leonard (USA) (WBC)
1987/8	Frank Tate (USA) (IBF)
1987/9	Sumbu Kalambay (Zaï) (WBA)
1987/8	Thomas Hearns (USA) (WBC)
1988/9	Iran Barkley (USA) (WBC)
1988/91	Michael Nunn (USA) (IBF)
1989/90	Roberto Duran (Pan) (WBC)
1989/90	Doug de Witt (USA) (WBO)
1989/91	Mike McCallum (Jam) (WBA)
1990	Nigel Benn (Eng) (WBO)
1990/1	Chris Eubank (Eng) (WBO)
1990/3	Julian Jackson (Virl) (WBC)
1991/3	James Toney (USA) (IBF)
1991/3	Gerald McClellan (USA) (WBO)
1992/3	Reggie Johnson (USA) (WBA)
1993–	Gerald McClellan (USA) (WBC)
1993/4	Chris Pyatt (Eng) (WBO)
1993–	Roy Jones (USA) (IBF)
1993–	John David Jackson (USA) (WBA)
1994–	Steve Collins (Ire) (WBO)

Light Middleweight

1962/3	Denny Moyer (USA) (WBA)
1963	Ralph Dupas (USA) (WBA)
1963/5	Sandro Mazzinghi (Ita) (WBA)
1965/6	Nino Benvenuti (Ita) (WBA)
1966/8	Ki-Soo Kim (SKo) (WBA)
1968/9	Sandro Mazzinghi (Ita) (WBA)
1969/70	Freddie Little (USA) (WBA)
1970/1	Carmelo Bossi (Ita) (WBA)
1971/4	Koichi Wajima (Jap) (WBA)
1974/5	Oscar Albarado (USA) (WBA)
1975	Koichi Wajima (Jap) (WBA)
1975	Miguel de Oliveira (Bra) (WBC)
1975/6	Jae-Do Yuh (SKo) (WBA)
1975/6	Elisha Obed (Bah) (WBC)
1976	Koichi Wajima (Jap) (WBA)
1976	José Duran (Spa) (WBA)
1976/7	Eckhard Dagge (Ger) (WBC)
1976/7	Miguel Castellini (Arg) (WBA)
1977/8	Eddie Gazo (Nic) (WBA)
1977/9	Rocky Mattioli (Ita) (WBC)
1978/9	Masashi Kudo (Jap) (WBA)
1979/81	Maurice Hope (Ant) (WBC)
1979/81	Ayub Kalule (Uga) (WBA)
1981/2	Wilfred Benitez (USA) (WBC)
1981	Sugar Ray Leonard (USA) (WBA)
1981/2	Tadashi Mihara (Jap) (WBA)
1982/3	Davey Moore (USA) (WBA)
1982/6	Thomas Hearns (USA) (WBC)
1983/4	Roberto Duran (Pan) (WBA)
1984	Mark Medal (USA) (IBF)
1984/7	Mike McCallum (Jam) (WBA)
1984/6	Carlos Santos (PuR) (IBF)
1986/7	Buster Drayton (USA) (IBF)
1986/7	Duane Thomas (USA) (WBC)
1987/8	Matthew Hilton (Can) (IBF)
1987	Lupe Aquino (Mex) (WBC)
1987/8	Gianfranco Rosi (Ita) (WBC)
1987/90	Julian Jackson (Virl) (WBA)
1988/9	Don Curry (USA) (WBC)
1988/9	Robert Hines (USA) (IBF)
1988/93	John David Jackson (USA) (WBO)
1989	Darrin van Horn (USA) (IBF)
1989	René Jacqot (Fra) (WBC)
1989/90	John Mugabi (Uga) (WBC)
1989–	Gianfranco Rosi (Ita) (IBF)
1990/3	Terry Norris (USA) (WBC)
1991	Gilbert Dele (Fra) (WBA)
1991/2	Vinnie Pazienza (USA) (WBA)
1992–	Julio Cesar Vasquez (Arg) (WBA)

1993–	Verno Phillips (USA) (WBO)
1993/4	Simon Brown (USA) (WBC)
1994–	Tony Norris (USA) (WBC)

Welterweight

1892/4	Mysterious Billy Smith (USA)
1894/8	Tommy Ryan (USA)
1898/1900	Mysterious Billy Smith (USA)
1900/1	Matty Matthews (USA)
1900	Eddie Connolly (USA)
1900	Rube Ferns (USA)
1901/4	Joe Walcott (Bar)
1904/5	Dixie Kid (USA)
1906/7	Honey Mellody (USA)
1907	Mike Twin Sullivan (USA)
1907/8	Mike Twin Sullivan (USA) (CALIF)
1907/8	Frank Mantell (USA) (OHIO)
1908/10	Harry Lewis (USA) (OHIO)
1908/10	Jimmy Gardner (USA) (LOUIS)
1910/2	Harry Lewis (USA) (GB/FR)
1910/2	Jimmy Clabby (USA) (USA/AUSTR)
1914	Waldemar Holberg (Den) (AUSTR)
1914	Tom McCormick (Ire) (AUSTR)
1914/5	Matt Wells (Eng) (AUSTR)
1915	Mike Glover (USA) (USA)
1915	Jack Britton (USA) (USA)
1915/6	Ted Kid Lewis (Eng)
1916/7	Jack Britton (USA)
1917/9	Ted Kid Lewis (Eng)
1919/22	Jack Britton (USA)
1922/6	Mickey Walker (USA)
1926/7	Pete Latzo (USA)
1927/9	Joe Dundee (Ita)
1929	Joe Dundee (Ita) (NY)
1929	Jackie Fields (USA) (NBA)
1929/30	Jackie Fields (USA)
1930	Young Jack Thompson (USA)
1930/1	Tommy Freeman (USA)
1931	Young Jack Thompson (USA)
1931/2	Lou Brouillard (Can)
1932/3	Jackie Fields (USA)
1933	Young Corbett III (Ita)
1933/4	Jimmy McLarnin (Ire)
1934	Barney Ross (USA)
1934/5	Jimmy McLarnin (Ire)
1935/8	Barney Ross (USA)
1938/40	Henry Armstrong (USA)
1940/1	Fritzie Zivic (USA)
1941/6	Red Cochrane (USA)
1946	Marty Servo (USA)
1946/51	Sugar Ray Robinson (USA)

1951	Johnny Bratton (USA) (NBA)
1951/2	Kid Gavilan (Cub) (NBA/NY)
1952/4	Kid Gavilan (Cub)
1954/5	Johnny Saxton (USA)
1955	Tony de Marco (USA)
1955/6	Carmen Basilio (USA)
1956	Johnny Saxton (USA)
1956/7	Carmen Basilio (USA)
1958	Virgil Akins (USA)
1958/60	Don Jordan (DoR)
1960/1	Benny Kid Paret (Cub)
1961	Emile Griffith (Virl)
1961/2	Benny Kid Paret (Cub)
1962/3	Emile Griffith (Virl)
1963	Luis Rodriguez (Cub)
1963/6	Emile Griffith (Virl)
1966/7	Curtis Cokes (USA) (WBA)
1966/7	Charley Shipes (USA) (CALIF)
1967/9	Curtis Cokes (USA)
1969/70	José Napoles (Cub)
1970/1	Billy Backus (USA)
1971/5	José Napoles (Cub)
1972/4	José Napoles (Cub) (WBA/WBC)
1972/4	Hedgemon Lewis (USA) (NY)
1974/5	José Napoles (Cub)
1975	José Napoles (Cub) (WBC)
1975/6	Angel Espada (PuR) (WBA)
1975/6	John H. Stracey (Eng) (WBC)
1976/9	Carlos Palomino (Mex) (WBC)
1976/80	Pipino Cuevas (Mex) (WBA)
1979	Wilfred Benitez (USA) (WBC)
1979/80	Sugar Ray Leonard (USA) (WBC)
1980	Roberto Duran (Pan) (WBC)
1980/1	Thomas Hearns (USA) (WBA)
1980/1	Sugar Ray Leonard (USA) (WBC)
1981/2	Sugar Ray Leonard (USA)
1983/4	Don Curry (USA) (WBA)
1983/5	Milton McCrory (USA) (WBC)
1984/5	Don Curry (USA) (WBA/IBF)
1985/6	Don Curry (USA)
1986	Lloyd Honeyghan (Jam)
1986/7	Lloyd Honeyghan (Jam) (WBC/IBF)
1987	Mark Breland (USA) (WBA)
1987/8	Marlon Starling (USA) (WBA)
1987/8	Jorge Vaca (Mex) (WBC)
1988/9	Lloyd Honeyghan (Jam) (WBC)
1988/91	Simon Brown (Jam) (IBF)
1988	Tomas Molinares (Col) (WBA)
1989/90	Mark Breland (USA) (WBA)
1989/90	Marlon Starling (USA) (WBC)

1989	Genaro Leon (Mex) (WBO)
1989/93	Manning Galloway (USA) (WBO)
1990/1	Aaron Davis (USA) (WBA)
1990	Maurice Blocker (USA) (WBC)
1991/2	Meldrick Taylor (USA) (WBA)
1991	Simon Brown (Jam) (WBC/IBF)
1991	Simon Brown (Jam) (WBC)
1991/3	Maurice Blocker (USA) (IBF)
1991/3	James McGirt (USA) (WBC)
1992/4	Crisanto Espana (Ven) (WBA)
1993	Gert Bo Jacobsen (Den) (WBO)
1993–	Pernell Whitaker (USA) (WBC)
1993–	Felix Trinidad (PuR) (IBF)
1993–	Eamon Loughran (GB) (WBO)
1994	Ike Quartey (Gha) (WBA)

Light Welterweight

1926/9	Mushy Callahan (USA) (NBA/NY)
1929/30	Mushy Callahan (USA) (NBA)
1930/1	Jackie Kid Berg (Eng) (NBA)
1931/2	Tony Canzoneri (USA) (NBA)
1932/3	Johnny Jadick (USA) (NBA)
1933	Battling Shaw (Mex) (NBA)
1933	Tony Canzoneri (USA) (NBA)
1933/5	Barney Ross (USA) (NBA)
1946/7	Tippy Larkin (USA) (MASS/NY)
1959/60	Carlos Ortiz (PuR) (NBA)
1960/2	Duilio Loi (Ita) (NBA)
1962	Eddie Perkins (USA) (NBA)
1962/3	Duilio Loi (Ita) (NBA)
1963	Roberto Cruz (Phi) (WBA)
1963/5	Eddie Perkins (USA) (WBA)
1965/6	Carlos Hernandez (Ven) (WBA)
1966/7	Sandro Lopopolo (Ita) (WBA)
1967/8	Paul Fujii (Haw) (WBA)
1968/72	Nicolino Loche (Arg) (WBA)
1968/70	Pedro Adigue (Phi) (WBC)
1970/4	Bruno Arcari (Ita) (WBC)
1972	Alfonso Frazer (Pan) (WBA)
1972/6	Antonio Cervantes (Col) (WBA)
1974/5	Perico Fernandez (Spa) (WBC)
1975/6	SaensakMuangsurin(Tha)(WBC)
1976/7	Wilfred Benitez (USA) (WBA)
1976	Miguel Velasquez (Spa) (WBC)
1976/8	SaensakMuangsurin(Tha)(WBC)
1977/80	Antonio Cervantes (Col) (WBA)
1977	Wilfred Benitez (USA) (NY)
1978/80	Sang-Hyun Kim (SKo) (WBC)
1980/2	Saoul Mamby (USA) (WBC)
1980/3	Aaron Pryor (USA) (WBA)
1982/3	Leroy Haley (USA) (WBC)

1983/4	Bruce Curry (USA) (WBC)
1984	Johnny Bumphus (USA) (WBA)
1984/5	Bill Costello (USA) (WBC)
1984/5	Gene Hatcher (USA) (IBF)
1984/6	Aaron Pryor (USA) (IBF)
1985/6	Ubaldo Sacco (Arg) (WBA)
1985/6	Lonnie Smith (USA) (WBC)
1986/7	Patrizio Oliva (Ita) (WBA)
1986	Gary Hinton (USA) (IBF)
1986	Rene Arredondo (Mex) (WBC)
1986/7	Tsuyoshi Hamada (Jap) (WBC)
1986/7	Joe Manley (USA) (IBF)
1987	Terry Marsh (Eng) (IBF)
1987/90	Juan M. Coggi (Arg) (WBA)
1987	Rene Arredondo (Mex) (WBC)
1987/9	Roger Mayweather (USA) (WBC)
1988	James McGirt (USA) (IBF)
1988/90	Meldrick Taylor (USA) (IBF)
1989/91	Hector Camacho (PuR) (WBO)
1989/90	Julio Cesar Chavez (Mex) (WBC)
1990/1	Julio Cesar Chavez (Mex) (IBF/WBC)
1990/1	Loreto Garza (USA) (WBA)
1991	Greg Haugen (USA) (WBO)
1991/2	Hector Camacho (PuR) (WBO)
1991/2	Edwin Rosario (PuR) (WBA)
1991/4	Julio Cesar Chavez (Mex) (WBC)
1991/2	Rafael Pineda (Col) (IBF)
1992	Akinobu Hiranaka (Jap) (WBA)
1992/3	Carlos Gonzalez (Mex) (WBO)
1992/3	Pernell Whitaker (USA) (IBF)
1992/3	Morris East (Phi) (WBA)
1993–	Juan M. Coggi (Arg) (WBA)
1993/4	Charles Murray (USA) (IBF)
1993–	Zack Padilla (USA) (WBO)
1994	Frankie Randall (USA) (WBC)
1994–	Julio Cesar Chavez (Mex) (WBC)
1994–	Jake Rodriguez (USA) (IBF)

Lightweight

1890/5	Jack McAuliffe (Ire) (USA)
1896/9	George Lavigne (USA)
1899/1902	Frank Erne (Swi)
1902/4	Joe Gans (USA)
1904/5	Jimmy Britt (USA)
1905/6	Battling Nelson (Den)
1906/8	Joe Gans (USA)
1908/10	Battling Nelson (Den)
1910/2	Ad Wolgast (USA)
1912/4	Willie Ritchie (USA)
1914/7	Freddie Welsh (Wal)

1917/25	Benny Leonard (USA)
1925	Jimmy Goodrich (USA) (NY)
1925/6	Rocky Kansas (USA)
1926/30	Sammy Mandell (USA)
1930	Al Singer (USA)
1930/3	Tony Canzoneri (USA)
1933/5	Barney Ross (USA)
1935/6	Tony Canzoneri (USA)
1936/8	Lou Ambers (USA)
1938/9	Henry Armstrong (USA)
1939/40	Lou Ambers (USA)
1940/1	Sammy Angott (USA) (NBA)
1940/1	Lew Jenkins (USA) (NY)
1941/2	Sammy Angott (USA)
1942/3	Beau Jack (USA) (NY)
1943	Slugger White (USA) (MARY)
1943	Bob Montgomery (USA) (NY)
1943/4	Sammy Angott (USA) (NBA)
1943/4	Beau Jack (USA) (NY)
1944/7	Bob Montgomery (USA) (NY)
1944/5	Juan Zurita (Mex) (NBA)
1945/7	Ike Williams (USA) (NBA)
1947/51	Ike Williams (USA)
1951/2	Jimmy Carter (USA)
1952	Lauro Salas (Mex)
1952/4	Jimmy Carter (USA)
1954	Paddy de Marco (USA)
1954/5	Jimmy Carter (USA)
1955/6	Wallace Bud Smith (USA)
1956/62	Joe Brown (USA)
1962/5	Carlos Ortiz (PuR)
1965	Ismael Laguna (Pan)
1965/8	Carlos Ortiz (PuR)
1968/9	Carlos Teo Cruz (DoR)
1969/70	Mando Ramos (USA)
1970	Ismael Laguna (Pan)
1970/1	Ken Buchanan (Sco)
1971/2	Ken Buchanan (Sco) (WBA)
1971/2	Pedro Carrasco (Spa) (WBC)
1972	Mando Ramos (USA) (WBC)
1972/8	Roberto Duran (Pan) (WBA)
1972	Chango Carmona (Mex) (WBC)
1972/4	Rodolfo Gonzalez (Mex) (WBC)
1974/6	Guts Ishimatsu (Jap) (WBC)
1976/8	Esteban de Jesus (PuR) (WBC)
1978/9	Roberto Duran (Pan)
1979/81	Jim Watt (Sco) (WBC)
1979/80	Ernesto Espana (Ven) (WBA)
1980/1	Hilmer Kenty (USA) (WBA)
1981	Sean O'Grady (USA) (WBA)
1981/3	Alexis Arguello (Nic) (WBC)

1981	Claude Noel (Tri) (WBA)
1981/2	Arturo Frias (USA) (WBA)
1982/4	Ray Mancini (USA) (WBA)
1983/4	Edwin Rosario (PuR) (WBC)
1984	Charlie Brown (USA) (IBF)
1984/5	Harry Arroyo (USA) (IBF)
1984/6	Livingstone Bramble (USA) (WBA)
1984/5	Jose Luis Ramirez (Mex) (WBC)
1985/6	Jimmy Paul (USA) (IBF)
1985/7	Hector Camacho (PuR) (WBC)
1986/7	Edwin Rosario (PuR) (WBA)
1986/7	Greg Haugen (USA) (IBF)
1987/8	Vinnie Pazienza (USA) (IBF)
1987/8	Jose Luis Ramirez (Mex) (WBC)
1987/8	Julio Cesar Chavez (Mex) (WBA)
1988/9	Greg Haugen (USA) (IBF)
1988/9	Julio Cesar Chavez (Mex) (WBA/ WBC)
1989/90	Maurizio Aceves (Mex) (WBO)
1989	Pernell Whitaker (USA) (IBF)
1989/90	Edwin Rosario (PuR) (WBA)
1989/90	Pernell Whitaker (USA) (IBF/WBC)
1990	Juan Nazario (PuR) (WBA)
1990/2	Pernell Whitaker (USA) (IBF/ WBC/WBA)
1990/2	Dingaan Thobela (SAf) (WBO)
1992	Joey Gamache (USA) (WBA)
1992–	Giovanni Parisi (Ita) (WBO)
1992/3	Tony Lopez (USA) (WBA)
1992–	Miguel Gonzalez (Mex) (WBC)
1993/4	Fred Pendleton (USA) (IBF)
1993	Dingaan Thobela (SAf) (WBA)
1993–	Obzubek Nazarov (Rus) (WBA)
1994–	Rafael Ruelas (Mex) (IBF)

Super Featherweight

1921/3	Johnny Dundee (Ita) (NY)
1923	Jack Bernstein (USA) (NBA/NY)
1923/4	Johnny Dundee (Ita) (NBA/NY)
1924/5	Kid Sullivan (USA) (NBA/NY)
1925	Mike Ballerino (USA) (NBA/NY)
1925/9	Tod Morgan (USA) (NBA/NY)
1929	Benny Bass (Rus) (NBA/NY)
1929/31	Benny Bass (Rus) (NBA)
1931/3	Kid Chocolate (Cub) (NBA)
1933/4	Frankie Klick (USA) (NBA)
1949/50	Sandy Saddler (USA) (OHIO)
1959/60	Harold Gomes (USA) (NBA)
1960/7	Flash Elorde (Phi) (NBA)
1967	Yoshiaki Numata (Jap) (WBA)
1967/71	Hiroshi Kobayashi (Jap) (WBA)

1969/70	Rene Barrientos (Phi) (WBC)
1970/1	Yoshiaki Numata (Jap) (WBC)
1971/2	Alfredo Marcano (Ven) (WBA)
1971/4	Ricardo Arredondo (Mex) (WBC)
1972/3	Ben Villaflor (Phi) (WBA)
1973	Kuniaki Shibata (Jap) (WBA)
1973/6	Ben Villaflor (Phi) (WBA)
1974/5	Kuniaki Shibata (Jap) (WBC)
1975/8	Alfredo Escalera (PuR) (WBC)
1976/80	Sam Serrano (PuR) (WBA)
1978/80	Alexis Arguello (Nic) (WBC)
1980/1	Yasutsune Uehara (Jap) (WBA)
1980/1	Rafael Limon (Mex) (WBC)
1981	Cornelius Boza-Edwards (Uga) (WBC)
1981/3	Sam Serrano (PuR) (WBA)
1981/2	Roland Navarrete (Phi) (WBC)
1982	Rafael Limon (Mex) (WBC)
1982/3	Bobby Chacon (USA) (WBC)
1983/4	Roger Mayweather (USA) (WBA)
1983/4	Hector Camacho (PuR) (WBC)
1984/5	Rocky Lockridge (USA) (WBA)
1984/5	Hwan-Kil Yuh (SKo) (IBF)
1984/7	Julio Cesar Chavez (Mex) (WBC)
1985	Lester Ellis (Eng) (IBF)
1985/6	Wilfredo Gomez (PuR) (WBA)
1985/7	Barry Michael (Eng) (IBF)
1986	Alfredo Layne (Pan) (WBA)
1986/91	Brian Mitchell (SAf) (WBA)
1987/8	Rocky Lockridge (USA) (IBF)
1988/94	Azumah Nelson (Gha) (WBC)
1988/9	Tony Lopez (USA) (IBF)
1989	Juan Molina (PuR) (WBO)
1989/90	Juan Molina (PuR) (IBF)
1989/92	Kamel Bou Ali (Tun) (WBO)
1990/1	Tony Lopez (USA) (IBF)
1991	Joey Gamache (USA) (WBA)
1991/2	Brian Mitchell (SAf) (IBF)
1991–	Genaro Hernandez (USA) (WBA)
1992–	Juan Molina (PuR) (IBF)
1992	Daniel Londas (Fra) (WBO)
1992/4	Jimmy Bredahl (Den) (WBO)
1994–	James Leija (USA) (WBC)
1994–	Oscar De La Hoya (USA) (WBO)

Featherweight

1890	Billy Murphy (NZ) (AUSTR)
1890/1	Young Griffo (Aus) (AUSTR)
1891/2	George Dixon (Can) (USA)
1892/7	George Dixon (Can)
1897/8	Solly Smith (USA)

1898	Solly Smith (USA) (USA)
1898/9	Ben Jordan (Eng) (GB)
1898	Dave Sullivan (Ire) (USA)
1899/1900	George Dixon (Can) (USA)
1899/1900	George Dixon (Can)
1900/1	Terry McGovern (USA)
1901/3	Young Corbett II (USA)
1903/4	Abe Attell (USA)
1904/5	Tommy Sullivan (USA)
1906/12	Abe Attell (USA)
1912	Abe Attell (USA) (USA)
1912/3	Jim Driscoll (Wal) (GB/IBU)
1912/3	Johnny Kilbane (USA) (USA)
1913/22	Johnny Kilbane (USA)
1922/3	Johnny Kilbane (USA) (NBA)
1922/3	Johnny Dundee (Ita) (NY)
1923	Eugene Criqui (Fra)
1923/4	Johnny Dundee (Ita)
1925/6	Kid Kaplan (Rus)
1926/7	Honeyboy Finnegan (USA) (MASS)
1927/8	Benny Bass (Rus) (NBA)
1927/8	Tony Canzoneri (USA) (NY)
1928	Tony Canzoneri (USA)
1928/9	André Routis (Fra)
1929/32	Bat Battalino (USA)
1932/3	Tommy Paul (USA) (NBA)
1932/3	Kid Chocolate (Cub) (NY)
1933/6	Freddie Miller (USA) (NBA)
1934/5	Baby Arizmendi (Mex) (NY)
1935/6	Baby Arizmendi (Mex) (CALIF)
1936/7	Petey Sarron (USA) (NBA)
1936/7	Henry Armstrong (USA) (CALIF)
1936	Mike Belloise (USA) (NY)
1937/8	Maurice Holtzer (Fra) (IBU)
1937/8	Henry Armstrong (USA) (NBA/ NY/CALIF)
1938/9	Leo Rodak (USA) (NBA)
1938/9	Joey Archibald (USA) (NY)
1939/40	Joey Archibald (USA)
1940	Joey Archibald (USA) (NY)
1940	Jimmy Perrin (USA) (LOUIS)
1940/1	Petey Scalzo (USA) (NBA)
1940/1	Harry Jeffra (USA) (NY)
1941	Joey Archibald (USA) (NY)
1941	Richie Lemos (USA) (NBA)
1941/2	Chalky Wright (Mex) (NY)
1941/2	Harry Jeffra (USA) (MARY)
1941/3	Jackie Wilson (USA) (NBA)
1942/6	Willie Pep (USA) (NY)
1943	Jackie Callura (Can) (NBA)

1943/4	Phil Terranova (USA) (NBA)
1944/6	Sal Bartolo (USA) (NBA)
1946/8	Willie Pep (USA)
1948/9	Sandy Saddler (USA)
1949/50	Willie Pep (USA)
1950/7	Sandy Saddler (USA)
1957/9	Hogan Kid Bassey (Nig)
1959/63	Davey Moore (USA)
1963/4	Sugar Ramos (Cub)
1964/7	Vicente Saldivar (Mex)
1967/8	Raul Rojas (USA) (WBA)
1968	Howard Winstone (Wal) (WBC)
1968/9	Jose Legra (Cub) (WBC)
1969/71	Shozo Saijyo (Jap) (WBA)
1969/70	Johnny Famechon (Fra) (WBC)
1970	Vicente Saldivar (Mex) (WBC)
1970/2	Kuniaki Shibata (Jap) (WBC)
1971/2	Antonio Gomez (Ven) (WBA)
1972	Clemente Sanchez (Mex) (WBC)
1972/4	Ernesto Marcel (Pan) (WBA)
1972/3	Jose Legra (Cub) (WBC)
1973/4	Eder Jofre (Bra) (WBC)
1974	Ruben Olivares (Mex) (WBA)
1974/5	Bobby Chacon (USA) (WBC)
1974/7	Alexis Arguello (Nic) (WBA)
1975	Ruben Olivares (Mex) (WBC)
1975/6	David Kotey (Gha) (WBC)
1976/80	Danny Lopez (USA) (WBC)
1977	Rafael Ortega (Pan) (WBA)
1977/8	Cecilio Lastra (Spa) (WBA)
1978/85	Eusebio Pedroza (Pan) (WBA)
1980/2	Salvador Sanchez (Mex) (WBC)
1982/4	Juan Laporte (PuR) (WBC)
1984/5	Min-Keun Chung (SKo) (IBF)
1984	Wilfredo Gomez (PuR) (WBC)
1984/7	Azumah Nelson (Gha) (WBC)
1985/6	Barry McGuigan (Ire) (WBA)
1985/6	Ki-Yung Chung (SKo) (IBF)
1986/7	Steve Cruz (USA) (WBA)
1986/7	Antonio Rivera (PuR) (IBF)
1987/91	Antonio Esparragoza (Ven) (WBF)
1988	Calvin Grove (USA) (IBF)
1988/9	Jeff Fenech (Aus) (WBC)
1988/90	Jorge Paez (Mex) (IBF)
1989/92	Maurizio Stecca (Ita) (WBO)
1989/90	Louie Espinosa (USA) (WBO)
1990/1	Jorge Paez (Mex) (IBF/WBO)
1990/1	Marcos Villasana (Mex) (WBC)
1991/3	Kyun-Yung Park (SKo) (WBA)
1991	Troy Dorsey (USA) (IBF)
1991/2	Maurizio Stecca (Ita) (WBO)

1991/3	Manuel Medina (Mex) (IBF)
1991/3	Paul Hodkinson (Eng) (WBC)
1992	Colin McMillan (Eng) (WBO)
1992/3	Ruben Palacio (Col) (WBO)
1993–	Tom Johnson (USA) (IBF)
1993–	Steve Robinson (Wal) (WBO)
1993	Gregorio Vargas (Mex) (WBC)
1993–	Kevin Kelley (USA) (WBC)
1993–	Eloy Rojas (Ven) (WBA)

Super Bantamweight

1922/3	Jack Kid Wolfe (USA) (NY)
1976	Rigoberto Riasco (Pan) (WBC)
1976	Royal Kobayashi (Jap) (WBC)
1976/7	Dong-Kyun Yum (SKo) (WBC)
1977/83	Wilfredo Gomez (PuR) (WBC)
1977/8	Soo-Hwan Hong (SKo) (WBA)
1978/80	Ricardo Cardona (Col) (WBA)
1980	Leo Randolph (USA) (WBA)
1980/2	Sergio Palma (Arg) (WBA)
1982/4	Leonardo Cruz (DoR) (WBA)
1983/4	Jaime Garza (USA) (WBC)
1983/4	Bobby Berna (Phi) (IBF)
1984	Loris Stecca (Ita) (WBA)
1984/5	Seung-In Suh (SKo) (IBF)
1984/6	Victor Callejas (PuR) (WBA)
1984/5	Juan Meza (Mex) (WBC)
1985/6	Ji-Won Kim (SKo) (IBF)
1985/6	Lupe Pintor (Mex) (WBC)
1986/7	Samart Payakarun (Tha) (WBC)
1987	Louie Espinosa (USA) (WBA)
1987/8	Seung-Hoon Lee (SKo) (IBF)
1987/8	Jeff Fenech (Aus) (WBC)
1987/8	Julio Gervacio (DoR) (WBA)
1988	Bernardo Pinango (Ven) (WBA)
1988/90	Daniel Zaragoza (Mex) (WBC)
1988/9	Jose Sanabria (Ven) (IBF)
1988/9	Juan J. Estrada (Mex) (WBA)
1989/90	Fabrice Benichou (Spa) (IBF)
1989	Kenny Mitchell (USA) (WBO)
1989/90	Valerio Nati (Ita) (WBO)
1989/90	Jesus Salud (USA) (WBA)
1990/2	Welcome Ncita (SAf) (IBF)
1990	Paul Banke (USA) (WBC)
1990/1	Orlando Fernandez (PuR) (WBO)
1990/1	Luis Mendoza (Col) (WBA)
1990/1	Pedro Decima (Arg) (WBC)
1991	Kiyoshi Hatanaka (Jap) (WBC)
1991/2	Jesse Benavides (USA) (WBO)
1991/2	Daniel Zaragoza (Mex) (WBC)
1991/2	Raul Perez (Mex) (WBA)

1992	Thierry Jacob (Fra) (WBC)
1992–	Wilfredo Vasquez (PuR) (WBA)
1992–	Tracy Harris Patterson (USA) (WBC)
1992/3	Duke McKenzie (Eng) (WBO)
1992–	Kennedy McKinney (USA) (IBF)
1993–	Daniel Jimenez (PuR) (WBO)

Bantamweight

1890/2	George Dixon (Can)
1892/5	Billy Plimmer (Eng)
1895/9	Pedlar Palmer (Eng)
1899/1900	Terry McGovern (USA)
1900/1	Dan Dougherty (USA)
1901/3	Harry Forbes (USA)
1903/4	Frankie Neil (USA)
1904/5	Joe Bowker (Eng)
1905/7	Jimmy Walsh (USA)
1907	Owen Moran (Eng) (GB)
1908/9	Johnny Coulon (Can) (USA)
1909/10	Monte Attell (USA) (CALIF)
1909/11	Johnny Coulon (Can) (LOUIS)
1910/1	Frankie Conley (Ita) (CALIF)
1910/2	Digger Stanley (Eng) (GB/IBU)
1911/4	Johnny Coulon (Can) (USA)
1912/3	Charles Ledoux (Fra) (GB/IBU)
1913/4	Eddie Campi (USA) (GB/IBU)
1914	Kid Williams (Den) (GB/IBU)
1914/7	Kid Williams (Den)
1917/20	Pete Herman (USA)
1920/1	Joe Lynch (USA)
1921	Pete Herman (USA)
1921/2	Johnny Buff (USA)
1922/3	Joe Lynch (USA)
1923/4	Joe Lynch (USA) (NBA)
1923/4	Abe Goldstein (USA) (NY)
1924	Abe Goldstein (USA)
1924/5	Eddie Martin (USA)
1925/7	Charlie Rosenberg (USA)
1927/8	Bud Taylor (USA) (NBA)
1927	Teddy Baldock (Eng) (GB)
1927/9	Willie Smith (SAf) (GB)
1928/9	Bushy Graham (Ita) (NY)
1929/31	Al Brown (Pan) (NY/IBU)
1931	Pete Sanstol (Nor) (NBA)
1931/4	Al Brown (Pan)
1934/5	Sixto Escobar (PuR) (NBA)
1934/5	Al Brown (Pan) (NY/IBU)
1935/6	BaltazarSangchilli(Spa)(NY/IBU)
1935	Lou Salica (USA) (NBA)
1935/6	Sixto Escobar (PuR) (NBA)

1936	Tony Marino (USA) (NY/IBU)
1936/7	Sixto Escobar (PuR)
1937/8	Harry Jeffra (USA)
1938/9	Sixto Escobar (PuR)
1940/2	Lou Salica (USA)
1942/7	Manuel Ortiz (USA)
1947	Harold Dade (USA)
1947/50	Manuel Ortiz (USA)
1950/2	Vic Toweel (SAf)
1952/4	Jimmy Carruthers (Aus)
1954/6	Robert Cohen (Alg) (NY/EBU)
1955/7	Raton Macias (Mex) (NBA)
1956/7	Mario D'Agata (Ita) (NY/EBU)
1957	Alphonse Halimi (Alg) (NY/EBU)
1957/9	Alphonse Halimi (Alg)
1959/60	Joe Becerra (Mex)
1960/1	Alphonse Halimi (Alg) (EBU)
1960/2	Eder Jofre (Bra) (NBA)
1961/2	Johnny Caldwell (Ire) (EBU)
1962/5	Eder Jofre (Bra)
1965/8	Fighting Harada (Jap)
1968/9	Lionel Rose (Aus)
1969/70	Ruben Olivares (Mex)
1970/1	Chuchu Castillo (Mex)
1971/2	Ruben Olivares (Mex)
1972	Rafael Herrera (Mex)
1972	Enrique Pinder (Pan)
1972/3	Enrique Pinder (Pan) (WBC)
1973	Romeo Anaya (Mex) (WBA)
1973/4	Rafael Herrera (Mex) (WBC)
1973/4	Arnold Taylor (SAf) (WBA)
1974/5	Soo-Hwan Hong (SKo) (WBA)
1974/6	Rodolfo Martinez (Mex) (WBC)
1975/7	Alfonso Zamora (Mex) (WBA)
1976/9	Carlos Zarate (Mex) (WBC)
1977/80	Jorge Lujan (Pan) (WBA)
1979/83	Lupe Pintor (Mex) (WBC)
1980	Julian Solis (PuR) (WBA)
1980/4	Jeff Chandler (USA) (WBA)
1983/5	Albert Davila (USA) (WBC)
1984/6	Richard Sandoval (USA) (WBA)
1984/5	Satoshi Shingaki (Jap) (IBF)
1985/7	Jeff Fenech (Aus) (IBF)
1985	Daniel Zaragoza (Mex) (WBC)
1985/8	Miguel Lora (Col) (WBC)
1986	Gaby Canizales (USA) (WBA)
1986/7	Bernardo Pinango (Ven) (WBA)
1987	Takuya Muguruma (Jap) (WBA)
1987/8	Kelvin Seabrooks (USA) (IBF)
1987	Chan-Yung Park (SKo) (WBA)
1987/8	Wilfredo Vasquez (PuR) (WBA)

1988	Kaokor Galaxy (Tha) (WBA)
1988–	Orlando Canizales (USA) (IBF)
1988/9	Sung-Il Moon (SKo) (WBA)
1988/91	Raul Perez (Mex) (WBC)
1989/91	Israel Contrerras (Ven) (WBO)
1989	Kaokor Galaxy (Tha) (WBA)
1989/91	Luisito Espinosa (Phi) (WBA)
1991	Greg Richardson (USA) (WBC)
1991	Gaby Canizales (USA) (WBO)
1991/2	Duke McKenzie (Eng) (WBO)
1991/2	Joichiro Tatsuyushi (Jap) (WBC)
1991/2	Israel Contrerras (Ven) (WBA)
1992	Eddie Cook (USA) (WBA)
1992/3	Victor Rabanales (Mex) (WBC)
1992–	Rafael del Valle (PuR) (WBO)
1992/3	Jorge Eliecer Julio (Col) (WBA)
1993	Il-Jung Byun (SKo) (WBC)
1993–	Yasuei Yakushiji (Jap) (WBC)
1993/4	Junior Jones (USA) (WBA)
1994–	John Michael Johnson (USA) (WBA)

Super Flyweight

1980/1	Rafael Orono (Ven) (WBC)
1981/2	Chul-Ho Kim (SKo) (WBC)
1981	Gustavo Ballas (Arg) (WBA)
1981/2	Rafael Pedroza (Pan) (WBA)
1982/4	Jiro Watanabe (Jap) (WBA)
1982/3	Rafael Orono (Ven) (WBC)
1983/4	Payao Poontarat (Tha) (WBC)
1983/5	Joo-Do Chun (SKo) (IBF)
1984/6	Jiro Watanabe (Jap) (WBC)
1985/6	Elly Pical (Ina) (IBF)
1984/91	Kaosai Galaxy (Tha) (WBA)
1986	Cesar Polanco (DoR) (IBF)
1986/7	Gilberto Roman (Mex) (WBC)
1986/7	Elly Pical (Ina) (IBF)
1987	Santos Laciar (Arg) (WBC)
1987	Tae-Il Chang (SKo) (IBF)
1987/8	Jesus Rojas (Col) (WBC)
1987/9	Elly Pical (Ina) (IBF)
1988/9	Gilberto Roman (Mex) (WBC)
1989/92	Jose Ruiz (PuR) (WBO)
1989/90	Juan Polo Perez (Col) (IBF)
1989/90	Nana Yaw Konadu (Gha) (WBC)
1990/3	Sung-Il Moon (SKo) (WBC)
1990/3	Robert Quiroga (USA) (IBF)
1992	Jose Quirino (Mex) (WBO)
1992–	Katsuya Onizuka (Jap) (WBA)
1992–	Johnny Bredahl (Den) (WBO)
1993–	Julio Cesar Borboa (Mex) (IBF)

1993/4	Jose Luis Bueno (Mex) (WBC)
1994–	Hiroshi Kawashima (Jap) (WBC)

Flyweight

1913	Sid Smith (Eng) (GB/IBU)
1913/4	Bill Ladbury (Eng) (GB/IBU)
1914	Percy Jones (Wal) (GB/IBU)
1915	Tancy Lee (Sco) (GB/IBU)
1915/6	Joe Symonds (Eng) (GB/IBU)
1916	Jimmy Wilde (Wal) (GB/IBU)
1916/23	Jimmy Wilde (Wal)
1923/5	Pancho Villa (Phi)
1925/7	Fidel la Barba (USA)
1927/8	Johnny McCoy (USA) (CALIF)
1927/8	Frenchy Belanger (Can) (NBA)
1927/9	Izzy Schwartz (USA) (NY)
1928	Newsboy Brown (Rus) (CALIF)
1928/9	Frankie Genaro (USA) (NBA)
1928/9	Johnny Hill (Sco) (GB/CALIF)
1929	Emile Pladner (Fra) (NBA/IBU)
1929/31	Frankie Genaro (USA) (NBA/IBU)
1929/30	Willie la Morte (USA) (NY)
1930/5	Midget Wolgast (USA) (NY)
1931/2	Young Perez (Tun) (NBA/IBU)
1932/5	Jackie Brown (Eng) (NBA/IBU)
1935/7	Benny Lynch (Sco) (NBA)
1935/7	Small Montana (Phi) (NY/CALIF)
1936/7	Valentin Angelmann (Fra) (IBU)
1937	Benny Lynch (Sco)
1938/40	Peter Kane (Eng) (NY/IBU)
1938/40	Young Dado (Phi) (NBA/CALIF)
1940/3	Peter Kane (Eng)
1943/7	Jackie Paterson (Sco)
1947/8	Jackie Paterson (Sco) (GB/NY)
1947/8	Rinty Monaghan (Ire) (NBA)
1948/50	Rinty Monaghan (Ire)
1950	Terry Allen (Eng)
1950/2	Dado Marino (Haw)
1952/4	Yoshio Shirai (Jap)
1954/60	Pascual Perez (Arg)
1960/2	Pone Kingpetch (Tha)
1962/3	Fighting Harada (Jap)
1963	Pone Kingpetch (Tha)
1963/4	Hiroyuki Ebihara (Jap)
1964/5	Pone Kingpetch (Tha)
1965	Salvatore Burruni (Ita)
1965/6	Salvatore Burruni (Ita) (WBC)
1966/8	Horacio Accavallo (Arg) (WBA)
1966	Walter McGowan (Sco) (WBC)
1966/9	Chartchai Chionoi (Tha) (WBC)
1969/70	Efren Torres (Mex) (WBC)

1969	Hiroyuki Ebihara (Jap) (WBA)
1969/70	Bernabe Villacampo (Phi) (WBA)
1970	Chartchai Chionoi (Tha) (WBC)
1970	Berkerk Chartvanchai (Tha) (WBA)
1970/3	Masao Ohba (Jap) (WBA)
1970/1	Erbito Salavarria (Phi) (WBC)
1972	Betulio Gonzalez (Ven) (WBC)
1972/3	Venice Borkorsor (Tha) (WBC)
1973/4	Chartchai Chionoi (Tha) (WBA)
1973/4	Betulio Gonzalez (Ven) (WBC)
1974/5	Shoji Oguma (Jap) (WBC)
1974/5	Susumu Hanagata (Jap) (WBA)
1975/9	Miguel Canto (Mex) (WBC)
1975/6	Erbito Salavarria (Phi) (WBA)
1976	Alfonso Lopez (Pan) (WBA)
1976/8	Guty Espadas (Mex) (WBA)
1978/9	Betulio Gonzalez (Ven) (WBA)
1979/80	Chan-Hee Park (SKo) (WBC)
1979/80	Luis Ibarra (Pan) (WBA)
1980	Tae-Shik Kim (SKo) (WBA)
1980/1	Shoji Oguma (Jap) (WBC)
1980/1	Peter Mathebula (SAf) (WBA)
1981	Santos Laciar (Arg) (WBA)
1981/2	Antonio Avelar (Mex) (WBC)
1981	Luis Ibarra (Pan) (WBA)
1981/2	Juan Herrera (Mex) (WBA)
1982	Prudencio Cardona (Col) (WBC)
1982/5	Santos Laciar (Arg) (WBA)
1982	Freddie Castillo (Mex) (WBC)
1982/3	Eleoncio Mercedes (DoR) (WBC)
1983	Charlie Magri (Tun) (WBC)
1983/4	Frank Cedeno (Phi) (WBC)
1983/5	Soon-Chun Kwon (SKo) (IBF)
1984	Koji Kobayashi (Jap) (WBC)
1984	Gabriel Bernal (Mex) (WBC)
1984/8	Sot Chitalada (Tha) (WBC)
1985/7	Hilario Zapata (Pan) (WBA)
1985/6	Chong-Kwan Chung (SKo) (IBF)
1986	Bi-Won Chung (SKo) (IBF)
1986/7	Hi-Sup Shin (SKo) (IBF)
1987/9	Fidel Bassa (Col) (WBA)
1987	Dodie Penalosa (Phi) (IBF)
1987/8	Chang-Ho Choi (SKo) (IBF)
1988	Rolando Bohol (Phi) (IBF)
1988/9	Yong-Kang Kim (SKo) (WBC)
1989	Elvis Alvarez (Col) (WBO)
1988/9	Duke McKenzie (Eng) (IBF)
1989/91	Sot Chitalada (Tha) (WBC)
1989/92	Dave McAuley (Ire) (IBF)
1989/90	Jesus Rojas (Ven) (WBA)
1990	Yul-Woo Lee (SKo) (WBA)

1990/2	Isidro Perez (Mex) (WBO)
1990	Yukihito Tamakuma (Jap) (WBA)
1991/2	Muangchai Kitikasem (Tha) (WBC)
1991	Elvis Alvarez (Col) (WBA)
1991/2	Yong-Kang Kim (SKo) (WBA)
1992/3	Pat Clinton (Sco) (WBO)
1992	Rodolfo Blanco (Col) (IBF)
1992–	Yuri Arbachakov (Rus) (WBC)
1992	Aquiles Guzman (Ven) (WBA)
1992–	Pichit Sitbangprachan (Tha) (IBF)
1992/4	David Griman (Ven) (WBA)
1993–	Jacob Matlala (SAf) (WBO)
1994–	Sayen Sor Ploenchit (Tha) (WBA)

Light Flyweight

1975	Franco Udella (Ita) (WBC)
1975/6	Jaime Rios (Pan) (WBA)
1975/8	Luis Estaba (Ven) (WBC)
1976	Juan Guzman (DoR) (WBA)
1976/81	Yoko Gushiken (Jap) (WBA)
1978	Freddie Castillo (Mex) (WBC)
1978	Sor Vorasingh (Tha) (WBC)
1978/80	Sun-Jun Kim (SKo) (WBC)
1980	Shigeo Nakajima (Jap) (WBC)
1980/2	Hilario Zapata (Pan) (WBC)
1981	Pedro Flores (Mex) (WBA)
1981	Hwan-Jin Kim (SKo) (WBA)
1981/3	Katsuo Tokashiki (Jap) (WBA)
1982	Amado Ursua (Mex) (WBC)
1982	Tadashi Tomori (Jap) (WBC)
1982/3	Hilario Zapata (Pan) (WBC)
1983/8	Jung-Koo Chang (SKo) (WBC)
1983/4	Lupe Madera (Mex) (WBA)
1983/6	Dodie Penalosa (Phi) (IBF)
1984/5	Francisco Quiroz (DoR) (WBA)
1985	Joey Olivo (USA) (WBA)
1985/91	Myung-Woo Yuh (SKo) (WBA)
1987/8	Jum-Hwan Choi (SKo) (IBF)
1988/9	Tacy Macalos (Phi) (IBF)
1988/9	German Torres (Mex) (WBC)
1989	Yul-Woo Lee (SKo) (WBC)
1989/90	Muangchai Kitikasem (Tha) (IBF)
1989/92	Jose de Jesus (PuR) (WBO)
1989/90	Humberto Gonzalez (Mex) (WBC)
1990/3	Michael Carbajal (USA) (IBF)
1990/1	Rolando Pascua (Phi) (WBC)
1991	Melchor Cob Castro (Mex) (WBC)
1991/3	Humberto Gonzalez (Mex) (WBC)
1991/2	Hiroki Ioka (Jap) (WBA)
1992–	Josue Camacho (PuR) (WBO)

1992/3	Myung-Woo Yuh (SKo) (WBA)
1993/4	Michael Carbajal (USA) (IBF/WBC)
1993–	Luis Gamez (Ven) (WBA)
1994–	Humberto Gonzalez (Mex) (IBF/WBC)

Mini-Flyweight

1987/8	Kyung-Yung Lee (SKo) (IBF)
1987/8	Hiroki Ioka (Jap) (WBC)
1988/9	Luis Gamez (Ven) (WBA)
1988/9	Samuth Sithnaruepol (Tha) (IBF)
1988/9	Napa Kiatwanchai (Tha) (WBC)
1989/91	Bong-Jun Kim (SKo) (WBA)
1989	Nico Thomas (Ina) (IBF)

1989/92	Rafael Torres (DoR) (WBO)
1989/90	Eric Chavez (Phi) (IBF)
1989/90	Jum-Hwan Choi (SKo) (WBC)
1990	Hideyuki Ohashi (Jap) (WBC)
1990/2	Fahlan Lukmingkwan (Tha) (IBF)
1990–	Ricardo Lopez (Mex) (WBC)
1991/2	Hi-Yon Choi (SKo) (WBA)
1992	Manny Melchor (Phi) (IBF)
1992/3	Hideyuki Ohashi (Jap) (WBA)
1992–	Ratanapol Sowvoraphin (Tha) (IBF)
1993–	Chana Porpaoin (Tha) (WBA)
1993/4	Paul Weir (Sco) (WBO)
1994–	Alex Sanchez (PuR)(WBO)
1993–	Chana Porpeirin (Tha) (WBA)

OLYMPIC GAMES

Super Heavyweight

1984	Tyrell Bigg (USA)
1988	Lennox Lewis (Can)
1992	Roberto Balado (Cub)

Heavyweight

1904	Samuel Berger (USA)
1908	Albert Oldham (UK)
1920	Ronald Rawson (UK)
1924	Otto von Porat (Nor)
1928	Arturo Rodriguez Jurado (Arg)
1932	Santiago Lovell (Arg)
1936	Herbert Runge (Ger)
1948	Rafael Iglesias (Arg)
1952	Edward Sanders (USA)
1956	Peter Rademacher (USA)
1960	Franco de Piccoli (Ita)
1964	Joe Frazier (USA)
1968	George Foreman (USA)
1972	Teofilo Stevenson (Cub)
1976	Teofilo Stevenson (Cub)
1980	Teofilo Stevenson (Cub)
1984	Henry Tillman (USA)
1988	Ray Mercer (USA)
1992	Félix Savon (Cub)

Light Heavyweight

1920	Eddie Eagan (USA)
1924	Harry Mitchell (GB)
1928	Victor Avendano (Arg)
1932	David Carstens (SAf)
1936	Roger Michelot (Fra)
1948	George Hunter (SAf)
1952	Norvel Lee (USA)

1956	James Boyd (USA)
1960	Cassius Clay (USA)
1964	Cosimo Pinto (Ita)
1968	Dan Poznyak (USSR)
1972	Mate Parlov (Yug)
1976	Leon Spinks (USA)
1980	Slobodan Kacar (Yug)
1984	Anton Jospovic (Yug)
1988	Andrew Maynard (USA)
1992	Torsten May (Ger)

Middleweight

1904	Charles Mayer (USA)
1908	John Douglas (UK)
1920	Harry Mallin (UK)
1924	Harry Mallin (UK)
1928	Piero Toscani (Ita)
1932	Carmen Barth (USA)
1936	Jean Despeaux (Fra)
1948	László Papp (Hun)
1952	Floyd Patterson (USA)
1956	Gennadiy Schatkov (USSR)
1960	Edward Crook (USA)
1964	Valeriy Popenchenko (USSR)
1968	Chris Finnegan (UK)
1972	Vyacheslav Lemeschev (USSR)
1976	Michael Spinks (USA)
1980	José Gomez (Cub)
1984	Joon-sup Shin (SKo)
1988	Henry Maske (GDR)
1992	Ariel Hernández (Cub)

Light Middleweight

1952	László Papp (Hun)

1956	László Papp (Hun)
1960	Wilbert McClure (USA)
1964	Boris Lagutin (USSR)
1968	Boris Lagutin (USSR)
1972	Dieter Kottysch (FRG)
1976	Jerzy Rybicki (Pol)
1980	Armando Martinez (Cub)
1984	Frank Tate (USA)
1988	Si-hun Park (SKo)
1992	Juan Carlos Lemus (Cub)

Welterweight

1904	Albert Young (USA)
1920	Albert Schneider (Can)
1924	Jean Delarge (Bel)
1928	Edward Morgan (NZ)
1932	Edward Flynn (USA)
1936	Sten Suvio (Fin)
1948	Julius Torma (Cze)
1952	Zygmunt Chychla (Pol)
1956	Nicolae Linca (Rom)
1960	Giovanni Benvenuti (Ita)
1964	Marian Kasprzyk (Pol)
1968	Manfred Wolke (GDR)
1972	Emilio Correa (Cub)
1976	Jochen Bachfeld (GDR)
1980	Andrés Aldama (Cub)
1984	Mark Breland (USA)
1988	Robert Wangila (Ken)
1992	Michael Carruth (Ire)

Light Welterweight

1952	Charles Adkins (USA)
1956	Vladimir Yengibaryan (USSR)
1960	Bohumil Nemecek (Cze)
1964	Jerzy Kulej (Pol)
1968	Jerzy Kulej (Pol)
1972	Ray Seales (USA)
1976	Ray Leonard (USA)
1980	Patrizio Oliva (Ita)
1984	Jerry Page (USA)
1988	Vyacheslav Yanovsky (USSR)
1992	Héctor Vincent (Cub)

Lightweight

1904	Harry Spangler (USA)
1908	Frederick Grace (UK)
1920	Samuel Mossberg (USA)
1924	Hans Neilsen (Den)
1928	Carlo Orlando (Ita)
1932	Lawrence Stevens (SAf)
1936	Imre Harangi (Hun)

1948	Gerald Dreyer (SAf)
1952	Aureliano Bolognesi (Ita)
1956	Dick McTaggart (UK)
1960	Kazimierz Pazdzior (Pol)
1964	Józef Grudzien (Pol)
1968	Ron Harris (USA)
1972	Jan Szczepanski (Pol)
1976	Howard Davis (USA)
1980	Angel Herrera (Cub)
1984	Pernell Whitaker (USA)
1988	Andreas Zuelow (GDR)
1992	Oscar de la Hoya (USA)

Featherweight

1904	Oliver Kirk (USA)
1908	Richard Gunn (UK)
1920	Paul Fritsch (Fra)
1924	John Fields (USA)
1928	Lambertus van Klaveren (Hol)
1932	Carmelo Robledo (Arg)
1936	Oscar Casanova (Arg)
1948	Ernesto Formenti (Ita)
1952	Jan Zachara (Cze)
1956	Vladimir Safronov (USSR)
1960	Francesco Musso (Ita)
1964	Stanislav Stepashkin (USSR)
1968	Antonio Roldan (Mex)
1972	Boris Kuznetsov (Bul)
1976	Angel Herrera (Cub)
1980	Rudi Fink (GDR)
1984	Meldrick Taylor (USA)
1988	Giovanni Parisi (Ita)
1992	Andreas Tews (Ger)

Bantamweight

1904	Oliver Kirk (USA)
1908	Henry Thomas (UK)
1920	Clarence Walker (SAf)
1924	William Smith (SAf)
1928	Vittorio Tamagnini (Ita)
1932	Horace Gwynne (Can)
1936	Ulderico Sergo (Ita)
1948	Tibor Csik (Hun)
1952	Pentti Hämäläinen (Fin)
1956	Wolfgang Behrendt (FRG)
1960	Oleg Grigoryev (USSR)
1964	Takao Sakurai (Jap)
1968	Valeriy Sokolov (USSR)
1972	Orlando Martinez (Cub)
1976	Yung-jo Gu (NKo)
1980	Juan Hernández (Cub)
1984	Maurizio Stecca (Ita)

| 1988 | Kennedy McKinney (USA) |
| 1992 | Joel Casamayor (Cub) |

Flyweight

1904	George Finnegan (USA)
1920	Frankie Genaro (USA)
1924	Fidel La Barba (USA)
1928	Antal Kocsis (Hun)
1932	István Énekes (Hun)
1936	Willi Kaiser (Ger)
1948	Pascual Perez (Arg)
1952	Nathan Brooks (USA)
1956	Terry Spinks (UK)
1960	Gyula Török (Hun)
1964	Fernando Atzori (Ita)
1968	Ricardo Delgado (Mex)

1972	Georgi Kostadinov (Bul)
1976	Leo Randolph (USA)
1980	Petar Lessov (Bul)
1984	Steve McCrory (USA)
1988	Kwang-sun Kim (SKo)
1992	Choi-su Choi (NKo)

Light Flyweight

1968	Francisco Rodriguez (Ven)
1972	György Gedo (Hun)
1976	Jorge Hernández (Cub)
1980	Shamil Sabirov (USSR)
1984	Paul Gonzales (USA)
1988	Ivailo Hrisrov (Bul)
1992	Rogelio Marcelo (Cub)

BRAVERY

THE VICTORIA CROSS

The highest award for bravery in Britain is the Victoria Cross, founded by Royal Warrant on 29 January 1856. It was originally intended to be awarded solely to members of the Royal Navy and British Army who, serving in the presence of the enemy, had have performed some signal act of valour or devotion to their country.

In due course, further Royal Warrants enlarged the scope of the award to admit other categories, but the overriding requirement for winning it remained conspicuous bravery.

It was to be conferred by the Sovereign alone, upon advice, and was to be utterly beyond reproach.

Some 1354 individuals have been awarded the VC, the last two being awarded for service in the 1982 Falklands War.

STANHOPE GOLD MEDAL

Among other bravery awards (such as the George Cross) mention should be made of the awards of the Royal Humane Society. The most prestigious award of the Royal Humane Society is the Stanhope Gold Medal, awarded since 1873. The winners since 1945 have been:

1945	Cyril G. L. Brown, NFS
1946	Alan E. Ravani
1947	Mrs Petronella Ferguson
1948	Thomas Matson Roberts
1949	Lieut. (E) (AE) Robert Colin Pearson, RN
1950	Roland Bulteaux
1951	John Williams, Konongo Gold Mines
1952	Peter Strachan, Fishing Vessel *Three Bells*

1953	Thomas Frederick Gill
1954	Mehmet Mustafa Shemmedi
1955	Petty Officer Ivor Laurence Beale
1956	Lieut.-Col. Hugh Barry O'Sullivan, MC, Royal Tank Regiment (decd)
1957	William Robertson
1958	Lieut. David John Nowell Hall, RN
1962	Graham Morris Jorgensen
1963	Frederick John Knight
1964	Teehu Makimare
1965	Lieut. Barry John Campbell, 1st

	Field Regiment, Royal Australian Artillery	1979	Bruce Wallace McPherson
1966	Chief Petty Officer Paul	1980	Station Officer John McNab
	Greengrass, HMS *St Angelo*	1981	Dulcie Kalms
1967	Junior Engineer Jack Milne	1982	Joseph Kaleak
	Easton, MN	1983	Stephen Jury
1968	Robert John Ryan	1984	Victor Leanard Golding
1970	John Christopher Broekmeulen	1985	David Michael Garner
1971	Thomas Nicol	1986	Gordon William Sonnichsen
1972	Malcolm Aspeslet	1987	James George Smith
1974	Abraham Starr	1988	Rupert Novis
1975	Terry Haydon Gleeson	1989	Trevor Allan Viney
1976	Graham Thomas Robson	1990	Elaine Walsh
1977	Randy Sherman Davey	1991	WPC Lesley Allison Moore
1978	Ian Richard Howard	1992	Rodney Stephen Peters
		1993	Beryl Ellen Smith

BRIDES

CLOTHES SHOW BRIDE OF THE YEAR

This annual award for the Clothes Show Bride of the Year (when some 3,000 hopefuls compete) was won in 1994 by Kerry Doyland. Kerry and her bridegroom, Steven Thorne, were married at the Anglican Church alongside Venice's Grand Canal, with her wedding outfit made by Romeo Gigli and with a honeymoon in Barbados for the newlyweds.

BUDGERIGAR BREEDING

The World Budgerigar Championships were held in November 1993 at Doncaster in South Yorkshire. Strongman Geoff Capes was voted the world's no. 1 budgie breeder with his bird Fenland Giant. The house lived in by Geoff Capes is home to no less than 300 budgies.

BUSINESS

Among the many awards for top businessmen and companies are the following:

HAMBRO BUSINESSMAN OF THE YEAR

1993   Sir Christopher Hogg, chairman of chemicals group Courtaulds. Chosen for his 'unswerving commitment and personal example which inspires admiration inside and outside Courtaulds'.

GUARDIAN YOUNG BUSINESSMAN OF THE YEAR

This award, which began in 1970, is made for a significant contribution to business, not only at a personal and company level but also in the national context. The judges are usually the Directors General of the British Institute of Management, the Institute of Directors and the Confederation of British Industry, and the Chairman of the *Guardian*. Some famous winners include (1972) James Gulliver of Fine Fare Group, (1975) Michael Edwardes, Chief Executive of the Chloride Group, and (1978) Nigel Broackes, then chairman of Trafalgar House.

BUSINESS ENTERPRISE AWARD

The Business Enterprise Award, effectively the search for the Company of the Year, is sponsored by Midland Bank, Henley Management College and the *Sunday Telegraph*. Any UK company or UK subsidiary of an overseas company with an annual turnover of at least £5 million is eligible. Companies are judged on their economic contribution to British society in terms of wealth created and employment generated and on the degree of enterprise they have shown in the design, manufacture and marketing of their products and services. All award proceeds are donated to the charity Mencap. The award, launched in 1980, has seen quite a variety of winners:

1980	Barratt Developments	1987	Body Shop International
1981	J. Sainsbury	1988	Iceland Frozen Foods
1982	Racal Electronics	1989	William Cook
1983	S. R. Gent	1990	Spring Ram
1984	Apricot Computers	1991	Rentokil
1985	Virgin Group	1992	Vodafone
1986	{ Derwent Valley Foods Ltd Marlborough Technical Management	1993	Serco

Other finalists in 1993 were Airtours, Betterware, Carpetright, Harrington Kilbride, Holliday Chemicals, Micro Focus, Pace Micro Technology and John Wood.

See also **Women**.

CALLIGRAPHY

NATIONAL SCHOOLS HANDWRITING COMPETITION

More than 18,000 pupils from 500 schools entered the 1993 National Schools Handwriting Competition which is sponsored by Osmiroid. Entries in four age groups are judged on legibility, flow, consistency, layout and tidiness. The children in each group are asked to copy a different poem. The category winners were:

Class A (5–7-year-olds)
Thomas Greenhouse (6), Hamsey Green
  County First School, Warlingham,
  Surrey

Class B (8–11-year-olds)
Kerry McCarthy (11), Canongate Primary
  School, St Andrews, Scotland

Class C (12–14-year-olds)
Annabelinda Tindall, St Mary's School,
  Cambridge

Best School (overall collection of entries)
Cranford House, near Wallingford, Oxon

CAMERAS

CAMERAS OF THE YEAR

Each year the photography magazine *Amateur Photographer* assesses with its team of experts the best new cameras, lenses, films and accessories available on the market. Its 1994 winners were:

Overall Camera of the Year Minolta Dynax 700si
SLR Camera of the Year Minolta Dynax 700si
Zoom Camera of the Year Canon Sureshot Z-115
Compact Camera of the Year Nikon AF-600

Lens of the Year Sigma 70 20-210mm f/4-5-6 UC apo
Film of the Year Fuji Super G400
Accessory of the Year Uniloc System 1700 Tripod
Innovation of the Year Durst Magico Enlarger

See also **Photography**

CANOEING

OLYMPIC GAMES

Men's Kayak 500m Singles

1976	Vasile Diba (Rom)
1980	Vladimir Parfenovich (USSR)
1984	Ian Ferguson (NZ)
1988	Zsolt Gyulay (Hun)
1992	Mikko Kolehmainen (Fin)

Men's Kayak 1000m Singles

1936	Gregor Hradetzky (Aut)
1948	Gert Fredriksson (Swe)
1952	Gert Fredriksson (Swe)
1956	Gert Fredriksson (Swe)
1960	Erik Hansen (Den)
1964	Rolf Peterson (Swe)
1968	Mihaly Hesz (Hun)
1972	Alexandr Shaperenko (USSR)
1976	Rudiger Helm (GDR)
1980	Rudiger Helm (GDR)
1984	Alan Thompson (NZ)
1988	Greg Barton (USA)
1992	Clint Robinson (Aus)

Women's Kayak 500m Singles

1948	Karen Hoff (Den)
1952	Sylvi Saimo (Fin)
1956	Elisaveta Dementyeva (USSR)
1960	Anatonina Seredina (USSR)
1964	Lyudmila Khvedosyuk (USSR)
1968	Lyudmila Pinayeva (USSR)
1972	Yulia Ryabchinskaya (USSR)
1976	Carola Zirzow (GDR)
1980	Brigit Fischer (GDR)
1984	Agneta Anderson (Swe)
1988	Vania Guecheva (USSR)
1992	Brigit Schmidt (Ger)

Men's Slalom Singles

1972	Siegbert Horn (GDR)
1992	Pierpaolo Ferrazzi (Ita)

Women's Slalom Singles

1972	Angelika Bahmann (GDR)
1992	Elisabeth Micheler (Ger)

Men's 500m Pairs

1976	East Germany
1980	USSR
1984	New Zealand
1988	New Zealand
1992	Germany

Men's 1000m Pairs

1936	Austria
1948	Sweden
1952	Finland
1956	West Germany
1960	Sweden
1964	Sweden
1968	USSR
1972	USSR
1976	USSR
1980	USSR
1984	Canada
1988	USA
1992	Germany

Women's 500m Pairs

1960	USSR
1964	West Germany
1968	West Germany
1972	USSR
1976	USSR
1980	East Germany
1984	Sweden
1988	East Germany
1992	Germany

Women's 500m Fours

1984	Romania
1988	East Germany
1992	Hungary

Men's 1000m Fours

1964	USSR
1968	Norway
1972	USSR
1976	USSR
1980	East Germany
1984	New Zealand
1988	Hungary
1992	Germany

Men's Canadian 500m Singles

1976	Alexandr Rogov (USSR)
1980	Sergey Postrekhin (USSR)
1984	Larry Cain (Can)
1988	Olaf Heukrodt (GDR)

1992	Nikolai Boukhalov (Bul)

Men's Canadian 1000m Singles

1936	Francis Amyot (Can)
1948	Josef Holecek (Cze)
1952	Josef Holecek (Cze)
1956	Leon Roptman (Rom)
1960	Josef Parti (Hun)
1964	Jurgen Eschert (Ger)
1968	Tibor Tatai (Hun)
1972	Ivan Patzaichin (Rom)
1976	Matija Ljubek (Yug)
1980	Lubomir Lubenov (Bul)
1984	Ulrich Eicke (FRG)
1988	Ivan Klementiev (USSR)
1992	Nikolai Boukhalov (Bul)

Men's Canadian 500m Pairs

1976	USSR
1980	Hungary
1984	Yugoslavia
1988	USSR
1992	CIS

Men's Canadian 1000m Pairs

1936	Czechoslovakia
1948	Czechoslovakia
1952	Denmark
1956	Romania
1960	USSR
1964	USSR
1968	Romania
1972	USSR
1976	USSR
1980	Romania
1984	Romania
1988	USSR
1992	Germany

Men's Slalom Singles

1972	Reinhard Eiben (GDR)
1992	Lukas Pollert (Cze)

Men's Slalom Pairs

1972	East Germany
1992	USA

CARS

CAR OF THE YEAR

Each year, *What Car?* magazine runs a competition to find the 'Car of the Year'.

1978	Renault 20TS	1986	Saab 9000 Turbo 16
1979	Peugeot 305	1987	Renault 21 Savanna GTX
1980	Vauxhall Astra	1988	BMW 735i
1981	VW Golf GTi	1989	Ford Fiesta 1.1 LX
1982	Mercedes-Benz 200T	1990	Rover 214 Si
1983	MG Metro	1991	Rover Metro 1.1 L
1984	Peugeot 205 GR	1992	Volkswagen Golf 1.8 GL
1985	Volkswagen Golf GL	1993	Ford Mondeo 1.8 GLX

Category winners for 1993 were:

Best Supermini Nissan Micra 1.0 LX

Best Small Hatchback Citroën ZX
  Avantage 1.4

Best Small Saloon Rover 414 Si

Best Family Car Ford Mondeo 1.8 GLX

Best Hot Hatchback Nissan Sunny 2.0e
  GTi

Best Coupé Mazda MX-6

Best Performance Car TVR Griffith 4.3

  Targa

Best Estate Car Audi 100 2.0E Estate

Best Off-Road Car Isuzu Trooper Citation
  TD LWB

Best Diesel Car Audi 100 TDi

Best Small Executive Car BMW 318i

Best Executive Car Renault Safrane RT
  2.0

Best Luxury Car Jaguar XJ6 3.2

BBC *TOP GEAR* GOOD CAR GUIDE AWARDS

Similar awards are made by the BBC *Top Gear* programme. Awards for 1993–4 include:

Best Luxury Car Alfa Romeo 164

Best Off Roader Ford Maverick

Best Hatch Volkswagen Golf

Best Family Car Ford Mondeo

Best Wild Car Escort Cosworth

Lowest Depreciation BMW 3-series

Best Fast Saloon BMW 5-series

Best Diesel Citroën 2X

Best Value Ford Fiesta

Best Fast Coupé Honda NSX

Best Small Car Nissan Micra

Best Convertible Mazda MX-5

Best Estate Peugeot 405

Best Hot Hatch Volkswagen Golf VR6

Best Small Hatch Peugeot 106

Best Company Car Vauxhall Cavalier

EUROPEAN CAR OF THE YEAR

This prestigious award is the continent's top accolade for new models. For 1994 there were 15 eligible cars and the award was decided by the votes of 58 senior motoring writers from 20 European countries. The winner was the Ford Mondeo. It was the first time Ford had won the title since 1986, when the award went to the Scorpio/Granada.

THE BVRLA ANTI-THEFT AWARDS

These annual awards, which date from 1988, are presented to the motor manufacturer who is judged to have done most to prevent vehicle-related crime during the previous twelve months.

1987	Vauxhall Motors	1990	Vauxhall Motors
1988	Vauxhall Motors	1991	Rover (for its 800 series)
1989	*no award*	1992	Vauxhall Motors

Vauxhall Motors demonstrated to the panel of judges – comprising of representatives of the police, Home Office, insurers and the media and chaired by BVRLA President Freddie Aldous – in 1992 that it remained a clear leader in the field.

CHEFS

BBC *MASTERCHEF* AWARD

Amateur cooks from all the regions of Britain compete for the annual Masterchef award. This very popular BBC programme is effectively the British 'Grand Prix' for amateur chefs. The Masterchef competition was devised by Franc Roddam who was determined to put down those who decried British food. The programme has cast its net wide – in Loyd Grossman's words, 'The cooks have come in all ages, shapes and sizes!'

In 1992 all the finalists were women. In 1993, all were men. The 1993 final was judged by Sir John Harvey-Jones and Michel Roux.

1990	Joan Bunting	1993	Derek Johns (first ever male
1991	Sue Lawrence		Masterchef)
1992	Vanessa Binns	1994	Gerry Goldwyre

Derek Johns's winning menu in 1993 was:

Pasta with Globe Artichoke and Wild Mushrooms
Rosettes of Turbot with a Leek Sauce
Thin-crust Apple and Mango Tart with a Caramel and Gingered Kiwi Sauce

See also **Restaurants**.

CHEMISTRY

NOBEL PRIZE FOR CHEMISTRY

This was first awarded in 1901. Details of the various Nobel prizes are given on p. 206. The following Britons received the award prior to 1945:

1904	Sir William Ramsay		Eulor-Chelpin (Swe, German-
1908	Ernest Rutherford		born)
1921	Frederick Soddy	1937	Walter N. Haworth (with Paul
1922	Francis W. Aston		Karrer (Swi, Russian-born)
1928	Arthur Harden (with Hans von		

Winners since 1945 have been:

1945	Artturi I. Virtanen (Fin)	1949	William F. Giauque (USA)
1946	James B. Sumner (USA)	1950	Kurt Alder (Ger)
	John H. Northrop (USA)		Otto P. H. Diels (GDR)
	Wendell M. Stanley (USA)	1951	Edwin M. McMillan (USA)
1947	Sir Robert Robinson (GB)		Glenn T. Seaborg (USA)
1948	Arne W. K. Tiselius (Swe)		

1952	Archer J. P. Martin (GB) Richard L. M. Synge (GB)
1953	Hermann Staudinger (GDR)
1954	Linus C. Pauling (USA)
1955	Vincent du Vigneaud (USA)
1956	Sir Cyril N. Hinshelwood (GB) Nikolai N. Semenov (USSR)
1957	Lord Todd (Alexander R. Todd) (GB)
1958	Frederick Sanger (GB)
1959	Jaroslav Heyrovsky (Cze)
1960	Willard F. Libby (USA)
1961	Melvin Calvin (USA)
1962	Sir John C. Kendrew (GB) Max F. Perutz (GB, Austrian-born)
1963	Giulio Natta (Ita) Karl Ziegler (GDR)
1964	Dorothy Crowfoot Hodgkin (GB)
1965	Robert B. Woodward (USA)
1966	Robert S. Mulliken (USA)
1967	Manfred Eigen (Ger) Ronald G. W. Norrish (GB) Sir George Porter (GB)
1968	Lars Onsager (USA, Norwegian-born)
1969	Derek H. R. Barton (GB) Odd Hassel (Nor)
1970	Luis F. Leloir (Arg, French-born)
1971	Gerhard Herzberg (Can, German-born)
1972	Christian B. Anifinsen (USA) Stanford Moore (USA) William H. Stein (USA)
1973	Ernest Otto Fischer (GDR) Geoffrey Wilkinson (GB)
1974	Paul J. Flory (USA)

1975	John W. Cornforth (GB) Vladimir Prelog (Swi, Yugoslavian-born)
1976	William N. Lipscomb Jr (USA)
1977	Ilya Prigogine (Bel, Russian-born)
1978	Peter Mitchell (GB)
1979	Herbert C. Brown (USA) Gerry Wittig (GDR)
1980	Frederick Sanger (GB) Paul Berg (USA) Walter Gilbert (USA)
1981	Roald Hoffman (USA) Kenichi Fukui (Jap)
1982	Aaron Klug (GB)
1983	Henry Taube (USA)
1984	R. Bruce Merrifield (USA)
1985	Herbert A. Hauptman (USA) Jerome Karle (USA)
1986	Dudley Herschbach (USA) Yuan T. Lee (USA) John C. Polanyi (Can)
1987	Donald J. Cram (USA) Charles J. Paderson (USA) Jean-Marie Lehn (Fra)
1988	Johan Deisenhofer (Ger) Robert Huber (Ger) Hartmut Michel (Ger)
1989	Thomas R. Cech (USA) Sidney Altman (USA)
1990	Elias J. Corey (USA)
1991	Richard R. Ernst (Swi)
1992	Rudolph Marcus (USA, Canadian-born)
1993	Michael Smith (Can, British-born) Kary Mullis (USA)

CHESS

WORLD CHAMPIONSHIPS

Enormous interest in chess at all ages was highlighted by the televising of the 1993 World Championships in London between Gary Kasparov, the Russian holder, and Britain's first ever challenger, Nigel Short.

The world championship began in 1885 with a match in St Louis won by Wilhelm Steinitz.

1885–94	Wilhelm Steinitz (Aus)	1927–35	Alexander Alekhine (Fra)
1894–1921	Emmanuel Lasker (Ger)	1935–7	Max Euwe (Hol)
1921–7	José Copablanca (Cub)	1937–47	Alexander Alekhine (Fra)

1948–57	Mikhail Botvinnik (USSR)		1963–9	Tigran Petrosian (USSR)
1957–8	Vassily Smyslov (USSR)		1969–72	Boris Spassky (USSR)
1958–60	Mikhail Botvinnik (USSR)		1972–5	Bobby Fischer (USA)
1960–1	Mikhail Tal (USSR)		1975–85	Anatoly Karpov (USSR)
1961–3	Mikhail Botvinnik (USSR)		1985–	Gary Kasparov (USSR)

BRITISH CHESS FEDERATION (BCF) CHAMPIONSHIPS

British Men's Champion

1946	R. F. Combe
1947	H. Golombek
1948	R. J. Broadbent
1949	H. Golombek
1950	R. J. Broadbent
1951	E. Klein
1952	R. G. Wade
1953	D. A. Yanofsky
1954	{ L. W. Barden / A. Phillips
1955	H. Golombek
1956	C. H. O'D. Alexander
1957	Dr S. Fazekas
1958	J. Penrose
1959	J. Penrose
1960	J. Penrose
1961	J. Penrose
1962	J. Penrose
1963	J. Penrose
1964	M. J. Haygarth
1965	P. N. Lee
1966	Dr J. Penrose
1967	Dr J. Penrose
1968	Dr J. Penrose
1969	Dr J. Penrose
1970	R. G. Wade
1971	R. D. Keene
1972	B. R. Eley
1973	W. R. Hartston
1974	G. S. Botterill
1975	W. R. Hartston
1976	A. J. Mestel
1977	G. S. Botterill
1978	J. S. Speelman
1979	R. Bellin
1980	Dr J. D. M. Nunn
1981	P. E. Littlewood
1982	A. J. Miles
1983	A. J. Mestel
1984	N. D. Short
1985	J. S. Speelman

1986	J. S. Speelman
1987	N. D. Short
1988	A. J. Mestel
1989	M. Adams
1990	H. J. Plaskett
1991	J. M. Hodgson
1992	J. M. Hodgson
1993	M. Hennigan

British Lady Champion

1946	Miss E. Saunders
1947	Miss E. Tranmer
1948	Miss E. C. Price
1949	Miss E. Tranmer
1950	Mrs R. M. Bruce
1951	Mrs R. M. Bruce
1952	*no contest*
1953	Miss E. Tranmer
1954	Mrs R. M. Bruce
1955	{ Miss J. F. Doulton / Mrs R. M. Bruce
1956	Mrs E. Pritchard
1957	Capt. P. A. Sunnucks
1958	Capt. P. A. Sunnucks
1959	Mrs R. M. Bruce
1960	Mrs R. M. Bruce
1961	Miss E. Tranmer
1962	Mrs R. M. Bruce
1963	Mrs R. M. Bruce
1964	Capt. P. A. Sunnucks
1965	Mrs E. Pritchard
1966	{ Mrs M. E. E. Clarke / Miss G. Moore
1967	{ Mrs R. M. Bruce / Miss D. Dobson
1968	Miss D. Dobson
1969	{ Mrs R. M. Bruce / Miss D. Dobson
1970	Mrs J. Hartston
1971	Mrs J. Hartston
1972	Mrs J. Hartston
1973	Mrs J. Hartston
1974	Mrs J. Hartston

1975	Miss S. Jackson
1976	Dr J. Hartston
1977	Dr J. Hartston
1978	Miss S. Jackson
1979	Dr J. Miles
1980	Miss S. Jackson
1981	Miss S. Jackson
1982	Miss J. Garwell
1983	Mrs R. Hamid Mrs H. Milligan
1984	Miss B. Sathe Mrs V. Unni
1985	Mrs R. Hamid
1986	Mrs S. K. Arkell
1987	Miss C. Forbes
1988	Miss C. Forbes
1989	Mrs R. Hamid
1990	Mrs S. K. Arkell
1991	Mrs S. K. Arkell
1992	Mrs S. K. Arkell
1993	Mrs S. Dhar

Veteran Championships

1982	P. C. Hoad
1983	P. C. Hoad
1984	H. Golombek P. C. Hoad
1985	D. Andrew H. Golombek P. C. Hoad
1986	P. C. Hoad
1987	P. C. Hoad
1988	D. Baldwin
1989	P. C. Hoad
1990	P. C. Hoad
1991	J. Soesan
1992	J. Soesan
1993	Lim K.-A. R. D. Westra

BCF Junior Championships (Under 21)

1953	D. F. Griffiths
1954	B. Cafferty
1955	J. D. Taylor
1956–60	*no contest*
1961	D. G. Wells

1962	K. B. Richardson
1963	M. J. Basman R. A. Harris
1964	C. F. Woodcock
1965	A. J. Whiteley
1966	B. J. Denman A. T. Ludgate
1967	L. S. Tate
1968	L. de Veauce
1969	R. G. Eales
1970	D. M. Wise
1971	A. J. Miles
1972	J. M. Quinn
1973	L. D. Marks
1974	J. G. Nicholson
1975	P. Littlewood
1976	R. L. Britton C. R. Chandler R. W. Haldane
1977	J. M. Hodgson W. N. Watson
1978	D. Shuttleworth T. M. Clarke A. J. Muir J. Hall
1979	N. R. Davies
1980	A. P. Lewis
1981	M. P. Townsend
1982	M. Kerridge
1983	N. Thomas C. Dawson F. Khan B. Lund
1984	S. C. Brown
1985	M. Condie
1986	M. Adams M. Condie S. Conquest N. R. McDonald
1987	S. Conquest
1988	M. Adams
1989	M. Adams
1990	M. Adams
1991	M. Hennigan
1992	D. Kumaran
1993	D. Kumaran

BCF Junior Championships are also awarded to Under 18s, Under 16s etc. down to Under 8s.

BRITISH OPEN RAPIDPLAY CHAMPIONSHIP

1986	N. Short	1989	J. Nunn
1987	N. Davies		⎧ M. Hebden
	⎧ M. Chandler	1990	⎨ J. Hodgson
	⎪ G. Flear		⎩ J. Speelman
1988	⎨ M. Hebden	1991	⎧ L. Polugaevsky
	⎪ J. Hodgson		⎩ J. Speelman
	⎩ J. Nunn	1992	W. Watson

COUNTY CHAMPIONSHIP

1908	Middlesex	1938	Lancashire	1970	Cambridgeshire
1909	Middlesex	1939–45	*no contest*	1971	Cambridgeshire
1910	Middlesex	1946	Lancashire	1972	Cambridgeshire
1911	Surrey	1947	Middlesex	1973	Essex
1912	Kent	1948	Lancashire	1974	Yorkshire
1913	Middlesex	1949	Middlesex	1975	Kent
1914	Middlesex	1950	Middlesex	1976	Kent
1915–19	*no contest*	1951	Oxfordshire	1977	Lancashire
1920	Surrey	1952	Oxfordshire	1978	Lancashire
1921	Yorkshire	1953	Middlesex	1979	Middlesex
1922	Lancashire	1954	Surrey	1980	Middlesex
1923	Lancashire	1955	Middlesex	1981	Kent
1924	Surrey	1956	Middlesex	1982	Yorkshire
1925	Middlesex	1957	Warwickshire	1983	Kent
1926	Lancashire	1958	Essex	1984	Kent
1927	Middlesex	1959	Lancashire	1985	Middlesex
1928	Middlesex	1960	Lancashire	1986	Middlesex
1929	Surrey	1961	Warwickshire	1987	Middlesex
1930	Lancashire	1962	Warwickshire	1988	Kent
1931	Middlesex	1963	Middlesex	1989	Middlesex
1932	Middlesex	1964	Middlesex	1990	Greater
1933	Lancashire	1965	Middlesex		Manchester
1934	Middlesex	1966	Lancashire	1991	Kent
1935	Lancashire	1967	Lancashire	1992	Staffordshire
1936	Middlesex	1968	Lancashire	1993	Kent
1937	Middlesex	1969	Lancashire		

THE TIMES BRITISH SCHOOLS TOURNAMENT

(formerly the Sunday Times *National Schools Championship)*

1958	Calday Grange Grammar School	1967	Battersea Grammar School
1959	Calday Grange Grammar School	1968	Bolton School
1960	Wolverhampton Grammar School	1969	Dundee High School
1961	Colfe's Grammar School	1970	Dulwich College
1962	Liverpool Institute	1971	Ayr Academy
1963	Hove Grammar School	1972	Ayr Academy
1964	Liverpool Institute	1973	Bolton School
1965	Dulwich College	1974	Southern Grammar School,
1966	Dulwich College		Portsmouth

1975	St Paul's, London		Newcastle upon Tyne
1976	Bolton School	1985	St Paul's, London
1977	Bluecoat School, Birmingham	1986	Plymouth College
1978	St Paul's, London	1987	Queen Mary's Grammar School,
1979	St Paul's, London		Walsall
1980	King Edward VI, Southampton	1988	St Paul's, London
1981	St Paul's, London	1989	St Paul's, London
1982	St Paul's, London	1990	St Paul's, London
1983	Queen Mary's Grammar School,	1991	Manchester Grammar School
	Walsall	1992	Nottingham High School
1984	Royal Grammar School,	1993	Truro School

NATIONAL CLUB CHAMPIONSHIP

Sponsored by Leigh Interests plc

1950	Cambridge University	1972	Cambridge University
1951	Lud Eagle	1973	Cambridge University
1952	Oxford University	1974	Cambridge University
1953	Ilford	1975	Cambridge University
1954	Cheltenham	1976	Athenaeum
1955	Cheltenham	1977	Atticus
1956	Ilford	1978	Islington
1957	Leicestershire	1979	Oxford University
1958	Cambridge University	1980	King's Head
1959	Cheltenham	1981	King's Head
1960	Cambridge University	1982	Rugby
1961	Sutton Coldfield	1983	Oxford University
1962	West Ham	1984	Cambridge University
1963	Manchester	1985	Streatham and Brixton
1964	Ilford	1986	Cambridge University
1965	York	1987	Wood Green
1966	Oxford University	1988	Glasgow Polytechnic
1967	Bradford	1989	Wood Green
1968	Islington and North London	1990	Wood Green
1969	Cambridge University	1991	Barbican
1970	Oxford University	1992	Barbican
1971	Cambridge University	1993	Wood Green

OPEN PLATE TOURNAMENT

1976	Streatham	1986	Sale
1977	Islington and North London	1987	King's Head
1978	South Manchester	1988	Powder Mill
1979	Mushrooms	1989	Streatham / Brixton
1980	London Central YMCA		
1981	PERME Waltham Abbey	1990	Richmond
1982	Writtle	1991	Atticus
1983	Leeds University	1992	Wood Green
1984	Canterbury	1993	Slough (Lady Haig)
1985	Kynoch		

NATIONAL MAJOR CLUB CHAMPIONSHIP

Sponsored by Leigh Interests plc

1984	Tunbridge Wells	1989	Oldham
1985	King's Head	1990	Fulham
1986	Hastings and St Leonards	1991	Warley Quinborne
1987	Lichfield	1992	Kingston-on-Thames
1988	Cambridge University	1993	Southend-on-Sea

CHILDREN

Among the many national competitions which are centred around children are the following:

MISS PEARS

Since 1958 this much loved competition has invited the entry of photographs of little girls nationwide aged between 3 and 9, with the winner becoming 'princess for a day' and the bearer of the famous Miss Pears title for one year.

The competition has changed very little since its first winner was crowned in 1958 and now reaps around 20,000 entries every year. Miss Pears also plays an important part in continuing the long-running association Pears has always had with the Arts. Part of the prestigious Miss Pears prize is the opportunity for the winner to have her portrait painted by a popular artist of the time.

1958	Susan Cadge, 3, of Bristol	1970	Belinda-Jane Anderson, 7, of Rosneath, Nr Helensburgh, Scotland
1959	Susan Fowler, 3, of Harrow, Middx	1971	Louise Stewart, 3, of Cullercoats, Northumberland
1960	Suzanne Lowndes, 4, of Carmarthen, Wales	1972	Louise Payne, 3, of Walton-on-Thames, Surrey
1961	Julie Williams, 3, of Newport Pagnell, Bucks	1973	Natalie Clark, 5, of Loughton, Essex
1962	Peggy Ross, 5, of Hammersmith, London	1974	Katie Goodwin, 4, of Stalybridge, Cheshire
1963	Elizabeth MacFarlane, 4, of Tarbert, Loch Fyne, Scotland	1975	Sharon Fitton, 5, of Horncastle, Lincs
1964	Corrienne Robb, 4, of Belfast, Northern Ireland	1976	Sarah Coombs, 3, of Hayling Island, Hants
1965	Catherine Hancock, 4, of Whitefield, Manchester	1977	Sarah Worth, 4, of Timperley, Cheshire
1966	Tessa Roberts, 4, of Teddington, Middx	1978	Kirsty Leighton, 6, of Wylam, Northumberland
1967	Deborah Perryman, 4, of Wembley, Middx	1979	Christine Cashman, 4, of South Croydon, Surrey
1968	Susan Wood, 3, of Leek, Staffs	1980	Natalie Norgrove, 5, of Kidderminster, West Midlands
1969	Justine Hornby, 3, of Formby, Liverpool		

1981	Emma Mason, 4, of Blyth, Northumberland	1988	Sarah Cowie, 5, of Aberdeen, Scotland
1982	Ellena Lartey, 3, of Barry, South Glamorgan	1989	Lisa West, 5, of Raynes Park, London
1983	Gemma Plant, 4, of Cheddleton, Leek, Staffs	1990	Robyn Parker, 3, of Epsom, Surrey
1984	Jenny Curran, 3, of Shepperton, Middx	1991	Sarah Bell, 4, of Ambleside, Cumbria
1985	Joanne Fearnley, 3, of Leeds	1992	Sophie Johnson, 4, of Swanlands, Hull
1986	Hannah Phillips, 4, of Quorn, Leics	1993	Candice Carpenter, 4, of Harlow, Essex
1987	Claire Moogan, 3, of Liverpool		

BISTO KIDS OF THE YEAR

The Bisto Kids of the Year competition is an annual search for a couple of 'today's' kids who best personify the famous pair of Bisto characters. The competition, though, is not based on appearance alone; the judges look for children who are also helpful and considerate of others' needs. The 1993 competition changed from the normal format by asking the children to dress as they thought the Bisto Kids would look in the year 2525.

To enter the competition, all you have to do is be between 7 and 10 years old, and send in a photo of yourself dressed in a Bisto outfit, striking the original cheeky 'Ahh! Bisto' pose.

The Bisto Kids characters were first created by illustrator Will Owen in 1919, when he designed a poster featuring two ragamuffin children sniffing the aroma from a hot pie, uttering the immortal words 'Ahh! Bisto'. Ever since, children have had great fun dressing up and portraying these lovable yet cheeky characters. From the mid-1920s, Bisto kids outfits were loaned free of charge from the Bisto factory on condition that a photograph of the wearers was returned with the outfits. Recent winners have been:

1987	Robin Denis and Charlotte Orly	1991	Helen and Alexander Jacksons
1988	Lorelei and Alex Harwood	1992	Adam and Catherine Milligan
1989	Sarah and Jonothan Chapman	1993	Claira and Liam Salter
1990	Jody and Carly McMillan		

The winners of the competition spend their year as ambassadors for Bisto at various events around the country, and raising money for charity. Claira and Liam Salter, the 1993 Bisto Kids of the Year, spent their year helping to raise £125,000 for the Bisto Helping Hands appeal.

CHILDREN OF COURAGE AWARDS

These awards, sponsored by the magazine *Woman's Own*, are to honour children whose lives have been devastated by tragedy.

The 1993 awards, to eight very courageous children, were made by Dame Betty Boothroyd, MP, Speaker of the House of Commons, during a carol service at Westminster Abbey. They included Leigh Ann Johns (10), who lost both legs in a car accident involving a drunken driver; Edhem Dedovic (11), evacuated from Bosnia during Operation Irma; Samantha Thompson (14), badly injured by Warrington IRA bomb; and Kayleigh Moore (5), born with all her organs back to front. The other winners were Tomas Zippo (8) from Milton Keynes, Dawn Foster (13) from Norfolk, Stuart Abbot (11) from Hull and Neika Chetwyn (9) from Manchester.

Among the 1994 winners, announced in February, were 12-year-old James Dixon from Cheshire (who has undergone a heart and lung transplant to help overcome cystic fibrosis) and Kerri Wyatt, who suffers from spastic quadriplegia.

CHILD OF ACHIEVEMENT

The annual McDonalds' Restaurants Child of Achievement Awards are given to those who have made a special service to others or overcome particular adversity. Some 150 awards were made in 1993 (the eleventh year of the award).

Child of Achievement: Music in the Community Award

This is also sponsored by McDonalds. Choirs and bands are judged on their community involvement as well as enthusiasm and love of music, rather than pure technical excellence.

1987	Burnt Mill School Choir	1992/3 *Choir Section*	Ratton School Choir
1988	Burnt Mill School Choir		⎧ Anonymata
1989	Penygroes County Primary School Choir	*Band Section*	⎨ West Cheshire Schools Concert
1990	Llandybie Primary School Choir		⎩ Board
1991	⎧ Bryn Haford School Choir ⎨ Chosen Hill School Choir		

EUROPEAN CHILD OF ACHIEVEMENT

These new awards were inaugurated in Paris on 1 November 1992. They bring together the children of Europe at one central Child of Achievement Awards Ceremony. The 50 European Child of Achievement Awards show that humanity, compassion and an ability to achieve against outstanding odds are being shown each and every day by children in each and every European country.

CHILDREN'S LITERATURE

BRITISH BOOK AWARDS

Among the many British Book Awards (see p. 55) are the following specifically for children's books:

The Children's Author of the Year

1989	Roald Dahl
1990	Anne Fine
1991	Dick King-Smith
1992	Raymond Briggs
1993	Anne Fine

The Bowater Illustrated Children's Book of the Year

1990	Nicola Bayley for *The Mousehole Cat*
1991	Helen Oxenbury for *Farmer Duck*
1992	Mick Inkpen for *Penguin Small*
1993	Babette Cole for *Mummy Laid an Egg*

GUARDIAN CHILDREN'S FICTION AWARD

£1,000 is awarded to a work of fiction published in the previous calendar year in Britain and written by a British or Commonwealth author. It excludes picture books and books by previous winners. Books should be for children of approximately seven years or over.

1967	Leon Garfield, *Devil In The Fog*	1982	Michelle Magorian, *Goodnight Mister Tom*
1968	Alan Garner, *The Owl Service*		
1969	Joan Aiken, *The Whispering Mountain*	1983	Anita Desai, *The Village By The Sea*
1970	K. M. Peyton, *Flambards*	1984	Dick King-Smith, *The Sheep-Pig*
1971	John Christopher, *The Guardians*	1985	Ted Hughes, *What Is The Truth?*
		1986	Ann Pilling, *Henry's Leg*
1972	Gillian Avery, *A Likely Lad*	1987	James Aldridge, *The True Story Of Spit MacPhee*
1973	Richard Adams, *Watership Down*		
1974	Barbara Willard, *The Iron Lily*	1988	Ruth Thomas, *The Runaways*
1975	Winifred Cawley, *Gran at Colegate*	1989	Geraldine McCaughrean, *A Pack Of Lies*
1976	Nina Bawden, *The Peppermint Pig*	1990	Anne Fine, *Goggle-eyes*
		1991	Robert Westall, *The Kingdom By The Sea*
1977	Peter Dickinson, *The Blue Hawk*		
1978	Diana Wynne Jones, *Charmed Life*	1992	Rachel Anderson, *Paper Faces* / Hilary McKay, *The Exiles*
1979	Andrew Davies, *Conrad's War*	1993	William Mayne, *Low Tide*
1980	Ann Schlee, *The Vandal*	1994	Sylvia Waugh, *Menyms*
1981	Peter Carter, *The Sentinels*		

MOTHER GOOSE AWARD

The Mother Goose Award was established in 1979 for 'the most exciting newcomer to British children's book illustration'. Its aim is to encourage children's book illustrators at the beginning of their careers by drawing critical attention to their work, and to encourage publishers to continue to foster new talent in the field of illustration for children.

1979	Michelle Cartlidge for *Pippin and Pod*	1987	Patrick James Lynch for *A Bag of Moonshine*
1980	Reg Cartwright for *Mr Potter's Pigeon*	1988	Emma Chichester-Clark for *Listen To This*
1981	Juan Wijngaard for *Green Finger House*	1989	Charles Fuge for *Bush Vark's First Day Out*
1982	Jan Ormerod for *Sunshine*	1990	David Hughes for *Strat and Chatto*
1983	Satoshi Kitamura for *Angry Arthur*	1991	Amanda Harvey for *A Close Call*
1984	Patrick Benson for *The Hob Stories*	1992	Ted Dewan for *Inside the Whale*
		1993	Clare Fletcher for *The Seashell Song*
1985	Susan Varley for *Badger's Parting Gifts*	1994	Lisa Flather for *Where the Great Bear Watches*
1986	not awarded		

SMARTIES BOOK PRIZE

With annual prize money totalling £12,000, this prize is the biggest children's book prize in the world. It is sponsored by Nestlé Rowntree and administered by the Book Trust. There are three categories: 5 years and under, 6–8 years and 9–11 years. The winner of each category receives £2,000 and a certificate. The overall winner, chosen from one of the category winners, receives a further £6,000 and the Book Prize Trophy for the year.

The prize seeks to reward excellence in writing for children, stimulate interest in children's books and encourage children to read.

1985	Jill Paton Walsh, *Gaffer Samson's Luck* (illustrated by Brock Cole)	1989	Michael Rosen and Helen Oxenbury, *We're Going on a Bear Hunt*
1986	Jenny Nimmo, *The Snow Spider* (illustrated by Joanna Carey)	1990	Pauline Fisk, *Midnight Blue*
1987	James Berry, *A Thief in the Village*	1991	Martin Waddell and Helen Oxenbury, *Farmer Duck*
1988	Martin Waddell and Barbara Firth, *Can't You Sleep Little Bear?*	1992	Gillian Cross, *The Great Elephant Chase*
		1993	Michael Foreman, *War Game*

CHOIRS

CHOIRBOY/CHOIRGIRL OF THE YEAR

The Choirboy and Choirgirl of the Year Competitions are designed to encourage young choristers to sing in their local church choirs and therefore within their local communities.

The competitions are open to local church and chapel choristers throughout the UK who enter by submitting a cassette tape of their singing. The tapes are divided up into regions and seven boys and seven girls are selected to go forward to each of the eight regional finals held in Leeds, Manchester, Birmingham, Bristol, Norwich, London, Brighton and Cardiff. The winning boy and girl from each regional final go forward to the national final of the competitions held in London during October.

The Choirboy of the Year contest began in 1975, the Choirgirl of the Year in 1989. Up until the end of 1991, both competitions were sponsored by BET plc. Since then, pending new sponsors, only one competition has been held – in 1992. It was run and managed, on behalf of the Royal School of Church Music, by Kestrel Communications, the consultants who created the competition.

The 1992 Choirgirl of the Year was Fiona Wight, 14, of Sutton Valence School Chapel Choir, Kent. To compete Fiona had to sing two pieces. These were the set piece, 'Come into Him' from Handel's *Messiah*, and her own choice piece, 'Make Joyful Noise unto the Lord' by Michael Head.

The 1992 Choirboy of the Year was Gavin Moralee, 12, of St Barnabas Church Choir, Dulwich. To compete Gavin had to sing two pieces. These were the set piece, 'How Beautiful are the Feet' from Handel's *Messiah*, and his own choice piece, 'The Monk and his Cat' by Samuel Barber.

SAINSBURY'S CHOIR OF THE YEAR

The sixth biennial contest for the Sainsbury's Choir of the Year took place in 1994. With over £9,000 in prize money and seven rounds televised on BBC2, the competition is the UK's major amateur choral event. There were two titles to be won: the 1994 Sainsbury's

Adult Choir of the Year and, for choirs whose members are aged 19 or under, the 1994 Sainsbury's Youth Choir of the Year. Each title is worth £2,000, with an extra £1,000 for the commissioning of a new choral work. Past Sainsbury's Choir of the Year finalists have gone on to make successful recordings, TV appearances and concert tours. The 1994 winner was awaited as this volume went to press. The last winners (in 1992) were Canzonetta (Manchester) and, in the Youth Section, Farnham Youth Choir.

CIDER

CIDER OF THE YEAR

CAMRA (the Campaign for Real Ale) organizes not only numerous beer and pub championships (see pp. 225–6), but also an annual Cider of the Year Award at its Cider and Perry Competition at its Great British Beer Festival. Recent winners have been:

1991	Theobolds
1992	Theobolds
1993	Bibbenden

The 1993 winning tipple was Bibbenden's Strong Kentish Cider brewed by Julian Barnes from fruit grown around Maidstone and Ashford, Kent. It is still, pale yellow, 8.5 per cent alcohol by volume, with a definite apple flavour.

CINEMA

THE HOLLYWOOD ACADEMY AWARDS (OSCARS)

The film industry's most glittering prize remains the Hollywood Academy Award, or 'Oscar'. The Oscar came about as a result of the formation of the Academy of Motion Picture Arts and Sciences in 1927. The Academy thought it would gain additional prestige and publicity if it gave out annual awards for artistic and technical merit. The first awards ceremony was in May 1929 and was a modest affair; nowadays the ceremony is a lavish spectacle watched by countless millions on worldwide television.

The Oscar itself is a gold-plated statuette of a knight holding a crusader's sword and standing on a reel of film whose five spokes symbolize the original branches of the Academy (actors, directors, producers, technicians and writers). Legend has it that the name comes from a secretary Margaret Herrick, later an executive director of the Academy, who commented one day that the statuette 'reminds me of my uncle Oscar'.

Ben Hur (1959) holds the record number of Oscars – 11. *West Side Story* (1961) won 10; *Gone With the Wind* (1939), *Gigi* (1958) and *The Last Emperor* (1987) each won 9. Katharine Hepburn has won more major acting Oscars than any other star – 4. Bette Davis, Louise Rainer, Olivia de Havilland, Ingrid Bergman, Glenda Jackson, Jane Fonda, Sally Field and Jodie Foster have won Best Actress twice; Spencer Tracy, Fredric March, Gary Cooper, Marlon Brando and Dustin Hoffman have done the same as Best Actor.

Academy Award for Best Film

1927/8 *Wings* (USA)
1928/9 (March) *Broadway Melody* (USA)
1929/30 (Nov) *All Quiet on the Western Front* (USA)
1930/1 *Cimarron* (USA)
1931/2 *Grand Hotel* (USA)
1932/3 *Cavalcade* (USA)
1934 *It Happened One Night* (USA)
1935 *Mutiny on the Bounty* (USA)
1936 *The Great Ziegfeld* (USA)
1937 *The Life of Emile Zola* (USA)
1938 *You Can't Take It With You* (USA)
1939 *Gone With the Wind* (USA)
1940 *Rebecca* (USA)
1941 *How Green Was My Valley* (USA)
1942 *Mrs Miniver* (USA)
1943 *Casablanca* (USA)
1944 *Going My Way* (USA)
1945 *The Lost Weekend* (USA)
1946 *The Best Years of Our Lives* (USA)
1947 *Gentleman's Agreement* (USA)
1948 *Hamlet* (GB)
1949 *All the King's Men* (USA)
1950 *All About Eve* (USA)
1951 *An American in Paris* (USA)
1952 *The Greatest Show on Earth* (USA)
1953 *From Here to Eternity* (USA)
1954 *On the Waterfront* (USA)
1955 *Marty* (USA)
1956 *Around the World in Eighty Days* (USA)
1957 *The Bridge on the River Kwai* (GB)
1958 *Gigi* (USA)
1959 *Ben Hur* (USA)
1960 *The Apartment* (USA)
1961 *West Side Story* (USA)
1962 *Lawrence of Arabia* (GB)
1963 *Tom Jones* (GB)
1964 *My Fair Lady* (USA)
1965 *The Sound of Music* (USA)
1966 *A Man for All Seasons* (GB)
1967 *In the Heat of the Night* (USA)
1968 *Oliver!* (GB)
1969 *Midnight Cowboy* (USA)
1970 *Patton* (USA)
1971 *The French Connection* (USA)
1972 *The Godfather* (USA)
1973 *The Sting* (USA)
1974 *The Godfather, Part II* (USA)
1975 *One Flew Over the Cuckoo's Nest* (USA)
1976 *Rocky* (USA)
1977 *Annie Hall* (USA)
1978 *The Deer Hunter* (USA)
1979 *Kramer vs Kramer* (USA)
1980 *Ordinary People* (USA)
1981 *Chariots of Fire* (GB)
1982 *Gandhi* (GB)
1983 *Terms of Endearment* (USA)
1984 *Amadeus* (USA)
1985 *Out of Africa* (USA)
1986 *Platoon* (USA)
1987 *The Last Emperor* (Ita/GB/Chn)
1988 *Rain Man* (USA)
1989 *Driving Miss Daisy* (USA)
1990 *Dances with Wolves* (USA)
1991 *The Silence of the Lambs* (USA)
1992 *Unforgiven* (USA)
1993 *Schindler's List* (USA)

Best Actor

1927/8 Emil Jannings, *The Way of All Flesh*
1928/9 Warner Baxter, *In Old Arizona*
1929/30 George Arliss, *Disraeli*
1930/1 Lionel Barrymore, *A Free Soul*
1931/2 { Fredric March, *Dr Jekyll and Mr Hyde* / Wallace Beery, *The Champ*
1932/3 Charles Laughton, *The Private Life of Henry VIII*
1934 Clark Gable, *It Happened One Night*
1935 Victor McLaglen, *The Informer*
1936 Paul Muni, *The Story of Louis Pasteur*
1937 Spencer Tracy, *Captains Courageous*
1938 Spencer Tracy, *Boys' Town*
1939 Robert Donat, *Goodbye Mr Chips*
1940 James Stewart, *The Philadelphia Story*
1941 Gary Cooper, *Sergeant York*
1942 James Cagney, *Yankee Doodle Dandy*
1943 Paul Lukas, *Watch on the Rhine*

1944	Bing Crosby, *Going My Way*
1945	Ray Milland, *The Lost Weekend*
1946	Fredric March, *The Best Years of Our Lives*
1947	Ronald Colman, *A Double Life*
1948	Laurence Olivier, *Hamlet*
1949	Broderick Crawford, *All the King's Men*
1950	José Ferrer, *Cyrano de Bergerac*
1951	Humphrey Bogart, *The African Queen*
1952	Gary Cooper, *High Noon*
1953	William Holden, *Stalag 17*
1954	Marlon Brando, *On the Waterfront*
1955	Ernest Borgnine, *Marty*
1956	Yul Brynner, *The King and I*
1957	Alec Guinness, *The Bridge on the River Kwai*
1958	David Niven, *Separate Tables*
1959	Charlton Heston, *Ben Hur*
1960	Burt Lancaster, *Elmer Gantry*
1961	Maximilian Schell, *Judgment at Nuremberg*
1962	Gregory Peck, *To Kill a Mockingbird*
1963	Sidney Poitier, *Lilies of the Field*
1964	Rex Harrison, *My Fair Lady*
1965	Lee Marvin, *Cat Ballou*
1966	Paul Scofield, *A Man for All Seasons*
1967	Rod Steiger, *In the Heat of the Night*
1968	Cliff Robertson, *Charly*
1969	John Wayne, *True Grit*
1970	George C. Scott, *Patton* (refused)
1971	Gene Hackman, *The French Connection*
1972	Marlon Brando, *The Godfather* (refused)
1973	Jack Lemmon, *Save the Tiger*
1974	Art Carney, *Harry and Tonto*
1975	Jack Nicholson, *One Flew Over the Cuckoo's Nest*
1976	Peter Finch, *Network*
1977	Richard Dreyfuss, *The Goodbye Girl*
1978	Jon Voigt, *Coming Home*
1979	Dustin Hoffman, *Kramer vs Kramer*
1980	Robert DeNiro, *Raging Bull*
1981	Henry Fonda, *On Golden Pond*

1982	Ben Kingsley, *Gandhi*
1983	Robert Duvall, *Tender Mercies*
1984	F. Murray Abraham, *Amadeus*
1985	William Hurt, *Kiss of the Spider Woman*
1986	Paul Newman, *The Color of Money*
1987	Michael Douglas, *Wall Street*
1988	Dustin Hoffman, *Rain Man*
1989	Daniel Day-Lewis, *My Left Foot*
1990	Jeremy Irons, *Reversal of Fortune*
1991	Anthony Hopkins, *The Silence of the Lambs*
1992	Al Pacino, *Scent of a Woman*
1993	Tom Hanks, *Philadelphia*

Best Actress

1927/8	Janet Gaynor, *Seventh Heaven*
1928/9	Mary Pickford, *Coquette*
1929/30	Norma Shearer, *The Divorcee*
1930/1	Marie Dressler, *Min and Bill*
1931/2	Helen Hayes, *Sin of Madelon Claudet*
1932/3	Katharine Hepburn, *Morning Glory*
1934	Claudette Colbert, *It Happened One Night*
1935	Bette Davis, *Dangerous*
1936	Louise Rainer, *The Great Ziegfeld*
1937	Louise Rainer, *The Good Earth*
1938	Bette Davis, *Jezebel*
1939	Vivien Leigh, *Gone With the Wind*
1940	Ginger Rogers, *Kitty Foyle*
1941	Joan Fontaine, *Suspicion*
1942	Greer Garson, *Mrs Miniver*
1943	Jennifer Jones, *The Song of Bernadette*
1944	Ingrid Bergman, *Gaslight*
1945	Joan Crawford, *Mildred Pierce*
1946	Olivia de Havilland, *To Each His Own*
1947	Loretta Young, *The Farmer's Daughter*
1948	Jane Wyman, *Johnny Belinda*
1949	Olivia de Havilland, *The Heiress*
1950	Judy Holliday, *Born Yesterday*
1951	Vivien Leigh, *A Streetcar Named Desire*
1952	Shirley Booth, *Come Back, Little Sheba*

1953	Audrey Hepburn, *Roman Holiday*
1954	Grace Kelly, *Country Girl*
1955	Anna Magnani, *The Rose Tattoo*
1956	Ingrid Bergman, *Anastasia*
1957	Joanne Woodward, *The Three Faces of Eve*
1958	Susan Hayward, *I Want to Live*
1959	Simone Signoret, *Room at the Top*
1960	Elizabeth Taylor, *Butterfield 8*
1961	Sophia Loren, *Two Women*
1962	Anne Bancroft, *The Miracle Worker*
1963	Patricia Neal, *Hud*
1964	Julie Andrews, *Mary Poppins*
1965	Julie Christie, *Darling*
1966	Elizabeth Taylor, *Who's Afraid of Virginia Woolf?*
1967	Katharine Hepburn, *Guess Who's Coming to Dinner*
1968	Katharine Hepburn, *The Lion in Winter* / Barbra Streisand, *Funny Girl*
1969	Maggie Smith, *The Prime of Miss Jean Brodie*
1970	Glenda Jackson, *Women in Love*
1971	Jane Fonda, *Klute*
1972	Liza Minelli, *Cabaret*
1973	Glenda Jackson, *A Touch of Class*
1974	Ellen Burstyn, *Alice Doesn't Live Here Anymore*
1975	Louise Fletcher, *One Flew Over the Cuckoo's Nest*
1976	Faye Dunaway, *Network*
1977	Diane Keaton, *Annie Hall*
1978	Jane Fonda, *Coming Home*
1979	Sally Field, *Norma Rae*
1980	Sissy Spacek, *Coal Miner's Daughter*
1981	Katharine Hepburn, *On Golden Pond*
1982	Meryl Streep, *Sophie's Choice*
1983	Shirley MacLaine, *Terms of Endearment*
1984	Sally Field, *Places in the Heart*
1985	Geraldine Page, *The Trip to Bountiful*
1986	Marlee Matlin, *Children of a Lesser God*
1987	Cher, *Moonstruck*
1988	Jodie Foster, *The Accused*
1989	Jessica Tandy, *Driving Miss Daisy*

1990	Kathy Bates, *Misery*
1991	Jodie Foster, *The Silence of the Lambs*
1992	Emma Thompson, *Howards End*
1993	Holly Hunter, *The Piano*

Best Director

1927/8	Frank Borzage, *Seventh Heaven* / Lewis Milestone, *Two Arabian Knights*
1928/9	Frank Lloyd, *The Divine Lady*
1929/30	Lewis Milestone, *All Quiet on the Western Front*
1930/1	Norman Taurog, *Skippy*
1931/2	Frank Borzage, *Bad Girl*
1932/3	Frank Lloyd, *Cavalcade*
1934	Frank Capra, *It Happened One Night*
1935	John Ford, *The Informer*
1936	Frank Capra, *Mr Deeds Goes to Town*
1937	Leo McCarey, *The Awful Truth*
1938	Frank Capra, *You Can't Take It With You*
1939	Victor Fleming, *Gone With The Wind*
1940	John Ford, *The Grapes of Wrath*
1941	John Ford, *How Green Was My Valley*
1942	William Wyler, *Mrs Miniver*
1943	Michael Curtiz, *Casablanca*
1944	Leo McCarey, *Going My Way*
1945	Billy Wilder, *The Lost Weekend*
1946	William Wyler, *The Best Years of Our Lives*
1947	Elia Kazan, *Gentleman's Agreement*
1948	John Huston, *Treasure of Sierra Madre*
1949	Joseph L. Mankiewicz, *A Letter to Three Wives*
1950	Joseph L. Mankiewicz, *All About Eve*
1951	George Stevens, *A Place in the Sun*
1952	John Ford, *The Quiet Man*
1953	Fred Zinnemann, *From Here to Eternity*

1954	Elia Kazan, *On the Waterfront*	1975	Milos Forman, *One Flew Over the Cuckoo's Nest*
1955	Delbert Mann, *Marty*		
1956	George Stevens, *Giant*	1976	John Avildsen, *Rocky*
1957	David Lean, *The Bridge on the River Kwai*	1977	Woody Allen, *Annie Hall*
		1978	Michael Cimino, *The Deer Hunter*
1958	Vincente Minnelli, *Gigi*	1979	Robert Benton, *Kramer vs Kramer*
1959	William Wyler, *Ben Hur*		
1960	Billy Wilder, *The Apartment*	1980	Robert Redford, *Ordinary People*
1961	Jerome Robbins and Robert Wise, *West Side Story*	1981	Warren Beatty, *Reds*
		1982	Richard Attenborough, *Gandhi*
1962	David Lean, *Lawrence of Arabia*	1983	James L. Brooks, *Terms of Endearment*
1963	Tony Richardson, *Tom Jones*		
1964	George Cukor, *My Fair Lady*	1984	Milos Forman, *Amadeus*
1965	Robert Wise, *The Sound of Music*	1985	Sydney Pollack, *Out of Africa*
1966	Fred Zinnemann, *A Man for All Seasons*	1986	Oliver Stone, *Platoon*
		1987	Bernardo Bertolucci, *The Last Emperor*
1967	Mike Nichols, *The Graduate*		
1968	Sir Carol Reed, *Oliver!*	1988	Barry Levinson, *Rain Man*
1969	John Schlesinger, *Midnight Cowboy*	1989	Oliver Stone, *Born on the Fourth of July*
1970	Franklin J. Schaffner, *Patton*	1990	Kevin Costner, *Dances with Wolves*
1971	William Friedkin, *The French Connection*		
		1991	Jonathan Demme, *The Silence of the Lambs*
1972	Bob Fosse, *Cabaret*		
1973	George Roy Hill, *The Sting*	1992	Clint Eastwood, *Unforgiven*
1974	Francis Ford Coppola, *The Godfather, Part II*	1993	Steven Spielberg, *Schindler's List*

VENICE FILM FESTIVAL

Venice is the oldest of the international film festivals, celebrating its fiftieth anniversary in 1993. Its initial aim was to 'raise the new art of the films to the level of the other arts'. Politically controversial in the 1930s (the best film award to Leni Riefenstahl's allegedly pro-Fascist film *Olympia* caused a particular storm), the Festival has often been dogged by financial and bureaucratic problems and abandoned its award system in 1969, only to reinstate it in 1980. Nevertheless, the Festival has a reputation for attracting specialist films of high artistic value, as can particularly be seen in its roster of winning films during the 1960s.

Best Foreign Film Award (1934–42)
Best Film Award (1946–68)
Golden Lion for Best Film (1980–)

1932	*no official award*	1938	*Olympia* (Ger)
1933	*no festival*	1939	*no award*
1934	*Man of Aran* (GB)	1940	*Der Postmeister* (Ger)
1935	*Anna Karenina* (USA)	1941	*Ohm Kruger* (Ger)
1936	*Der Kaiser von Kalifornien* (Ger)	1942	*Der grosse König* (Ger)
1937	*Un Carnet de Bal* (Fra)	1943	*no festival*
		1944	*no festival*
		1945	*no festival*
		1946	*The Southerner* (USA)
		1947	*Sirean* (Cze)

1948	Hamlet (GB)	Jury and award system discontinued	
1949	Manon (Fra)	1969–79	
1950	Justice is Done (Fra)	1980	Gloria (USA)
1951	Rashomon (Jap)		Atlantic City (Fra/Can)
1952	Forbidden Games (Fra)	1981	Die Bleierne Zeit (FRG)
1953	no award	1982	The State of Things (FRG)
1954	Romeo and Juliet (Ita/GB)	1983	Prénom Carmen (Fra/Swi)
1955	Ordet (Den)	1984	Year of the Quiet Sun (Pol)
1956	no award	1985	Sans toit ni loi aka Vagabonde
1957	Aparajito (Ind)		(Fra)
1958	Muhomatsu no Issho (Jap)	1986	Le Rayon Vert (Fra)
1959	Il Generale della Rovere (Ita)	1987	Au Revoir les Enfants (Fra)
1960	Le Passage du Rhin (Fra)	1988	The Legend of the Holy Drinker
1961	Last Year at Marienbad (Fra)		(Ita)
1962	Childhood of Ivan (USSR)	1989	A City of Sadness (Tai)
1963	Le Mani sulla Città (Ita)	1990	Rosencrantz and Guildenstern
1964	Red Desert (Ita)		Are Dead (GB)
1965	Of a Thousand Delights (Ita)	1991	Urga (USSR/Fra)
1966	Battle of Algiers (Ita)	1992	Qiu Ju Da Guansi (Chn)
1967	Belle de Jour (Fra)	1993	Short Cuts (USA)
1968	Die Aristen in der Zirkuskuppel		Three Colours Blue (Fra)
	(FRG)		

CANNES FILM FESTIVAL

Cannes is the most flamboyant, glamorous and commercially orientated of modern film festivals. It began in 1946 and has run in consecutive years ever since, apart from 1948 and 1950, when it was cancelled for financial reasons, and 1968, when political demonstrations, spearheaded by prominent French film-makers, brought the festival to a halt. Annually held in May, its top prize is the coveted Palme d'Or (Golden Palm) for best film.

Palme d'Or for Best Film

1946	La Bataille du Rail (Fra)	1961	Viridiana (Sp)
1947	Antoine et Antoinette (Fra)		Une Aussi Longue Absence (Fra)
1948	no festival	1962	The Given Word (Bra)
1949	The Third Man (GB)	1963	The Leopard (Ita)
1950	no festival	1964	The Umbrellas of Cherbourg (Fra)
1951	Miracle in Milan (Ita)	1965	The Knack (GB)
	Miss Julie (Swe)	1966	A Man and a Woman (Fra)
1952	Othello (Mor)		Signore e Signori (Ita)
	Two Cents Worth of Hope (Ita)	1967	Blow-Up (GB)
1953	The Wages of Fear (Fra)	1968	festival disrupted; no awards
1954	Gate of Hell (Jap)	1969	If (GB)
1955	Marty (USA)	1970	M*A*S*H (USA)
1956	World of Silence (Fra)	1971	The Go-Between (GB)
1957	Friendly Persuasion (USA)	1972	The Working Class Goes to
1958	The Cranes are Flying (USSR)		Paradise (Ita)
1959	Black Orpheus (Fra)		The Mattei Affair (Ita)
1960	La Dolce Vita (Ita)	1973	Scarecrow (USA)
			The Hireling (GB)

1974	The Conversation (USA)	1984	Paris, Texas (FRG)
1975	Chronicle of the Burning Years (Alg)	1985	When Father Was Away on Business (Yug)
1976	Taxi Driver (USA)	1986	The Mission (GB)
1977	Padre Padrone (Ita)	1987	Under the Sun of Satan (Fra)
1978	L'Albergo Degli Zoccoli (Ita)	1988	Pelle the Conqueror (Den)
1979	The Tin Drum (FRG) / Apocalypse Now (USA)	1989	Sex, Lies and Videotape (USA)
		1990	Wild at Heart (USA)
1980	All That Jazz (USA) / Kagemusha (Jap)	1991	Barton Fink (USA)
		1992	Best Intentions (Swe)
1981	Man of Iron (Pol)	1993	Farewell My Concubine (Chn) / The Piano (Aus)
1982	Missing (USA) / Yol (Tur)	1994	Pulp Fiction (USA)
1983	The Ballad of Narayama (Jap)		

THE BERLIN FILM FESTIVAL

The Berlin Film Festival was established in 1951 by Dr Alfred Bauer. There was no overall Best Film Award in the first year and between 1952 and 1956, as well as a jury, the audience was allowed to determine award-winners, a practice abandoned when the Festival received an 'A' classification from the International Federation of Film Producers' Associations. Less commercial than Cannes, less arty than Venice, the Festival has gained a reputation for showcasing more offbeat, independent films, particularly supporting young directors. In 1970, political demonstrations by young activists forced the Festival to close.

Award for Best Film

		1972	The Canterbury Tales (Ita)
		1973	Distant Thunder (Ind)
1952	She Danced for the Summer (Swe)	1974	The Apprenticeship of Duddy Kravitz (Can)
1953	The Wages of Fear (Fra)	1975	Orkobefogados (Hun)
1954	Hobson's Choice (GB)	1976	Buffalo Bill and the Indians (USA) – award declined
1955	The Rats (FRG)		
1956	Invitation to the Dance (GB)	1977	The Ascent (USSR)
1957	Twelve Angry Men (USA)	1978	The Trouts (Spa) / The Words of Max (Spa)
1958	The End of the Day (Swe)		
1959	The Cousins (Fra)	1979	David (FRG)
1960	Lazarillo de Tormes (Spa)	1980	Heartland (USA) / Palermo Oder Wolfsburg (FRG)
1961	La Notte (Ita)		
1962	A Kind of Loving (GB)	1981	Di Presa Di Presa (Spa)
1963	Oath of Obedience (FRG) / The Devil (Ita)	1982	Die Sehnsucht der Veronica Voss (FRG)
1964	Dry Summer (Tur)	1983	Ascendancy (GB) / The Beehive (Spa)
1965	Alphaville (Fra)		
1966	Cul de Sac (GB)	1984	Love Streams (USA)
1967	Le Départ (Bel)	1985	Wetherby (GB) / Die Frau und der Fremde (FRG)
1968	Ole Dole Doff (Swe)		
1969	Early Years (Yug)	1986	Stammheim (FRG)
1970	no award	1987	The Theme (USSR)
1971	The Garden of the Finzi-Continis (Ita)	1988	Red Sorghum (Chn)
		1989	Rain Man (USA)

1990	{ Music Box (USA)	1993	{ · The Woman from the Lake of
	Larks on a String (Cze)		Scented Souls (Chn)
1991	House of Smiles (Ita)		The Wedding Banquet (Tai/USA)
1992	Grand Canyon (USA)	1994	In the Name of the Father (USA/Ire)

BRITISH FILM ACADEMY AWARDS

The British Film Academy (BFA) was founded in 1948 and instituted the awards as an incentive to foster and improve creative standards in film-making. Later it merged with the Guild of Television Producers and Directors; and, after a further reorganization, became known as the British Academy of Film and Television Arts (BAFTA). It holds its BAFTA awards ceremony in March of every year.

Between 1948 and 1968 there were separate awards for the best British film of the year and for the best film from any source. From 1969, however, there has been just one Best Film award.

Best Film From Any Source (1947–67)

1947	The Best Years of Our Lives (USA)
1948	Hamlet (GB)
1949	Bicycle Thieves (Ita)
1950	All About Eve (USA)
1951	La Ronde (Fra)
1952	The Sound Barrier (GB)
1953	Forbidden Games (Fra)
1954	The Wages of Fear (Fra)
1955	Richard III (GB)
1956	Gervaise (Fra)
1957	The Bridge on the River Kwai (GB)
1958	Room at the Top (GB)
1959	Ben Hur (USA)
1960	The Apartment (USA)
1961	{ Ballad of a Soldier (USSR) / The Hustler (USA)
1962	Lawrence of Arabia (GB)
1963	Tom Jones (GB)
1964	Dr Strangelove (GB)
1965	My Fair Lady (USA)
1966	Who's Afraid of Virginia Woolf? (USA)
1967	A Man For All Seasons (GB)

The Best British Film of the Year (1947–67)

1947	Odd Man Out
1948	The Fallen Idol
1949	The Third Man
1950	The Blue Lamp
1951	The Lavender Hill Mob
1952	The Sound Barrier

1953	Genevieve
1954	Hobson's Choice
1955	Richard III
1956	Reach for the Sky
1957	The Bridge on the River Kwai
1958	Room at the Top
1959	Sapphire
1960	Saturday Night and Sunday Morning
1961	A Taste of Honey
1962	Lawrence of Arabia
1963	Tom Jones
1964	Dr Strangelove
1965	The Ipcress File
1966	The Spy Who Came in from the Cold
1967	A Man for all Seasons

Best Film (1968–93)

1968	The Graduate (USA)
1969	Midnight Cowboy (USA)
1970	Butch Cassidy and the Sundance Kid (USA)
1971	Sunday Bloody Sunday (GB)
1972	Cabaret (USA)
1973	{ La Nuit Américaine (Fra) / Day for Night (Fra)
1974	Lacombe, Lucien (Fra)
1975	Alice Doesn't Live Here Any More (USA)
1976	One Flew Over the Cuckoo's Nest (USA)
1977	Annie Hall (USA)
1978	Julia (USA)
1979	Manhattan (USA)
1980	The Elephant Man (GB)

John McCarthy and Jill Morrell, authors of *Some Other Rainbow*, the bestselling hardback book of 1993

Recent winners of the Children of Courage Award

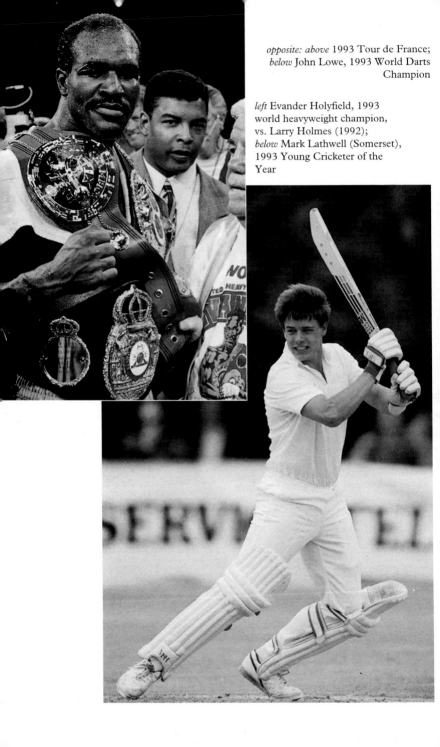

opposite: above 1993 Tour de France;
below John Lowe, 1993 World Darts
Champion

left Evander Holyfield, 1993
world heavyweight champion,
vs. Larry Holmes (1992);
below Mark Lathwell (Somerset),
1993 Young Cricketer of the
Year

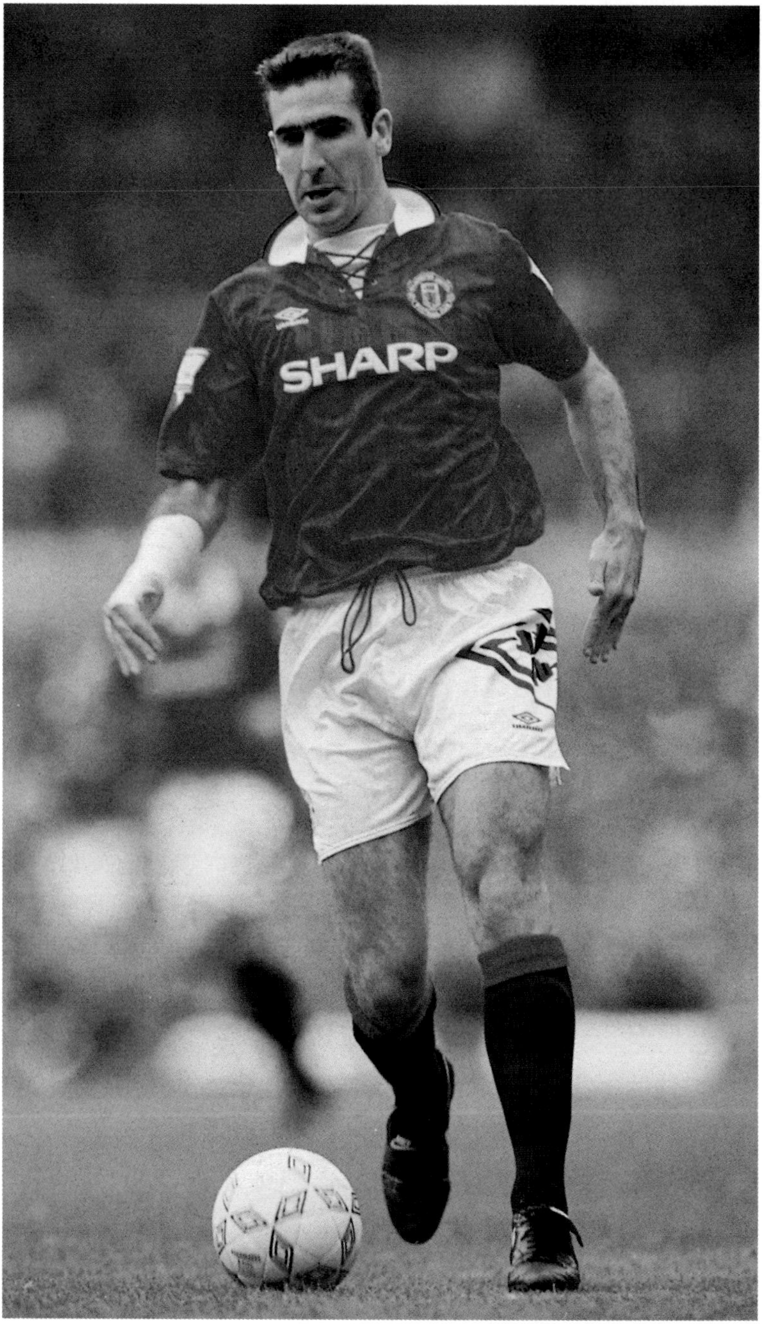
SHARP

opposite Eric Cantona (Manchester United), 1994 English PFA Footballer of the Year

right Greg Norman, winner of the 1993 British Open; *below* Richard Dunwoody, winner of the 1994 Grand National on Miinnehoma

above Australia winning the 1991 Rugby Union World Cup; *below* Stephen Hendry, the reigning Embassy World Professional champion

Jayne Torvill and Christopher Dean winning the pairs compulsory dance in the 1994 winter olympics

Crufts Supreme Champion 1994: Buttons, alias Champion Purston Hit and Miss from Brocolita, a Welsh terrier, with his handler Frank Kellett and owner Mrs Anne Maughan

Paddy Byrne with Nip, winners of the 1993 singles *One Man and His Dog* award

1993 *British Birds* magazine bird photograph of the year by Alan Williams of a hoopoe

1981	*Chariots of Fire* (GB)
1982	*Gandhi* (GB)
1983	*Educating Rita* (GB)
1984	*The Killing Fields* (GB)
1985	*The Purple Rose of Cairo* (USA)
1986	*A Room with a View* (GB)
1987	*Jean de Florette* (Fra)
1988	*The Last Emperor* (Ita/GB/Chn)
1989	*Dead Poets Society* (USA)
1990	*GoodFellas* (USA)
1991	*The Commitments* (USA/UK)
1992	*Howards End* (GB)
1993	*Schindler's List* (USA)

BAFTA Film Awards

The 1992 film awards were:

Best Film Howards End (Ismail Merchant/James Ivory)

Best Director Robert Altman (*The Player*)

Best Original Screenplay Husbands And Wives (Woody Allen)

Best Adapted Screenplay The Player (Michael Tolkin)

Best Actress Emma Thompson (*Howards End*)

Best Actor Robert Downey Jr (*Chaplin*)

Best Supporting Actress Miranda Richardson (*Damage*)

Best Supporting Actor Gene Hackman (*Unforgiven*)

Best Original Film Music Strictly Ballroom (David Hirschfielder)

Best Foreign Film Raise The Red Lantern (Chiu Fu-Sheng/Zhang Yimou)

Best Short Film Omnibus (Anne Bennet/ Sam Karmann)

Best Short Animated Film Daumier's Law (Ginger Gibbons/Geoff Dunbar)

Among the 1993 awards were:

Best Film Schindler's List

Best Director Steven Spielberg (*Schindler's List*)

Best Supporting Actor Ralph Fiennes (*Schindler's List*)

Best Actor Sir Anthony Hopkins (*Remains of the Day*)

Best Actress Holly Hunter (*The Piano*)

Best Supporting Actress Miriam Margolyes (*The Age of Innocence*)

EUROPEAN FILM AWARDS

These are the youngest of the major film awards, known as the 'Felix', named after the restaurant in Cannes from which the awards were launched. The first presentation ceremony took place in Berlin in 1988.

1988

Best film A Short Film About Killing (Pol)

Best actor Max Von Sydow, Pelle the Conqueror (Swe)

Best actress Carmen Maura, Women on the Verge of a Nervous Breakdown (Spa)

Best director Wim Wenders, Wings of Desire (FRG)

1989

Best film Landscape in the Mist (Gre/Ita)

Best actor Philippe Noiret, Life and Nothing But and Cinema Paradiso (Ita)

Best actress Ruth Sheen, High Hopes (UK)

Best director Geza Beremenyi, Eldorado (The Midas Touch) (Hun)

1990

Best film Open Doors (Ita)

Best actor Kenneth Branagh, Henry V (UK)

Best actress Carmen Maura, Ay Carmela! (Spa)

Best director no award

1991

Best film Riff-Raff (UK)

Best actor Michel Bouquet, Toto Lé Heros (Bel)

Best actress Clotilde Courou, Le Petit Criminel (Fra)

1992

Best film The Stolen Children (Ita)

Best actor Matti Pellonpaa, La Vie de Bohème (Fin)

Best actress Juliette Binoche, *Les Amants du Pont Neuf* (Fra)
Life Achievement Award Billy Wilder

1993

Best film *Urga* (Rus)

Best actor Daniel Auteuil, *Un Coeur en Hiver* (Fra)
Best actress Maia Morgenstern, *The Oak Tree* (Rom)
Life Achievement Award Michelangelo Antonioni

THE TEN BEST FILMS

Every ten years since 1952, *Sight and Sound* magazine has conducted an international poll of critics, archivists and film scholars to determine the ten best films of all time.

1952

1	De Sica's *Bicycle Thieves* (Ita)
2	Chaplin's *City Lights* (USA) Chaplin's *The Gold Rush* (USA)
4	Eisenstein's *Battleship Potemkin* (USSR)
5	Griffith's *Intolerance* (USA) Flaherty's *Louisiana Story* (USA)
7	Von Stroheim's *Greed* (USA) Carné's *Le Jour Se Lève* (Fra) Dreyer's *The Passion of Joan of Arc* (Fra) Lean's *Brief Encounter* (GB)
10	Clair's *Le Million* (Fra) Renoir's *La Règle du Jeu* (Fra)

1962

1	Welles's *Citizen Kane* (USA)
2	Antonioni's *L'avventura* (Ita)
3	Renoir's *La Règle du Jeu* (Fra)
4	Von Stroheim's *Greed* (USA) Mizoguchi's *Ugetsu Monogatari* (Jap) Eisenstein's *Battleship Potemkin* (USSR)
6	De Sica's *Bicycle Thieves* (Ita) Eisenstein's *Ivan the Terrible* (USSR)
9	Visconti's *La Terra Trema* (Ita)
10	Vigo's *L'Atalante* (Fra)

1972

1	Welles's *Citizen Kane* (USA)
2	Renoir's *La Règle du Jeu* (Fra)
3	Eisenstein's *Battleship Potemkin* (USSR)
4	Fellini's *8½* (Ita)
5	Antonioni's *L'avventura* (Ita) Bergman's *Persona* (Swe)

7	Dreyer's *The Passion of Joan of Arc* (Fra)
8	Keaton and Bruckman's *The General* (USA) Welles's *The Magnificent Ambersons* (USA)
10	Mizoguchi's *Ugetsu Monogatari* (Jap) Bergman's *Wild Strawberries* (Swe)

1982

1	Welles's *Citizen Kane* (USA)
2	Renoir's *La Règle du Jeu* (Fra)
3	Kurosawa's *Seven Samurai* (Jap) Donen and Kelly's *Singin' in the Rain* (USA)
5	Fellini's *8½* (Ita)
6	Eisenstein's *Battleship Potemkin* (USSR)
7	Antonioni's *L'avventura* (Ita) Welles' *The Magnificent Ambersons* (USA) Hitchcock's *Vertigo* (USA)
10	Keaton and Bruckman's *The General* (USA) Ford's *The Searchers* (USA)

1992

1	Welles' *Citizen Kane* (USA)
2	Renoir's *La Règle du Jeu* (Fra)
3	Ozu's *Tokyo Story* (Jap)
4	Hitchcock's *Vertigo* (USA)
5	Ford's *The Searchers* (USA)
6	Vigo's *L'Atalante* (Fra) Dreyer's *The Passion of Joan of Arc* (Fra) Ray's *Pather Panchali* (Ind) Eisenstein's *Battleship Potemkin* (USSR)
10	Kubrick's *2001: A Space Odyssey* (GB)

COMPUTERS

THE *PC PLUS* AWARDS

Each year *PC Plus*, the PC magazine, gives its annual awards for the best equipment on the market. The most recent winners, announced in its February 1994 issue, were:

Accounting Software   M.Y.O.B.

Communications   US Robotics Sportster 14400

Databases   FoxPro 2.5 for DOS and Windows

Desktop publishing   Microsoft Publisher 2.0

Networking   NetWare 4

Games   Sam and Max Hit the Road

Peripherals   Fargo Primera dye-sublimation printer

Operating Systems and Utilities   no award made

Personal Computers   Gateway 2000 4DX2-66V

Programming/Software Development   Bounds Checker 2.0 for Windows

Spreadsheets   Borland Quattro Pro for Windows

Graphics   Core1DRAW! 4.0

Word Processing   Q & A Write 3.0

Integrated Software   Lotus SmartSuite 2

Product of the Year   Quattro Pro 5

THE *PCW* AWARDS

Since 1991 the magazine *Personal Computer World* has listed its annual winners in a whole variety of categories. New categories in 1994 reflected the changing computer world, especially the 'year of the CD-ROM'. 1994 winners were:

Best Database   Microsoft Access

Best Spreadsheet   Microsoft Excel 5

Best Presentation Graphics Application   Lotus Freelance 2

Best Ast Application   Adobe Photoshop 2.5

Most Innovative or Influential Software   Windows NT

Most Innovative or Influential Hardware   Apple Newton

Best DTP/Best Budget DTP   Quark Xpress 3.x/Microsoft Publisher

Best Budget Printer   Hewlett Packard LaserJet 4L

Best Comms Software   CommWorks for Windows

Best Printer   Hewlett Packard LaserJet 4

Best Sub-Notebook   Toshiba T3400CT

Best Entry Level Notebook   Mitac 4020/G

Best Power Portable   Toshiba T6600C

Best Power User System   Silicon Graphics Indy

Best System under £1000   Apple Mac LC475

Best System under £2000   Dan for Multimedia

Best Game   X-Wing

Best Utility   Lotus Organizer

Best Suite   Microsoft Office

Best Programming Language   Microsoft Visual Basic

Best Network Product   Little Big Lan

Best Sound Card/Best CD-ROM Drive   Orchid SoundWave 32 – Pioneer 604X

Best Monitor/Best Graphics Card   Eizo Flexscan T660i-T – Rapier 24M

Turkey of the Year   Intel Pentium

CRICKET

WORLD CUP

1975	West Indies	1987	Australia
1979	West Indies	1992	Pakistan
1983	India		

COUNTY CHAMPIONSHIPS

1864	Surrey	1898	Yorkshire	1948	Glamorgan
1865	Nottinghamshire	1899	Surrey	1949	{ Middlesex / Yorkshire
1866	Middlesex	1900	Yorkshire		
1867	Yorkshire	1901	Yorkshire	1950	{ Lancashire / Surrey
1868	Nottinghamshire	1902	Yorkshire		
1869	{ Nottinghamshire / Yorkshire	1903	Middlesex	1951	Warwickshire
		1904	Lancashire	1952	Surrey
1870	Yorkshire	1905	Yorkshire	1953	Surrey
1871	Nottinghamshire	1906	Kent	1954	Surrey
1872	Nottinghamshire	1907	Nottinghamshire	1955	Surrey
1873	{ Gloucestershire / Nottinghamshire	1908	Yorkshire	1956	Surrey
		1909	Kent	1957	Surrey
1874	Gloucestershire	1910	Kent	1958	Surrey
1875	Nottinghamshire	1911	Warwickshire	1959	Yorkshire
1876	Gloucestershire	1912	Yorkshire	1960	Yorkshire
1877	Gloucestershire	1913	Kent	1961	Hampshire
1878	*undecided*	1914	Surrey	1962	Yorkshire
1879	{ Nottinghamshire / Lancashire	1919	Yorkshire	1963	Yorkshire
		1920	Middlesex	1964	Worcestershire
1880	Nottinghamshire	1921	Middlesex	1965	Worcestershire
1881	Lancashire	1922	Yorkshire	1966	Yorkshire
1882	{ Nottinghamshire / Lancashire	1923	Yorkshire	1967	Yorkshire
		1924	Yorkshire	1968	Yorkshire
1883	Nottinghamshire	1925	Yorkshire	1969	Glamorgan
1884	Nottinghamshire	1926	Lancashire	1970	Kent
1885	Nottinghamshire	1927	Lancashire	1971	Surrey
1886	Nottinghamshire	1928	Lancashire	1972	Warwickshire
1887	Surrey	1929	Nottinghamshire	1973	Hampshire
1888	Surrey	1930	Lancashire	1974	Worcestershire
1889	{ Surrey / Lancashire / Nottinghamshire	1931	Yorkshire	1975	Leicestershire
		1932	Yorkshire	1976	Middlesex
		1933	Yorkshire	1977	{ Middlesex / Kent
1890	Surrey	1934	Lancashire		
1891	Surrey	1935	Yorkshire	1978	Kent
1892	Surrey	1936	Derbyshire	1979	Essex
1893	Yorkshire	1937	Yorkshire	1980	Middlesex
1894	Surrey	1938	Yorkshire	1981	Nottinghamshire
1895	Surrey	1939	Yorkshire	1982	Middlesex
1896	Yorkshire	1946	Yorkshire	1983	Essex
1897	Lancashire	1947	Middlesex	1984	Essex

1985	Middlesex	1988	Worcestershire	1991	Essex
1986	Essex	1989	Worcestershire	1992	Essex
1987	Nottinghamshire	1990	Middlesex	1993	Middlesex

NATWEST BANK TROPHY

1963	Sussex	1974	Kent	1985	Essex
1964	Sussex	1975	Lancashire	1986	Sussex
1965	Yorkshire	1976	Northamptonshire	1987	Nottinghamshire
1966	Warwickshire	1977	Middlesex	1988	Middlesex
1967	Kent	1978	Sussex	1989	Warwickshire
1968	Warwickshire	1979	Somerset	1990	Lancashire
1969	Yorkshire	1980	Middlesex	1991	Hampshire
1970	Lancashire	1981	Derbyshire	1992	Northamptonshire
1971	Lancashire	1982	Surrey	1993	Warwickshire
1972	Lancashire	1983	Somerset		
1973	Gloucestershire	1984	Middlesex		

BENSON AND HEDGES CUP

1972	Leicestershire	1980	Northamptonshire	1988	Hampshire
1973	Kent	1981	Somerset	1989	Nottinghamshire
1974	Surrey	1982	Somerset	1990	Lancashire
1975	Leicestershire	1983	Middlesex	1991	Worcestershire
1976	Kent	1984	Lancashire	1992	Hampshire
1977	Gloucestershire	1985	Leicestershire	1993	Derbyshire
1978	Kent	1986	Middlesex	1994	Warwickshire
1979	Essex	1987	Yorkshire		

SUNDAY LEAGUE WINNERS

1969	Lancashire	1978	Hampshire	1987	Worcestershire
1970	Lancashire	1979	Somerset	1988	Worcestershire
1971	Worcestershire	1980	Warwickshire	1989	Lancashire
1972	Kent	1981	Essex	1990	Derbyshire
1973	Kent	1982	Sussex	1991	Nottinghamshire
1974	Leicestershire	1983	Yorkshire	1992	Middlesex
1975	Hampshire	1984	Essex	1993	Glamorgan
1976	Kent	1985	Essex		
1977	Leicestershire	1986	Hampshire		

WISDEN CRICKETERS OF THE YEAR

1947	A. V. Bedser, L. B. Fishlock, V. (M. H.) Mankad, T. P. B. Smith, C. Washbrook	1950	T. E. Bailey, R. O. Jenkins, J. G. Langridge, R. T. Simpson, B. Sutcliffe
1948	M. P. Donnelly, A. Melville, A. D. Nourse, J. D. Robertson, N. W. D. Yardley	1951	T. G. Evans, S. Ramadhin, A. L. Valentine, E. D. Weekes, F. M. M. Worrell
1949	A. L. Hassett, W. A. Johnston, R. R. Lindwall, A. R. Morris, D. Tallon	1952	R. Appleyard, H. E. Dollery, J. C. Laker, P. B. H. May, E. A. B. Rowan

1953	H. Gimblett, T. W. Graveney, D. S. Sheppard, W. S. Surridge, F. S. Trueman
1954	R. N. Harvey, G. A. R. Lock, K. R. Miller, J. H. Wardle, W. Watson
1955	B. Dooland, Fazal Mahmood, W. E. Hollies, J. B. Statham, G. E. Tribe
1956	M. C. Cowdrey, D. J. Insole, D. J. McGlew, H. J. Tayfield, F. H. Tyson
1957	D. Brookes, J. W. Burke, M. J. Hilton, G. R. A. Langley, P. E. Richardson
1958	P. J. Loader, A. J. W. McIntyre, O. G. Smith, M. J. Stewart, C. L. Walcott
1959	H. L. Jackson, R. E. Marshall, C. A. Milton, J. R. Reid, D. Shackleton
1960	K. F. Barrington, D. B. Carr, R. Illingworth, G. Pullar, M. J. K. Smith
1961	N. A. T. Adcock, E. R. Dexter, R. A. McLean, R. Subba Row, J. V. Wilson
1962	W. E. Alley, R. Benaud, A. K. Davidson, W. M. Lawry, N. C. O'Neill
1963	D. Kenyon, Mushtaq Mohammad, P. H. Parfitt, P. J. Sharpe, F. J. Titmus
1964	D. B. Close, C. C. Griffith, C. C. Hunte, R. B. Kanhai, G. S. Sobers
1965	G. Boycott, P. J. Burge, J. A. Flavell, G. D. McKenzie, R. B. Simpson
1966	K. C. Bland, J. H. Edrich, R. C. Motz, P. M. Pollock, R. G. Pollock
1967	R. W. Barber, B. L. D'Oliveira, C. Milburn, J. T. Murray, S. M. Nurse
1968	Asif Iqbal, Hanif Mohammad, K. Higgs, J. M. Parks, Nawab of Pataudi jun.
1969	J. G. Binks, D. M. Green, B. A. Richards, D. L. Underwood, O. S. Wheatley
1970	B. F. Butcher, A. P. E. Knott, Majid Khan, M. J. Procter, D. J. Shepherd
1971	J. D. Bond, C. H. Lloyd, B. W. Luckhurst, G. M. Turner, R. T. Virgin
1972	G. G. Arnold, B. S. Chandrasekhar, L. R. Gibbs, B. Taylor, Zaheer Abbas
1973	G. S. Chappell, D. K. Lillee, R. A. L. Massie, J. A. Snow, K. R. Stackpole
1974	K. D. Boyce, B. E. Congdon, K. W. R. Fletcher, R. C. Fredericks, P. J. Sainsbury
1975	D. L. Amiss, M. H. Denness, N. Gifford, A. W. Greig, A. M. E. Roberts
1976	I. M. Chappell, P. G. Lee, R. B. McCosker, D. S. Steele, R. A. Woolmer
1977	J. M. Brearley, C. G. Greenidge, M. A. Holding, I. V. A. Richards, R. W. Taylor
1978	I. T. Botham, M. Hendrick, A. Jones, K. S. McEwan, R. G. D. Willis
1979	D. I. Gower, J. K. Lever, C. M. Old, C. T. Radley, J. N. Shepherd
1980	J. Garner, S. M. Gavaskar, G. A. Gooch, D. W. Randall, B. C. Rose
1981	K. J. Hughes, R. D. Jackman, A. J. Lamb, C. E. B. Rice, V. A. P. van der Bijl
1982	T. M. Alderman, A. R. Border, J. Hadlee, Javed Miandad, R. W. Marsh
1983	Imran Khan, T. E. Jesty, A. I. Kallicharran, Kapil Dev, M. D. Marshall
1984	M. Amarnath, J. V. Coney, J. E. Emburey, M. W. Gatting, C. L. Smith
1985	M. D. Crowe, H. A. Gomes, G. W. Humpage, J. Simmons, S. Wettimuny
1986	P. Bainbridge, R. M. Ellison, C. J. McDermott, N. V. Radford, R. T. Robinson
1987	J. H. Childs, G. A. Hick, D. B. Vengsarkar, C. A. Walsh, J. J. Whitaker
1988	J. P. Agnew, N. A. Foster, D. P. Hughes, P. M. Roebuck, Salim Malik

1989	K. J. Barnett, P. J. L. Dujon, P. A. Neale, F. D. Stephenson, S. R. Waugh
1990	S. J. Cook, D. M. Jones, R. C. Russell, R. A. Smith, M. A. Taylor
1991	M. A. Atherton, M. Azharuddin, A. R. Butcher, D. L. Haynes, M. E. Waugh
1992	C. E. L. Ambrose, P. A. J. DeFreitas, A. A. Donald, R. B. Richardson, Waqar Younis.
1993	N. E. Briers, M. D. Moxon, I. D. K. Salisbury, A. J. Stewart, Wasim Akram
1994	D. C. Boon, I. A. Healy, M. G. Hughes, S. K. Warne, S. L. Watkin

YOUNG CRICKETER OF THE YEAR

Every September the Cricket Writers' Club select the season's best young cricketer.

1950	R. Tattersall
1951	P. B. H. May
1952	F. S. Trueman
1953	M. C. Cowdrey
1954	P. J. Loader
1955	K. F. Barrington
1956	B. Taylor
1957	M. J. Stewart
1958	A. C. D. Ingleby-Mackenzie
1959	G. Pullar
1960	D. A. Allen
1961	P. H. Parfitt
1962	P. J. Sharpe
1963	G. Boycott
1964	J. M. Brearley
1965	A. P. E. Knott
1966	D. L. Underwood
1967	A. W. Greig
1968	R. M. H. Cottam
1969	A. Ward
1970	C. M. Old
1971	J. Whitehouse
1972	D. R. Owen-Thomas
1973	M. Hendrick
1974	P. H. Edmonds
1975	A. Kennedy
1976	G. Miller
1977	I. T. Botham
1978	D. I. Gower
1979	P. W. G. Parker
1980	G. R. Dilley
1981	M. W. Gatting
1982	N. G. Cowans
1983	N. A. Foster
1984	R. J. Bailey
1985	D. V. Lawrence
1986	A. A. Metcalfe / J. J. Whitaker
1987	R. J. Blakey
1988	M. P. Maynard
1989	N. Hussain
1990	M. A. Atherton
1991	M. R. Ramprakash
1992	I. D. K. Salisbury
1993	M. N. Lathwell

WOMEN'S WORLD CUP

1973	England
1978	Australia
1982	Australia
1988	Australia
1993	England

CROSSWORDS

THE TIMES/KNOCKANDO CROSSWORD CHAMPIONSHIP

For over two decades, *The Times* Crossword Championship has occupied a special place in the crossword enthusiasts' calendar. During the 1970s, the champion *par excellence* was the late Dr John Sykes (winner from 1972 to 1975, and on later occasions). In 1980, he completed the four *Times* crosswords in 37 minutes 30 seconds.

The championship is now held in association with Knockando pure single malt whisky. The results of the 23rd Annual Championship in 1993 were:

1   Dr Peter Mayo
2   Michael Trollope
3   { John Henderson
    { Michael Macdonald-Cooper

Dr Peter Mayo, a senior lecturer in Russian and Slavonic Studies at Sheffield University, solved each of the four puzzles in an average of 11 minutes 15 seconds.

CYCLING

OLYMPIC GAMES

Men's Sprint

1896	Paul Masson (Fra)
1900	Georges Taillandier (Fra)
1906	Francesco Verri (Ita)
1920	Maurice Peeters (Hol)
1924	Lucien Michard (Fra)
1928	Roger Beaufrand (Fra)
1932	Jacobus van Egmond (Hol)
1936	Toni Merkens (Ger)
1948	Mario Ghella (Ita)
1952	Enzo Sacchi (Ita)
1956	Michel Rousseau (Fra)
1960	Sante Gaiardoni (Ita)
1964	Giovanni Pettenella (Ita)
1968	Daniel Morelon (Fra)
1972	Daniel Morelon (Fra)
1976	Anton Tkác (Cze)
1980	Lutz Hesslich (GDR)
1984	Mark Gorski (USA)
1988	Lutz Hesslich (GDR)
1992	Jens Fiedler (Ger)

1968	Pierre Trentin (Fra)
1972	Niels-Christian Fredborg (Den)
1976	Klaus-Jurgen Grünke (GDR)
1980	Lothar Thoms (GDR)
1984	Freddy Schmidtke (FRG)
1988	Aleksandr Kirichenko (USSR)
1992	José Manuel Moreno (Spa)

Men's 4000m Individual Pursuit

1964	Jiri Daler (Cze)
1968	Daniel Rebillard (Fra)
1972	Knut Knudsen (Nor)
1976	Gregor Braun (GDR)
1980	Robert Dill-Bundi (Swi)
1984	Steve Hegg (USA)
1988	Gintautas Umaras (USSR)
1992	Chris Boardman (UK)

Men's 50km Points Race

1984	Roger Ilegems (Bel)
1988	Dan Frost (Den)
1992	Giovanni Lombardi (Ita)

Men's 1000m Time Trial

1896	Paul Masson (Fra)
1906	Francesco Verri (Ita)
1928	Willy Falck-Hansen (Den)
1932	Edgar Gray (Aus)
1936	Arie van Vliet (Hol)
1948	Jacques Dupont (Fra)
1952	Russell Mockridge (Aus)
1956	Leandro Faggin (Ita)
1960	Sante Gaiardoni (Ita)
1964	Patrick Sercu (Bel)

Men's Individual Road Race

1896	Aristidis Konstantinidis (Gre)
1906	Fernand Vast (Fra)
1912	Rudolph Lewis (SAf)
1920	Harry Stenqvist (Swe)
1924	Armand Blanchonnet (Fra)
1928	Henry Hansen (Den)
1932	Attilio Pavesi (Ita)
1936	Robert Charpentier (Fra)
1948	José Beyaert (Fra)
1952	André Noyelle (Bel)

1956	Ercole Baldini (Ita)
1960	Viktor Kapitonov (USSR)
1964	Mario Zanin (Ita)
1968	Pierfranco Vianelli (Ita)
1972	Hennie Kuiper (Hol)
1976	Bernt Johansson (Swe)
1980	Sergey Sukhoruchenkov (USSR)
1984	Alexi Grewal (USA)
1988	Olaf Ludwig (GDR)
1992	Fabio Casartelli (Ita)

Men's 4000m Team Pursuit

1908	Great Britain
1920	Italy
1924	Italy
1928	Italy
1932	Italy
1936	France
1948	France
1952	Italy
1956	Italy
1960	Italy
1964	West Germany
1968	Denmark
1972	West Germany
1976	West Germany

1980	USSR
1984	Australia
1988	USSR
1992	Germany

Men's 100km Team Time Trial

1960	Italy
1964	Holland
1968	Holland
1972	USSR
1976	USSR
1980	USSR
1984	Italy
1988	East Germany
1992	Germany

Women's Road Race

1984	Connie Carpenter-Phinney (USA)
1988	Monique Knol (Hol)
1992	Kathryn Watt (Aus)

Women's 1000m Sprint

1988	Erika Salumyae (USSR)
1992	Erika Salumyae (Est)

Women's 3000m Individual Pursuit

1992	Petra Rossner (Ger)

TOUR DE FRANCE

1903	Maurice Garin (Fra)
1904	Henri Cornet (Fra)
1905	Louis Trousselier (Fra)
1906	René Pottier (Fra)
1907	Lucien Petit-Breton (Fra)
1908	Lucien Petit-Breton (Fra)
1909	François Faber (Lux)
1910	Octave Lapize (Fra)
1911	Gustave Garrigou (Fra)
1912	Odile Defraye (Bel)
1913	Philippe Thys (Bel)
1914	Philippe Thys (Bel)
1919	Firmin Lambot (Bel)
1920	Philippe Thys (Bel)
1921	Léon Scieur (Bel)
1922	Firmin Lambot (Bel)
1923	Henri Pélissier (Fra)
1924	Ottavio Bottecchia (Ita)
1925	Ottavio Bottecchia (Ita)
1926	Lucien Buysse (Bel)
1927	Nicholas Frantz (Lux)
1928	Nicholas Frantz (Lux)

1929	Maurice De Waele (Bel)
1930	André Leducq (Fra)
1931	Antonin Magne (Fra)
1932	André Leducq (Fra)
1933	Georges Speicher (Fra)
1934	Antonin Magne (Fra)
1935	Romain Maës (Bel)
1936	Sylvere Maës (Bel)
1937	Roger Lapébie (Fra)
1938	Gino Bartali (Ita)
1939	Sylvere Maës (Bel)
1947	Jean Robic (Fra)
1948	Gino Bartali (Ita)
1949	Fausto Coppi (Ita)
1950	Ferdinand Kebler (Swi)
1951	Hugo Koblet (Swi)
1952	Fausto Coppi (Ita)
1953	Louison Bobet (Fra)
1954	Louison Bobet (Fra)
1955	Louison Bobet (Fra)
1956	Roger Walkowiak (Fra)
1957	Jacques Anquetil (Fra)

1958	Charly Gaul (Lux)	1977	Bernard Thevenet (Fra)
1959	Federico Bahamontès (Spa)	1978	Bernard Hinault (Fra)
1960	Gastone Nencini (Ita)	1979	Bernard Hinault (Fra)
1961	Jacques Anquetil (Fra)	1980	Joop Zoetemelk (Hol)
1962	Jacques Anquetil (Fra)	1981	Bernard Hinault (Fra)
1963	Jacques Anquetil (Fra)	1982	Bernard Hinault (Fra)
1964	Jacques Anquetil (Fra)	1983	Laurent Fignon (Fra)
1965	Felice Gimondi (Ita)	1984	Laurent Fignon (Fra)
1966	Lucien Aimar (Fra)	1985	Bernard Hinault (Fra)
1967	Roger Pingeon (Fra)	1986	Greg LeMond (USA)
1968	Jan Janssen (Hol)	1987	Stephen Roche (Ire)
1969	Eddy Merckx (Bel)	1988	Pedro Delgado (Spa)
1970	Eddy Merckx (Bel)	1989	Greg LeMond (USA)
1971	Eddy Merckx (Bel)	1990	Greg LeMond (USA)
1972	Eddy Merckx (Bel)	1991	Miguel Induráin (Spa)
1973	Luis Ocana (Spa)	1992	Miguel Induráin (Spa)
1974	Eddy Merckx (Bel)	1993	Miguel Induráin (Spa)
1975	Bernard Thevenet (Fra)	1994	Miguel Induráin (Spa)
1976	Lucien van Impe (Bel)		

MILK RACE

1951	Ian Steel (GB)	1974	Roy Schuiten (Hol)
1952	Ken Russell (GB)	1975	Bernt Johansson (Swe)
1953	Gordon Thomas (GB)	1976	Bill Nickson (GB)
1954	Eugène Tamburlini (Fra)	1977	Said Gusseinov (USSR)
1955	Anthony Hewson (GB)	1978	Jan Brzezny (Pol)
1958	Richard Durlacher (Aut)	1979	Yuriy Kashirin (USSR)
1959	Bill Bradley (GB)	1980	Ivan Mitchtenko (USSR)
1960	Bill Bradley (GB)	1981	Sergey Krivocheyev (USSR)
1961	Billy Holmes (GB)	1982	Yuriy Kashirin (USSR)
1962	Eugen Pokorny (Pol)	1983	Matt Eaton (USA)
1963	Peter Chisman (GB)	1984	Oleg Czougeda (USSR)
1964	Arthur Metcalfe (GB)	1985	Eric van Lancker (Bel)
1965	Les West (GB)	1986	Joey McLoughlin (GB)
1966	Josef Gawliczek (Pol)	1987	Malcolm Elliott (GB)
1967	Les West (GB)	1988	Vasiliy Zhdanov (USSR)
1968	Gosta Pettersson (Swe)	1989	Brian Walton (Can)
1969	Fedor Den Hertog (Hol)	1990	Shane Sutton (Aus)
1970	Jiri Mainus (Cze)	1991	Chris Walker (GB)
1971	Fedor Den Hertog (Hol)	1992	Conor Henry (Ire)
1972	Hennie Kuiper (Hol)	1993	Chris Lillywhite (GB)
1973	Piet van Katwijk (Hol)		

DARTS

WORLD CHAMPIONSHIPS

1978	Leighton Rees (Wal)	1980	Eric Bristow (Eng)
1979	John Lowe (Eng)	1981	Eric Bristow (Eng)

1982	Jocky Wilson (Sco)	1988	Bob Anderson (Eng)
1983	Keith Deller (Eng)	1989	Jocky Wilson (Sco)
1984	Eric Bristow (Eng)	1990	Phil Taylor (Eng)
1985	Eric Bristow (Eng)	1991	Dennis Priestley (Eng)
1986	Eric Bristow (Eng)	1992	Phil Taylor (Eng)
1987	John Lowe (Eng)	1993	John Lowe (Eng)

DOCTORS

BUPA MEDICAL FOUNDATION DOCTOR OF THE YEAR AWARD

In 1993 this coveted title went to Bryan Williams of the Leicester Royal Infirmary. The 1994 award went to a consultant surgeon also from the Leicester Royal Infirmary: Nick London, who has conducted research which brings hope of cure for diabetes.

DOGS

CRUFT'S DOG SHOW

Although the first dog show was held at Newcastle-upon-Tyne in 1859, Cruft's was not started until 1886. This famous national dog show now enjoys both tremendous popular interest and an international reputation. The first award for Best in Show was made in 1928. Recent winners of the Cruft's Supreme Champion award were:

1993 Champion Pencloe Dutch Gold, whippet, owned by Miss Morag Bolton – the first Scottish-owned dog to become Supreme Champion since 1929.

1994 Buttons (a Welsh terrier, whose grandiose kennel name is Champion Purston Hit and Miss from Brocolitia). Owned by Mrs Anne Maughan from Newcastle-upon-Tyne, handled by Frank Kellett.

WESTMINSTER DOG OF THE YEAR

A rather different competition (but known as Parliament's own Cruft's) is the annual search for the top dog belonging to an MP. In 1994, and judged on loyalty and obedience, the three top prizes in the contest organized by the Canine Defence League and held in Victoria Tower Gardens, were awarded as follows:

1 Baz, a Labrador owned by Conservative MP for Thanet North, Roger Gale.

2 Bijou, a collie belonging to Conservative MP for Brentford, Nirj Deva.

3 Kizzy, a mongrel belonging to Conservative MP for Stockton South, Tim Devlin, who declared 'The good thing about a dog is that whatever happens in politics he's always pleased to see you.'

NATIONAL SCRUFTS SHOW

A world removed from Cruft's, but with an appeal all its own, was the 1993 National Scrufts Show at Chobham, Surrey on 25 July – an alternative dog show definitely for non-pedigree pets.

The proud (or at least very cheerful) winner, owned by 10-year-old Christopher Chance, was Tramp. Tramp, a truly scruffy 2-year-old cross-breed, was saved from a rubbish tip by Christopher's father Philip, of Redworth, Co. Durham, who nursed him back to health. Tramp wowed the judges, including Worzel Gummidge star Jon Pertwee and Pam 'Ma Larkin' Ferris, at the RSPCA competition.

ECONOMICS

NOBEL PRIZE FOR ECONOMICS

The Nobel Prize for Economics is the most recent of the Nobel Prizes, having been established in 1969. (For a background note on the Nobel Prizes, see p. 208.)

1969	Ragnar Frisch (Nor) / Jan Tinbergen (Hol)	1980	Lawrence Klein (USA)
		1981	James Tobin (USA)
1970	Paul A. Samuelson (USA)	1982	George J. Stigler (USA)
1971	Simon Kuznets (USA)	1983	Gerard Debreu (USA)
1972	Kenneth J. Arrow (USA) / Sir John R. Hicks (GB)	1984	Sir Richard Stone (GB)
		1985	Franco Modigliani (USA, Italian-born)
1973	Vassily Leontief (USA) (Russian-born)		
		1986	James M. Buchanan (USA)
1974	Gunnar Myrdal (Swe) / Friedrich A. von Hayek (Aut)	1987	Robert M. Solow (USA)
		1988	Maurice Allais (Fra)
1975	Leonid V. Kantorovich (USSR) / Tjalling C. Koopmans (USA) (Dutch-born)	1989	Trygve Haavelmo (Nor)
		1990	Harry M. Markowitz (USA) / William F. Sharpe (USA) / Merton H. Miller (USA)
1976	Milton Friedman (USA)		
1977	Bertil Ohlin (Swe) / James Edward Meade (GB)	1991	Ronald H. Coase (GB/USA)
		1992	Gary Becker (USA)
1978	Herbert Simon (USA)	1993	Robert W. Fogel (USA) / Douglass C. North (USA)
1979	Sir Arthur Lewis (GB) (St Lucien-born) / Theodore W. Schultz (USA)		

The 1993 prizewinners gained their award for research that helps to explain Japan's strong economy and why the former Soviet bloc has gone downhill, by using modern statistical methods to re-examine economies of the past. They won a prize of 6.7 million kronor (£540,000).

EISTEDDFOD

THE CHAIR (competition for a poem in strict metre)

	Place	Winner and poem
1980	Dyffryn Lliw	Donald Evans, 'Y Ffwrnais'
1981	Machynlleth	John Gwilym Jones, 'Y Frwydr'
1982	Abertawe a'r Cylch	Gerallt Lloyd Owen, 'Climeri'
1983	Ynys Môn	Einion Evans, 'Ynys'
1984	Llanbedr Pont Steffan	Aled Rhys Wiliam, 'Y Pethau Bychain'
1985	Y Rhyl	Robat Powel, 'Cynefin'
1986	Abergwaun	Gwynn ap Gwilym, 'Y Cwmwl'
1987	Bro Madog	Ieuan Wyn, 'Llanw a Thrai'
1988	Casnewydd	Elwyn Edwards, 'Storm'
1989	Dyffryn Conwy a'r Cyffiniau	Idris Reynolds, 'Y Daith'
1990	Cwm Rhymni	Myrddin ap Dafydd, 'Gwythiennau'
1991	Bro Delyn	Robin Llwyd ap Owain, 'Awdl Foliant Merch ein
1992	Ceredigion, Aberystwyth	Idris Reynolds, 'A Fo Ben'
1993	Neath Valley	Merion McIntyre Huws.

THE CROWN (competition for poetry in free verse)

	Place	Winner and poem
1980	Dyffryn Lliw	Donald Evans, 'Dilyniant o Gerddi'
1981	Machynlleth	Siôn Aled, 'Wynebau'
1982	Abertawe a'r Cylch	Eirwyn George, 'Dilyniant o Gerddi'
1983	Ynys Môn	Eluned Phillips, 'Clymau'
1984	Llanbedr Pont Steffan	John Roderick Rees, 'Llygaid'
1985	Y Rhyl	John Roderick Rees, 'Glannau'
1986	Abergwaun	T. James Jones, 'Llwch'
1987	Bro Madog	John Gruffydd Jones, 'Casgliad o Gerddi'
1988	Casnewydd	T. James Jones, 'Ffin'
1989	Dyffryn Conwy a'r Cyffiniau	Selwyn Griffith, 'Dilyniant o Gerddi'
1990	Cwm Rhymni	Iwan Llwyd, 'Gwreichion'
1991	Bro Delyn	Einir Jones, 'Pelydrau'
1992	Ceredigion, Aberystwyth	Cyril Jones, 'Cyfrannu'
1993	Neath Valley	Eirwyn George.

PROSE MEDAL

	Winner and subject
1980	Robyn Lewis, 'Esgid yn Gwasgu'
1981	John Griffith Jones, 'Cysgodion ar y Pared'
1982	Gwilym Meredith Jones, 'Ochr arall y Geiniog'
1983	T. Wilson Evans, 'Y Pabi Coch'
1984	John Idris Owen, 'Y Tŷ Haearn'
1985	Meg Elis, 'Cyn Daw'r Gaeaf'
1986	Ray Evans, 'Y Llyffant'
1987	Margiad Roberts, 'Sna'm llonydd i' ga'I'

1988	*no award*
1989	Irma Chilton, 'Mochyn Gwydr'
1990	*no award*
1991	Angharad Tomos, 'Si hei lwli'
1992	Robin Llywelyn, 'Seren Wen ar Gefndir Gwyn'
1993	Mihangel Morgan

W. TOWYN ROBERTS AWARD

Another major competition at the National Eisteddfod each year is the Towyn Roberts award, established to promote solo singing in Wales.

1982	Mari Ffion Williams	1988	Gail Pearson
	Vaughan Howells		Nicola Railton
1983	Meinir Williams	1989	Sharon Evans
1984	Aneirin Mason Hughes		Mark Luther
1985	Leah Marian Jones	1990	Jeffrey Roberts
1986	Helen Hessey White	1991	Eldrydd Cynan Jones
1987	Rhian Owen	1992	Elizabeth Stevens
	Bryn Terfel	1993	Elen Môn

ELECTIONS

GENERAL ELECTIONS 1900–92 (IN BRITAIN)

	1st	2nd	3rd	Others	Turnout (per cent)
28 Sept–24 Oct 1900	Conservative 402	Liberal 184	Labour 2	Other 82	74·6
12 Jan–7 Feb 1906	Liberal 400	Conservative 157	Labour 30	Others 83	82·6
14 Jan–9 Feb 1910	Liberal 275	Conservative 273	Labour 40	Others 82	86·6
2–19 Dec 1910	Liberal 272	Conservative 272	Labour 42	Others 84	81·1
14 Dec 1918	Conservative 383	Liberal 161	Labour 73	Others 90	58·9
15 Nov 1922	Conservative 345	Labour 142	Liberal 116	Others 12	71·3
6 Dec 1923	Conservative 258	Labour 191	Liberal 159	Others 7	70·8
29 Oct 1924	Conservative 419	Labour 151	Liberal 40	Others 5	76·6
30 May 1929	Labour 288	Conservative 260	Liberal 59	Others 8	76·1
27 Oct 1931	Conservative 521	Labour 52	Liberal 37	Others 5	76·3
14 Nov 1935	Conservative 432	Labour 154	Liberal 20	Others 9	71·2
5 July 1945	Labour 393	Conservative 213	Liberal 12	Others 22	72·7
23 Feb 1950	Labour 315	Conservative 298	Liberal 9	Others 3	84·0
25 Oct 1951	Conservative 321	Labour 295	Liberal 6	Others 3	82·5
25 May 1955	Conservative 344	Labour 277	Liberal 6	Others 3	76·7
8 Oct 1959	Conservative 365	Labour 258	Liberal 6	Others 1	78·8
15 Oct 1964	Labour 317	Conservative 303	Liberal 9	Others 1	77·1
31 Mar 1966	Labour 363	Conservative 253	Liberal 12	Others 2	75·9
18 June 1970	Conservative 330	Labour 288	Liberal 6	Others 6	72·0
28 Feb 1974	Labour 301	Conservative 297	Liberal 14	Others 23	78·8
10 Oct 1974	Labour 319	Conservative 277	Liberal 13	Others 26	72·8
3 May 1979	Conservative 339	Labour 268	Liberal 11	Others 17	76·0
9 June 1983	Conservative 397	Labour 209	Liberal 23†	Others 21	73·0
11 June 1987	Conservative 376	Labour 229	Liberal 22†	Others 23	75·0
9 Apr 1992	Conservative 336	Labour 271	Liberal 20†	Others 24	78·0

† Alliance in 1983 and 1987, Liberal Democrats in 1992.

FAMOUS BY-ELECTIONS (SINCE 1958)

Date	Winner	Party	Constituency	
27 Mar 1958	Mark Bonham Carter	Liberal	Torrington	First Liberal victory at a by-election since 1929.
14 Mar 1962	Eric Lubbock	Liberal	Orpington	The most sensational Liberal victory of the 1960s. The party swept to victory in a safe Conservative seat.
7 Nov 1963	Sir Alec Douglas-Home	Conservative	Kinross and W. Perthshire	The by-election in which the former 14th Earl of Home returned to the Commons as Sir Alec Douglas-Home.
21 Jan 1965	Ronald Buxton	Conservative	Leyton	The Conservatives defeated Labour's Foreign Secretary, Patrick Gordon Walker, in a normally safe East London Labour stronghold.
24 Mar 1965	David Steel	Liberal	Roxburgh, Selkirk and Peebles	David Steel won a safe Conservative seat to become the 'baby of the House' and eventual Liberal Party leader.
14 July 1966	Gwynfor Evans	Plaid Cymru	Carmarthen	The first – and so far the only – Welsh Nationalist to win a seat in a by-election.
2 Nov 1967	Winifred Ewing	Scottish National Party	Hamilton	The first SNP by-election victory since the party won Motherwell in a wartime by-election in April 1945.
28 Mar 1968	Don Williams	Conservative	Dudley	The by-election which saw the largest swing ever recorded to the Conservatives during the 1966–70 Wilson Government.
26 Oct 1972	Cyril Smith	Liberal	Rochdale	First of the famous series of Liberal by-election victories of 1972–73.
7 Dec 1972	Graham Tope	Liberal	Sutton and Cheam	A sensational Liberal victory in one of the safest Tory areas – the London suburbs.
1 Mar 1973	Dick Taverne	Democratic Labour	Lincoln	Dick Taverne won a personal triumph as a Democratic Labour candidate, having previously been the town's Labour MP.
8 Nov 1973	Margo MacDonald	Scottish National Party	Glasgow Govan	The first SNP by-election victory since Hamilton in 1967.
4 Nov 1976	R. G. Hodgson	Conservative	Walsall North	The safe Labour stronghold formerly held by John Stonehouse fell on a swing of 22·6 per cent to the Conservatives – the largest swing of the 1974–79 Parliament to a Conservative.
28 Apr 1977	Austin Mitchell	Labour	Grimsby	Labour's best result of the 1974–79 Parliament – held the same day that Ashfield fell to the Tories on a 20·8 per cent swing.

Date	Winner	Party	Constituency	
29 Mar 1979	David Alton	Liberal	Liverpool Edge Hill	A sweeping Liberal victory by 8133 votes in a hitherto safe Labour seat.
26 Nov 1981	Shirley Williams	SDP	Crosby	First SDP by-election victory, on a swing of 25·6 per cent from the Conservatives.
25 Mar 1982	Roy Jenkins	SDP	Glasgow Hillhead	Second SDP victory returned Roy Jenkins to Westminster
26 Feb 1987	Rosie Barnes	SDP	Greenwich	Sensational SDP victory from Labour.
29 July 1993	Diana Maddock	Lib. Dem.	Christchurch	Following on from Newbury, Lib. Dems take Conservative stronghold on biggest swing in a by-election this century.

ENVIRONMENT

BAYER JOURNALISM AWARDS FOR SCIENCE IN THE ENVIRONMENT

The Bayer Journalism Awards for Science in the Environment are presented annually in recognition of excellence in the accurate, objective and understandable reporting of man's impact on the environment, and in particular the contribution of science to these issues. The winners, announced in November 1993, were:

National Newspapers Steve Connor (*The Independent on Sunday*: 'Why Our World is a Mite Too Stuffy')

Regional Newspapers James McGhee (*Edinburgh Evening News*: 'The Air That We Breathe', 'The Hole Story', 'Nature Fights Back')

Trade/Technical/National Magazines Richard House (*Institutional Investor*: 'Balance Sheet Poison')

INTERNATIONAL COSMOS PRIZE

Forty million yen (£250,000) is given 'to reward the endeavours of researchers and scientists for excellence and understanding' in their field. The Prize Committee was established with profits from the 1990 Expo in Osaka. The 1993 winner was Ghillean Prance, the Director of Kew Gardens, who was awarded the prize for his work in the South American rainforests.

CLEANEST EUROPEAN CAPITAL CITIES

Organized by the Tidy Britain Group, this survey was conducted in November 1993 and its results published in February 1994. The tests for cleanliness were carried out within a 1km circle of the area around each country's national Parliament. Scores were awarded (out of a maximum of 100).

The top three were:
London   77
Berne   76 (the 1992 winner)
Paris   69

The bottom three were:
Brussels   51
Madrid   45
Athens   45

In the graffiti section, London and Berne were the joint winners, Amsterdam came bottom. Madrid was named the worst European capital for dog-fouling.

EQUESTRIANISM

OLYMPIC GAMES

Individual Showjumping

	Rider	Horse
	Rider	*Horse*
1900	Aimé Haegeman (Bel)	Benton II
1912	Jean Cariou (Fra)	Mignon
1920	Tommaso Lequio (Ita)	Trebecco
1924	Alphonse Gemuseus (Swi)	Lucette
1928	Frantisek Ventura (Cze)	Eliot
1932	Takeichi Nishi (Jap)	Uranus
1936	Kürt Hasse (Ger)	Tora
1948	Humberto Mariles Cortés (Mex)	Arete
1952	Pierre Jonquères d'Oriola (Fra)	Ali Baba
1956	Hans Günter Winkler (Ger)	Halla
1960	Raimondo d'Inzeo (Ita)	Posillipo
1964	Pierre Jonquères d'Oriola (Fra)	Lutteur B
1968	William Steinkraus (USA)	Snowbound
1972	Graziano Mancinelli (Ita)	Ambassador
1976	Alwin Schockemöhle (FRG)	Warwick Rex
1980	Jan Kowalczyk (Pol)	Artemor
1984	Joe Fargis (USA)	Touch of Class
1988	Pierre Durand (Fra)	Jappeloup
1992	Ludger Beerbaum (Ger)	Classic Touch

Team Showjumping

1912	Sweden
1920	Sweden
1924	Sweden
1928	Spain
1936	Germany
1948	Mexico
1952	Great Britain
1956	Germany
1960	Germany
1964	Germany
1968	Canada
1972	Germany
1976	France
1980	USSR
1984	USA
1988	West Germany
1992	Holland

Individual Three-day Eventing

	Rider	Horse
	Rider	*Horse*
1912	Axel Nordlander (Swe)	Lady Artist
1920	Helmer Mörner (Swe)	Germania
1924	Adolph van de Voort van Zijp (Hol)	Silver Piece
1928	Charles Pahud de Mortanges (Hol)	Marcroix
1932	Charles Pahud de Mortanges (Hol)	Marcroix
1936	Ludwig Stubbendorff (Ger)	Nurmi
1948	Bernard Chevallier (Fra)	Aiglonne
1952	Hans von Blixen-Finecke Jr (Swe)	Jubal
1956	Petrus Kastenman (Swe)	Iluster
1960	Lawrence Morgan (USA)	Salad Days
1964	Mauro Checcoli (Ita)	Surbean
1968	Jean-Jacques Guyon (Fra)	Pitou
1972	Richard Meade (UK)	Laurieston
1976	Edmund Coffin (USA)	Bally-C or
1980	Federico Roman (Ita)	Rossinan
1984	Mark Todd (NZ)	Charisma
1988	Mark Todd (NZ)	Charisma
1992	Matthew Ryan (Aus)	Kibah Tic Toc

Team Three-day Eventing

1912	Sweden
1920	Sweden
1924	Holland
1928	Holland
1932	USA
1936	Germany
1948	USA
1952	Sweden
1956	Great Britain
1960	Australia
1964	Italy
1968	Great Britain
1972	Great Britain
1976	USA
1980	USSR
1984	USA
1988	West Germany
1992	Australia

Individual Dressage Champions

	Rider	Horse
1912	Carl Bonde (Swe)	Emperor
1920	Janne Lundblad (Swe)	Uno
1924	Ernst Linder (Swe)	Piccolomini
1928	Carl von Langen (Ger)	Draufgänger
1932	Xavier Lesage (Fra)	Taine
1936	Heinz Pollay (Ger)	Kronos
1948	Hans Moser (Swi)	Hummer
1952	Henri St Cyr (Swe)	Master Rufus
1956	Henri St Cyr (Swe)	Juli
1960	Sergey Filatov (USSR)	Absent
1964	Henri Chammartin (Swi)	Woermann
1968	Ivan Kizimov (USSR)	Ichor
1972	Liselott Linsenhoff (FRG)	Piaff
1976	Christine Stückelberger (Swi)	Granat
1980	Elisabeth Theurer (Aut)	Mon Chéri
1984	Reiner Klimke (FRG)	Ahlerich
1988	Nicole Uphoff (FRG)	Rembrandt
1992	Nicole Uphoff (Ger)	Rembrandt

Team Dressage

1928	Germany
1932	France
1936	Germany
1948	France
1952	Sweden
1956	Sweden
1964	Germany
1968	West Germany
1972	USSR
1976	West Germany
1980	USSR
1984	West Germany
1988	West Germany
1992	Germany

BRITISH SHOWJUMPING DERBY

	Rider	Horse
1961	Seamus Hayes (Ire)	Goodbye III
1962	Pat Smythe (GB)	Flanagan
1963	Nelson Pessoa (Bra)	Gran Geste
1964	Seamus Hayes (Ire)	Goodbye III
1965	Nelson Pessoa (Bra)	Gran Geste
1966	David Broome (GB)	Mister Softee
1967	Marion Coakes (GB)	Stroller
1968	Alison Westwood (GB)	The Maverick VII
1969	Anneli Drummond-Hay (GB)	Xanthos
1970	Harvey Smith (GB)	Mattie Brown
1971	Harvey Smith (GB)	Mattie Brown
1972	Hendrick Snoek (FRG)	Shirokko
1973	Alison Dawes (née Westwood) (GB)	Mr Banbury
1974	Harvey Smith (GB)	Salvador
1975	Paul Darragh (Ire)	Pele
1976	Eddie Macken (Ire)	Boomerang
1977	Eddie Macken (Ire)	Boomerang
1978	Eddie Macken (Ire)	Boomerang
1979	Eddie Macken (Ire)	Boomerang
1980	Michael Whitaker (GB)	Owen Gregory
1981	Harvey Smith (GB)	Sanyo Video
1982	Paul Schockemohle (FRG)	Deister
1983	John Whitaker (GB)	Ryan's Son
1984	John Ledingham (Ire)	Gabhram
1985	Paul Schockemohle (FRG)	Lorenzo
1986	Paul Schockemohle (FRG)	Next Deister
1987	Nick Skelton (GB)	Raffles

	Rider	*Horse*
1988	Nick Skelton (GB)	Apollo
1989	Nick Skelton (GB)	Apollo
1990	Joe Turi (GB)	Vital
1991	Michael Whitaker (GB)	Monsanta
1992	Michael Whitaker (GB)	Monsanta
1993	Michael Whitaker (GB)	Monsanta

FENCING

OLYMPIC GAMES

Men's Team Foil

1904	Cuba
1920	Italy
1924	France
1928	Italy
1932	France
1936	Italy
1948	France
1952	France
1956	Italy
1960	USSR
1964	USSR
1968	France
1972	Poland
1976	West Germany
1980	France
1984	Italy
1988	USSR
1992	Germany

Men's Team Epée

1908	France
1912	Belgium
1920	Italy
1924	France
1928	Italy
1932	France
1936	Italy
1948	France
1952	Italy
1956	Italy
1960	Italy
1964	Hungary
1968	Hungary
1972	Hungary
1976	Sweden
1980	France

1984	West Germany
1988	France
1992	Germany

Men's Team Sabre

1908	Hungary
1912	Hungary
1920	Italy
1924	Italy
1928	Hungary
1932	Hungary
1936	Hungary
1948	Hungary
1952	Hungary
1956	Hungary
1960	Hungary
1964	USSR
1968	USSR
1972	Italy
1976	USSR
1980	USSR
1984	Italy
1988	Hungary
1992	CIS

Men's Individual Foil

1896	Emile Gravelotte (Fra)
1900	Emile Coste (Fra)
1904	Ramon Fonst (Cub)
1912	Nedo Nadi (Ita)
1920	Nedo Nadi (Ita)
1924	Roger Ducret (Fra)
1928	Lucien Gaudin (Fra)
1932	Gustavo Marzi (Ita)
1936	Giulio Gaudini (Ita)
1948	Jean Buhan (Fra)
1952	Christian d'Oriola (Fra)

1956	Christian d'Oriola (Fra)
1960	Viktor Zhadanovich (USSR)
1964	Egon Franke (Pol)
1968	Ion Drimba (Rom)
1972	Witold Woyda (Pol)
1976	Fabio Dal Zotto (Ita)
1980	Vladimir Smirnov (USSR)
1984	Mauro Numa (Ita)
1988	Stefano Cerioni (Ita)
1992	Philippè Omnes (Fra)

Men's Individual Epée

1900	Ramon Fonst (Cub)
1904	Ramon Fonst (Cub)
1908	Gaston Alibert (Fra)
1912	Paul Anspach (Bel)
1920	Armand Massard (Fra)
1924	Charles Delport (Bel)
1928	Lucien Gaudin (Fra)
1932	Giancarlo Cornaggia-Medici (Ita)
1936	Franco Riccardi (Ita)
1948	Luigi Cantone (Ita)
1952	Edoardo Mangiarotti (Ita)
1956	Carlo Pavesi (Ita)
1960	Giuseppe Delfino (Ita)
1964	Grigoriy Kriss (USSR)
1968	Gyozo Kulcsar (Hun)
1972	Csaba Fenyvesi (Hun)
1976	Alexander Pusch (FRG)
1980	Johan Harmenberg (Swe)
1984	Philippe Boisse (Fra)
1988	Arnd Schmitt (FRG)
1992	Eric Srecki (Fra)

Men's Individual Sabre

1896	Jean Georgiadis (Gre)
1900	Georges de la Falaise (Fra)
1904	Manuel Diaz (Cub)
1908	Jeno Fuchs (Hun)
1912	Jeno Fuchs (Hun)
1920	Nedo Nadi (Ita)
1924	Sandor Posta (Hun)
1928	Odon Tersztyanszky (Hun)

1932	Gyorgy Piller (Hun)
1936	Endre Kabos (Hun)
1948	Aldar Gerevich (Hun)
1952	Pal Kovacs (Hun)
1956	Rudolf Karpati (Hun)
1960	Rudolf Karpati (Hun)
1964	Tibor Pezsa (Hun)
1968	Jerzy Pawlowski (Pol)
1972	Viktor Sidiak (USSR)
1976	Viktor Krovopuskov (USSR)
1980	Viktor Krovopuskov (USSR)
1984	Jean-François Lamour (Fra)
1988	Jean-François Lamour (Fra)
1992	Bence Szabo (Hun)

Women's Team Foil

1960	USSR
1964	Hungary
1968	USSR
1972	USSR
1976	USSR
1980	France
1984	West Germany
1988	West Germany
1992	Italy

Women's Individual Foil

1924	Ellen Osiier (Den)
1928	Helene Mayer (Ger)
1932	Ellen Preis (Aut)
1936	Ilona Elek (Hun)
1948	Ilona Elek (Hun)
1952	Irene Camber (Ita)
1956	Gillian Sheen (UK)
1960	Heidi Schmid (FRG)
1964	Ildikó Ujlaki-Rejtö (Hun)
1968	Yelena Novikova (USSR)
1972	Antonella Ragno-Lonzi (Ita)
1976	Ildikó Schwarczenberger (Hun)
1980	Pascale Trinquet (Fra)
1984	Luan Jujie (Chn)
1988	Anja Fichtel (FRG)
1992	Giovanna Trillini (Ita)

FIELD GUNS

ROYAL NAVY FIELD GUN COMPETITION

The world-famous Royal Navy Field Gun Competition is one of the main highlights of the Royal Tournament. Three teams representing the naval commands of Portsmouth,

Devonport and the Fleet Air Arm compete against each other every day at the Royal Tournament in a fiercely contested fight for four important trophies.

The Royal Navy Field Gun Competition originates from the South African War when, in 1899, guns from HMS *Terrible* and HMS *Powerful* were taken ashore and transported hundreds of miles across land before going into action.

The competition in its present form was first run in 1907. The three crews are each made up of 18 men aged 18 to 40, all of whom are volunteers. Competition for a place in one of the teams is very fierce – over 1000 men from all ranks apply to take part – even though it involves nine weeks of intensive training (including carrying a gun that weighs more than a mini car!).

The Royal Navy Field Gun Competition is the most dangerous event at the Royal Tournament, and even though injuries are quite often sustained – the most common being broken arms, legs, collar bones and crushed feet – one participant has celebrated eight years in the Portsmouth crew. The 1992 winners were the Fleet Air Arm (3 out of 4 trophies).

FLOWERS

Among the countless festivals of flowers (and flower arranging) the pride of place goes to the Royal Horticultural Society's annual Chelsea Flower Show. Each May, this much loved institution offers an abundance of plants, vegetables, flowers and shrubs all at their peak of perfection.

Each category has its winner and the very long list of winners is published each year in *The Times*.

Equally prestigious is the Olympic Spring Gardening Fair. At the 1994 Spring Gardening Fair at Olympia, five gardens were awarded gold, including *The Times* French garden, a formal garden featuring mixed beds of flowers, vegetables and herbs, edged with low-box hedging; and the *News of the World* family garden, which made good use of space.

The other gold medal winners were a Victorian garden from Brent Council; a Japanese garden from Hilliers Garden Centres, of Ampfield, Hampshire; and a garden of camellias from Trehane Camellia Nursery, of Wimborne, Dorset.

FOOD AND DRINK

GLENFIDDICH AWARDS

These awards recognize excellence in writing, publishing and broadcasting relating to the subjects of food and drink. The winner of each of twelve categories receives £800, a case of Glenfiddich Pure Malt Scotch Whisky, and an engraved commemorative quaich. The overall winner, chosen from the winners of the categories, receives the Glenfiddich Trophy, which is held for a year, and a further cheque for £3,000. The awards were created and are sponsored by William Grant and Sons, the distillers of Glenfiddich Pure Malt Scotch Whisky.

1990

Book author – food   Margaret Visser
Book author – drink   Hugh Johnson
Food writer   Joanna Blythman
Drink writer   Tim Atkin

Restaurant writer   Jonathan Meades
Whisky writer   Matt Phillips
Regional writer   Colin Pressdee
Trade writer   Tom Stevenson
Radio programme   *Woman's Hour*, BBC
   Radio 4

TV programme   *This Food Business*
Visual category   Dorling Kindersley

Special award   { Patrick Rance
London Food
commission

Glenfiddich trophy winner   Patrick Rance

1991

Book author – food   Pierre Koffmann
Book author – drink   Burton Anderson
Food writer   Matthew Fort
Drink writer   Kathryn McWhirter
Restaurant writer   Craig Brown
Whisky writer   Michael Jackson
Regional writer   Robert Cockcroft
Trade writer   Andrew Barr
Radio programme   *Table Talk*, BBC Radio 3
TV programme   *The Beer Hunter*
Visual category   *The Complete Book of Spices*
Special award   *Arena Food Night*, BBC2 TV
Glenfiddich trophy winner   Jill Norman

1992

Book author – food   Elisabeth Luard
Book author – drink   Oz Clarke
Food writer   Claudia Roden
Drink writer   Joanna Simon
Cookery writer   Lynda Brown
Restaurant writer   Matthew Fort
Whisky writer   Jim Murray
Trade writer   { John Harvey
Richard Wilson
Radio programme   'Designer Genes', *One Step Beyond*
TV programme   *Matters of Taste*
Visual category   Joy Davies, Robin Broadbent and Robin Harvey for *Harpers & Queen*
Special awards   { Arabella Boxer
Adnam's Wine Merchants
CAMRA
Glenfiddich trophy winner   Claudia Roden

1993

Book author – food   Margaret Shaida
Book author – drink   Simon Loftus
Food writer   Emily Green
Drink writer   Tim Atkin
Cookery writer   Josceline Dimbleby
Restaurant writer   Tom Jaine
Whisky writer   Rose Murray Brown
Regional writer   John McKenna
Trade writer   Tom Stevenson
TV programme   Jenny Stevens and the BBC Continuing Education and Training team
Radio programme   'Women Chefs in Scotland', *Woman's Hour*, BBC Radio 4
Visual category   Ralph Steadman (for *The Grapes of Ralph*)
Special awards   { Alan Davidson
Sainsbury's
Future Cooks Awards, Anna Best and Peta Brown
Glenfiddich trophy winner   Alan Davidson

1994

Book author – food   Alastair Little and Richard Whittington
Book author – drink   Michael Jackson
Food writer   Michael Raffael
Drink writer   Anthony Rose
Cookery writer   Frances Bissell
Restaurant writer   John Lanchester
Whisky writer   Jim Murray
Regional writer   Joanna Blythman
Magazine of the Year   *Wine*
TV programme   MasterChef 1993
Radio programme   Food on the Radio (RTE, Dublin)
Special awards   { Fay Maschler
Serif Publishing
Glenfiddich trophy winner   Michael Jackson (for *Michael Jackson's Beer Companion*)

GAELIC FOOTBALL

ALL-IRELAND CHAMPIONSHIP

1887	Limerick	1923	Dublin	1959	Kerry
1888	*No event*	1924	Kerry	1960	Down
1889	Tipperary	1925	Galway	1961	Down
1890	Cork	1926	Kerry	1962	Kerry
1891	Dublin	1927	Kildare	1963	Dublin
1892	Dublin	1928	Kildare	1964	Galway
1893	Wexford	1929	Kerry	1965	Galway
1894	Dublin	1930	Kerry	1966	Galway
1895	Tipperary	1931	Kerry	1967	Meath
1896	Limerick	1932	Kerry	1968	Down
1897	Dublin	1933	Cavan	1969	Kerry
1898	Dublin	1934	Galway	1970	Kerry
1899	Dublin	1935	Cavan	1971	Offaly
1900	Tipperary	1936	Mayo	1972	Offaly
1901	Dublin	1937	Kerry	1973	Cork
1902	Dublin	1938	Galway	1974	Dublin
1903	Kerry	1939	Kerry	1975	Kerry
1904	Kerry	1940	Kerry	1976	Dublin
1905	Kildare	1941	Kerry	1977	Dublin
1906	Dublin	1942	Dublin	1978	Kerry
1907	Dublin	1943	Roscommon	1979	Kerry
1908	Dublin	1944	Roscommon	1980	Kerry
1909	Kerry	1945	Cork	1981	Kerry
1910	Louth	1946	Kerry	1982	Offaly
1911	Cork	1947	Cavan	1983	Dublin
1912	Louth	1948	Cavan	1984	Kerry
1913	Kerry	1949	Meath	1985	Kerry
1914	Kerry	1950	Mayo	1986	Kerry
1915	Wexford	1951	Mayo	1987	Meath
1916	Wexford	1952	Cavan	1988	Meath
1917	Wexford	1953	Kerry	1989	Cork
1918	Wexford	1954	Meath	1990	Cork
1919	Kildare	1955	Kerry	1991	Down
1920	Tipperary	1956	Galway	1992	Donegal
1921	Dublin	1957	Louth	1993	Derry
1922	Dublin	1958	Dublin		

GARDENS

GARDEN OF THE YEAR

This annual award is presented by Christie's, in conjunction with the Historic Houses Association. The award recognizes both public enjoyment and horticultural interest.

The 1993 award went to Forde Abbey in Dorset, a twelfth-century Cistercian foundation. The Abbey is near Chard, on the border with Somerset, and its 50-acre grounds provided constantly changing colour throughout the seasons and attracted 33,500 visitors. There is a wide variety of species including Asiatic primulas, redwood trees from California and a rare incense cedar from north-west America.

The 1994 award went to the terraced gardens at Haddon Hall, the Derbyshire home of the Duke of Rutland. The gardens, which were deserted in the eighteenth and nineteenth centuries (when the dukes lived at Belvoir Castle) were lovingly restored from the 1920s by the 9th Duke.

BEST GARDEN AWARD

This coveted accolade is awarded at the annual Chelsea Flower Show. In 1993 the winning award (and a fourth consecutive gold medal) went to Mrs Julie Toll for her wild flower and seaside design which had more than 10,000 plants lurking among the sand dunes, shell paths and rabbit burrows.

GOLF

BRITISH OPEN

1900	John H. Taylor (UK)	1933	Densmore Shute (USA)
1901	James Braid (UK)	1934	Henry Cotton (UK)
1902	Sandy Herd (UK)	1935	Alfred Perry (UK)
1903	Harry Vardon (UK)	1936	Alfred Padgham (UK)
1904	Jack White (UK)	1937	Henry Cotton (UK)
1905	James Braid (UK)	1938	Reg Whitcombe (UK)
1906	James Braid (UK)	1939	Dick Burton (UK)
1907	Arnaud Massy (Fra)	1946	Sam Snead (USA)
1908	James Braid (UK)	1947	Fred Daly (UK)
1909	John H. Taylor (UK)	1948	Henry Cotton (UK)
1910	James Braid (UK)	1949	Bobby Locke (SAf)
1911	Harry Vardon (UK)	1950	Bobby Locke (SAf)
1912	Edward Ray (UK)	1951	Max Faulkner (UK)
1913	John H. Taylor (UK)	1952	Bobby Locke (SAf)
1914	Harry Vardon (UK)	1953	Ben Hogan (USA)
1920	George Duncan (UK)	1954	Peter Thomson (Aus)
1921	Jock Hutchinson (USA)	1955	Peter Thomson (Aus)
1922	Walter Hagen (USA)	1956	Peter Thomson (Aus)
1923	Arthur Havers (UK)	1957	Bobby Locke (SAf)
1924	Walter Hagen (USA)	1958	Peter Thomson (Aus)
1925	Jim Barnes (USA)	1959	Gary Player (SAf)
1926	Bobby Jones (USA)	1960	Kel Nagle (Aus)
1927	Bobby Jones (USA)	1961	Arnold Palmer (USA)
1928	Walter Hagen (USA)	1962	Arnold Palmer (USA)
1929	Walter Hagen (USA)	1963	Bob Charles (NZ)
1930	Bobby Jones (USA)	1964	Tony Lema (USA)
1931	Tommy Armour (USA)	1965	Peter Thomson (Aus)
1932	Gene Sarazen (USA)	1966	Jack Nicklaus (USA)

1967	Roberto de Vicenzo (Arg)	1981	Bill Rogers (USA)
1968	Gary Player (SAf)	1982	Tom Watson (USA)
1969	Tony Jacklin (UK)	1983	Tom Watson (USA)
1970	Jack Nicklaus (USA)	1984	Seve Ballesteros (Spa)
1971	Lee Trevino (USA)	1985	Sandy Lyle (UK)
1972	Lee Trevino (USA)	1986	Greg Norman (Aus)
1973	Tom Weiskopf (USA)	1987	Nick Faldo (UK)
1974	Gary Player (SAf)	1988	Seve Ballesteros (Spa)
1975	Tom Watson (USA)	1989	Mark Calcavecchia (USA)
1976	Johnny Miller (USA)	1990	Nick Faldo (UK)
1977	Tom Watson (USA)	1991	Ian Baker-Finch (Aus)
1978	Jack Nicklaus (USA)	1992	Nick Faldo (UK)
1979	Seve Ballesteros (Spa)	1993	Greg Norman (Aus)
1980	Tom Watson (USA)	1994	Nick Price (Zim)

US OPEN

1895	Horace Rawlins (USA)	1932	Gene Sarazen (USA)
1896	James Foulis (USA)	1933	Johnny Goodman (USA)
1897	Joe Lloyd (USA)	1934	Olin Dutra (USA)
1898	Fred Herd (USA)	1935	Sam Parks, Jnr (USA)
1899	Willie Smith (USA)	1936	Tony Manero (USA)
1900	Harry Vardon (UK)	1937	Ralph Guldahl (USA)
1901	Willie Anderson (USA)	1938	Ralph Guldahl (USA)
1902	Laurie Auchterlonie (USA)	1939	Byron Nelson (USA)
1903	Willie Anderson (USA)	1940	Lawson Little (USA)
1904	Willie Anderson (USA)	1941	Craig Wood (USA)
1905	Willie Anderson (USA)	1946	Lloyd Mangrum (USA)
1906	Alex Smith (USA)	1947	Lew Worsham (USA)
1907	Alex Ross (USA)	1948	Ben Hogan (USA)
1908	Fred McLeod (USA)	1949	Cary Middlecoff (USA)
1909	George Sargent (USA)	1950	Ben Hogan (USA)
1910	Alex Smith (USA)	1951	Ben Hogan (USA)
1911	John McDermott (USA)	1952	Julius Boros (USA)
1912	John McDermott (USA)	1953	Ben Hogan (USA)
1913	Francis Ouimet (USA)	1954	Ed Furgol (USA)
1914	Walter Hagen (USA)	1955	Jack Fleck (USA)
1915	Jerome Travers (USA)	1956	Cary Middlecoff (USA)
1916	Charles Evans, Jnr (USA)	1957	Dick Mayer (USA)
1919	Walter Hagen (USA)	1958	Tommy Bolt (USA)
1920	Edward Ray (UK)	1959	Billy Casper (USA)
1921	Jim Barnes (USA)	1960	Arnold Palmer (USA)
1922	Gene Sarazen (USA)	1961	Gene Littler (USA)
1923	Bobby Jones (USA)	1962	Jack Nicklaus (USA)
1924	Cyril Walker (USA)	1963	Julius Boros (USA)
1925	Willie Macfarlane (USA)	1964	Ken Venturi (USA)
1926	Bobby Jones (USA)	1965	Gary Player (SAf)
1927	Tommy Armour (USA)	1966	Billy Casper (USA)
1928	Johnny Farrell (USA)	1967	Jack Nicklaus (USA)
1929	Bobby Jones (USA)	1968	Lee Trevino (USA)
1930	Bobby Jones (USA)	1969	Orville Moody (USA)
1931	Billy Burke (USA)	1970	Tony Jacklin (UK)

1971	Lee Trevino (USA)	1983	Larry Nelson (USA)
1972	Jack Nicklaus (USA)	1984	Fuzzy Zoeller (USA)
1973	Johnny Miller (USA)	1985	Andy North (USA)
1974	Hale Irwin (USA)	1986	Raymond Floyd (USA)
1975	Lou Graham (USA)	1987	Scott Simpson (USA)
1976	Jerry Pate (USA)	1988	Curtis Strange (USA)
1977	Hubert Green (USA)	1989	Curtis Strange (USA)
1978	Andy North (USA)	1990	Hale Irwin (USA)
1979	Hale Irwin (USA)	1991	Payne Stewart (USA)
1980	Jack Nicklaus (USA)	1992	Tom Kite (USA)
1981	David Graham (Aus)	1993	Lee Janzen (USA)
1982	Tom Watson (USA)	1994	Ernie Els (SAf)

US MASTERS

1934	Horton Smith (USA)	1966	Jack Nicklaus (USA)
1935	Gene Sarazen (USA)	1967	Gay Brewer (USA)
1936	Horton Smith (USA)	1968	Bob Goalby (USA)
1937	Byron Nelson (USA)	1969	George Archer (USA)
1938	Henry Picard (USA)	1970	Billy Casper (USA)
1939	Ralph Guldahl (USA)	1971	Charles Coody (USA)
1940	Jimmy Demaret (USA)	1972	Jack Nicklaus (USA)
1941	Craig Wood (USA)	1973	Tommy Aaron (USA)
1942	Byron Nelson (USA)	1974	Gary Player (SAf)
1946	Herman Keiser (USA)	1975	Jack Nicklaus (USA)
1947	Jimmy Demaret (USA)	1976	Raymond Floyd (USA)
1948	Claude Harmon (USA)	1977	Tom Watson (USA)
1949	Sam Snead (USA)	1978	Gary Player (SAf)
1950	Jimmy Demaret (USA)	1979	Fuzzy Zoeller (USA)
1951	Ben Hogan (USA)	1980	Seve Ballesteros (Spa)
1952	Sam Snead (USA)	1981	Tom Watson (USA)
1953	Ben Hogan (USA)	1982	Craig Stadler (USA)
1954	Sam Snead (USA)	1983	Seve Ballesteros (Spa)
1955	Cary Middlecoff (USA)	1984	Ben Crenshaw (USA)
1956	Jack Burke, Jnr (USA)	1985	Bernhard Langer (FRG)
1957	Doug Ford (USA)	1986	Jack Nicklaus (USA)
1958	Arnold Palmer (USA)	1987	Larry Mize (USA)
1959	Art Wall, Jnr (USA)	1988	Sandy Lyle (UK)
1960	Arnold Palmer (USA)	1989	Nick Faldo (UK)
1961	Gary Player (SAf)	1990	Nick Faldo (UK)
1962	Arnold Palmer (USA)	1991	Ian Woosnam (UK)
1963	Jack Nicklaus (USA)	1992	Fred Couples (USA)
1964	Arnold Palmer (USA)	1993	Bernhard Langer (Ger)
1965	Jack Nicklaus (USA)		

US PROFESSIONAL GOLFERS ASSOCIATION

1916	Jim Barnes (USA)	1921	Walter Hagen (USA)
1919	Jim Barnes (USA)	1922	Gene Sarazen (USA)
1920	Jock Hutchison (USA)	1923	Gene Sarazen (USA)

1924	Walter Hagen (USA)	1961	Jerry Barber (USA)
1925	Walter Hagen (USA)	1962	Gary Player (SAf)
1926	Walter Hagen (USA)	1963	Jack Nicklaus (USA)
1927	Walter Hagen (USA)	1964	Bobby Nichols (USA)
1928	Leo Diegel (USA)	1965	Dave Marr (USA)
1929	Leo Diegel (USA)	1966	Al Geiberger (USA)
1930	Tommy Armour (USA)	1967	Don January (USA)
1931	Tom Creavy (USA)	1968	Julius Boros (USA)
1932	Olin Dutra (USA)	1969	Raymond Floyd (USA)
1933	Gene Sarazen (USA)	1970	Dave Stockton (USA)
1934	Paul Runyan (USA)	1971	Jack Nicklaus (USA)
1935	Johnny Revolta (USA)	1972	Gary Player (SAf)
1936	Densmore Shute (USA)	1973	Jack Nicklaus (USA)
1937	Densmore Shute (USA)	1974	Lee Trevino (USA)
1938	Paul Runyan (USA)	1975	Jack Nicklaus (USA)
1939	Henry Picard (USA)	1976	Dave Stockton (USA)
1940	Byron Nelson (USA)	1977	Lanny Wadkins (USA)
1941	Vic Ghezzi (USA)	1978	John Mahaffey (USA)
1942	Sam Snead (USA)	1979	David Graham (Aus)
1944	Bob Hamilton (USA)	1980	Jack Nicklaus (USA)
1945	Byron Nelson (USA)	1981	Larry Nelson (USA)
1946	Ben Hogan (USA)	1982	Raymond Floyd (USA)
1947	Jim Ferrier (USA)	1983	Hal Sutton (USA)
1948	Ben Hogan (USA)	1984	Lee Trevino (USA)
1949	Sam Snead (USA)	1985	Hubert Green (USA)
1950	Chandler Harper (USA)	1986	Bob Tway (USA)
1951	Sam Snead (USA)	1987	Larry Nelson (USA)
1952	Jim Turnesa (USA)	1988	Jeff Sluman (USA)
1953	Walter Burkemo (USA)	1989	Payne Stewart (USA)
1954	Chick Harbert (USA)	1990	Wayne Grady (Aus)
1955	Doug Ford (USA)	1991	John Daly (USA)
1956	Jack Burke (USA)	1992	Nick Price (Zim)
1957	Lionel Hebert (USA)	1993	Paul Azinger (USA)
1958	Dow Finsterwald (USA)	1994	José-Maria Olazabal (Spa)
1959	Bob Rosburg (USA)		
1960	Jay Hebert (USA)		

RYDER CUP

1927	USA	1955	USA	1975	USA
1929	Great Britain	1957	Great Britain	1977	USA
1931	USA	1959	USA	1979	USA
1933	Great Britain	1961	USA	1981	USA
1935	USA	1963	USA	1983	USA
1937	USA	1965	USA	1985	Europe
1947	USA	1967	USA	1987	Europe
1949	USA	1969	*tied*	1989	*tied*
1951	USA	1971	USA	1991	USA
1953	USA	1973	USA	1993	USA

GOVERNMENT

A new class of award made a welcome entry in 1994 – the 'Bad Government' awards inaugurated by the pressure group for constitutional reform, Charter 88, to mark its fifth birthday. Among the little-sought-after titles (known as Golden Cockroaches) were:

Illusionist of the Year	The Labour Party (for creating the image of an opposition)
Demolition of Local Government Award	John Redwood (for the proliferation of non-accountable quangos in Wales)
The King John Award for the Grossest Abuse of a Fundamental Right	Michael Howard (for his plans to abolish the right to silence in court cases)
Alan Clark Memorial Award for Greatest Economy with the Truth	Tristan Garel-Jones, Sir Robin Butler and William Waldegrave (over the Matrix Churchill affair)
Government Department Award (for the least idea where it is going)	Department of Trade and Industry (for its energy policy)
Rip Van Winkle Award (for the person most wedded to the past)	Michael Portillo (for reviving the Victorian concept of the undeserving poor)
Award for Institution Hanging On Against All The Odds	The House of Lords (or the House of Codgers as it was irreverently referred to)

GREYHOUND RACING

GREYHOUND DERBY

1927	Entry Badge	1952	Endless Gossip	1973	Patricia's Hope
1928	Boher Ash	1953	Daws Dancer	1974	Jimsun
1929	Mick the Miller	1954	Paul's Fun	1975	Tartan Khan
1930	Mick the Miller	1955	Rushton Mack	1976	Mutts Silver
1931	Seldom Lad	1956	Dunmore King	1977	Balliniska Band
1932	Wild Woolley	1957	Ford Spartan	1978	Lacca Champion
1933	Future Cutlet	1958	Pigalle Wonder	1979	Sarah's Bunny
1934	Davesland	1959	Mile Bush Pride	1980	Indian Joe
1935	Greta Ranee	1960	Duleek Dandy	1981	Parkdown Jet
1936	Fine Jubilee	1961	Palm's Printer	1982	Laurie's Panther
1937	Wattle Bark	1962	The Grand Canal	1983	I'm Slippy
1938	Lone Keel	1963	Lucky Boy Boy	1984	Whisper Wishes
1939	Highland Rum	1964	Hack Up Chieftain	1985	Pagan Swallow
1940	G. R. Archduke	1965	Chittering Clapton	1986	Tico
1945	Ballyhennessy Seal	1966	Faithful Hope	1987	Signal Spark
1946	Monday's News	1967	Tric-Trac	1988	Hit the Lid
1947	Trev's Perfection	1968	Camira Flash	1989	Lartigue Note
1948	Priceless Border	1969	Sand Star	1990	Slippy Blue
1949	Narrogar Ann	1970	John Silver	1991	Ballinderry Ash
1950	Ballymac Ball	1971	Dolores Rocket	1992	Farloe Melody
1951	Ballylanigan Tanist	1972	Patricia's Hope	1993	Ringa Hustle

GYMNASTICS

OLYMPIC GAMES

Men's Combined

1900	Gustave Sandras (Fra)
1904	Julius Lenhart (Aut)
1908	Alberto Braglia (Ita)
1912	Alberto Braglia (Ita)
1920	Giorgio Zampori (Ita)
1924	Leon Stukelj (Yug)
1928	Georges Miez (Swi)
1932	Romeo Neri (Ita)
1936	Alfred Schwarzmann (Ger)
1948	Veikko Huhtanen (Fin)
1952	Viktor Chukarin (USSR)
1956	Viktor Chukarin (USSR)
1960	Boris Shakhlin (USSR)
1964	Yukio Endo (Jap)
1968	Sawao Kato (Jap)
1972	Sawao Kato (Jap)
1976	Nikolay Andrianov (USSR)
1980	Aleksandr Ditiatin (USSR)
1984	Koji Gushiken (Jap)
1988	Vladimir Artemov (USSR)
1992	Vitaliy Shcherbo (CIS)

Men's Floor

1932	Istavan Pelle (Hun)
1936	Georges Miez (Swi)
1948	Ferenc Pataki (Hun)
1952	William Thoresson (Swe)
1956	Valentin Muratov (USSR)
1960	Nobuyuki Aihara (Jap)
1964	Franco Menichelli (Ita)
1968	Sawao Kato (Jap)
1972	Nikolay Andrianov (USSR)
1976	Nikolay Andrianov (USSR)
1980	Roland Brückner (GDR)
1984	Li Ning (Chn)
1988	Sergey Kharikov (USSR)
1992	Li Xiaosahuang (Chn)

Men's Parallel Bars

1896	Alfred Flatow (Ger)
1904	George Eyser (USA)
1908	August Güttinger (Swi)
1928	Ladislav Vacha (Cze)
1932	Romeo Neri (Ita)
1936	Konrad Frey (Ger)

1948	Michael Reusch (Swi)
1952	Hans Eugster (Swi)
1956	Viktor Chukarin (USSR)
1960	Boris Shakhlin (USSR)
1964	Yukio Endo (Jap)
1968	Akinori Nakayama (Jap)
1972	Sawao Kato (Jap)
1976	Sawao Kato (Jap)
1980	Aleksandr Tkachev (USSR)
1984	Bart Conner (USA)
1988	Vladimir Artemov (USSR)
1992	Vitaliy Shcherbo (CIS)

Men's Pommel Horse

1896	Louis Zutter (Swi)
1904	Anton Heida (USA)
1924	Josef Wilhelm (Swi)
1928	Hermann Hanggi (Swi)
1932	Istvan Pelle (Hun)
1936	Konrad Frey (Ger)
1948	Paavo Aaltonen (Fin) / Veikko Huhtanen (Fin) / Heikki Savolainen (Fin)
1952	Viktor Chukarin (USSR)
1956	Boris Shakhlin (USSR)
1960	Eugen Ekman (Fin) / Boris Shakhlin (USSR)
1964	Miroslav Cerar (Yug)
1968	Miroslav Cerar (Yug)
1972	Viktor Klimenko (USSR)
1976	Zoltán Magyar (Hun)
1980	Zoltán Magyar (Hun)
1984	Li Ning (Chn) / Peter Vidmar (USA)
1988	Lyubomir Gueraskov (Bul) / Zsolt Borkai (Hun) / Dmitri Belozerchev (USSR)
1992	Vitaliy Shcherbo (CIS) / Pae Gil-Su (NKo)

Men's Rings

1896	Ioannis Mitropoulos (Gre)
1904	Hermann Glass (USA)
1924	Francesco Martino (Ita)
1928	Leon Skutelj (Yug)
1932	George Gulack (USA)
1936	Alois Hudec (Cze)

1948	Karl Frei (Swi)
1952	Grant Shaginyan (USSR)
1956	Albert Azaryan (USSR)
1960	Albert Azaryan (USSR)
1964	Takuji Hayata (Jap)
1968	Akinori Nakayama (Jap)
1972	Akinori Nakayama (Jap)
1976	Nikolay Andrianov (USSR)
1980	Aleksandr Ditiatin (USSR)
1984	Koji Gushiken (Jap) Li Ning (Chn)
1988	Holger Behrendt (GDR) Dmitri Belozerchev (USSR)
1992	Vitaliy Shcherbo (CIS)

Men's Horizontal Bars

1896	Hermann Weingärtner (Ger)
1904	Anton Heida (USA) Edward Hennig (USA)
1924	Leon Stukelj (Yug)
1928	Georges Miez (Swi)
1932	Dallas Bixler (USA)
1936	Aleksanteri Saavala (Fin)
1948	Josef Stadler (Swi)
1952	Jack Günthard (Swi)
1956	Takashi Ono (Jap)
1960	Takashi Ono (Jap)
1964	Boris Shakhlin (USSR)
1968	Mikhail Voronin (USSR) Akinori Nakayama (Jap)
1972	Mitsuo Tsukahara (Jap)
1976	Mitsuo Tsukahara (Jap)
1980	Stoyan Deltchev (Bul)
1984	Shinji Morisue (Jap)
1988	Vladimir Artemov (USSR) Valeri Lyukine (USSR)
1992	Trent Dimas (USA)

Men's Vault

1896	Carl Schumann (Ger)
1904	Anton Heida (USA) George Eyser (USA)
1924	Frank Kriz (USA)
1928	Eugen Mack (Swi)
1932	Savino Guglielmetti (Ita)
1936	Alfred Schwarzmann (Ger)
1948	Paavo Aaltonen (Fin)
1952	Viktor Chukarin (USSR)
1956	Helmuth Bantz (Ger) Valentin Muratov (USSR)
1960	Takashi Ono (Jap) Boris Shahlkin (USSR)

1964	Haruhiro Yamashita (Jap)
1968	Mikhail Voronin (USSR)
1972	Klaus Köste (GDR)
1976	Nikolay Andrianov (USSR)
1980	Nikolay Andrianov (USSR)
1984	Lou Yun (Chn)
1988	Lou Yun (Chn)
1992	Vitaliy Shcherbo (CIS)

Men's Team

1904	USA
1908	Sweden
1912	Italy
1920	Italy
1924	Italy
1928	Switzerland
1932	Italy
1936	Germany
1948	Finland
1952	USSR
1956	USSR
1960	Japan
1964	Japan
1968	Japan
1972	Japan
1976	Japan
1980	USSR
1984	USA
1988	USSR
1992	CIS

Women's Combined

1952	Maria Gorokhovskaya (USSR)
1956	Larissa Latynina (USSR)
1960	Larissa Latynina (USSR)
1964	Vera Cáslavská (Cze)
1968	Vera Cáslavská (Cze)
1972	Lyudmila Tourischeva (USSR)
1976	Nadia Comaneci (Rom)
1980	Yelena Davydova (USSR)
1984	Mary Lou Retton (US)
1988	Yelena Shoushounova (USSR)
1992	Tatyana Gutsu (CIS)

Women's Asymmetrical Bars

1952	Margit Korondi (Hun)
1956	Agnes Keleti (Hun)
1960	Polina Astakhova (USSR)
1964	Polina Astakhova (USSR)
1968	Vera Cáslavská (Cze)
1972	Karin Janz (GDR)
1976	Nadia Comaneci (Rom)
1980	Maxi Gnauck (GDR)

1984	Ma Yanhong (Chn)
	Julianne McNamara (USA)
1988	Daniela Silivas (Rom)
1992	Li Lu (Chn)

Women's Beam

1952	Nina Bocharova (USSR)
1956	Agnes Keleti (Hun)
1960	Eva Bosakova (Cze)
1964	Vera Cáslavská (Cze)
1968	Natalya Kuchinskaya (USSR)
1972	Olga Korbut (USSR)
1976	Nadia Comaneci (Rom)
1980	Nadia Comaneci (Rom)
1984	Simona Pauca (Rom)
	Ecaterina Szabo (Rom)
1988	Daniela Silivas (Rom)
1992	Tatyana Lysenko (CIS)

Women's Floor

1952	Agnes Keleti (Hun)
1956	Larissa Latynina (USSR)
	Agnes Keleti (Hun)
1960	Larissa Latynina (USSR)
1964	Larissa Latynina (USSR)
1968	Larissa Petrik (USSR)
	Vera Cáslavská (Cze)
1972	Olga Korbut (USSR)
1976	Nelli Kim (USSR)
1980	Nelli Kim (USSR)
	Nadia Comaneci (Rom)
1984	Ecaterina Szabo (Rom)
1988	Daniela Silivas (Rom)
1992	Lavinia Milosovici (Rom)

Women's Vault

1952	Yekaterina Kalinchuk (USSR)
1956	Larissa Latynina (USSR)
1960	Margarita Nikolayeva (USSR)
1964	Vera Cáslavská (Cze)
1968	Vera Cáslavská (Cze)
1972	Karin Janz (GDR)
1976	Nelli Kim (USSR)
1980	Natalya Shaposhnikova (USSR)
1984	Ecaterina Szabo (Rom)
1988	Svetlana Boginskaya (USSR)
1992	Lavinia Milosovici (Rom)
	Henrietta Ónodi (Hun)

Women's Rhythmic Gymnastics

1984	Lori Fung (Can)
1988	Marina Lobach (USSR)
1992	Aleksandra Timoschenko (CIS)

Women's Team

1928	Holland
1936	Germany
1948	Czechoslovakia
1952	USSR
1956	USSR
1960	USSR
1964	USSR
1968	USSR
1972	USSR
1976	USSR
1980	USSR
1984	Romania
1988	USSR
1992	CIS

HAIRDRESSING

BRITISH HAIRDRESSING AWARDS

Dubbed 'the awards that are a cut above the Oscars', the annual British Hairdressing Awards attract enormous excitement and attention. The black tie event, presented by *Hairdressers Journal* and sponsored by Schwarzkopf, produced the following winners of the fifteen 1993 awards:

British Hairdresser of the Year Andrew Collinge

Avant Garde Hairdresser of the Year Michael Barnes

Men's Hairdresser of the Year Guy Kremer

Newcomer of the Year Joe McGivern

Afro Hairdresser of the Year Errol Douglas

Artistic Team of the Year Toni and Guy

Session Hairdresser of the Year Guido

The Regional Hairdresser of the Year Awards were won by the following:

Southern	Robert Smith	*London*	Charles Worthington
Wales and South-west	Phil Smith	*Northern*	Mark Hill
Midland	Stephen Blyth	*Scottish*	Alan Edwards
Eastern	Terry Calvert	*Northern Ireland*	Paul Stafford

HANDBALL

OLYMPIC GAMES

Men's		**Women's**	
1936	Germany	1976	USSR
1972	Yugoslavia	1980	USSR
1976	USSR	1984	Yugoslavia
1980	East Germany	1988	South Korea
1984	Yugoslavia	1992	South Korea
1988	USSR		
1992	CIS		

HOCKEY

WORLD CUP

Men's		**Women's**	
1971	Pakistan	1974	Holland
1973	Holland	1976	West Germany
1975	India	1978	Holland
1978	Pakistan	1981	West Germany
1982	Pakistan	1983	Holland
1986	Australia	1986	Holland
1990	Holland	1990	Holland

OLYMPIC GAMES

Men's			
1908	England	1972	West Germany
1920	Great Britain	1976	New Zealand
1928	India	1980	India
1932	India	1984	Pakistan
1936	India	1988	Great Britain
1948	India	1992	Germany
1952	India		
1956	India	**Women's**	
1960	Pakistan	1980	Zimbabwe
1964	India	1984	Holland
1968	Pakistan	1988	Australia
		1992	Spain

ENGLISH LEAGUE

Men

1975	Bedfordshire Eagles
1976	Slough
1977	Southgate
1978	Southgate
1979	Isca
1980	Slough
1981	Slough
1982	Slough
1983	Slough
1984	Neston
1985	East Grinstead
1986	East Grinstead
1987	Slough
1988	Southgate
1989	Southgate
1990	Hounslow
1991	Havant
1992	Havant
1993	Hounslow

Women

1990	Slough
1991	Slough
1992	Slough
1993	Ipswich

HOMES

THE INDIVIDUAL HOMES AWARDS

Organized by the *Daily Telegraph* since 1992, the awards have come in response to the growing numbers of people who are having their homes individually built (about one in three of new detached houses are now in this category). The 1993 judging panel included Lord Rodgers of Quarry Bank, Director General of the Royal Institute of British Architects; Dr Mary Archer, Chairman of the National Energy Foundation; Peter Harris, Editor of *Individual Homes* magazine; and Barbara Kay of the Individual House Builders Association.

The 1993 winner was Tressour Wood, Weem, Aberfeldy, Scotland.

HORSE-RACING

1000 GUINEAS

	Horse				
1900	Winifreda	1914	Princess Dorrie	1928	Scuttle
1901	Aida	1915	Vaucluse	1929	Taj Mah
1902	Sceptre	1916	Canyon	1930	Fair Isle
1903	Quintessence	1917	Diadem	1931	Four Course
1904	Pretty Polly	1918	Ferry	1932	Kandy
1905	Cherry Lass	1919	Roseway	1933	Betty Brown
1906	Flair	1920	Cinna	1934	Campanula
1907	Witch Elm	1921	Bettina	1935	Mesa
1908	Rhodora	1922	Silver Urn	1936	Tide-Way
1909	Electra	1923	Tranquil	1937	Exhibitionist
1910	Winkipop	1924	Plack	1938	Ruckfel
1911	Atmah	1925	Saucy Sue	1939	Galatea II
1912	Tagalie	1926	Pillion	1940	Godiva
1913	Jest	1927	Cresta Run	1941	Dancing Time

	Horse				
1942	Sun Chariot	1960	Never Too Late	1978	Enstone Spark
1943	Herringbone	1961	Sweet Solera	1979	One in a Million
1944	Picture Play	1962	Abermaid	1980	Quick as Lightning
1945	Sun Stream	1963	Hula Dancer	1981	Fairy Footsteps
1946	Hypericum	1964	Pourparler	1982	On the House
1947	Imprudence	1965	Night Off	1983	Ma Biche
1948	Queenpot	1966	Glad Rags	1984	Pebbles
1949	Musidora	1967	Fleet	1985	Oh So Sharp
1950	Camaree	1968	Caergwrie	1986	Midway Lady
1951	Belle of All	1969	Full Dress II	1987	Miesque
1952	Zabara	1970	Humble Duty	1988	Ravinella
1953	Happy Laughter	1971	Altesse Royale	1989	Musical Bliss
1954	Festoon	1972	Waterloo	1990	Salsabil
1955	Meld	1973	Mysterious	1991	Shadayid
1956	Honeylight	1974	Highclere	1992	Hatoof
1957	Rose Royale II	1975	Nocturnal Spree	1993	Sayyedati
1958	Bella Paola	1976	Flying Water	1994	Las Meninas
1959	Petite Etoile	1977	Mrs McArdy		

2000 GUINEAS

	Horse				
1900	Diamond Jubilee	1929	Mr Jinks	1958	Pall Mall
1901	Handicapper	1930	Diolite	1959	Taboun
1902	Sceptre	1931	Cameronian	1960	Martial
1903	Rock Sand	1932	Orwell	1961	Rockavon
1904	St Amant	1933	Rodosto	1962	Privy Councillor
1905	Vedas	1934	Colombo	1963	Only for Life
1906	Gorgos	1935	Bahram	1964	Baldric II
1907	Slieve Gallion	1936	Pay Up	1965	Niksar
1908	Norman III	1937	Le Ksar	1966	Kashmir II
1909	Minoru	1938	Pasch	1967	Royal Palace
1910	Neil Gow	1939	Blue Peter	1968	Sir Ivor
1911	Sunstar	1940	Djebel	1969	Right Tack
1912	Sweeper II	1941	Lambert Simnel	1970	Nijinsky
1913	Louvis	1942	Big Game	1971	Brigadier Gerard
1914	Kennymore	1943	Kingsway	1972	High Top
1915	Pommern	1944	Garden Path	1973	Mon Fils
1916	Clarissimus	1945	Court Martial	1974	Nonoaico
1917	Gay Crusader	1946	Happy Knight	1975	Bolkonski
1918	Gainsborough	1947	Tudor Minstrel	1976	Wollow
1919	The Panther	1948	My Babu	1977	Nebbiolo
1920	Tetratema	1949	Nimbus	1978	Roland Gardens
1921	Criag an Eran	1950	Palestine	1979	Tap On Wood
1922	St Louis	1951	Ki Ming	1980	Known Fact
1923	Ellangowan	1952	Thunderhead II	1981	To-Agori-Mou
1924	Diophon	1953	Nearula	1982	Zino
1925	Manna	1954	Darius	1983	Lomond
1926	Colorado	1955	Our Babu	1984	El Gran Señor
1927	Adam's Apple	1956	Gilles de Retz	1985	Shaheed
1928	Flamingo	1957	Crepello	1986	Dancing Brave

1987	Don't Forget Me	1990	Tirol	1993	Zafonic
1988	Doyoun	1991	Mystiko	1994	Mr Bailey's
1989	Nashwan	1992	RodrigodeTriano		

THE DERBY

	Horse				
1900	Diamond Jubilee	1932	April the Fifth	1964	Santa Claus
1901	Volodyovski	1933	Hyperion	1965	Sea Bird II
1902	Ard Patrick	1934	Windsor Lad	1966	Charlottown
1903	Rock Sand	1935	Bahram	1967	Royal Palace
1904	St Amant	1936	Mahmoud	1968	Sir Ivor
1905	Cicero	1937	Mid-day Sun	1969	Blakeney
1906	Spearmint	1938	Bois Roussel	1970	Nijinsky
1907	Orby	1939	Blue Peter	1971	Mill Reef
1908	Signorinetta	1940	Pont l'Eveque	1972	Roberto
1909	Minoru	1941	Owen Tudor	1973	Morston
1910	Lemberg	1942	Watling Street	1974	Snow Knight
1911	Sunstar	1943	Straight Deal	1975	Grundy
1912	Tagalie	1944	Ocean Swell	1976	Empery
1913	Aboyeur	1945	Dante	1977	The Minstrel
1914	Durbar II	1946	Airborne	1978	Shirley Heights
1915	Pommern	1947	Pearl Diver	1979	Troy
1916	Fifinella	1948	My Love	1980	Henbit
1917	Gay Crusader	1949	Nimbus	1981	Shergar
1918	Gainsborough	1950	Galcador	1982	Golden Fleece
1919	Grand Parade	1951	Arctic Prince	1983	Teenoso
1920	Spion Kop	1952	Tulyar	1984	Secreto
1921	Humorist	1953	Pinza	1985	Slip Anchor
1922	Captain Cuttle	1954	Never Say Die	1986	Shahrastani
1923	Papyrus	1955	Phil Drake	1987	Reference Point
1924	Sansovino	1956	Lavandin	1988	Kahyasi
1925	Manna	1957	Crepello	1989	Nashwan
1926	Coronach	1958	Hard Ridden	1990	Quest For Fame
1927	Call Boy	1959	Parthia	1991	Generous
1928	Fellstead	1960	St Paddy	1992	Dr Devious
1929	Trigo	1961	Psidium	1993	Commander in
1930	Blenheim	1962	Larkspur		Chief
1931	Cameronian	1963	Relko	1994	Erhaab

THE OAKS

	Horse				
1779	Bridget	1788	Nightshade	1797	Nike
1780	Tetoum	1789	Tag	1798	Bellissima
1781	Faith	1790	Hippolyta	1799	Bellina
1782	Ceres	1791	Portia	1800	Ephemera
1783	Maid of the Oaks	1792	Volante	1801	Eleanor
1784	Stella	1793	Caelia	1802	Scotia
1785	Trifle	1794	Hermione	1803	Theophania
1786	Yellow Filly	1795	Platina	1804	Pelisse
1787	Annette	1796	Pasiot	1805	Meteora

Horse

1806	Bronze	1857	Blink Bonny	1906	Keystone II
1807	Briseis	1858	Governess	1907	Glass Doll
1808	Morel	1859	Summerside	1908	Signorinetta
1809	Maid of Orleans	1860	Butterfly	1909	Perola
1810	Oriana	1861	Brown Duchess	1910	Rosedrop
1811	Sorcery	1862	Feu de Joie	1911	Cherimoya
1812	Manuella	1863	Queen Bertha	1912	Mirska
1813	Music	1864	Fille de L'Air	1913	Jest
1814	Medora	1865	Regalia	1914	Princess Dorrie
1815	Minuet	1866	Tormentor	1915	Snow Marten
1816	Landscape	1867	Hippia	1916	Fifinella
1817	Neva	1868	Formosa	1917	Sunny Jane
1818	Corinne	1869	Brigantine	1918	My Dear
1819	Shoveler	1870	Gamos	1919	Bayuda
1820	Caroline	1871	Hannah	1920	Charlebelle
1821	Augusta	1872	Reine	1921	Love in Idleness
1822	Pastille	1873	Marie Stuart	1922	Pogrom
1823	Zinc	1874	Apology	1923	Brownhylda
1824	Cobweb	1875	Spinaway	1924	Straitlace
1825	Wings	1876	Enguerrande ⎱ dead	1925	Saucy Sue
1826	Lilias		Camelia ⎰ heat	1926	Short Story
1827	Gulnare	1877	Placida	1927	Beam
1828	Turquoise	1878	Jannette	1928	Toboggan
1829	Green Mantle	1879	Wheel of Fortune	1929	Pennycomequick
1830	Variation	1880	Jenny Howlet	1930	Rose of England
1831	Oxygen	1881	Thebais	1931	Brulette
1832	Galata	1882	Geheimniss	1932	Udaipur
1833	Vespa	1883	Bonny Jean	1933	Chatelaine
1834	Pussy	1884	Busybody	1934	Light Brocade
1835	Queen of Trumps	1885	Lonely	1935	Quashed
1836	Cyprian	1886	Miss Jummy	1936	Lovely Rosa
1837	Miss Letty	1887	Rêve d'Or	1937	Exhibitionist
1838	Industry	1888	Seabreeze	1938	Rockfel
1839	Deception	1889	L'Abbesse de	1939	Galatea II
1840	Crucifix		Jouarre	1940	Godiva
1841	Ghunznee	1890	Memoir	1941	Commotion
1842	Our Nell	1891	Mimi	1942	Sun Chariot
1843	Poison	1892	La Flèche	1943	Why Hurry
1844	The Princess	1893	Mrs Butterwick	1944	Hycilla
1845	Refraction	1894	Amiable	1945	Sun Stream
1846	Mendicant	1895	La Sagesse	1946	Steady Aim
1847	Miami	1896	Canterbury Pilgrim	1947	Imprudence
1848	Cymba	1897	Limasol	1948	Masaka
1849	Lady Evelyn	1898	Airs and Graces	1949	Musidora
1850	Rhedycina	1899	Musa	1950	Asmena
1851	Iris	1900	La Roche	1951	Neasham Belle
1852	Songstress	1901	Caps and Bells II	1952	Frieze
1853	Catherine Hayes	1902	Sceptre	1953	Ambiguity
1854	Mincemeat	1903	Our Lassie	1954	Sun Cap
1855	Marchioness	1904	Pretty Polly	1955	Meld
1856	Mincepie	1905	Cherry Lass	1956	Sicarelle

1957	Carrozza	1970	Lupe	1983	Sun Princess
1958	Bella Paola	1971	Altesse Royale	1984	Circus Plume
1959	Petite Etoile	1972	Ginevra	1985	Oh So Sharp
1960	Never Too Late	1973	Mysterious	1986	Midway Lady
1961	Sweet Solera	1974	Polygamy	1987	Unite
1962	Monade	1975	Juliette Marny	1988	Diminuendo
1963	Noblesse	1976	Pawneese	1989	Snow Bride
1964	Homeward Bound	1977	Dunfermline	1990	Salsabil
1965	Long Look	1978	Fari Salinia	1991	Jet Ski Lady
1966	Valoris	1979	Scintillate	1992	User Friendly
1967	Pia	1980	Bireme	1993	Bob's Return
1968	La Lagune	1981	Blue Wind	1994	Balanchine
1969	Sleeping Partner	1982	Time Charter		

ST LEGER

	Horse				
1776	Allabaculia	1810	Octavian	1844	Foig a Ballagh
1777	Bourbon	1811	Soothsayer	1845	The Baron
1778	Hollandaise	1812	Otterington	1846	Sir Tatton Sykes
1779	Tommy	1813	Altisidora	1847	Van Tromp
1780	Ruler	1814	William	1848	Surplice
1781	Serina	1815	Filho da Puta	1849	The Flying Dutchman
1782	Imperatrix	1816	The Duchess	1850	Voltigeur
1783	Phenomenon	1817	Ebor	1851	Newminster
1784	Omphale	1818	Reveller	1852	Stockwell
1785	Cowslip	1819	Antonio	1853	West Australian
1786	Paragon	1820	St Patrick	1854	Knight of St George
1787	Spadille	1821	Jack Spigot	1855	Saucebox
1788	Young Flora	1822	Theodore	1856	Warlock
1789	Pewett	1823	Barefoot	1857	Impérieuse
1790	Ambidexter	1824	Jerry	1858	Sunbeam
1791	Young Traveller	1825	Memnon	1859	Gamester
1792	Tartar	1826	Tarrare	1860	St Albans
1793	Ninety-Three	1827	Matilda	1861	Caller Out
1794	Beningbrough	1828	The Colonel	1862	The Marquis
1795	Hambletonian	1829	Rowton	1863	Lord Clifden
1796	Ambrosio	1830	Birmingham	1864	Blair Athol
1797	Lounger	1831	Chorister	1865	Gladiateur
1798	Symmetry	1832	Margrave	1866	Lord Lyon
1799	Cockfighter	1833	Rockingham	1867	Achievement
1800	Champion	1834	Touchstone	1868	Formosa
1801	Quiz	1835	Queen of Trumps	1869	Pero Gomez
1802	Orville	1836	Elis	1870	Hawthornden
1803	Remembrancer	1837	Mango	1871	Hannah
1804	Sancho	1838	Don John	1872	Wenlock
1805	Staveley	1839	Charles the Twelfth	1873	Marie Stuart
1806	Fyldener	1840	Launcelot	1874	Apology
1807	Paulina	1841	Satirist	1875	Craig Millar
1808	Petronius	1842	The Blue Bonnet	1876	Petrarch
1809	Ashton	1843	Nutwith	1877	Silvio

	Horse				
1878	Jannette	1917	Gay Crusader	1956	Cambremer
1879	Rayon d'Or	1918	Gainsborough	1957	Ballymoss
1880	Robert the Devil	1919	Keysoe	1958	Alcide
1881	Iroquois	1920	Caligula	1959	Cantelo
1882	Dutch Oven	1921	Polemarch	1960	St Paddy
1883	Ossian	1922	Royal Lancer	1961	Aurelius
1884	The Lambkin	1923	Tranquil	1962	Hethersett
1885	Melton	1924	Salmon-Trout	1963	Ragusa
1886	Ormonde	1925	Solario	1964	Indiana
1887	Kilwarlin	1926	Coronach	1965	Provoke
1888	Seabreeze	1927	Book Law	1966	Sodium
1889	Donovan	1928	Fairway	1967	Ribocco
1890	Memoir	1929	Trigo	1968	Ribero
1891	Common	1930	Singapore	1969	Intermezzo
1892	La Flèche	1931	Sandwich	1970	Nijinsky
1893	Isinglass	1932	Firdaussi	1971	Athens Wood
1894	Throstle	1933	Hyperion	1972	Boucher
1895	Sir Visto	1934	Windsor Lad	1973	Peleid
1896	Persimmon	1935	Bahram	1974	Bustino
1897	Galtee More	1936	Boswell	1975	Bruni
1898	Wildfowler	1937	Chulmleigh	1976	Crow
1899	Flying Fox	1938	Scottish Union	1977	Dunfermline
1900	Diamond Jubilee	1939	*no race*	1978	Julio Mariner
1901	Doricles	1940	Turkham	1979	Son of Love
1902	Sceptre	1941	Sun Castle	1980	Light Cavalry
1903	Rock Sand	1942	Sun Chariot	1981	Cut Above
1904	Pretty Polly	1943	Herringbone	1982	Touching Wood
1905	Challacombe	1944	Tehran	1983	Sun Princess
1906	Troutbeck	1945	Chamossaire	1984	Commanche Run
1907	Wool Winder	1946	Airborne	1985	Oh So Sharp
1908	Your Majesty	1947	Sayajirao	1986	Moon Madness
1909	Bayardo	1948	Black Tarquin	1987	Reference Point
1910	Swynford	1949	Ridge Wood	1988	Minster Son
1911	Prince Palatine	1950	Scratch II	1989	Michelozzo
1912	Tracery	1951	Talma II	1990	Snurge
1913	Night Hawk	1952	Tulyar	1991	Toulon
1914	Black Jester	1953	Premonition	1992	User Friendly
1915	Pommern	1954	Never Say Die	1993	Bob's Return
1916	Hurry On	1955	Meld		

GRAND NATIONAL

	Horse				
1836	The Duke	1844	Discount	1852	Miss Mowbray
1837	The Duke	1845	Cureall	1853	Peter Simple
1838	Sir William	1846	Pioneer	1854	Bourton
1839	Lottery	1847	Matthew	1855	Wanderer
1840	Jerry	1848	Chandler	1856	Freetrader
1841	Charity	1849	Peter Simple	1857	Emigrant
1842	Gay Lad	1850	Abd-el-Kader	1858	Little Charley
1843	Vanguard	1851	Abd-el-Kader	1859	Half Caste

1860	Anatis	1903	Drumcree	1951	Nickel Coin
1861	Jealousy	1904	Moifaa	1952	Teal
1862	Huntsman	1905	Kirkland	1953	Early Mist
1863	Emblem	1906	Ascetic's Silver	1954	Royal Tan
1864	Emblematic	1907	Eremon	1955	Quare Times
1865	Alcibiade	1908	Rubio	1956	E.S.B.
1866	Salamander	1909	Lutteur III	1957	Sundew
1867	Cortolvin	1910	Jenkinstown	1958	Mr What
1868	The Lamb	1911	Glenside	1959	Oxo
1869	The Colonel	1912	Jerry M	1960	Merryman II
1870	The Colonel	1913	Covertcoat	1961	Nicolaus Silver
1871	The Lamb	1914	Sunloch	1962	Kilmore
1872	Casse Tête	1915	Ally Sloper	1963	Ayala
1873	Disturbance	1916	Vermouth	1964	Team Spirit
1874	Reugny	1917	Ballymacad	1965	Jay Trump
1875	Pathfinder	1918	Poethlyn	1966	Anglo
1876	Regal	1919	Poethlyn	1967	Foinavon
1877	Austerlitz	1920	Troytown	1968	Red Alligator
1878	Shifnal	1921	Shaun Spadah	1969	Highland Wedding
1879	The Liberator	1922	Music Hall	1970	Gay Trip
1880	Empress	1923	Sergeant Murphy	1971	Specify
1881	Woodbrook		Bennett	1972	Well To Do
1882	Seaman	1924	Master Robert	1973	Red Rum
1883	Zoëdone	1925	Double Chance	1974	Red Rum
1884	Voluptuary	1926	Jack Horner	1975	L'Escargot
1885	Roquefort	1927	Sprig	1976	Rag Trade
1886	Old Joe	1928	Tipperary Tim	1977	Red Rum
1887	Gamecock	1929	Gregalach	1978	Lucius
1888	Playfair	1930	Shaun Goilin	1979	Rubstic
1889	Frigate	1931	Grakle	1980	Ben Nevis
1890	Ilex	1932	Forbra	1981	Aldaniti
1891	Come Away	1933	Kellsboro' Jack	1982	Grittar
1892	Father O'Flynn	1934	Golden Miller	1983	Corbière
1893	Cloister	1935	Reynoldstown	1984	Hallo Dandy
1894	Why Not	1936	Reynoldstown	1985	Last Suspect
1895	Wild Man from	1937	Royal Mail	1986	West Tip
	Borneo	1938	Battleship	1987	Maori Venture
1896	The Soarer	1939	Workman	1988	Rhyme 'N Reason
1897	Manifesto	1940	Bogskar	1989	Little Polveir
1898	Drogheda	1946	Lovely Cottage	1990	Mr Frisk
1899	Manifesto	1947	Caughoo	1991	Seagram
1900	Ambush II	1948	Sheila's Cottage	1992	Party Politics
1901	Grudon	1949	Russian Hero	1993	*no race*
1902	Shannon Lass	1950	Freebooter	1994	Miinnehoma

CHELTENHAM GOLD CUP

	Horse				
1924	Red Splash	1927	Thrown In	1930	Easter Hero
1925	Ballinode	1928	Patron Saint	1932	Golden Miller
1926	Koko	1929	Easter Hero	1933	Golden Miller

	Horse				
1934	Golden Miller	1956	Limber Hill	1976	Royal Frolic
1935	Golden Miller	1957	Linwell	1977	Davy Lad
1936	Golden Miller	1958	Kerstin	1978	Midnight Court
1937	No race	1959	Roddy Owen	1979	Alverton
1938	Morse Code	1960	Pas Seul	1980	Master Smudge
1939	Brendan's Cottage	1961	Saffron Tartan	1981	Little Owl
1940	Roman Hackle	1962	Mandarin	1982	Silver Buck
1941	Poet Prince	1963	Mill House	1983	Bregawn
1942	Médoc II	1964	Arkle	1984	Burrough Hill Lad
1945	Red Rower	1965	Arkle	1985	Forgive 'N' Forget
1946	Prince Regent	1966	Arkle	1986	Dawn Run
1947	Fortina	1967	Woodland Venture	1987	The Thinker
1948	Cottage Rake	1968	Fort Leney	1988	Charter Party
1949	Cottage Rake	1969	What a Myth	1989	Desert Orchid
1950	Cottage Rake	1970	L'Escargot	1990	Norton's Coin
1951	Silver Fame	1971	L'Escargot	1991	Garrison Savannah
1952	Mont Tremblant	1972	Glencaraig Lady	1992	Cool Ground
1953	Knock Hard	1973	The Dikler	1993	Jodami
1954	Four Ten	1974	Captain Christy	1994	The Fellow
1955	Gay Donald	1975	Ten Up		

CHAMPION HURDLE

	Horse				
1927	Blaris	1951	Hatton's Grace	1973	Comedy of Errors
1928	Brown Jack	1952	Sir Ken	1974	Lanzarote
1929	Royal Falcon	1953	Sir Ken	1975	Comedy of Errors
1930	Brown Tony	1954	Sir Ken	1976	Night Nurse
1931	No race	1955	Clair Soleil	1977	Night Nurse
1932	Insurance	1956	Doorknocker	1978	Monksfield
1933	Insurance	1957	Merry Deal	1979	Monksfield
1934	Chenango	1958	Bandalore	1980	Sea Pigeon
1935	Lion Courage	1959	Fare Time	1981	Sea Pigeon
1936	Victor Norman	1960	Another Flash	1982	For Auction
1937	Free Fare	1961	Eborneezer	1983	Gaye Brief
1938	Our Hope	1962	Anzio	1984	Dawn Run
1939	African Sister	1963	Winning Fair	1985	See You Then
1940	Solford	1964	Magic Court	1986	See You Then
1941	Seneca	1965	Kirriemuir	1987	See You Then
1942	Forestation	1966	Salmon Spray	1988	Celtic Shot
1945	Brains Trust	1967	Saucy Kit	1989	Beech Road
1946	Distel	1968	Persian War	1990	Kribensis
1947	National Spirit	1969	Persian War	1991	Morley Street
1948	National Spirit	1970	Persian War	1992	Royal Gait
1949	Hatton's Grace	1971	Bula	1993	Granville Again
1950	Hatton's Grace	1972	Bula	1994	Flakey Dove

JOCKEY OF THE YEAR

The Jockeys' Association awards, voted by members and sponsored by *Racing Post*:

1990

Jockey Pat Eddery
Flat Jockey Pat Eddery
National Hunt Jockey Richard
  Dunwoody
Apprentice Jimmy Fortune
Lady Jockey Alex Greaves
Personality Lester Piggott

1991

Jockey Alan Munro
Flat Jockey Pat Eddery
National Hunt Jockey Peter Niven
Apprentice Darryll Holland
Lady Jockey Alex Greaves
Personality Lester Piggott

1992

Jockey Michael Roberts
Flat Jockey Michael Roberts

National Hunt Jockey Richard
  Dunwoody
Apprentice David Harrison
Lady Jockey Emma O'Gorman
Personality Lester Piggott

1993

Jockey Adrian Maguire
Flat Jockey Frankie Dettori
National Hunt Jockey Richard
  Dunwoody
Apprentice Jason Weaver
Lady Jockey Diane Clay
Personality { Frankie Dettori / Peter Scudamore }
Readers' Award (Riding Achievement of the Year) Graham Bradley
Jockeys' Association Council (Special Award) Peter Scudamore

RACEHORSE OF THE YEAR

Racegoers' Club annual poll for Racehorse of the Year:

Flat		**National Hunt**	
1988	Mtoto	1988/89	Desert Orchid
1989	Nashwan	1989/90	Desert Orchid
1990	Dayjur	1990/1	Morley Street
1991	Generous	1991/2	Remittance Man
1992	User Friendly	1992/3	Jodami

CHAMPION HORSES

Timeform annual champion horses/highest rated, racehorses and hurdlers and steeplechasers:

	Flat	Rated		National Hunt	Rated
1988	Warning	136	1987/8	Desert Orchid	177
1989	Zilzal	137	1988/9	Desert Orchid	182
1990	Dayjur	137	1989/90	Desert Orchid	187
1991	Generous	139	1990/1	Morley Street	174
1992	St Jovite	135	1991/2	Carvill's Hill	182
1993	Opera House	131	1992/3	Jodami	174

HOTELS

EGON RONAY AWARDS

Pre-eminent among the many awards in the category of hotels and restaurants are those conferred by the gourmet and critic, Egon Ronay. Among the Egon Ronay awards are:

Egon Ronay Hotel of the Year

This annual award in Britain for the best hotel is made to a hotel whose consistent excellence or enterprise is found to be outstanding. The winner receives and keeps for a year an engraved plate. The first winner, in 1969, was the Lygon Arms, Broadway, Hereford and Worcester. Among famous London hotels to win in the early years were the Inn on the Park (1970), the Berkeley Hotel (1972), the Ritz (1978) and the Connaught Hotel (1979). Winners in recent years have been:

1987	Homewood Park, Freshford
1988	Park Hotel, Kenmare
1989	The Savoy, London
1990	Gidleigh Park, Chagford, Devon
1991	Longueville Manor, St Saviour, Jersey
1992	The Dorchester, London
1993	The Chester Grosvenor, Chester
1994	One Devonshire Gardens, Glasgow

Egon Ronay Hosts of the Year

1992	Woodhayes, Whimple, Devon
1993	Stock Hill House, Gillingham, Dorset
1994	Sharrow Bay, Ullswater, Cumbria

Egon Ronay Cellnet Guide All-time Top Ten Hotels

All of these have been open at least ten years. The list (in gazetteer order) is:

The Connaught, London
Le Gavroche, London
La Tante Claire, London
Waterside Inn, Bray-on-Thames, Berks
Carved Angel, Dartmouth, Devon
Le Manoir aux Quat'Saisons, Great Milton, Oxon
Sharrow Bay, Ullswater, Cumbria
Inverlochy Castle, Fort William, Scotland
Walnut Tree, Abergavenny, Wales
Ballymaloe House, Shanagarry, Scotland

Egon Ronay Cellnet Guide Top Romantic Hotels

Blake's, London
Dorchester Terrace, London
Launceston Place, London
Odin's, London
Savoy River Room, London
Midsummer House, Cambridge

Le Talbooth, Dedham, Essex
Leatherne Bottel, Goring-on-Thames, Oxon
Michael's Nook, Grasmere, Cumbria
Pink Geranium, Melbourn, Cambs
Woodhayes, Whimple, Devon
Clifton Hotel, Nairn, Scotland
Auchterarder House, Auchterarder, Scotland
Inverlochy Castle, Fort William, Scotland
Old Rectory, Llansanffraid Glan Conwy, Wales
Château la Chaire, Rozel Bay, Jersey
Marlfield House, Gorey, Jersey

Egon Ronay's Top Twelve for Classic British Cooking

The Dorchester Grill, London
Greenhouse, London
Savoy Grill Room, London
Amberley Castle, Amberley, W. Sussex
Bond's, Castle Cary, Somerset
Belfry, Handforth, Cheshire
Weavers, Haworth, N. Yorks
Cliveden, Taplow, Bucks
Castle, Taunton, Somerset
Raemoir House, Banchory, Scotland
The Balmoral, Scotland Grill Room, Edinburgh
Champany Inn, Linlithgow

Egon Ronay Heinz Guide Awards

Recent awards, given for hotels and restaurants catering for families with children.

1992 Family Hotel of the Year Woolley Grange, Woolley Green, Bradford-on-Avon, Wilts
1992 Family Restaurant of the Year Bluebeckers, Odiham, Hants

MICHELIN HOTEL GUIDE, 1994

The 1994 awards from one of the longest-existing hotel guides were not good news for Britain. Indeed, there were murmurings in the kitchens of several fine restaurants when only 2 of the coveted '3-star' ratings went to British restaurants, and only 8 '2-star' ratings (France won 19 '3-star' and 84 '2-star' ratings).

3-star Awards

The Waterside Inn, Bray-on-Thames, Berks
La Tante Claire, London

2-star Awards

Le Gavroche, London
Chez Nico (Grosvenor House Hotel),
   London

The Restaurant (Hyde Park Hotel),
   London
Lettonie, Bristol
Paul Heathcote's, Longridge, Scotland
Le Manoir aux Quat' Saisons, Great Milton,
   Oxon
L'Ortolan, Reading, Berks
Altnaharrie Inn, Ullapool, Scotland

AA SELECTED HOTELS OF THE YEAR

Equally prestigious are the hotel awards given by the AA. Its top category of award is the Red Star. Some 96 hotels received this accolade in 1992–3.

A new award developed by the AA is its Selected Hotels of the Year. This new award was introduced for 1993 to recognize the AA hotel inspectors' top hotels in England, Scotland, Wales and Ireland.

Each year the AA's inspectors make a total of some four thousand visits, looking at every element of a hotel's operation. They are uniquely qualified to judge hotels ranging from the simplest to the most magnificent.

For this award there are no rigid guidelines for the hotels to meet, which means that every single one in the AA scheme has the chance of winning this accolade.

The four 1992–3 winners were:

England   Woolley Grange, Bradford-on-Avon, Wilts
Scotland   Loch Melford, Arduaine, Strathclyde
Wales   Ty Mawr, Brechfa, Dyfed
Ireland   Cromleach Lodge Country House, Castlebaldwin, Co. Sligo

GOOD HOTEL GUIDE CÉSAR AWARDS

The annual awards of Césars – named after the celebrated hotelier, César Ritz – are given for different sorts of excellence among hotels in Britain and Ireland. The categories listed below for 1994 show the wide range of hotels, inns and guest houses which fall within the *Good Hotel Guide* scope. Categories may vary from year to year.

For maintaining highest standards of hotelmanship through three generations

The Goring, London

For keeping untarnished the traditional values of the family seaside hotel

Treglos, Constantine Bay, Cornwall

Epitome of the English country hotel

Congham Hall, Grimston, Leics

Cottage idyll: No. 1 in the Dolls' House division

Little Hodgeham, Bethersden, Kent

For Scottish hospitality at its incomparable best	The Airds, Port Appin
Welsh hospitality at its best	The Old Rectory, Llansanffraid Glan Conwy
Irish hotel of the year	Hilton Park, Clones
Family hotel of the year	Philipburn House, Selkirk, Scotland
Excellence on Exmoor	Ashwick House, Dulverton, Somerset
For utterly enjoyable mild eccentricity	Hodgkinson's, Matlock Bath, Derbyshire

---

WHICH? HOTEL GUIDE HOTELS OF THE YEAR

Hotels have also attracted the eagle eye of the *Which? Hotel Guide*. Its 1994 edition picks out one hotel from each county that particularly caught its eye. They are not necessarily the most luxurious or expensive – indeed, there are several bed and breakfasts among them – but they all offer individual attention, comfort, a warm welcome and something just a little bit unusual. Not all counties have an award winner. The 1994 awards were:

London

London	Pippa Pop-ins

England

Avon	Queensberry, Bath
Bucks	Hartwell House, Aylesbury
Cambs	Chiswick House, Meldreth
Cheshire	White House Manor, Prestbury
Cornwall	Manor Farm, Crackington Haven
Cumbria	New House Farm, Lorton
Derbyshire	Hucklow Hall, Great Hucklow
Devon	Blackaller Hotel, North Bovey
Dorset	Hams Plot, Beaminster
Co. Durham	Lumley Castle, Chester-le-Street
E. Sussex	Netherfield Place, Netherfield
Essex	Whitehall, Broxted
Glos	Swan, Bibury
Greater Manchester	Victoria & Albert, Manchester
Hants	Gordleton Mill, Lymington
Hereford & Worcester	The Steppes, Ullingswick
Herts	Hall House, Hertford
Humberside	Winteringham Fields, Winteringham
Isle of Wight	Seaview Hotel, Seaview
Kent	Hancocks Farmhouse, Cranbrook
Lancs	River House, Poulton-le-Fylde
Lincs	Guy Wells, Whaplode
Norfolk	Morston Hall, Morston
Northants	Falcon, Castle Ashby
Northumberland	Low Barns, Corbridge
N. Yorks	White House, Harrogate
Oxon	Upper Green Farm, Towersey
Shropshire	Severn Lodge, Ironbridge
Somerset	Periton Park, Minehead

Staffs	Old Beams, Waterhouses
Suffolk	Otley House, Otley
Warwicks	Caterham House, Stratford-upon-Avon
West Midlands	Jonathans, Oldbury
W. Sussex	Angel, Midhurst
W. Yorks	Wellfield House, Huddersfield
Wilts	Old Vicarage, Burbage

Scotland

Borders	The Ley, Innerleithen
Dumfries & Galloway	Riverside Inn, Canonbie
Fife	Peat Inn, Peat Inn, nr Cupar
Grampian	Leslie Castle, Leslie
Highland	Tigh an Eilean, Shieldaig
Lothian	28 Northumberland Street, Edinburgh
Strathclyde	Crinan Hotel, Crinan
Tayside	Kinloch House, Blairgowrie

Wales

Clwyd	Starlings Castle, Chirk
Dyfed	Cnapan, Newport
Gwynedd	Ty'n Rhos, Llanddeiniolen
Powys	Monaughty Poeth, Llanfair Waterdine
South Glamorgan	Egerton Grey, Porthkerry

Channel Islands

| Guernsey | Idlerocks, St Martin's |

THE TIMES TOP TEN BEDROOMS

Announced in April 1994, the winners chosen by Robin Young for *The Times* (with prices in parentheses) were:

1. The Oliver Messel Suite, The Dorchester Hotel, Park Lane, London (£1000 plus VAT per night)

2. The Pasha Suite, Blakes Hotel, 33 Roland Gardens, London (£295 per night including service and tax)

3. The Round Bed Room, Portobello Hotel, 22 Stanley Gardens, London (£180 per night including breakfast and VAT)

4. The Lady Gretton Room, Stapleford Park, Stapleford, near Melton Mowbray, Leics (£210 per night, including VAT and continental breakfast)

5. The Gold Silk Room, The Sloane Hotel, 29 Draycott Place, London (£190 plus VAT per night)

6. Room No. 75, Croquet Lawn Room, Chewton Glen Hotel, New Milton, Hants (£280 per night including service and tax)

7. The Penthouse Suite, 42 The Calls, Leeds, Yorks (£185 per night including VAT and service)

8. The Dovecote, Manoir aux Quat'Saisons, Great Milton, Oxon (£325 per night including service and VAT)

9. The Lady Astor Suite, Cliveden, Taplow, near Maidenhead, Berks (£580 per night including service and VAT)

10. The Octagonal Four-poster Room, Franklin Hotel, 28 Egerton Gardens, London (£210 plus VAT per night)

HURLING

ALL-IRELAND CHAMPIONSHIPS

1945	Tipperary	1962	Tipperary	1979	Kilkenny
1946	Cork	1963	Kilkenny	1980	Galway
1947	Kilkenny	1964	Tipperary	1981	Offaly
1948	Waterford	1965	Tipperary	1982	Kilkenny
1949	Tipperary	1966	Cork	1983	Kilkenny
1950	Tipperary	1967	Kilkenny	1984	Cork
1951	Tipperary	1968	Wexford	1985	Offaly
1952	Cork	1969	Kilkenny	1986	Cork
1953	Cork	1970	Cork	1987	Galway
1954	Cork	1971	Tipperary	1988	Galway
1955	Wexford	1972	Kilkenny	1989	Tipperary
1956	Wexford	1973	Limerick	1990	Cork
1957	Kilkenny	1974	Kilkenny	1991	Tipperary
1958	Tipperary	1975	Kilkenny	1992	Limerick
1959	Waterford	1976	Cork	1993	Kilkenny
1960	Wexford	1977	Cork		
1961	Tipperary	1978	Cork		

HYMNS

The accolade for the most popular hymn goes to 'Dear Lord and Father of Mankind', according to a survey compiled by BBC1's *Songs of Praise* programme in 1992. The top six hymns requested for *Songs of Praise* were:

1. 'Dear Lord and Father of Mankind'
2. 'The Day Thou Gavest, Lord, Has Ended'
3. 'The Old Rugged Cross'
4. 'How Great Thou Art'
5. 'Abide With Me'
6. 'Shine, Jesus, Shine'

ICE HOCKEY

WORLD CHAMPIONSHIPS

1920	Canada	1935	Canada	1950	Canada
1924	Canada	1936	Great Britain	1951	Canada
1928	Canada	1937	Canada	1952	Canada
1930	Canada	1938	Canada	1953	Sweden
1931	Canada	1939	Canada	1954	USSR
1932	Canada	1947	Czechoslovakia	1955	Canada
1933	USA	1948	Canada	1956	USSR
1934	Canada	1949	Czechoslovakia	1957	Sweden

1958	Canada	1970	USSR	1982	USSR
1959	Canada	1971	USSR	1983	USSR
1960	USA	1972	Czechoslovakia	1984	USSR
1961	Canada	1973	USSR	1985	Czechoslovakia
1962	Sweden	1974	USSR	1986	USSR
1963	USSR	1975	USSR	1987	Sweden
1964	USSR	1976	Czechoslovakia	1988	USSR
1965	USSR	1977	Czechoslovakia	1989	USSR
1966	USSR	1978	USSR	1990	USSR
1967	USSR	1979	USSR	1991	Sweden
1968	USSR	1980	USA	1992	Sweden
1969	USSR	1981	USSR	1993	Russia

OLYMPIC GAMES

1920	Canada	1952	Canada	1976	USSR
1924	Canada	1956	USSR	1980	USA
1928	Canada	1960	USA	1984	USSR
1932	Canada	1964	USSR	1988	USSR
1936	Great Britain	1968	USSR	1992	CIS
1948	Canada	1972	USSR	1994	Sweden

BRITISH CHAMPIONSHIPS

1982	Dundee Rockets	1986	Murrayfield Racers	1990	Cardiff Devils
1983	Dundee Rockets	1987	Durham Wasps	1991	Durham Wasps
1984	Dundee Rockets	1988	Durham Wasps	1992	Durham Wasps
1985	Fife Flyers	1989	Nottingham Panthers	1993	Cardiff Devils

NORTH AMERICAN NATIONAL HOCKEY LEAGUE

1945	Toronto Maple Leafs	1964	Toronto Maple Leafs
1946	Montreal Canadiens	1965	Montreal Canadiens
1947	Toronto Maple Leafs	1966	Montreal Canadiens
1948	Toronto Maple Leafs	1967	Toronto Maple Leafs
1949	Toronto Maple Leafs	1968	Montreal Canadiens
1950	Detroit Red Wings	1969	Montreal Canadiens
1951	Toronto Maple Leafs	1970	Boston Bruins
1952	Detroit Red Wings	1971	Montreal Canadiens
1953	Montreal Canadiens	1972	Boston Bruins
1954	Detroit Red Wings	1973	Montreal Canadiens
1955	Detroit Red Wings	1974	Philadelphia Flyers
1956	Montreal Canadiens	1975	Philadelphia Flyers
1957	Montreal Canadiens	1976	Montreal Canadiens
1958	Montreal Canadiens	1977	Montreal Canadiens
1959	Montreal Canadiens	1978	Montreal Canadiens
1960	Montreal Canadiens	1979	Montreal Canadiens
1961	Chicago Black Hawks	1980	New York Islanders
1962	Toronto Maple Leafs	1981	New York Islanders
1963	Toronto Maple Leafs	1982	New York Islanders

1983	New York Islanders	1989	Calgary Flames
1984	Edmonton Oilers	1990	Edmonton Oilers
1985	Edmonton Oilers	1991	Pittsburgh Penguins
1986	Montreal Canadiens	1992	Pittsburgh Penguins
1987	Edmonton Oilers	1993	Montreal Canadiens
1988	Edmonton Oilers		

ICE SKATING

OLYMPIC GAMES

Men's Figure Skating

1908	Ulrich Salchow (Swe)
1920	Gillis Grafstrom (Swe)
1924	Gillis Grafstrom (Swe)
1928	Gillis Grafstrom (Swe)
1932	Karl Schafer (Aut)
1936	Karl Schafer (Aut)
1948	Richard Button (USA)
1952	Richard Button (USA)
1956	Hayes Alan Jenkins (USA)
1960	David Jenkins (USA)
1964	Manfred Schneldorfer (FRG)
1968	Wolfgang Schwarz (Aut)
1972	Ondrej Napela (Cze)
1976	John Curry (GB)
1980	Robin Cousins (GB)
1984	Scott Hamilton (USA)
1988	Brian Boitano (USA)
1992	Viktor Petrenko (CIS)
1994	Aleksi Urmanov (Rus)

Women's Figure Skating

1908	Madge Syers (GB)
1920	Magda Julin (Swe)
1924	Herma Planck-Szabo (Aut)
1928	Sonja Henie (Nor)
1932	Sonja Henie (Nor)
1936	Sonja Henie (Nor)
1948	Barbara Ann Scott (Can)
1952	Jeanette Altwegg (GB)
1956	Tenley Albright (USA)
1960	Carol Heiss (USA)
1964	Sjoukje Dijkstra (Hol)
1968	Peggy Fleming (USA)
1972	Beatrix Schuba (Aut)
1976	Dorothy Hamill (USA)
1980	Anett Potzsch (GDR)
1984	Katarina Witt (GDR)
1988	Katarina Witt (GDR)
1992	Kristi Yamaguchi (USA)
1994	Oksana Baiul (Ukr)

Pairs

1908	Anna Hubler and Heinrich Burger (Ger)
1920	Ludovika Jakobsson and Walter Jakobsson (Fin)
1924	Helene Engelmann and Alfred Berger (Aut)
1928	Andrée Joly and Pierre Brunet (Fra)
1932	Andrée Brunet (née Joly) and Pierre Brunet (Fra)
1936	Maxi Herber and Ernst Baier (Ger)
1948	Micheline Lannoy and Pierre Baugniet (Bel)
1952	Ria Falk and Paul Falk (Ger)
1956	Elisabeth Schwartz and Kurt Oppelt (Aut)
1960	Barbara Wagner and Robert Paul (Can)
1964	Lyudmila Belousova and Oleg Protopopov (USSR)
1968	Lyudmila Belousova and Oleg Protopopov (USSR)
1972	Irina Rodnina and Aleksey Ulanov (USSR)
1976	Irina Rodnina and Aleksandr Zaitsev (USSR)
1980	Irina Rodnina and Aleksandr Zaitsev (USSR)
1984	Yelena Valova and Oleg Vasiliev (USSR)

1988	Yekaterina Gordeyeva and Sergey Grinkov (USSR)
1992	Natalya Mishkutienok and Artur Dmitriyev (CIS)
1994	Ekaterina Gordeeva and Sergei Krinkov (Rus)

Ice Dancing

1976	Lyudmila Pakhomova and Aleksandr Gorshkov (USSR)
1980	Natalya Linitschuck and Gannadiy Karponosov (USSR)
1984	Jayne Torvill and Christopher Dean (GB)
1988	Natalya Bestemianova and Andre Bukin (USSR)
1992	Marina Klimova and Sergey Ponomarenko (CIS)
1994	Oksana Grichtuk and Yevgeny Platov (Rus)

Men's 500m Speed Skating

1924	Charles Jewtraw (USA)
1928	Bernt Evensen (Nor)
1932	John Shea (USA)
1936	Ivar Ballangrud (Nor)
1948	Finn Helgesen (Nor)
1952	Kenneth Henry (USA)
1956	Yevgeny Grishin (USSR)
1960	Yevgeny Grishin (USSR)
1964	Richard McDermott (USA)
1968	Erhard Keller (Ger)
1972	Erhard Keller (Ger)
1976	Yevgeny Kulikov (USSR)
1980	Eric Heiden (USA)
1984	Sergei Fokichev (USSR)
1988	Uwe-Jens Mey (GDR)
1992	Uwe-Jens Mey (Ger)
1994	Aleksandr Golubev (Rus)

Men's 1000m Speed Skating

1976	Peter Mueller (USA)
1980	Eric Heiden (USA)
1984	Gaetan Boucher (Can)
1988	Nikolay Gulyayev (USSR)
1992	Olaf Zinke (Ger)
1994	Daniel Jansen (USA)

Men's 1500m Speed Skating

1924	Claus Thunberg (Fin)
1928	Claus Thunberg (Fin)

1932	John Shea (USA)
1936	Charles Mathisen (Nor)
1948	Sverre Farstad (Nor)
1952	Hjalmar Andersen (Nor)
1956	Yevgeny Grishin (USSR)
1960	Roald Aas (Nor)
1964	Ants Antson (USSR)
1968	Cornelis Verkerk (Hol)
1972	Adrianus Schenk (Hol)
1976	Jan Egil Storholt (Nor)
1980	Eric Heiden (USA)
1984	Gaetan Boucher (Can)
1988	Andre Hoffman (GDR)
1992	Johann Olav Koss (Nor)
1994	Johann Olav Koss (Nor)

Men's 5000m Speed Skating

1924	Claus Thunberg (Fin)
1928	Ivar Ballangrud (Nor)
1932	Irving Jaffee (USA)
1936	Ivar Ballangrud (Nor)
1948	Reider Liaklev (Nor)
1952	Hjalmar Andersen (Nor)
1956	Boris Shilkov (USSR)
1960	Viktor Kosichkin (USSR)
1964	Knut Johannesen (Nor)
1968	Fred Anton Maier (Nor)
1972	Adrianus Schenk (Hol)
1976	Sten Stensen (Nor)
1980	Eric Heiden (USA)
1984	Tomas Gustafsson (Swe)
1988	Tomas Gustafsson (Swe)
1992	Geir Karlsrad (Nor)
1994	Johann Olav Koss (Nor)

Men's 10,000m Speed Skating

1924	Julius Skutnabb (Fin)
1932	Irving Jaffee (USA)
1936	Ivar Ballangrud (Nor)
1948	Ake Seyffarth (Swe)
1952	Hjalmar Andersen (Nor)
1956	Sigvard Ericsson (Swe)
1960	Knut Johannesen (Nor)
1964	Jonny Nilsson (Swe)
1968	Johnny Hoglin (Swe)
1972	Adrianus Schenk (Hol)
1976	Piet Kleine (Hol)
1980	Eric Heiden (USA)
1984	Igor Malkov (USSR)
1988	Tomas Gustafsson (Swe)
1992	Bart Veldkamp (Hol)
1994	Johann Olav Koss (Nor)

Women's 500m Speed Skating

1960	Helga Haase (GDR)
1964	Lydia Skoblikova (USSR)
1968	Lyudmila Titova (USSR)
1972	Anne Henning (USA)
1976	Sheila Young (USA)
1980	Karin Enke (GDR)
1984	Christa Rothenburger (GDR)
1988	Bonnie Blair (USA)
1992	Bonnie Blair (USA)
1994	Bonnie Blair (USA)

Women's 1000m Speed Skating

1960	Klara Guseva (USSR)
1964	Lydia Skoblikova (USSR)
1968	Carolina Geijssen (Hol)
1972	Monika Pflug (Ger)
1976	Tatiana Averina (USSR)
1980	Natalia Petruseva (USSR)
1984	Karin Enke (GDR)
1988	Christa Rothenburger (Hol)
1992	Bonnie Blair (USA)
1994	Bonnie Blair (USA)

Women's 1500m Speed Skating

1960	Lydia Skoblikova (USSR)
1964	Lydia Skoblikova (USSR)
1968	Kaija Mustonen (Fin)
1972	Dianne Holum (USA)
1976	Galina Stepanskaya (USSR)
1980	Annie Borckink (Hol)
1984	Karin Enke (GDR)
1988	Yvonne van Gennip (Hol)
1992	Jacqueline Berner (Ger)
1994	Emese Hunyadi (Aut)

Women's 3000m Speed Skating

1960	Lydia Skoblikova (USSR)
1964	Lydia Skoblikova (USSR)
1968	Johanna Schut (Hol)
1972	Christina Baas-Kaiser (Hol)
1976	Tatiana Averina (USSR)
1980	Bjorg Eva Jensen (Nor)
1984	Andrea Schone (GDR)
1988	Yvonne van Gennip (Hol)
1992	Gunda Niemann (Ger)
1994	Svetlana Bazhanova (Rus)

Women's 5000m Speed Skating

1988	Yvonne van Gennip (Hol)
1992	Gunda Niemann (Ger)
1994	Claudia Pechstein (Ger)

JUDO

OLYMPIC GAMES

Men's Over-95kg

1964	Isao Inokuma (Jap)
1972	Willem Ruska (Hol)
1976	Sergey Novikov (USSR)
1980	Angelo Parisi (Fra)
1984	Hitoshi Saito (Jap)
1988	Hitoshi Saito (Jap)
1992	Davici Khakkaleichvili (CIS)

Men's Under-95kg

1972	Shota Chochoshvili (USSR)
1976	Kazuhiro Ninomiya (Jap)
1980	Robert Van de Walle (Bel)
1984	Hyeung-Zoo Ha (SKo)
1988	Aurelio Miguel (Bra)
1992	Antal Kovacs (Hun)

Men's Under-86kg

1964	Isao Okano (Jap)
1972	Shinobu Sekine (Jap)
1976	Isamu Sonoda (Jap)
1980	Jurg Rothlisberger (Swi)
1984	Peter Seisenbacher (Aut)
1988	Peter Seisenbacher (Aut)
1992	Waldemar Legien (Pol)

Men's Under-78kg

1980	Shota Khabareli (USSR)
1984	Frank Weineke (FRG)
1988	Waldemar Legien (Pol)
1992	Hidehiko Yoshida (Jap)

Men's Under-71kg

1964	Takehide Nakatani (Jap)
1972	Toyokazu Nomura (Jap)
1976	Vladimir Nevzorov (USSR)
1980	Ezio Gamba (Ita)
1984	Byeong-Kuen Ahn (SKo)
1988	Marc Alexandre (Fra)
1992	Toshihiko Koga (Jap)

Men's Under-65kg

1972	Takao Kawaguchi (Jap)
1976	Hector Rodriguez (Cub)
1980	Nikoli Soludukhin (USSR)
1984	Yoshiyuki Matsuoda (Jap)
1988	Lee Kuung-Keun (SKo)
1992	Rogerio Sampalo (Bra)

Men's Under-60kg

1980	Thierry Rey (Fra)
1984	Shinji Hosokawa (Jap)
1988	Kim Jae-Yup (SKo)
1992	Nazim Gusseinov (CIS)

Women's Over-72kg

1992	Zhuang Xiaoyan (Chn)

Women's Under-72kg

1992	Mi-Jung Kim (SKo)

Women's Under-66kg

1992	Odalis Reve (Cub)

Women's Under-61kg

1992	Catherine Fleury (Fra)

Women's Under-56kg

1992	Miriam Blasco (Spa)

Women's Under-52kg

1992	Aimudena Munoz (Spa)

Women's Under-48kg

1992	Cécile Nowak (Fra)

KNITTING

THE CHILDREN'S SOCIETY SPONSORED KNITATHLON

This annual competition has been running since 1980. Two prizes are available, one for the individual raising the most money from a sponsored knit, the other for the greatest amount being raised by one of the Society's local fundraising committees. The prize for the individual raising the most money has always been a cut rose bowl. In 1992 an extra prize category of the most unusual venue for a 'knit-in' was introduced.

Since it began the competition has raised an average figure of £44,000 per annum. Over the years sponsorship has also been received from companies such as Patons and Baldwins (wool manufacturers), Littlewoods and *Prima* Magazine.

Some winning individuals who raised the most money were:

1985	Mrs J. Coe, Romney Marsh, Kent	1991	Mrs K. Swindells, Didcot, Oxon
1986	Mrs E. Gudgin, Hertford	1992	Mrs D. Cranmer, Abingdon, Oxon

LACROSSE

WORLD CHAMPIONSHIPS

Men's

1967	USA	1982	USA
1974	USA	1986	USA
1978	Canada	1990	USA

Women's

1982	USA		1989	USA
1986	Australia		1993	USA

LETTER-WRITING

ROYAL MAIL'S YOUNG LETTER-WRITER OF THE YEAR

This competition, organized by the Post Office in 1993, attracted 315,000 entries. Of the four prize-winners, perhaps the most surprising was twelve-year-old Japanese girl Yuki Imoto, who could not speak English when she first arrived in the country.

In her winning letter, Yuki wrote a letter back to Mars from a Martian inspector who had come to Earth and discovered terrible environment problems. 'He suggested the Martian Prime Minister should conquer Earth until it was better again, and not set us free until we had learned our lesson.'

LITERATURE

JAMES TAIT BLACK MEMORIAL PRIZES

Two prizes of £1,500 are awarded annually, one for the best biography (listed first below) or work of that nature and the other for the best work of fiction published during the calendar year (listed second below). The prizes were founded in memory of the partner in the publishing firm of A. & C. Black Ltd, and since 1979 they have been supplemented by the Scottish Arts Council.

1980	Robert Bernard Martin, *Tennyson: The Unquiet Heart* J. M. Coetzee, *Waiting for the Barbarians*	1985	David Nokes, *A Hypocrite Reversed* Robert Edric, *Winter Garden*
1981	Victoria Glendinning, *Edith Sitwell: A Unicorn among Lions* { Salman Rushdie, *Midnight's Children* Paul Théroux, *The Mosquito Coast*	1986	{ D. Felicitas Corrigan, *Helen Waddell* Jenny Joseph, *Persephone*
		1987	{ Ruth Dudley Edwards, *Victor Gollancz: a Biography* George Mackay Brown, *The Golden Bird: Two Orkney Stories*
1982	Richard Ellmann, *James Joyce* Bruce Chatwin, *On the Black Hill*	1988	Brian McGuinness, *Wittgenstein: A Life: Young Ludwig (1889–1921)* Piers Paul Read, *A Season in the West*
1983	Alan Walker, *Franz Liszt: The Virtuoso Years* Jonathan Keates, *Allegro Postillions*		
1984	Lyndall Gordon, *Virginia Woolf: a Writer's Life* { J. G. Ballard, *Empire of the Sun* Angela Carter, *Nights at the Circus*	1989	Ian Gibson, *Federico Garcia Lorca: A Life* James Kelman, *A Disaffection*
		1990	Claire Tomalin, *The Invisible Woman* William Boyd, *Brazzaville Beach*

1991	Adrian Desmond and James Moore, *Darwin*		Rose Tremain, *Sacred Country*
	Iain Sinclair, *Downriver*	1993	Caryll Phillips, *Crossing the River*
1992	Charles Nicholl, *The Reckoning: The Murder of Christopher Marlowe*		Richard Holmes, *Dr Johnson and Mr Savage*

BOOKER PRIZE FOR FICTION

£20,000 is awarded for the best full-length novel published in the UK and written in English by a citizen of Britain, the Commonwealth or the Republic of Ireland. Its intention is to reward merit, raise the stature of the author in the eyes of the public and increase the sale of books. This literary prize attracts more attention in the media than any other and its award is televised annually.

1980	Sir William Golding, *Rites of Passage*	1988	Peter Carey, *Oscar and Lucinda*
1981	Salman Rushdie, *Midnight's Children*	1989	Kazuo Ishiguro, *The Remains of the Day*
1982	Thomas Keneally, *Schindler's Ark*	1990	A. S. Byatt, *Possession*
1983	J. M. Coetzee, *Life and Times of Michael K*	1991	Ben Okri, *The Famished Road*
1984	Anita Brookner, *Hotel du Lac*	1992	Michael Ondaatje, *The English Patient* / Barry Unsworth, *Sacred Hunger*
1985	Keri Hulme, *The Bone People*	1993	Roddy Doyle, *Paddy Clarke Ha Ha Ha*
1986	Kingsley Amis, *The Old Devils*		
1987	Penelope Lively, *Moon Tiger*		

In 1993, the 25th anniversary of the prize, the 'Booker of Bookers', chosen as the best of all the prize-winning novels, was Salman Rushdie's *Midnight's Children* (1981).

ARTHUR C. CLARKE AWARD

£1,000 is awarded for the best science fiction novel published in the UK. The award is named after the celebrated author of science fiction, Arthur C. Clarke (b. 1917).

1987	Margaret Atwood, *The Handmaid's Tale*	1990	Geoff Ryman, *The Child Garden*
1988	George Turner, *The Sea and the Summer*	1991	Colin Greenland, *Take Back Plenty*
1989	Rachel Pollack, *Unquenchable Fire*	1992	Pat Cadigan, *Synners*
		1993	Marge Piercy, *Body of Glass*
		1994	Jeff Noon, *Ringpull*

DAVID COHEN BRITISH LITERATURE PRIZE

This prize of £30,000, derived from the trust fund of the David Cohen Family Charitable Trust, is the biggest literary award in Britain. It is administered by the Arts Council in partnership with the bankers Coutts & Co. and is awarded every two years. The prize is given to a living British writer, novelist, short-story writer, poet, essayist or dramatist in recognition of his or her entire body of work. Another £10,000 is given by the Arts Council to enable the winner to commission new writing.

1993   Sir V. S. Naipaul

COMMONWEALTH WRITERS' PRIZE

These prizes, sponsored by the Commonwealth Foundation, are awarded for works of fiction (a novel or a collection of short stories) written in English by a citizen of the Commonwealth and published in the preceding year. Since 1989, the Commonwealth Writers' Prize of £10,000 has been awarded for the best book and a further prize of £2,000 for the best first published book (listed second below).

1987	Olive Senior (Jam), *Summer Lightning*		Pauline Melville (Guy), *Shape-Shifter*
1988	Festus Iyayi (Nig), *Heroes*	1992	Rohinton Mistry (Can), *Such a Long Journey*
1989	Janet Frame (NZ), *The Carpathians*		Robert Antoni (Bah), *Divina Trace*
	Bonnie Burnard (Can), *Women of Influence*	1993	Alex Miller (Aus), *The Ancestor Game*
1990	Mordecai Richler (Can), *Solomon Gursky was Here*		Githa Hariharan (Ind), *The Thousand Faces of Night*
	John Cranna (NZ), *Visitors*		
1991	David Malouf (Aus), *The Great World*		

THE DUFF COOPER PRIZE

£500 is awarded for a biographical or literary work, published by a recognized publisher in English or French during the preceding two years. Alfred Duff Cooper, the first Viscount Norwich (1890–1954), was a prominent politician, diplomatist and author, who held several ministerial posts and was the ambassador to France in 1944–47. After his death, an endowment fund was established in his memory. The judges are Artemis Cooper, Lord Norwich's granddaughter, and the Warden of New College, Oxford.

1980	Robert Bernard Martin, *Tennyson: the Unquiet Heart*	1988	Humphrey Carpenter, *A Serious Character: the Life of Ezra Pound*
1981	Victoria Glendinning, *Edith Sitwell: A Unicorn among Lions*	1989	Ian Gibson, *Federico Garcia Lorca: a Life*
1982	Richard Ellmann, *James Joyce*	1990	Hugh and Mirabel Cecil, *Clever Hearts*
1983	Peter Porter, *Collected Poems*		
1984	Hilary Spurling, *Ivy Compton-Burnett*	1991	Ray Monk, *Ludwig Wittgenstein: the Duty of Genius*
1985	Ann Thwaite, *Edmund Gosse: A Literary Landscape*	1992	Peter Hennessy, *Never Again: 1945–51*
1986	Alan Crawford, *C. R. Ashbee: Architect, Designer and Romantic Socialist*	1993	John Keegan, *A History of Warfare*
1987	Robert Hughes, *The Fatal Shore*		

CRIME WRITERS' ASSOCIATION AWARDS

John Creasey, the popular author of detective fiction, convened the first meeting of the Crime Writers' Association on 5 November 1953, and was its chairman from 1953 to 1957.

1980	Gold Dagger: H. R. F. Keating, *The Murder of the Maharajah* Silver Dagger: Ellis Peters, *Monk's Hood*
1981	Gold Dagger: Martin Cruz Smith, *Gorky Park* Silver Dagger: Colin Dexter, *The Dead of Jericho*
1982	Gold Dagger: Peter Lovesey, *The False Inspector Dew* Silver Dagger: S. T. Hamon, *Ritual Murder*
1983	Gold Dagger: John Hutton, *Accidental Crimes* Silver Dagger: William McIlvanney, *The Papers of Tony Veitch*
1984	Gold Dagger: B. M. Gill, *The Twelfth Juror* Silver Dagger: Ruth Rendell, *The Tree of Hands*
1985	Gold Dagger: Paula Gosling, *Monkey Puzzle* Silver Dagger: Dorothy Simpson, *Last Seen Alive*
1986	Diamond Dagger: Eric Ambler Gold Dagger: Ruth Rendell, *Live Flesh* Silver Dagger: P. D. James, *A Taste for Death*
1987	Diamond Dagger: P. D. James Gold Dagger: Barbara Vine (Ruth Rendell), *A Fatal Inversion* Silver Dagger: Scott Turow, *Presumed Innocent*

1988	Diamond Dagger: John le Carré Gold Dagger: Michael Dibdin, *Ratking* Silver Dagger: Sara Paretsky, *Toxic Shock*
1989	Diamond Dagger: Dick Francis Gold Dagger: Colin Dexter, *The Wench is Dead* Silver Dagger: Desmond Lowden, *The Shadow Run*
1990	Diamond Dagger: Julian Symons Gold Dagger: Reginald Hill, *Bones and Silence* Silver Dagger: Mike Phillips, *The Late Candidate*
1991	Diamond Dagger: Ruth Rendell Gold Dagger: Barbara Vine, *King Solomon's Carpet* Silver Dagger: Frances Fyfield, *Deep Sleep*
1992	Diamond Dagger: Leslie Charteris Gold Dagger: Colin Dexter, *The Way Through the Woods* Silver Dagger: Liza Cody, *Bucket Nut*
1993	Diamond Dagger: Ellis Peters Gold Dagger: Patricia Cornwell, *Cruel and Unusual* Silver Dagger: Sarah Dunant, *Fatlands*

FAWCETT SOCIETY BOOK PRIZE

£500 is awarded to the author of a book that has substantially contributed to the understanding of women's social position today. The prize is given alternately to works of fiction and non-fiction. Dame Millicent (Mrs Henry) Fawcett (1847–1929) was a leader of the women's suffrage movement from the 1860s onwards. The Fawcett Society has campaigned for equality between men and women since 1866. All the works submitted for the prize are placed in the Fawcett Library of the London Guildhall University.

| 1982 | Margaret Stacey and Marion Price, *Women, Power and Politics* |
| 1983 | Pat Barker, *Union Street* Zee Edgell, *Beka Lamb* |

1984	Caroline Steedman, *The Tidy House*
1985	Zoe Fairbairns, *Here Today*
1986	Marina Warner, *Monuments and Maidens*

1987	Shena Mackay, *Redhill Rococo*		Lucy Hughes-Hallett, *Cleopatra:*
1988	Beatrix Campbell, *Iron Ladies: Why do Women Vote Tory?*	1992	*Histories, Dreams and Distortions* Jacqueline Rose, *The Haunting*
1989	Stevie Smith, *Boy Blue*		*of Sylvia Plath*
1990	Jill Liddington, *The Long Road to Greenham*	1993	Jung Chang, *Wild Swans*
1991	Jennifer Dawson, *Judasland*	1994	Margaret Forster, *Daphne du Maurier*

PRIX GONCOURT

50 francs is awarded for the best prose work in French. This is the most prestigious of French literary awards. The Brothers Goncourt (Edmond 1822–96 and Jules 1830–70) were a celebrated literary partnership. Edmond Goncourt left money to found the Académie Goncourt, which awards the prize.

1980	Yves Navarre, *Le Jardin d'acclimatation*	1988	Erik Orsenna, *L'Exposition Coloniale*
1981	Lucien Bodard, *Anne-Marie*	1989	Jean Vautrin, *Un grand pas vers le bon Dieu*
1982	Dominique Fernandez, *Dans la main de l'ange*	1990	Jean Rouaud, *Les Champs d'Honneur*
1983	Frédérick Tristan, *Les Egarés*		
1984	Marguerite Duras, *L'Amant*	1991	Pierre Combescot, *Les Filles du Calvaire*
1985	Yann Queffelec, *Les Noces Barbares*	1992	Patrick Chamoiseau, *Texaco*
1986	Michel Host, *Valet de Nuit*	1993	Amin Maalouf, *Le Rocher de Tanios*
1987	Tahar Ben Jelloun, *La Nuit sacrée*		

GUARDIAN FICTION AWARD

A total of £3,500 (£2,000 for the winner and £500 for each of three others in the short list) is given for works of fiction by authors of British, Commonwealth or Irish origins that show promise and originality. There is a bias in favour of a first book and a tradition that the prize does not go to anyone who has already won a major prize.

1980	J. L. Carr, *A Month in the Country*	1986	Jim Crace, *Continent*
1981	John Banville, *Kepler*	1987	Peter Benson, *The Levels*
1982	Glyn Hughes, *Where I Used to Play on the Green*	1988	Lucy Ellmann, *Sweet Desserts*
		1989	Carol Lake, *Rose Hill*
1983	Graham Swift, *Waterland*	1990	Pauline Melville, *Shape Shifter*
1984	J. G. Ballard, *Empire of the Sun*	1991	Alan Judd, *The Devil's Own Work*
1985	Peter Ackroyd, *Hawksmoor*	1992	Alasdair Gray, *Poor Things*
		1993	Pat Barker, *The Eye in the Door*

HAWTHORNDEN PRIZE

£2,000 is awarded for a work of imaginative literature by a British subject under 41 years of age published during the previous year. The prize was founded by Miss Alice Warrender. Winners in its earlier years included Siegfried Sassoon, Robert Graves, Evelyn Waugh and Graham Greene.

1980	Christopher Reid, *Arcadia*	1981	Douglas Dunn, *St Kilda's Parliament*

1982	Timothy Mo, *Sour Sweet*		1990	Kit Wright, *Short Afternoons*
1983	Jonathan Keates, *Allegro Postillions*		1991	Claire Tomalin, *The Invisible Woman*
1984–7	no awards		1992	Ferdinand Mount, *Of Love and Asthma*
1988	Colin Thubron, *Behind the Wall*			
1989	Alan Bennett, *Talking Heads*		1993	Andrew Barrow, *The Tap Dancer*

WILLIAM HILL SPORTS BOOK OF THE YEAR

The prizes given in this annual award are a £3,000 cheque, a £500 free bet, and a leatherbound copy of the winning book.

1989	Patrick Robinson, *Daniel Topolski: True Blue*	1991	Thomas Hauser, *Muhammad Ali*
		1992	Nick Hornby, *Fever Pitch*
1990	Paul Kimmage, *Rough Ride*	1993	Stephen Jones, *Endless Winter*

SIR PETER KENT CONSERVATION BOOK PRIZE

£5,000 is awarded in the adult category and £2,000 in the children's category. The prizes are given for the best books on environmental issues published in the UK in the preceding calendar year. Sir Peter Kent (1913–86), the distinguished geologist, was a member and later the chairman of the Natural Environment Research Council. The prize was established in 1987, the European Year of the Environment.

1987	Chris Baines, *The Wild Side of Town*		Fred Pearce and Ian Winton, *Ian & Fred's Big Green Book*
1988	Jeremy Purseglove, *Taming the Flood*	1992	Iain and Oria Douglas-Hamilton, *Battle for the Elephants*
1989	Philip Wayre, *Operation Otter*		no children's winner
1990	Jonathan Kingdon, *Island Africa*		
1991	George Monbiot, *Amazon Watershed*	1993	Edward O. Wilson, *The Diversity of Life*
	Children's joint winners: Marie Friend, *Small Wonder*		Jo Readman, *Muck and Magic*

THE *MAIL ON SUNDAY* JOHN LLEWELLYN RHYS PRIZE

£5,000 is awarded for a work of fiction, poetry, drama or non-fiction by a writer under the age of 35 at the time of publication. The prize was founded by Jane Oliver, the widow of a writer killed in action in the Second World War, and is now sponsored by the *Mail on Sunday*.

1980	Desmond Hogan, *The Diamonds at the Bottom of the Sea*	1987	Jeanette Winterson, *The Passion*
		1988	Matthew Yorke, *The March Fence*
1981	A. N. Wilson, *The Laird of Abbotsford*	1989	Claire Harman, *Sylvia Townsend Warner*
1982	William Boyd, *An Ice-Cream War*	1990	Ray Monk, *Ludwig Wittgenstein*
1983	Lisa St Aubin de Teran, *The Slow Train to Milan*	1991	A. L. Kennedy, *Night Geometry and the Garscadden Trains*
1984	Andrew Motion, *Dangerous Play*	1992	Matthew Kneale, *Sweet Thames*
1985	John Milne, *Out of the Blue*	1993	Jason Goodwin, *On Foot to the Golden Horn*
1986	Tim Parks, *Loving Roger*		

SOMERSET MAUGHAM AWARDS

Three awards of £5,000–£6,000 each are given on the strength of the promise of a published work. Poetry, fiction, criticism, biography, history, philosophy, belles lettres, and travel books are all eligible for the awards, but not dramatic works. The winners are required to use the money for a period or periods of foreign travel. It was the intention of Somerset Maugham (1874–1965), the novelist, short-story writer and playwright, that young writers should be able to enrich their writing by experience in foreign countries.

1980	Max Hastings, *Bomber Command*		Carol Ann Duffy, *Selling Manhattan*
	Christopher Reid, *Arcadia*		Matthew Kneale, *Whore Banquets*
	Humphrey Carpenter, *The Inklings*	1989	Robert Christiansen, *Romantic Affinities*
1981	Julian Barnes, *Metroland*		Allan Hollinghurst, *The Swimming-Pool Library*
	Clive Sinclair, *Hearts of Gold*		
	A. N. Wilson, *The Healing Art*		Deirdre Madden, *The Bird of the Innocent Wood*
1982	William Boyd, *A Good Man in Africa*		
	Adam Mars-Jones, *Lantern Lecture*	1990	Mark Hudson, *Our Grandmothers' Drums*
1983	Lisa St Aubin de Teran, *Keepers of the House*		Sam North, *The Automatic Man*
			Nicholas Shakespeare, *The Vision of Elena Silves*
1984	Peter Ackroyd, *The Last Testament of Oscar Wilde*		
		1991	Peter Benson, *The Other Occupant*
	Timothy Garton Ash, *The Polish Revolution: Solidarity*		
			Lesley Glaister, *Honour Thy Father*
	Sean O'Brien, *The Indoor Park*		
1985	Blake Morrison, *Dark Glasses*		Helen Simpson, *Four Bare Legs on a Bed*
	Jeremy Reed, *By the Fisheries*		
	Jane Rogers, *Her Living Image*	1992	Geoff Dyer, *But Beautiful*
1986	Patricia Ferguson, *Family Myths and Legends*		Lawrence Norfolk, *Lemprière's Dictionary*
	Adam Nicolson, *Frontiers*		Gerard Woodward, *Householder*
	Tim Parks, *Tongues of Flame*	1992	Jackie Kay, *Other Lovers*
1987	Stephen Gregory, *The Cormorant*		A. L. Kennedy, *Looking for the Possible Dance*
	Ganni Howker, *Isaac Campion*		
	Andrew Motion, *The Lamberts*		Philip Marsden, *The Crossing Place*
1988	Jimmy Burns, *The Land that Lost its Heroes*		

THE McVITIE'S PRIZE FOR SCOTTISH WRITER OF THE YEAR

£10,000 is awarded to the overall winner, with £500 going to each of four other shortlisted writers. The prize is sponsored by United Biscuits (Holdings plc). Its aim is to encourage and promote Scottish literary excellence over a broad range of writing genres.

1987	David Thomson, *Nairn in Darkness and Light*	1990	Sorley MacLean, *From Wood to Ridge*
1988	Bernard MacLaverty, *The Great Profundo and Other Stories*	1991	William Boyd, *Brazzaville Beach*
		1992	John Purser, *Scotland's Music*
	Edwin Mickleburgh, *Antarctica: Beyond the Frozen Sea*	1993	John Prebble, *Landscapes and Memories*
1989	Alan Bold, *MacDiarmid*		

NATURAL WORLD BOOK OF THE YEAR AWARD

£500 is awarded for an outstanding book on British wildlife or the countryside. The book should inform and entertain its readers and be an original piece of work. The award was started in 1987.

1987	Norman Moore, *The Bird of Time*	1991	Jeremy Thomas and Richard
1988	David Macdonald, *Running with*		Lewington, *The Butterflies of*
	the Fox		*Britain and Ireland*
1989	Marjorie Blamey and Christopher	1992	Philippa Scott, *The Art of Peter*
	Grey-Wilson, *The Illustrated Flora*		*Scott*
	of Britain and Northern Europe	1993	Richard Fortey, *The Hidden*
1990	Janet Kear, *Man and Wildfowl*		*Landscape*

NCR BOOK AWARD

A first prize of £25,000 and three prizes of £1,500 for shortlisted authors are awarded for the best work of non-fiction published by a British publisher for the first time in the twelve months between 1 April and 31 March.

1988	David Thomson, *Nairn in*	1992	Jung Chang, *Wild Swans*
	Darkness and Light	1993	Peter Hennessy, *Never Again*
1989	Joe Simpson, *Touching the Void*	1994	John Campbell, *Edward Heath:*
1990	Simon Schama, *Citizens*		*a Biography*
1991	Claire Tomalin, *The Invisible Woman*		

NOBEL PRIZE FOR LITERATURE

For a note on the Nobel Prizes, see p. 206.

1945	Gabriela Mistral (Chi)	1964	Jean-Paul Sartre (Fra) Prize
1946	Hermann Hesse (Swi) (German-		declined
	born)	1965	Mikhail Sholokhov (USSR)
1947	André Gide (Fra)	1966	Shmuel Yosef Agnon (Isr)
1948	T. S. Eliot (GB) (USA-born)		(Austrian-born)
1949	William Faulkner (USA)		Nelly Sachs (Swe) (German-born)
1950	Bertrand Russell (GB)	1967	Miguel Angel Asturias (Gua)
1951	Par F. Lagerkvist (Swe)	1968	Yasunari Kawabata (Jap)
1952	François Mauriac (Fra)	1969	Samuel Beckett (Ire)
1953	Sir Winston Churchill (GB)	1970	Aleksandr. I. Solzhenitsyn (USSR)
1954	Ernest Hemingway (USA)	1971	Pablo Neruda (Chi)
1955	Halldor K. Laxness (Ice)	1972	Heinrich Boll (Ger)
1956	Juan Ramon Jimenez (PR)	1973	Patrick White (Aus)
	(Spanish-born)	1974	Eyvind Johnson (Swe)
1957	Albert Camus (Fra)		Harry Edmund Martinson (Swe)
1958	Boris L. Pasternak (USSR) Prize	1975	Eugenio Montale (Ita)
	declined	1976	Saul Bellow (USA)
1959	Salvatore Quasimodo (Ita)	1977	Vicente Aleixandre (Spa)
1960	Saint-John Perse (Fra)	1978	Isaac Bashevis Singer (USA)
1961	Ivo Andric (Yug)	1979	Odysseus Elytis (Odysseus
1962	John Steinbeck (USA)		Alepoudelis) (Gre)
1963	George Seferis (Gre)	1980	Czeslaw Milosz (Pol)

1981	Elias Canetti (GB, Bulgarian-born)	1987	Joseph Brodsky (US, USSR-born)
1982	Gabriel Garcia Márquez (Mex, Columbian-born)	1988	Naguib Mahfouz (Egy)
		1989	Camilo José Cela (Spa)
		1990	Octavio Paz (Mex)
1983	William Golding (GB)	1991	Nadine Gordimer (SAf)
1984	Jaroslav Seifert (Cze)	1992	Derek Walcott (StL)
1985	Claude Simon (Fra)	1993	Toni Morrison (USA)
1986	Wole Soyinka (Nig)		

PEN LITERARY PRIZES

PEN, a world association of writers, was founded in 1921 by C. A. Dawson Scott under the presidency of John Galsworthy. The prizes are the J. R. Ackerley Prize for Autobiography (£2,000), the Macmillan Silver Pen Award for Fiction (£500 and a silver pen) and the Time Life Silver Pen Award for Non-fiction (£1,000 and a silver pen).

The Silver Pen Award

| 1984 | Tony Gould, *Inside Outsider* |
| 1985 | Colin Thubron, *A Cruel Madness* |

Macmillan Silver Pen Award for Fiction

1986	A. S. Byatt, *Still Life*
1987	Lewis Nkosi, *Mating Birds*
1988	A. L. Barker, *The Gooseboy*
1989	Molly Keane, *Loving and Giving* / Marina Warner, *The Lost Father*
1990	V. S. Pritchett, *A Careless Widow, and other stories*
1991	Pauline Melville, *Shape-Shifter*
1992	John Arden, *Cogs Tyrannic*
1993	George Steiner, *Proofs and Three Parables*
1994	Nicola Barker, *Love Your enemies* / Clive Collins, *Misunderstandings*

Time Life Silver Pen Award for Non-fiction

1986	Michael Scammell, *Solzhenitsyn*
1987	Patrick Leigh Fermor, *Between the Woods and the Water*
1988	John Miller, *Friends and Romans: On the Run in Wartime Italy*
1989	Brenda Maddox, *Nora*
1990	William St Clair, *The Godwins and the Shelleys*
1991	Susan Richards, *Epics of Everyday Life*
1992	Alan Bullock, *Hitler and Stalin: Parallel Lives*
1993	Brian Keenan, *An Evil Cradling*
1994	John Hale, *The Civilisation of Europe in the Renaissance*

J. R. Ackerley Prize for Autobiography

1982	Edward Blishen, *Shaky Relations*
1983	Kathleen Dayus, *Her People* / Ted Walker, *The High Path*
1984	Richard Cobb, *Still Life*
1985	Angelica Garnett, *Deceived with Kindness*
1986	Dan Jacobson, *Time and Time Again*
1987	Diana Athill, *After the Funeral*
1988	Anthony Burgess, *Little Wilson and Big God*
1989	John Healy, *The Grass Arena*
1990	Germaine Greer, *Daddy We Hardly Knew You*
1991	Paul Binding, *St Martin's Ride*
1992	John Osborne, *Almost A Gentleman*
1993	Barry Humphries, *More, Please*
1994	Blake Morrison, *And When Did You Last See Your Father?*

PULITZER PRIZES

These awards are made by Columbia University, New York. Awards (currently worth $3,000 each) are given for American work in various categories of journalism, letters and music (i.e., composition). Fellowships worth $5,000 each are awarded to graduates of the Graduate School of Journalism of the University. Joseph Pulitzer (1847–1911) was a reporter, editor and publisher, who founded the Graduate School and the prizes. He expressly hoped that the prizes would encourage 'public service, public morals, American literature and the advancement of education'. Perhaps the most well-known of these in the UK is that for fiction.

Fiction

1980	Norman Mailer, *The Executioner's Song*
1981	John Kennedy Toole, *A Confederacy of Dunces*
1982	John Updike, *Rabbit is Rich*
1983	Alice Walker, *The Color Purple*
1984	William Kennedy, *Ironweed*
1985	Alison Lurie, *Foreign Affairs*
1986	Larry McMurtry, *Lonesome Dove*
1987	Peter Taylor, *A Summons to Memphis*
1988	Toni Morrison, *Beloved*
1989	Anne Tyler, *Breathing Lessons*
1990	Oscar Hijuelos, *The Mambo Kings Play Songs of Love*
1991	John Updike, *Rabbit at Rest*
1992	Jane Smiley, *A Thousand Acres*
1993	Robert Olen Butler, *A Good Scent from a Strange Mountain*

THE SALTIRE LITERARY AWARDS

£5,000 is awarded for the Scottish Book of the Year and, from 1988, £1,500 for the Scottish First Book of the Year. The awards are sponsored by the *Scotsman* and Scottish Television and administered by the Saltire Society. They are given for any new book by an author (A) or poet (P) of Scottish descent or living in Scotland, or to a book by anyone which deals with the work or life of a Scot or with a Scottish question, event or situation.

Scottish Book of the Year

1984	David Daiches (A/P), *God and the Poets* Tom Leonard (A), *Intimate Voices*
1985	Norman MacCaig (P), *Collected Poems*
1986	Stuart Hood (A), *A Storm from Paradise*
1987	Muriel Spark (A), *The Stories of Muriel Spark*
1988	Neal Ascherson (A), *Games with Shadows* Tom Nairn (A), *The Enchanted Glass*
1989	Allan Massie (A), *A Question of Loyalties*
1990	Sorley MacLean (P), *From Wood to Ridge*
1991	Duncan MacMillan (A), *Scottish Art: 1460–1990*
1992	Iain Crichton Smith (P), *Collected Poems*
1993	James Mackay (A), *Robert Burns: A Biography*

Scottish First Book of the Year

1988	Raymond Vettese (A), *The Richt Noise*
1989	Sian Hayton (A), *Cells of Knowledge*
1990	Harry Tait (A), *The Ballad of Sawney Bain*
1991	A. L. Kennedy (A), *Night Geometry and the Garscadden Trains*
1992	Jackie Kay (P), *The Adoption Papers* Crisdean Whyte (P), *Uirsgeul: myth*
1993	Ian Bell (A), *Dreams of Exile: A Life of Robert Louis Stevenson*

SCIENCE BOOK PRIZES

The prizes, administered by COPUS (the Committee on the Public Understanding of Science) and the Science Museum, London, and sponsored since 1991 by Rhône-Poulenc Ltd, are awarded for books that contribute to public understanding of science and technology. The Rhône-Poulenc Prize of £10,000 is given for books intended for a general readership. A total sum of £10,000 is also given for books of a younger category written for children.

General Category

1988	British Medical Association Board of Science, *Living with Risk*
1989	Roger Lewin, *Bones of Contention*
1990	Roger Penrose, *The Emperor's New Mind*
1991	Stephen Jay Gould, *Wonderful Life*
1992	Jared Diamond, *The Rise and Fall of the Third Chimpanzee*
1993	Steven Rose, *The Making of Memory*
1994	Steve Jones, *The Language of the Genes*

Younger Category

1988	Roger Kerrod, *Science Alive – Living Things*
1989	David Macaulay and Neil Ardley, *The Way Things Work*
1990	(under-14) Susan Mayes, *Starting Point Science Series:*

What Makes a Flower Grow?
What Makes It Rain?
What's Under the Ground?
Where Does Electricity Come From?
(under-8)
Ian Ridpath, *The Giant Book of Space*

1991	Fran Balkwill and Mic Rolph, *Cells are Us* and *Cell Wars*
1992	Peter Rowan, *The Amazing Voyage of the Cucumber Sandwich* David Burnie, *How Nature Works*
1993	Thompson Yardley, *Mighty Microbes*
1994	Linda Gamlin, *Eyewitness Guide: Evolution* David Lambert, *The Ultimate Dinosaur Book* Rebecca Heddle and Paul Shipton, *Science with Weather*

W. H. SMITH LITERARY AWARD

£10,000 is awarded to the Commonwealth author whose book makes, in the opinion of the judges, the most outstanding contribution to literature.

1980	Thom Gunn, *Selected Poems*	1988	Robert Hughes, *The Fatal Shore*
1981	Isabel Colegate, *The Shooting Party*	1989	Christopher Hill, *A Turbulent, Seditious and Factious People: John Bunyan and his Church*
1982	George Clare, *Last Waltz in Vienna*	1990	V. S. Pritchett, *A Careless Widow, and Other Stories*
1983	A. N. Wilson, *Wise Virgin*	1991	Derek Walcott, *Omeros*
1984	Philip Larkin, *Required Writing*	1992	Thomas Pakenham, *The Scramble for Africa*
1985	David Hughes, *The Pork Butcher*		
1986	Doris Lessing, *The Good Terrorist*	1993	Michèle Roberts, *Daughters of the House*
1987	Elizabeth Jennings, *Collected Poems*	1994	Vikram Seth, *A Suitable Boy*

BETTY TRASK AWARDS

A total of £26,000 for published or unpublished first novels of a traditional or romantic (and not experimental) nature by authors under thirty-five who are Commonwealth citizens. The numbers of prizewinners vary from year to year. According to Joanna Trollope, the chairman of the 1993 jury, Betty Trask 'wanted the prize to go to a mass-market book'.

1984	Ronald Frame, *Winter Journey*
	Claire Nonhebel, *Cold Showers*
1985	Susan Kay, *Legacy*
1986	Tim Parks, *Tongues of Flame*
	Patricia Ferguson, *Family Myths and Legends*
1987	James Maw, *Hard Luck*
1988	Alex Martin, *The General Interruptor*
	Candia McWilliam, *A Case of Knives*
1989	Nigel Watts, *The Life Game*
	William Riviere, *Watercolour Sky*
	Paul Horton, *Harry's Last Wedding*
	Alasdair McKee, *Uncle Henry's Last Stand*

1990	Robert McLiam Wilson, *Ripley Bogle*
	Elizabeth Chadwick, *The Wild Hunt*
	Rosemary Cohen, *No Strange Land*
	Nicholas Shakespeare, *The Vision of Elena Silves*
1991	Amit Chaudhuri, *A Strange and Sublime Address*
1992	Liane Jones, *The Dream Stone*
1993	Mark Blackaby, *You'll Never Be Here Again*
1994	Colin Bateman, *Divorcing Jack*
	Nadeem Aslam, *Season of the Rainbirds*

THOMAS COOK TRAVEL BOOK AWARDS

£7,500 is awarded for the best travel book, £2,500 for the best guide book and £1,000 for the best illustrated guide. The famous travel company began on 5 July 1841, the date of Thomas Cook's first excursion, and has archives dating from that time. It also runs an annual poetry competition to promote travel poetry.

Travel Books

1980	Robyn Davidson, *Tracks*
1981	Jonathan Raban, *Old Glory*
1982	Tim Severin, *The Sinbad Voyage*
1983	Vikram Seth, *From Heaven Lake*
1984	Geoffrey Moorhouse, *To the Frontier*
1985	Patrick Marnham, *So Far From God*
1986/7	Patrick Leigh Fermor, *Between the Woods and the Water*
1988	Colin Thubron, *Behind the Wall*
1989	Paul Theroux, *Riding the Iron Rooster*
1990	Mark Hudson, *Our Grandmothers' Drums*
1991	Jonathan Raban, *Hunting Mister Heartbreak*
1992	Norman Lewis, *A Goddess in the Stones*
	Gavin Young, *In Search of Conrad*
1993	Nik Cohn, *The Heart of the World*

Guide Books

| 1980 | John Brooks (ed), *The 1980 South American Handbook* |

1981	Evelyn Garside, *China Companion*
1982	G. Crowther, *Pa Raj* and T. Wheeler, *India*
1983	Michael Leapman, *Companion Guide to New York*
1984	Hugh McKnight, *Cruising French Waterways*
1985	Henry Thorold, *Shell Guide to Nottinghamshire*
1986/7	Fontana/Hachette *Guide to France*
1988	Stephen Batchelor, *The Tibet Guide*
	Charlie Waite and James Bentley, *Languedoc* (illustrated guide)
1989	John and Pat Underwood, *Landscapes of Madeira*
	Richard B. Fisher and Tom Ang, *The Marco Polo Expedition* (illustrated guide)
1990	Bernard McDonagh, *Blue Guide Turkey*
	Eric Newby, *What the Traveller Saw* (illustrated guide)
1991	Ben Box and Sarah Cameron, *Caribbean Islands Handbook*
1992	Fran Hazelton, *London's American Past*

Gordon Stainforth, *Eyes to the Hills* (illustrated guide)

1993 Paul Gray and Lucy Ridout, *Thailand*

TRAVEL WRITER OF THE YEAR

Among the many categories of British Book Awards (see p. 55) is the Travel Writer of the Year award. Recent winners were:

1989 Peter Mayle, *A Year in Provence*
1990 V. S. Naipaul, *India*
1991 Mark Shand, *Travels on my Elephant*

1992 Michael Palin, *Pole to Pole*

WELSH ARTS COUNCIL BOOK OF THE YEAR AWARD

These are awarded for works of exceptional merit by Welsh authors (by birth or residence) published during the previous calendar year. Separate prizes are given for works written in English and Welsh. Before 1992 prizes were awarded to more than one author; since 1992 there has been one prize of £3000. The awards are given by the Arts Council of Wales in association with the Principality Building Society.

Written in English

1985 David Hughes, *The Pork Butcher*
Christopher Meredith, *This*
J. P. Ward, *The Clearing*
Ivor Wilks, *South Wales and the Rising of 1839*

1986 Duncan Bush, *Salt*
Mary Jones, *Resistance*
Christopher Norris, *Contest of Faculties*
Oliver Reynolds, *Skevington's Daughter*
Gwyn A. Williams, *When Was Wales?*
Raymond Williams, *Loyalties*

1987 Dannie Abse, *Ask the Bloody Horse*
Stephen Gregory, *The Cormorant*
Douglas Houston, *With the Offal Eaters*
Frances Thomas, *Seeing Things*
Peter Thomas, *Strangers from a Secret Land*

1988 Hilary Llewellyn-Williams, *The Tree Calendar*
Sheenagh Pugh, *Beware Falling Tortoises*
Oliver Reynolds, *The Player Queen's Wife*

Bernice Rubens, *Our Father*
Glanmor Williams, *Recovery, Reorientation and Reformation*

1989 Tony Conran, *Blodeuwedd*
Catherine Fisher, *Immrama*
Christopher Meredith, *Shifts*
Leslie Norris, *The Girl from Cardigan*
Nigel Wells, *Wilderness/Just Bounce*

1990 John Barnie, *The King of Ashes*
Carol-Ann Courtney, *Morphine and Dolly Mixtures*
Christine Evans, *Cometary Phases*
David Jones, *Rebecca's Children*

1991 Russell Celyn Jones, *Soldiers and Innocents*
Moelwyn Merchant, *Fragments of Life*
Sheenagh Pugh, *Selected Poems*
Bernice Rubens, *Kingdom Come*
Robert Watson, *Whilom*

1992 Emyr Humphreys, *Bonds of Attachment*

1993 Robert Minhinnick, *Watching the Fire Eater*

1994 Paul Ferris, *Caitlin: The Life of Caitlin Thomas*

Written in Welsh

1985	Geraint Bowen, *Cerddi*
	Bryan Martin Davies, *Lleoedd*
	Glanmor Williams, *Grym*
	Tafodau Tân
1986	J. Eirian Davies, *Cerddi*
	Rhiannon Davies Jones,
	Dyddiadur Mari Gwyn
	Elwyn L. Jones, *Cyfrinach*
	Hannah
	Angharad Tomos, *Yma o Hyd*
1987	Nesta Wyn Jones, *Rhwng*
	Chwerthin a Chrio
	Alan Llwyd, *Barddoniaeth y*
	Chwedegau
	Gwylon Phillips, *Llofruddiaeth*
	Shadrach Lewis
	Beverley Smith, *Llywelyn ap*
	Gruffudd
	Rhydwen Williams, *Amser i Wylo*
1988	T. Glynne Davies, *Cerddi*
	Bobi Jones, *Llenyddiaeth*
	Gymraeg 1902–36
	Rhiannon Davies Jones, *Cribau*
	Eryri
	William Owen Roberts, *Y Pla*
	Huw Walters, *Canu'r Pwll a'r*
	Pulpud

1989	Donald Evans, *Iasau*
	Alan Llwyd, *Yn y Dirfawr Waq*
	D. Tecwyn Lloyd, *John Saunders*
	Lewis
	Prys Morgan, *Beibl i Gymru*
	Rhydwen Williams, *Liwsi Regina*
1990	Sioned Davies, *Pedeir Keinc y*
	Mabinogi
	Hywel Teifi Edwards, *Codi'r Hen*
	Wlad yn ei Hôl
	Alun Jones, *Plentyn y Bwtias*
	Dic Jones, *Os Hoffech Wybod*
	R. Gerallt Jones, *Cerddi 1955–*
	1989
	Selyf Roberts, *Gorwel Agos*
1991	John Davies, *Hanes Cymru*
	Menna Elfyn, *Aderyn Bach Mewn*
	Llaw
	Geraint H. Jenkins, *Cadw Tŷ*
	Mewn Cwmwl Tystion
	Bobi Jones, *Crio Chwerthin*
	Alan Llwyd, *Cerddi 1968–90*
	Gwyn Thomas, *Gwelaf Afon*
1992	Gerallt Lloyd Owen, *Cilmeri*
1993	Robin Llywelyn, *Seren Wen ar*
	Gefndir Gwyn
1994	Robin Chapman, *W. J. Gruffydd*

WHITBREAD LITERARY AWARDS

Up to 1985, the awards were given in separate categories as shown below: Novel (N), Biography (B), Poetry (P), Children's Book (CB), First Book (FB), First Novel (FN), Autobiography (A), Short Story (SS).

From 1986, a nomination goes forward from each of the following categories: Novel, First Novel, Children's Novel, Biography or Autobiography, and Poetry. Each nomination carries an award of £2,000. From these, one Book of the Year is chosen and its author receives an additional £20,500.

1980	David Lodge, *How Far Can You*
	Go? (N)
	Leon Garfield, *John Diamond*
	(CB)
	David Lodge, *How Far Can You*
	Go? (Book of the Year)
1981	Maurice Leitch, *Silver's City* (N)
	Nigel Hamilton, *Monty: The*
	Making of a General (B)
	Jane Gardam, *The Hollow Land*
	(CB)
	William Boyd, *A Good Man in*
	Africa (FN)

1982	John Wain, *Young Shoulders* (N)
	Edward Crankshaw, *Bismarck* (B)
	W. J. Corbett, *The Song of*
	Pentecost (CB)
	Kenneth Rose, *King George V* (B)
	Roald Dahl, *The Witches* (CB)
	John Fuller, *Flying to Nowhere*
	(FN)
1984	Christopher Hope, *Kruger's Alp*
	(N)
	Peter Ackroyd, *T. S. Eliot* (B)

Barbara Willard, *The Queen of the Pharisees' Children* (CB)

James Buchan, *A Parish of Rich Women* (FN)

Diane Rowe, *Tomorrow is our Permanent Address* (SS)

1985 Douglas Dunn, *Elegies* (Book of the Year)

1986 Kazuo Ishiguro, *An Artist of the Floating World* (Book of the Year)

1987 Christopher Nolan, *Under the Eye of the Clock* (Book of the Year)

1988 Paul Sayer, *The Comforts of Madness* (Book of the Year)

1989 Richard Holmes, *Coleridge: Early Visions* (Book of the Year)

1990 Nicholas Mosley, *Hopeful Monsters* (Book of the Year)

1991 John Richardson, *A Life of Picasso* (Book of the Year)

1992 Jeff Torrington, *Swing Hammer Swing!* (Book of the Year)

1993 Joan Brady, *Theory of War* (Book of the Year)

YORKSHIRE POST AWARDS

£1,200 is currently awarded to the best work of fiction or non-fiction published in the preceding year. £1,000 is awarded to a work by a new author published in the preceding year.

1984

First Prize Max Hastings, *Overlord*
Novel of the Year Kingsley Amis, *Stanley and the Women*
Best First Work Michael Parnell, *Eric Linklater: A Critical Biography*

1985

First Prize John Terraine, *The Right of the Line*
Novel of the Year Alice Thomas Ellis, *Unexplained Laughter*
Best First Work John David Morley, *Pictures from the Water Trade*

1986

Book of the Year Robert Rhodes James, *Anthony Eden*
Best First Work John Charmley, *Duff Cooper*

1987

Book of the Year Lyn MacDonald, *1914*
Best First Work Anne Spillard, *The Cartomancer*

1988

Book of the Year William Trevor, *The Silence in the Garden*
Best First Work Susha Guppy, *The Blindfold Horse*

1989

Book of the Year Simon Schama, *Citizens*
Best First Work William Dalrymple, *In Xanadu*

1990

Book of the Year Richard Mullen, *Anthony Trollope: A Victorian in his World*
Best First Work Susan Richards, *Epics of Everyday Life*

1991

Book of the Year Correlli Barnett, *Engage the Enemy More Closely*
Best First Work Harriet O'Brien, *The Forgotten Land*

1992

Book of the Year John Gross, *Shylock*
Best First Work Rory Maclean, *Stalin's Nose*

1993

Book of the Year Paul Preston, *Franco*
Best First Work Steve Jones, *The Language of the Genes*

MAGIC

THE MAGIC CIRCLE AWARDS

Young Magician of the Year

This is a direct competition open to those aged 12 to 18, who have to present a short magic act which is judged on standard of technique, ability, personality and presentation. The competition is held every 2 years and is open to entrants from all over the world. The eliminating rounds are held wherever necessary, with the final at a London theatre.

1961	Johnny Hart	1979	Philip Theodore
1963	Olavi Airaksinen	1981	Andrew O'Connor
1965	Keith Cooper	1983	Richard Pearson
1967	Colin Rose	1985	Jeremy Dane
1969	David Lait	1987	Andrew Chettleburgh
1971	Christopher Payne	1989	Richard Griffin
1973	Colin Boardman	1991	Philip Hitchcock
1975	David Owen / Martin Welford	1993	Simon Lee
1977	Stephen Hill / David Metcalfe		

The Maskelyne

This is given to the magician who has made an outstanding contribution either by performance, invention, writing or, in fact, in any way that will help to develop the art of magic. The award takes the shape of a bronze head of John Nevil Maskelyne, who was a great magician 100 years ago and who did much to help the Magic Circle when it was founded in 1905.

1970	Robert Harbin	1982	*no award*
1971	David Nixon	1983	*no award*
1972	Ali Bongo	1984	*no award*
1973	John Nevil Maskelyne (posthumously)	1985	*no award*
		1986	*no award*
1974	Peter Warlock	1987	*no award*
1975	*no award*	1988	Paul Daniels
1976	*no award*	1989	John Fisher
1977	*no award*	1990	Gil Leaney
1978	Goodliffe Neale	1991	Alan Shaxon
1979	*no award*	1992	Jeffery Atkins
1980	*no award*	1993	Harry Devano
1981	*no award*		

The Carlton Award

The Carlton Award is for comedy. Carlton achieved fame during the early part of this century as a top-of-the-bill performer of comedy magic. His unique appearance, dress and build earned him the title 'the Human Hairpin', outclassing his contemporaries both technically and in his mastery of the throwaway line.

1989	Larry Parker	1992	Terry Herbert
1990	Billy McComb	1993	Ali Bongo
1991	Jay Marshall		

The John Nevil Maskelyne Prize

Of the funds administered by the Magic Circle, the John Nevil Maskelyne Memorial Fund provides within its objects a monetary prize for noteworthy contributions by members or non-members of the Magic Circle to the art or literature of magic and to be known as the John Nevil Maskelyne Prize.

1988	Eddie Dawes	1991	Dennis Patten
1989	Robert Albo	1992	Bart Whaley
1990	Sam Sharpe	1993	Ruth Brandon

Cecil Lyle Award

The Magic Circular is the official magazine of the Magic Circle and the longest-continuous-running magic periodical in magic's history.

The Cecil Lyle Award, instituted many years ago by a distinguished past member of the Society, is for the best trick or illusion to be printed in *The Magic Circular* during the current year.

1989–90	Ian Adair	1992	Peter Jefferies
1991	Peter Jefferies	1993	Richard Wiseman

MANAGEMENT

BRITISH QUALITY OF MANAGEMENT AWARDS

The first winner of the new British Quality of Management Awards was announced in late 1993. The annual award, sponsored by MORI and Sundridge Park, the corporate and executive development group, is designed to assess management's capability in terms of a company's long-term development prospects and performance.

Almost 300 executives from Britain's top 500 companies, institutional fund managers and business editors were surveyed.

The eventual winner was BTR, the industrial conglomerate, with Alan Jackson as its chief executive and Kathleen O'Donovan as finance director. The two runners-up were Marks & Spencer and Glaxo.

MEDICINE

NOBEL PRIZE FOR MEDICINE

The Nobel Prize for Medicine dates from 1901 and, like the other Nobel Prizes, is the most prestigious award in its field. For a note on the Nobel Awards, see p. 206.

Up to 1945 the following British persons won the Nobel Prize:

1902	Sir Ronald Ross	1932	Edgar D. Adrian Sir Charles S. Sherrington
1922	Archibald V. Hill		
1929	Sir Frederick G. Hopkins (joint)	1936	Sir Henry H. Dale

Winners since 1945 were:

1945	Sir Alexander Fleming (GB) Ernst B. Chain (GB, German-born) Sir Howard W. Florey (GB, Australian-born)
1946	Hermann J. Muller (USA)
1947	Carl F. Cori (USA, Czech-born) Gerty T. Cori (USA, Czech-born) Bernardo A. Houssay (Arg)
1948	Paul H. Müller (Swi)
1949	Walter R. Hess (Swi) Antonio Moniz (Por)
1950	Philip S. Hench (USA) Edward C. Kendall (USA) Tadeus Reichstein (Swi, Polish-born)
1951	Max Theiler (USA, S. African-born)
1952	Selman A. Waksman (USA)
1953	Hans A. Krebs (GB, German-born) Fritz A. Lipmann (USA, German-born)
1954	John F. Enders (USA) Frederick C. Robbins (USA) Thomas H. Weller (USA)
1955	Alex H. T. Theorell (Swe)
1956	André F. Cournand (USA, French-born) Werner Forssmann (Ger) Dickinson W. Richards Jr (USA)
1957	Daniel Bovet (Ita, Swiss-born)
1958	George W. Beadle (USA) Edward L. Tatum (USA) Joshua Lederberg (USA)
1959	Arthur Kornberg (USA) Severo Ochoa (USA, Spanish-born)
1960	Sir F. Macfarlane Burnet (Aus) Peter B. Medawar (GB, Brazilian-born)
1961	Georg von Békèsy (USA, Hungarian-born)
1962	Francis H. C. Crick (GB) James D. Watson (USA) Maurice H. F. Wilkins (GB)
1963	Sir John C. Eccles (Aus) Alan L. Hodgkin (GB) Andrew F. Huxley (GB)
1964	Konrad E. Bloch (USA) Feodor Lynen (Ger)
1965	François Jacob (Fra) André Lwoff (Fra) Jacques Monod (Fra)
1966	Charles B. Huggins (USA) Francis Peyton Rous (USA)
1967	Ragnar Granit (Swe, Finnish-born) Haldan Keffer Hartline (USA) George Wald (USA)

1968	Robert W. Holley (USA)
	Har Gobind Khorana (USA, Indian-born)
	Marshall W. Nirenberg (USA)
1969	Max Delbrück (USA, German-born)
	Alfred D. Hershey (USA)
	Salvador D. Luria (USA, Italian-born)
1970	Julius Axelrod (USA)
	Ulf von Euler (Swe)
	Bernard Katz (GB)
1971	Earl W. Sutherland Jr (USA)
1972	Gerald M. Edelman (USA)
	Rodney Porter (GB)
1973	Karl von Frisch (Aut)
	Konrad Lorenz (Aut)
	Nikolaas Tinbergen (GB, Dutch-born)
1974	Albert Claude (USA, Luxembourg-born)
	Christian René de Duve (Bel)
	George Emil Palade (USA, Romanian-born)
1975	David Baltimore (USA)
	Howard Martin Temin (USA)
	Renato Dulbecco (USA, Italian-born)
1976	Baruch S. Blumberg (USA)
	D. Carleton Gajdusek (USA)
1977	Rosalyn S. Yalow (USA)
	Roger C. L. Guillemin (USA, French-born)
	Andrew V. Schally (USA)
1978	Werner Arber (Swi)
	Daniel Nathans (USA)
	Hamilton Smith (USA)
1979	Dr Hounsfield (GB)
	Allan Cormack (USA)
1980	Baruy Benacerraf (Ven)
	Jean Dausset (Fra)
	George Snell (USA)
1981	Roger W. Sperry (USA)
	David H. Hubel (USA)
	Torsten N. Wiesel (Swe)
1982	Sune Bergstrom (Swe)
	Bengt Samuelsson (Swe)
	John R. Vane (GB)
1983	Barbara McClintock (USA)
1984	Cesar Milstein (GB, Argentinian-born)
	Georges J. F. Kohler (FRG)
	Niels K. Jerne (GB, Danish-born)
1985	Michael S. Brown (USA)
	Joseph L. Goldstein (USA)
1986	Rita Levi-Montalcini (USA, Italian-born)
	Stanley Cohen (USA)
1987	Susumu Tonegawa (Jap)
1988	Gertrude B. Elion (USA)
	George H. Hitchings (USA)
	Sir James Black (GB)

1989	J. Michael Bishop (USA) Harold E. Varmus (USA)	1992	Edwin Krebs (USA) Edmond Fischer (USA)
1990	Joseph E. Murray (USA) E. Donnall Thomas (USA)	1993	Richard Roberts (UK) Phillip Sharp (USA)
1991	Edwin Neher (Ger) Bert Sakmann (Ger)		

MEMORY

MEMORIAD

In 1993 for the second year running the world memory championships were organized by the Brains Trust. Of the competitors at Memoriad '93 all were British except for Melik Duyar, the Turkish champion. The tasks the competitors had to perform included marathons such as committing a 2,000-digit number or 12 randomly shuffled packs of cards to memory in an hour, and sprints, in which only slightly less daunting tasks are tackled against the clock. Recent winners were:

1992	Dominic O'Brien	1994	Jonathan Hancock
1993	Dominic O'Brien		

Dominic O'Brien of Bishop's Stortford, Herts, retained his title at Memoriad '93, after a two-day battle of wits involving forty people. Among his incredible memory feats, he can memorize a shuffled pack of cards in 55.4 seconds, memorize 8 packs of cards in an hour and accurately recall two 100-digit numbers. He lost his title in 1994 to Oxford student Jonathan Hancock.

MILK

MILKMAN/MILKWOMAN OF THE YEAR

The search for the top Milkman of the Year is undertaken each year by the National Dairy Council. The competition in its present form has been organized since 1989.

Each year the winning milkman or milkwoman has received a Rover car and the nominator of the winner has received a two-week holiday in an exotic destination. Each runner-up milkperson receives a weekend for two in Paris and their nominators a year's supply of milk.

1989	Terry Brooks, Hastings, E. Sussex Saved two children from a fire.		
1990	Edwin Chapman, Darlington, Co. Durham Organized a surprise party for one of his customers and transported furniture on his float.		
1991	Nigel Matthews, Stoke-on-Trent, Staffs Ran a marathon to raise money		

for a new wheelchair for a customer's son. Delivered as normal the next day.

1992 Colin Dean, Brotherton, W. Yorks
The village community would collapse without Colin. Runs old people to church, organizes coffee mornings, produces pantomimes and plays.

1993 Irene Hall, Blackburn, Lancs

With her husband Kenneth, Mrs Hall has been rising at 4.30 a.m. most mornings for the last ten years to deliver milk in the Revidge and East Park Road areas of Blackburn. Irene knows all her customers by name and doesn't need a book to remember their orders. Has keys to her elderly customers' houses and checks on them after she has made sure they all get their milk by 8 a.m.

MODERN PENTATHLON

OLYMPIC GAMES

Team

1952	Hungary
1956	USSR
1960	Hungary
1964	USSR
1968	Hungary
1972	USSR
1976	Great Britain
1980	USSR
1984	Italy
1988	Hungary
1992	Poland

Individual

1912	Gosta Lilliehook (Swe)
1920	Gustaf Dryssen (Swe)
1924	Bo Lindman (Swe)
1928	Sven Thofelt (Swe)
1932	Johan Oxenstierna (Swe)
1936	Gotthardt Handrick (Ger)
1948	Willie Grut (Swe)
1952	Lars Hall (Swe)
1956	Lars Hall (Swe)
1960	Ferenc Nemeth (Hun)
1964	Ferenc Torok (Hun)
1968	Bjorn Ferm (Swe)
1972	Andras Balczo (Hun)
1976	Janusz Pyciak-Peciak (Pol)
1980	Anatoly Starostin (USSR)
1984	Daniele Masala (Ita)
1988	Janos Martinek (Hun)
1992	Arkadiusz Skrzypaszek (Pol)

MOTOR CYCLING

WORLD CHAMPIONSHIPS

1970

	Winner	Model
50cc	Angel Nieto (Spa)	Derbi
125cc	Dieter Braun (FRG)	Suzuki
250cc	Rod Gould (GB)	Yamaha
350cc	Giacomo Agostini (Ita)	MV
500cc	Giacomo Agostini (Ita)	MV
Sidecar	Klaus Enders (FRG)	BMW

1971

50cc	Jan de Vries (Hol)	Kreidler
125cc	Angel Nieto (Spa)	Derbi

	Winner	*Model*
250cc	Phil Read (GB)	Yamaha
350cc	Giacomo Agostini (Ita)	MV
500cc	Giacomo Agostini (Ita)	MV
Sidecar	Horst Owesle (FRG)	Munch

1972

50cc	Angel Nieto (Spa)	Derbi
125cc	Angel Nieto (Spa)	Derbi
250cc	Jarno Saarinen (Fin)	Yamaha
350cc	Giacomo Agostini (Ita)	MV
500cc	Giacomo Agostini (Ita)	MV
Sidecar	Klaus Enders(FRG)	BMW

1973

50cc	Jan de Vries (Hol)	Kreidler
125cc	Kent Andersson (Swe)	Yamaha
250cc	Dieter Braun (FRG)	Yamaha
350cc	Giacomo Agostini (Ita)	MV
500cc	Phil Read (GB)	MV
Sidecar	Klaus Enders (FRG)	BMW

1974

50cc	Henk van Kessell ((Hol)	Kreidler
125cc	Kent Andersson (Swe)	Yamaha
250cc	Walter Villa (Ita)	H-Davidson
350cc	Giacomo Agostini (Ita)	Yamaha
500cc	Phil Read (GB)	MV
Sidecar	Klaus Enders (FRG)	Busch BMW

1975

50cc	Angel Nieto (Spa)	Kreidler
125cc	Paolo Pileri (Ita)	Morbidelli
250cc	Walter Villa (Ita)	H-Davidson
350cc	Johnny Cecotto (Ven)	Yamaha
500cc	Giacomo Agostini (Ita)	Yamaha
Sidecar	Rolf Steinhausen (FRG)	Busch König

1976

50cc	Angel Nieto (Spa)	Bultaco
125cc	Pier-Paolo Bianchi (Ita)	Morbidelli
250cc	Walter Villa (Ita)	H-Davidson
350cc	Walter Villa (Ita)	H-Davidson
500cc	Barry Sheene (GB)	Suzuki
Sidecar	Rolf Steinhausen (FRG)	Busch König

1977

50cc	Angel Nieto (Spa)	Bultaco
125cc	Pier-Paolo Bianchi (Ita)	Morbidelli
250cc	Mario Lega (Ita)	Morbidelli
350cc	Takazumi Katayama (Jap)	Yamaha

	Winner	Model
500cc	Barry Sheene (GB)	Suzuki
750cc	Steve Baker (USA)	Yamaha
F1	Phil Read (GB)	Honda
Sidecar	George O'Dell (GB)	Yamaha

1978

50cc	Ricardo Tormo (Spa)	Bultaco
125cc	Eugenio Lazzarini (Ita)	MBA
250cc	Kork Ballington (SAf)	Kawasaki
350cc	Kork Ballington (SAf)	Kawasaki
500cc	Kenny Roberts (USA)	Yamaha
750cc	Johnny Cecotto (Ven)	Yamaha
F1	Mike Hailwood (GB)	Ducati
Sidecar	Rolf Biland (Swi)	Yamaha

1979

50cc	Eugenio Lazzarini (Ita)	Kreidler
125cc	Angel Nieto (Spa)	Morbidelli
250cc	Kork Ballington (SAf)	Kawasaki
350cc	Kork Ballington (SAf)	Kawasaki
500cc	Kenny Roberts (USA)	Yamaha
750cc	Patrick Pons (Fra)	Yamaha
F1	Ron Haslam (GB)	Honda
Sidecar	Rolf Biland (Swi)	Yamaha

1980

50cc	Eugenio Lazzarini (Ita)	Kreidler
125cc	Pier-Paolo Bianchi (Ita)	MBA
250cc	Anton Mang (FRG)	Kawasaki
350cc	John Ekerold (SAf)	Yamaha
500cc	Kenny Roberts (USA)	Yamaha
F1	Graeme Crosby (NZ)	Suzuki
Sidecar	Jock Taylor (GB)	Yamaha

1981

50cc	Ricardo Tormo (Spa)	Bultaco
125cc	Angel Nieto (Spa)	Minarelli
250cc	Anton Mang (FRG)	Kawasaki
350cc	Anton Mang (FRG)	Kawasaki
500cc	Marco Lucchinelli (Ita)	Suzuki
F1	Graeme Crosby (NZ)	Suzuki
Sidecar	Rolf Biland (Swi)	Yamaha

1982

50cc	Stefan Dorflinger (Swi)	MBA
125cc	Angel Nieto (Spa)	Garelli
250cc	Jean-Louis Tournadre (Fra)	Yamaha
350cc	Anton Mang (FRG)	Kawasaki
500cc	Franco Uncini (Ita)	Suzuki
Sidecar	Werner Schwarzel (FRG)	Yamaha
F1	Joey Dunlop (Ire)	Honda

	Winner	*Model*
1983		
50cc	Stefan Dorflinger (Swi)	Kreidler
125cc	Angel Nieto (Spa)	Garelli
250cc	Carlos Lavado (Ven)	Yamaha
500cc	Freddie Spencer (USA)	Honda
F1	Joey Dunlop (Ire)	Honda
Sidecar	Rolf Biland (Swi)	Yamaha
1984		
80cc	Stefan Dorflinger (Swi)	Zundapp
125cc	Angel Nieto (Spa)	Garelli
250cc	Christian Sarron (Fra)	Yamaha
500cc	Eddie Lawson (USA)	Yamaha
F1	Joey Dunlop (Ire)	Honda
Sidecar	Egbert Streuer (Hol)	Yamaha
1985		
80cc	Stefan Dorflinger (Swi)	Krauser
125cc	Fausto Gresini (Ita)	Garelli
250cc	Freddie Spencer (USA)	Honda
500cc	Freddie Spencer (USA)	Honda
F1	Joey Dunlop (Ire)	Honda
Sidecar	Egbert Streuer (Hol)	Yamaha
1986		
80cc	Jorge Martinez (Spa)	Derbi
125cc	Luca Cadalora (Ita)	Garelli
250cc	Carlos Lavado (Ven)	Yamaha
500cc	Eddie Lawson (USA)	Yamaha
F1	Joey Dunlop (Ire)	Honda
Sidecar	Egbert Streuer (Hol)	Yamaha
1987		
80cc	Jorge Martinez (Spa)	Derbi
125cc	Fausto Gresini (Ita)	Garelli
250cc	Anton Mang (FRG)	Honda
500cc	Wayne Gardner (Aus)	Honda
F1	Virginio Ferrari (Ita)	Yamaha
Sidecar	Steve Webster (GB)	LCR Krauser
1988		
80cc	Jorge Martinez (Spa)	Derbi
125cc	Jorge Martinez (Spa)	Derbi
250cc	Sito Pons (Spa)	Honda
500cc	Eddie Lawson (USA)	Yamaha
F1	Carl Fogarty (GB)	Honda
Sidecar	Steve Webster (GB)	LCR Krauser

1989

	Winner	Model
80cc	Champi Herreros (Spa)	Derbi
125cc	Alex Crivelle (Spa)	Cobas
250cc	Sito Pons (Spa)	Honda
500cc	Eddie Lawson (USA)	Honda
Sidecar	Steve Webster (GB)	Krauser

1990

125cc	Loris Capirossi (Ita)	Honda
250cc	John Kocinski (USA)	Yamaha
500cc	Wayne Rainey (USA)	Yamaha
Sidecar	Alain Michel (Fra)	Krauser

1991

125cc	Loris Capirossi (Ita)	Honda
250cc	Luca Cadalora (USA)	Honda
500cc	Wayne Rainey (USA)	Yamaha
Sidecar	Steve Webster (GB)	LCR

1992

125cc	Alessandro Gramigni (Ita)	Aprilia
250cc	Luca Cadalora (USA)	Honda
500cc	Wayne Rainey (USA)	Yamaha
Sidecar	Rolf Biland (Swi)	Yamaha

1993

125cc	Dirk Raudies (Ger)	Honda
250cc	Tetsuye Harada (Jap)	Yamaha
500cc	Kevin Schwantz (USA)	Suzuki
Sidecar	Rolf Biland (Swi)	Yamaha

ISLE OF MAN SENIOR TT

1947	Harold Daniell	1965	Mike Hailwood
1948	Artie Bell	1966	Mike Hailwood
1949	Harold Daniell	1967	Mike Hailwood
1950	Geoff Duke	1968	Giacomo Agostini (Ita)
1951	Geoff Duke	1969	Giacomo Agostini (Ita)
1952	Reg Armstrong	1970	Giacomo Agostini (Ita)
1953	Ray Amm (SRho)	1971	Giacomo Agostini (Ita)
1954	Ray Amm (SRho)	1972	Giacomo Agostini (Ita)
1955	Geoff Duke	1973	Jack Findlay
1956	John Surtees	1974	Phil Carpenter
1957	Bob McIntyre	1975	Mick Grant
1958	John Surtees	1976	Tom Herron
1959	John Surtees	1977	Phil Read
1960	John Surtees	1978	Tom Herron
1961	Mike Hailwood	1979	Mike Hailwood
1962	Gary Hockling (SRho)	1980	Graeme Crosby (NZ)
1963	Mike Hailwood	1981	Mick Grant
1964	Mike Hailwood	1982	Norman Brown

1983	*not held*	1989	Steve Hislop
1984	Rob McElnea	1990	Carl Fogarty
1985	Joey Dunlop	1991	Steve Hislop
1986	Roger Burnett	1992	Steve Hislop
1987	Joey Dunlop	1993	Nick Jeffries
1988	Joey Dunlop		

MOTOR RACING

FORMULA ONE WORLD CAR CHAMPIONSHIP

	Driver	Car	Constructors Cup
1950	Giuseppe Farina (Ita)	Alfa Romeo	
1951	Juan Manuel Fangio (Arg)	Alfa Romeo	
1952	Alberto Ascari (Ita)	Ferrari	
1953	Alberto Ascari (Ita)	Ferrari	
1954	Juan Manuel Fangio (Arg)	Maserati/Mercedes	
1955	Juan Manuel Fangio (Arg)	Mercedes-Benz	
1956	Juan Manuel Fangio (Arg)	Lancia-Ferrari	
1957	Juan Manuel Fangio (Arg)	Maserati	
1958	Mike Hawthorn (GB)	Ferrari	Vanwall
1959	Jack Brabham (Aus)	Cooper-Climax	Cooper-Climax
1960	Jack Brabham (Aus)	Cooper-Climax	Cooper-Climax
1961	Phil Hill (USA)	Ferrari	Ferrari
1962	Graham Hill (GB)	BRM	BRM
1963	Jim Clark (GB)	Lotus-Climax	Lotus-Climax
1964	John Surtees (GB)	Ferrari	Ferrari
1965	Jim Clark (GB)	Lotus-Climax	Lotus-Climax
1966	Jack Brabham (Aus)	Brabham-Repco	Brabham-Repco
1967	Denny Hulme (NZ)	Brabham-Repco	Brabham-Repco
1968	Graham Hill (GB)	Lotus-Ford	Lotus-Ford
1969	Jackie Stewart (GB)	Matra-Ford	Matra-Ford
1970	Jochen Rindt (Aut)	Lotus-Ford	Lotus-Ford
1971	Jackie Stewart (GB)	Tyrell-Ford	Tyrell-Ford
1972	Emerson Fittipaldi (Bra)	Lotus-Ford	Lotus-Ford
1973	Jackie Stewart (GB)	Tyrell-Ford	Lotus-Ford
1974	Emerson Fittipaldi (Bra)	McLaren-Ford	McLaren-Ford
1975	Niki Lauda (Aut)	Ferrari	Ferrari
1976	James Hunt (GB)	McLaren-Ford	Ferrari
1977	Niki Lauda (Aut)	Ferrari	Ferrari
1978	Mario Andretti (USA)	Lotus-Ford	Lotus-Ford
1979	Jody Scheckter (SAf)	Ferrari	Ferrari
1980	Alan Jones (Aus)	Williams-Ford	Williams-Ford
1981	Nelson Piquet (Bra)	Brabham-Ford	Williams-Ford
1982	Keke Rosberg (Fin)	Williams-Ford	Ferrari
1983	Nelson Piquet (Bra)	Brabham-BMW	Ferrari
1984	Niki Lauda (Aus)	McLaren-TAG	McLaren-Porsche

	Driver	Car	Constructors Cup
1985	Alain Prost (Fra)	McLaren-TAG	McLaren-TAG
1986	Alain Prost (Fra)	McLaren-TAG	Williams-Honda
1987	Nelson Piquet (Bra)	Williams-Honda	Williams-Honda
1988	Ayrton Senna (Bra)	McLaren-Honda	McLaren-Honda
1989	Alain Prost (Fra)	McLaren-Honda	McLaren-Honda
1990	Ayrton Senna (Bra)	McLaren-Honda	McLaren-Honda
1991	Ayrton Senna (Bra)	McLaren-Honda	McLaren-Honda
1992	Nigel Mansell (GB)	Williams-Renault	Williams-Renault
1993	Alain Prost (Fra)	Williams-Renault	Williams-Renault

BRITISH GRAND PRIX

1950	Giuseppe Farina (Ita)	1972	Emerson Fittipaldi (Bra)
1951	José Froilan Gonzalez (Arg)	1973	Peter Revson (USA)
1952	Alberto Ascari (Ita)	1974	Jody Scheckter (SAf)
1953	Alberto Ascari (Ita)	1975	Emerson Fittipaldi (Bra)
1954	José Froilan Gonzalez (Arg)	1976	Niki Lauda (Aut)
1955	Stirling Moss (UK)	1977	James Hunt (UK)
1956	Juan Manuel Fangio (Arg)	1978	Carlos Reutemann (Arg)
1957	Stirling Moss (UK) / Tony Brooks (UK)	1979	Clay Regazzoni (Swi)
		1980	Alan Jones (Aus)
1958	Peter Collins (UK)	1981	John Watson (UK)
1959	Jack Brabham (Aus)	1982	Niki Lauda (Aut)
1960	Jack Brabham (Aus)	1983	Alain Prost (Fra)
1961	Wolfgang von Trips (FRG)	1984	Nicki Lauda (Aut)
1962	Jim Clark (UK)	1985	Alain Prost (Fra)
1963	Jim Clark (UK)	1986	Nigel Mansell (UK)
1964	Jim Clark (UK)	1987	Nigel Mansell (UK)
1965	Jim Clark (UK)	1988	Ayrton Senna (Bra)
1966	Jack Brabham (Aus)	1989	Alain Prost (Fra)
1967	Jim Clark (UK)	1990	Alain Prost (Fra)
1968	Jo Siffert (Swi)	1991	Nigel Mansell (UK)
1969	Jackie Stewart (UK)	1992	Nigel Mansell (UK)
1970	Jochen Rindt (Aut)	1993	Alain Prost (Fra)
1971	Jackie Stewart (UK)	1994	Damon Hill (UK)

INDY CAR CHAMPIONSHIP

1946	Ted Horn	1958	Tony Bettenhausen, Sr
1947	Ted Horn	1959	Rodger Ward
1948	Ted Horn	1960	A. J. Foyt
1949	Johnny Parsons	1961	A. J. Foyt
1950	Henry Banks	1962	Rodger Ward
1951	Tony Bettenhausen, Sr	1963	A. J. Foyt
1952	Chuck Stevenson	1964	A. J. Foyt
1953	Sam Hanks	1965	Mario Andretti
1954	Jimmy Bryan	1966	Mario Andretti
1955	Bob Swikert	1967	A. J. Foyt
1956	Jimmy Bryan	1968	Bobby Unser
1957	Jimmy Bryan	1969	Mario Andretti

1970	Al Unser	1982	Rick Mears
1971	Joe Leonard	1983	Al Unser
1972	Joe Leonard	1984	Mario Andretti
1973	Roger McCluskey	1985	Al Unser
1974	Bobby Unser	1986	Bobby Rahal
1975	A. J. Foyt	1987	Bobby Rahal
1976	Gordon Johncock	1988	Danny Sullivan
1977	Tom Sneva	1989	Emerson Fittipaldi
1978	Tom Sneva	1990	Al Unser Jr
1979	A. J. Foyt / Rick Mears	1991	Michael Andretti
		1992	Bobby Rahal
1980	Johnny Rutherford	1993	Nigel Mansell
1981	Rick Mears		

LE MANS 24-HOUR RACE

	Winners	*Manufacturer*
1949	Luigi Chinetti (Ita), Lord Peter Selsdon (UK)	Ferrari
1950	Louis Rosier, Jean-Louis Rosier (Fra)	Talbot-Lago
1951	Peter Walker, Peter Whitehead (UK)	Jaguar
1952	Hermann Lang, Karl Riess (FRG)	Mercedes-Benz
1953	Tony Rolt, Duncan Hamilton (UK)	Jaguar
1954	Froilan Gonzalez (Arg), Maurice Trintignant (Fra)	Ferrari
1955	Mike Hawthorn, Ivor Bueb (UK)	Jaguar
1956	Ron Flockhart, Ninian Sanderson (UK)	Jaguar
1957	Ron Flockhart, Ivor Bueb (UK)	Jaguar
1958	Olivier Gendebien (Bel), Phil Hill (USA)	Ferrari
1959	Carroll Shelby, Roy Salvadori (UK)	Aston Martin
1960	Olivier Gendebien, Paul Frère (Bel)	Ferrari
1961	Olivier Gendebien (Bel), Phil Hill (USA)	Ferrari
1962	Olivier Gendebien (Bel), Phil Hill (USA)	Ferrari
1963	Ludovico Scarfiotti, Lorenzo Bandini (Ita)	Ferrari
1964	Jean Guichet (Fra), Nino Vaccarella (Ita)	Ferrari
1965	Jochen Rindt (Aut), Masten Gregory (USA)	Ferrari
1966	Chris Amon, Bruce McLaren (NZ)	Ford
1967	Dan Gurney, A. J. Foyt (USA)	Ford
1968	Pedro Rodriguez (Mex), Lucien Bianchi (Bel)	Ford
1969	Jacky Ickx (Bel), Jackie Oliver (UK)	Ford
1970	Hans Herrmann (FRG), Richard Attwood (UK)	Porsche
1971	Helmut Marko (Aut), Gijs van Lennep (Hol)	Porsche
1972	Henri Pescarolo (Fra), Graham Hill (UK)	Matra-Simca
1973	Henri Pescarolo, Gérard Larrousse (Fra)	Matra-Simca
1974	Henri Pescarolo, Gérard Larrousse (Fra)	Matra-Simca
1975	Jacky Ickx (Bel), Derek Bell (UK)	Mirage-Ford
1976	Jacky Ickx (Bel), Gijs van Lennep (Hol)	Porsche
1977	Jacky Ickx (Bel), Jürgen Barth (FRG), Hurley Haywood (USA)	Porsche
1978	Jean-Pierre Jaussaud, Didier Pironi (Fra)	Renault Alpine
1979	Klaus Ludwig (FRG), Bill Whittington (USA), Don Whittington (USA)	Porsche
1980	Jean-Pierre Jaussaud, Jean Rondeau (Fra)	Rondeau-Ford
1981	Jacky Ickx (Bel), Derek Bell (UK)	Porsche
1982	Jacky Ickx (Bel), Derek Bell (UK)	Porsche

	Winners	Manufacturer
1983	Vern Schuppan (Aut), Hurley Haywood (USA), Al Holbert (USA)	Porsche
1984	Klaus Ludwig (FRG), Henri Pescarolo(Fra)	Porsche
1985	Klaus Ludwig (FRG), Paulo Barillo (Ita), 'John Winter' (FRG)	Porsche
1986	Hans Stück (FRG), Derek Bell (UK), Al Holbert (USA)	Porsche
1987	Hans Stück (FRG), Derek Bell (UK), Al Holbert (USA)	Porsche
1988	Jan Lammers (Hol), Johnny Dumfries (UK), Andy Wallace (UK)	Jaguar
1989	Jochen Mass (FRG), Manuel Reuter (FRG), Stanley Dickens (Swe)	Mercedes
1990	John Nielsen (Den), Martin Brundle (UK), Price Cobb (USA)	Jaguar
1991	Johnny Herbert (UK), Bertrand Gachot (Bel), Volker Wendler (Ger)	Mazda
1992	Derek Warwick, Mark Blundell (UK), Yannick Dalmas (Fra)	Peugeot
1993	Erik Helery, Christopher Bolichet, Jeff Brabham (Aus)	Peugeot

MONTE CARLO RALLY

	Winner	Model
1911	Henri Rougier	Turcat-Mery
1912	J. Beutler	Berliet
1924	Jean Ledure	Bignan
1925	François Repusseau	Renault 40 CV
1926	Hon. Victor Bruce/W. J. Brunell	AC Bristol
1927	Lefebvre	Amilcar
1928	Jacques Bignan	Fiat
1929	Dr Sprenger van Eijk	Graham-Paige
1930	Hector Petit	Licorne
1931	Donald Healey	Invicta
1932	M. Vasselle	Hotchkiss
1933	M. Vasselle	Hotchkiss
1934	Jean Trevoux	Hotchkiss
1935	Christian Lahaye/R. Quatresous	Renault Nervasport
1936	I. Zamfirescu/J. Quinlin	Ford
1937	René le Begue/J. Quinlin	Delahaye
1938	G. Bakker Schut/Karel Ton	Ford
1939	Jean Trevoux/M. Lesurque	Hotchkiss
1949	Jean Trevoux/M. Lesurque	Hotchkiss
1950	Marcel Becquart/H. Secret	Hotchkiss
1951	Jean Trevoux/R. Crovetto	Delahaye
1952	Sidney Allard/Guy Warburton	Allard P2
1953	Maurice Gatsonides/P. Worledge	Ford Zephyr
1954	Louis Chiron/C. Basadonna	Lancia-Aurelia
1955	Per Malling/Gunnar Fadum	Sunbeam-Talbot
1956	Ronnie Adams/F. E. A. Bigger	Jaguar Mk VII
1957	*no race*	
1958	Guy Monraisse/J. Feret	Renault Dauphine
1959	Paul Coltelloni/P.Alexander	Citroen ID19
1960	Walter Schock/R. Moll	Mercedes 220SE
1961	Maurice Martin/Roger Bateau	Panhard PL17
1962	Erik Carlsson/Gunnar Haggbom	Saab 96
1963	Erik Carlsson/Gunnar Palm	Saab 96
1964	Paddy Hopkirk/Henry Liddon	Mini-Cooper 'S'
1965	Timo Mäkinen/Paul Easter	Mini-Cooper 'S'

	Winner	Model
1966	Pauli Toivonen/Ensio Mikander	Citroën DS21
1967	Rauno Aaltonen/Henry Liddon	Mini-Cooper 'S'
1968	Vic Elford/David Stone	Porsche 911T
1969	Björn Waldegärd/Lars Helmer	Porsche 911
1970	Björn Waldegärd/Lars Helmer	Porsche 911
1971	Ove Andersson/David Stone	Alpine Renault A110
1972	Sandro Munari/Mario Manucci	Lancia Fulvia
1973	Jean-Claude Andruet/'Biche'	Alpine Renault A110
1974	*no race*	
1975	Sandro Munari/Mario Manucci	Lancia Stratos
1976	Sandro Munari/Silvio Maiga	Lancia Stratos
1977	Sandro Munari/Mario Manucci	Lancia Stratos
1978	Jean-Pierre Nicolas/Vincent Laverne	Porsche Carrera 911
1979	Bernard Darniche/Alain Mahe	Lancia Stratos
1980	Walter Röhrl/Christian Geistdorfer	Fiat Abarth 131
1981	Jean Ragnotti/Jean-Marc André	Renault 5 Turbo
1982	Walter Röhrl/Christian Geistdorfer	Opel Ascona
1983	Walter Röhrl/Christian Geistdorfer	Opel Ascona
1984	Walter Röhrl/Christian Geistdorfer	Audi Quattro
1985	Ari Vatanen/Terry Harryman	Peugeot 205 Turbo 16
1986	Henri Toivonen/Sergio Cresto	Lancia Delta S4
1987	Mikki Biasion/Tiziano Siviero	Lancia Delta HF4
1988	Bruno Saby/Jean-François Fauchille	Lancia Delta HF4
1989	Mikki Biasion/Tiziano Siviero	Lancia Delta Integrale
1990	Didier Auriol/Bernard Occelli	Lancia Delta Integrale 16
1991	Carlos Sainz/Luis Moya	Toyota Celica GT4
1992	Didier Auriol/Bernard Occelli	Lancia HF Integrale
1993	Didier Auriol/Bernard Occelli	Toyota Celica Turbo

MUSEUMS

MUSEUM OF THE YEAR AWARD

This is an annual award, currently sponsored by IBM in conjunction with National Heritage, a voluntary organization which protects the interests of museums and galleries throughout the country. The award began in 1973 to induce industry to promote the arts. The museums are judged for their enterprise, general improvements and enhanced facilities. Hence the award recognizes and encourages new ventures and enterprises in one of society's greatest resources.

1973	Abbot Hall Museum, Kendal, Cumbria	1976	The Gladstone Pottery Museum, Stoke-on-Trent, Staffs
1974	The National Motor Museum, Beaulieu, Hants	1977	The Ironbridge Gorge Museum, Telford, Salop
1975	The Weald and Downland Open Air Museum, Singleton, W. Sussex	1978	{ The Museum of London { Erddig Hall, Wrexham, Wales

1979	Guernsey Museum and Art Gallery	1987	Manchester Museum
1980	British Museum (Natural History), London	1988	National Museum of Photography, Film and Television, Bradford
1981	The Hunday Farm Museum, Stocksfield, Northumberland	1989	National Portrait Gallery at Bodelwyddan Castle
1982	The City Museum and Art Gallery, Stoke-on-Trent, Staffs	1990	The Imperial War Museum, London and The Museum of Science and Industry, Manchester
1983	The Ulster Folk and Transport Museum, Holywood, N. Ireland		
1984	Quarry Bank Mill, Styal, Cheshire	1991	The National Railway Museum, York
1985	The Burrell Collection, Glasgow	1992	Manx National Heritage, Isle of Man
1986	Beamish: the North of England Open Air Museum, Co. Durham	1993	Jersey Museum

The 1993 winner, the new Jersey Museum at the Weighbridge, St Helier, succeeds in gathering together and presenting the historic collections of the island. The Jersey Heritage Trust devised a new building to link a merchant's house of 1817, the museum until recently, with a late eighteenth-century warehouse. The adjective 'sensational' is almost unknown in judges' reports, but it was used for this development. The apt variety of layout, the distinction of presentation and the excellent standard of facilities all received praise.

MUSIC

THE BRITS AWARDS

The British Record Industry Awards, organized by the British Phonographic Industry (BPI) and currently sponsored by Britannia Music Club, are meant as a showcase for the best of musical talent and a recognition of excellence and achievement in the careers of both British and international recording artists. The annual presentation of the awards is a popular television event.

1982

Best British

Male Artist Cliff Richard
Female Artist Randy Crawford
Group Police
Single 'Tainted Love' (Soft Cell)
Album Kings of the Wild Frontier (Adam and the Ants)
Newcomer Human League
Classical Recording Mahler's Symphony No. 10 (Bournemouth Symphony Orchestra)
Producer Martin Rushent

Best

Outstanding Contribution John Lennon

1983

Best British

Male Artist Paul McCartney
Female Artist Kim Wilde
Group Dire Straits
Single 'Come on Eileen' (Dexy's Midnight Runners)
Album Love Songs (Barbra Streisand)
Newcomer Yazoo
Classical Recording Portrait of John Williams
Producer Trevor Horn

International

Solo Artist   Kid Creole

Best

Outstanding Contribution   The Beatles

Other Awards

Special Award   Chris Wright

Sony Trophy for Technical
    Excellence   Paul McCartney

Life Achievement   Pete Townshend

1984

Best British

Male Artist   David Bowie

Female Artist   Annie Lennox

Group   Culture Club

Single   'Karma Chameleon' (Culture
    Club)

Album   Thriller (Michael Jackson)

Newcomer   Paul Young

Classical Recording   Songs of the
    Auvergne (Kiri Te Kanawa)

Producer   Steve Levine

International

Solo Artist   Michael Jackson

Best

Outstanding Contribution   George Martin

Other Awards

Sony Trophy for Technical
    Excellence   Spandau Ballet

1985

Best British

Male Artist   Paul Young

Female Artist   Alison Moyet

Group   Wham

Single   'Relax' (Frankie Goes to
    Hollywood)

Album   Diamond Life (Sade)

Newcomer   Frankie Goes to Hollywood

Classical Recording   Vivaldi's 'The Four
    Seasons' (Christopher Hogwood)

Producer   Trevor Horn

International

Solo Artist   Prince

Best

Music Video   Wild Boys (Duran Duran)

Soundtrack/Cast Recording   Purple Rain

Outstanding Contribution   Police

Other Awards

Best Comedy Record   Hole in My Shoe
    (Neil)

Special Award   Bob Geldof/Midge Ure

1986

Best British

Male Artist   Phil Collins

Female Artist   Annie Lennox

Group   Dire Straits

Single   'Everybody Wants to Rule the
    World' (Tears for Fears)

Album   No Jacket Required (Phil Collins)

Newcomer   Go West

Classical Recording   Elgar's Violin
    Concerto (Nigel Kennedy)

Producer   David Stewart

International

Solo Artist   Bruce Springsteen

Group   Huey Lewis and The News

Best

Music Video   Everytime You Go Away
    (Paul Young)

Outstanding Contribution   { Wham
                            { Elton John

1987

Best British

Male Artist   Peter Gabriel

Female Artist   Kate Bush

Group   Five Star

Single   'West End Girls' (Pet Shop Boys)

Album   Brothers in Arms (Dire Straits)

Newcomer   The Housemartins

Classical Recording   Elgar's Cello
    Concerto (Julian Lloyd-Webber)

Producer   David Stewart

International

Solo Artist   Paul Simon

Group   Bangles

Best

Music Video   Sledgehammer (Peter
    Gabriel)

Soundtrack/Cast Recording   Top Gun

Outstanding Contribution   Eric Clapton

1988

Best British

Male Artist   George Michael

Female Artist   Alison Moyet

Group   Pet Shop Boys
Single   'Never Gonna Give You Up' (Rick Astley)
Album   Nothing Like the Sun (Sting)
Newcomer   Wet Wet Wet
Classical Recording   Vaughan Williams's Symphony No. 5 (Vernon Handley)
Producer   Stock Aitken Waterman

International
Solo Artist   Michael Jackson
Group   U2
Newcomer   Terence Trent D'Arby

Best
Music Video   True Faith (New Order)
Soundtrack/Cast Recording   Phantom of the Opera
Outstanding Contribution   The Who

1989
Best British
Male Artist   Phil Collins
Female Artist   Annie Lennox
Group   Erasure
Single   'Perfect' (Fairground Attraction)
Album   First of a Million Kisses (Fairground Attraction)
Newcomer   Bros
Classical Recording   Handel's 'Messiah' (English Chamber Orchestra and Choir)

International
Solo Artist   { Tracy Chapman / Michael Jackson
Group   U2
Newcomer   Tracy Chapman

Best
Music Video   Smooth Criminal (Michael Jackson)
Soundtrack/Cast Recording   Buster
Outstanding Contribution   Cliff Richard

1990
Best British
Male Artist   Phil Collins
Female Artist   Annie Lennox
Group   Fine Young Cannibals
Single   'Another Day In Paradise' (Phil Collins)
Album   The Raw and the Cooked (Fine Young Cannibals)

Newcomer   Lisa Stansfield
Classical Recording   Gershwin's 'Porgy and Bess' (Simon Rattle)
Producer   David Stewart

International
Solo Artist   Neneh Cherry
Group   U2
Newcomer   Neneh Cherry

Best
Music Video   Lullaby (The Cure)
Soundtrack/Cast Recording   Batman
Outstanding Contribution   Queen

1991
Best British
Male Artist   Elton John
Female Artist   Lisa Stansfield
Group   The Cure
Single   'Enjoy the Silence' (Depeche Mode)
Album   Listen Without Prejudice Vol. 1 (George Michael)
Newcomer   Betty Boo
Classical Recording   Carreras, Domingo, Pavarotti in Concert
Producer   Chris Thomas

International
Solo Artist   { Sinead O'Connor / Michael Hutchence
Group   INXS
Newcomer   M. C. Hammer

Best
Music Video   A Little Time (Beautiful South)
Soundtrack/Cast Recording   Twin Peaks
Outstanding Contribution   Status Quo

1992
Best British
Male Artist   Seal
Female Artist   Lisa Stansfield
Group   { The KLF / Simply Red
Single   'These Are The Days of Our Lives' (Queen)
Album   Seal (Seal)
Newcomer   Beverley Craven
Classical Recording   Verdi's 'Otello' (Sir George Solti)
Producer   Trevor Horn

International

Solo Artist   Prince
Group   REM
Newcomer   P. M. Dawn

Best

Music Video   Killer (Seal)
Soundtrack/Cast Recording   The
   Commitments
Outstanding Contribution   Freddie
   Mercury

1993

Best British

Male Artist   Mick Hucknall
Female Artist   Annie Lennox
Group   Simply Red
Single   'Could it be Magic' (Take That)
Album   Diva (Annie Lennox)
Newcomer   Tasmin Archer
Classical Recording   Beethoven's Violin
   Concerto (Nigel Kennedy conducted by
   Klaus Tennstedt)
Producer   Peter Gabriel

International

Solo Artist   Prince
Group   REM
Newcomer   Nirvana

Best

Music Video   Stay (Shakespeare's Sister)
Soundtrack/Cast Recording   Wayne's
   World
Outstanding Contribution   Rod Stewart

Other Awards

Most Successful Live Band   U2

1994

The 1994 awards, sponsored by Britannia
Music Club, were dominated by young
and unfamiliar faces as the ceremony shed
its former rather conservative image.

Best British Group   Stereo MC's

Best Album by a British Artist   Stereo MC's
Best British Female Artist   Dina Carroll
Best International Newcomer   Bjork
Best International Female Singer   Bjork
Best Single   Take That
Best British Music Video   Take That
Best British Male Solo Artist   Sting
Best International Group   Crowded
   House
Best International Solo Artist   Lenny Kravitz
Best Newcomer   Gabrielle
Best New Dance Act   M-People
Best Soundtrack   The Bodyguard
Long Service Award   Van Morrison

CLASSICAL MUSIC AWARDS

The awards, made in association with Kenwood, celebrate excellence and honour the
highest achievements in international classical music. An international jury, chaired by
the editor of *The Independent*, selects winners in different categories. The Personality of
the Year is chosen as the result of a poll of the readers of *The Independent*, the *BBC
Music Magazine* in the UK and the USA, and *Onagu no Tomo*, the leading music
magazine in Japan. The 1994 awards were:

Personality of the Year   José Carreras
   (tenor)
Orchestra of the Year   New York
   Philharmonic
Chorus of the Year   Arnold Schoenberg
   Chorus
Female Singer of the Year   Cecilia Bartoli
   (soprano)
Conductor of the Year   Valery Gergiev
Opera Production of the
   Year   Stravinsky's Oedipus Rex at the

Saito Kinen Festival, Japan
Composition of the Year   Witold
   Lutoslawski's Symphony No. 4
Festival of the Year   Tender is the North,
   held at four London venues
Television Broadcast of the Year   The
   Vampyr, opera by Heinrich Marschner,
   on BBC TV
Instrumentalist of the Year   Yuri Bashmet
   (viola)
Recording of the Year   Henryk Gorecki's

Symphony No. 3, performed by the London Sinfonietta, with Dawn Upshaw, conducted by Paul Daniel
Chamber Group of the Year Kronos Quartet

Newcomer of the Year Sarah Chang (violin)
Male Singer of the Year Thomas Hampson (baritone)
Early Music Group of the Year Orchestra of the 18th Century

THE BP PETER PEARS AWARD

£5,000 and a London recital for the winner; 2nd prize, £2,000; 3rd and 4th prizes, £1,000 each. This international award for young professional singers was launched in memory of the tenor, Sir Peter Pears, who died in 1986. (It was discontinued when the period of sponsorship expired.) Winners were:

1989	Neal Davies (bass-baritone)	1991	Ann-Christine Goransson (soprano)
1990	David Mattinson (bass-baritone)		

CARDIFF SINGER OF THE WORLD COMPETITION

This competition is a biennial event, administered by BBC Wales and supported by BP.

1983	Karita Mattila (Fin)	1989	Dmitry Hvorostovsky (USSR)
1985	David Malis (USA)	1991	Lisa Gasteen (Aus)
1987	Valeria Esposito (Ita)	1993	Inger Dam-Jensen (Den)

Lieder Prize (introduced 1989)

1989	Bryn Terfel (Wal)	1993	Paul Whelan (NZ)
1991	Neal Davies (Wal)		

THE GRAMOPHONE AWARDS

The Gramophone Awards are given annually by *The Gramophone* for the best recordings of the year in a number of categories. One is chosen from these as the Record of the Year.

Record of the Year

	Category	Work recorded
1977	Operatic	Janáček, *Kátya Kabanová* (Vienna State Opera and Phil. Orch., Cond. Mackerras, Decca)
1978	Operatic	Puccini, *La Fanciulla del West* (Chorus and Orchestra of the Royal Opera House, Covent Garden, Cond. Mehta. Deutsche Grammophon)
1979	Chamber	Haydn, Piano Trios (Beaux Arts Trio, Philips)
1980	Operatic	Janáček, *From the House of the Dead* (Vienna State Opera, Cond. Mackerras, Decca)
1981	Opera	Wagner, *Parsifal* (Deutsche Oper, Berlin, Cond. von Karajan. Deutsche Grammophon)
1982–3	Concerto	Tippett, Triple Concerto (Pauk, Imai & Kirshbaum; LSO, Cond. Davis. Philips)
1984	Orchestral	Mahler, Symphony No. 9 (Berlin PO, Cond. von Karajan. Deutsche Grammophon)
1985	Concerto	Elgar, Violin Concerto (Kennedy; LPO Cond. Handley. EMI)
1986	Opera	Rossini, *Il Viaggio a Reims* (Soloists. Prague Phil. Chorus, Chamber Orch. of Europe, Cond. Abbado. Deutsche Grammophon)

	Category	Work recorded
1987	Early Music	Josquin Desprez, Masses (Tallis Scholars/Peter Philips. Gimell)
1988	Orchestral	Mahler, Symphony No. 2, 'Resurrection' (Soloists, City of Birmingham SO, Cond. Rattle. EMI)
1989	Chamber	Bartók, String Quartets Nos. 1–6 (Emerson Quartet. Deutsche Grammophon)
1990	Opera	Prokofiev, *The Love for Three Oranges* (Soloists, Lyon Opéra, Cond. Nagano. Virgin Classics)
1991	Choral	Beethoven, Mass in D major, 'Missa Solemnis' (Monteverdi Choir, Soloists, Cond. Gardiner. Archiv Produktion)
1992	Orchestral	Beethoven, Symphonies Nos. 1–9 (Chamber Orchestra of Europe, Cond. Harnocourt. Teldec)
1993	Solo vocal	Grieg, Songs (von Otter, Deutsche Grammophon)

Other awards for 1992 and 1993 were:

1992	Baroque – Vocal	Handel, *Giulio Cesare*
	Baroque – Non-Vocal	Rameau, Harpsichord Works
	Chamber	Szymanowski, String Quartets Nos. 1 and 2
	Choral	Britten, War Requiem Op. 66, Sinfonia da Requiem Op. 20 and *Ballad of Heroes* Op. 14
	Concerto	Medtner, Piano Concertos Nos. 2 and 3
	Contemporary	Tavener, *The Protecting Veil*
	Early Music	*The Rose and the Ostrich Feather*
	Engineering	Britten, War Requiem Op. 66, Sinfonia da Requiem Op.20 and *Ballad of Heroes* Op.14
	Historic – Non-Vocal	*The Elgar Edition*, Volume 1
	Historic – Vocal	*Covent Garden on Record*
	Instrumental	Alkan, 25 Préludes dans les tons majeurs et mineur Op. 31
	Music Theatre	Bernstein, *Candide*
	Opera	R. Strauss, *Die Frau Ohne Schatten*
	Solo Vocal	Schubert, Lieder
1993	Baroque –Non-Vocal	Heinichen, Dresden Concertos
	Baroque – Vocal	Stradella, *San Giovanni Battista*
	Chamber	Haydn, String Quartets Op. 20
	Choral	Mendelssohn, *Elijah*
	Concerto	Brahms, Piano Concerto No 1 and Two Songs Op. 91
	Contemporary	MacMillan, *Confessions of Isobel Gowdie*
	Early Music	Various, Venetian Vespers
	Engineering and Production	Debussy, *Le Martyre de Saint Sébastian*
	Historic – Non-Vocal	Rachmaninov, The Complete Recordings
	Historic – Vocal	Various Singers of Imperial Russia, Volumes 1–4
	Instrumental	Various, 80th birthday recital from Carnegie Hall, Shura Cherkassky
	Music Theatre	George and Ira Gershwin, *Lady Be Good*
	Opera	Poulenc, *Dialogues des Carmélites*
	Orchestral	Hindemith, Kammermusik
	Solo Vocal (Record of the Year)	Grieg, Songs (Anne Sofie von Otter)

KERRANG MAGAZINE AWARDS

Here are the results of the readers' polls for rock and heavy metal awards since the foundation of the magazine in 1981:

1981

Best Band AC/DC
Best Guitarist Ritchie Blackmore
Best Male Vocal David Coverdale
Best Female Vocalist Pat Benatar
Best Bassist Lemmy
Best Drummer Cozy Powell
Best New Band Rose Tattoo
Best Radio DJ Tommy Vance

1982

Best Band AC/DC
Best Guitarist Angus Young
Best Male Vocal Ian Gillian
Best Female Vocalist Pat Benatar
Best Bassist Cliff Williams
Best Drummer Cozy Powell
Best Live Gig Tour AC/DC
Best New Band Asia
Best Radio DJ Tommy Vance

1983

Best Band Kiss
Best Guitarist Ritchie Blackmore
Best Male Vocal Dio Ronnie James
Best Female Vocalist Pat Benatar
Best Bassist Steve Harris
Best Drummer Cozy Powell
Best Live Gig Tour Kiss
Best New Band Dio
Best Promotional Video Bark at the Moon, Ozzy Osbourne
Best Radio DJ Tommy Vance

1984

Best Band Iron Maiden
Best Guitarist Ritchie Blackmore
Best Male Vocal Dio Ronnie James
Best Female Vocalist Pat Benatar
Best Bassist Steve Harris
Best Drummer Nicko McBrain
Best Live Gig Tour Iron Maiden
Best New Band Bon Jovi
Best Promotional Video Gimme All Your Lovin' (ZZ Top)
Best Radio DJ Tommy Vance

1985

Best Band Iron Maiden

Best Guitarist Gary Moore
Best Male Vocal Bruce Dickinson
Best Female Vocalist Lee Aaron
Best Bassist Steve Harris
Best Drummer Nicko McBrain
Best Live Gig-Tour Knebworth
Best New Band Warlock
Best Promotional Video (no award)
Best Retail Video Live After Dark, Iron Maiden
Best Radio DJ Tommy Vance

1986

Best Band Iron Maiden
Best Guitarist Steve Vai
Best Male Vocal Bruce Dickinson
Best Female Vocalist Doro Pesch
Best Bassist Steve Harris
Best Drummer Nicko McBrain
Best Live Gig-Tour Iron Maiden
Best New Band Europe
Best Promotional Video Livin' on a Prayer, Bon Jovi
Best Retail Video Live After Dark, Iron Maiden
Best Radio DJ Tommy Vance

1987

Best Band Whitesnake
Best Guitarist Kirk Hammett
Best Male Vocal David Coverdale
Best Female Vocalist Doro Pesch
Best Bassist Steve Harris
Best Drummer Rick Allen
Best Live Gig Tour Anthrax
Best New Band Guns 'n' Roses
Best Promotional Video Suite of the Night, Whitesnake
Best Retail Video 12 Wasted Years, Iron Maiden
Best Radio DJ Tommy Vance

1988

Best Band Guns 'n' Roses
Best Guitarist Slash
Best Male Vocal W. Axl Rose
Best Female Vocalist Lita Ford

Best Bassist　Steve Harris
Best Drummer　Lars Ulrich
Best Live Gig Tour　Donnington
Best New Band　Guns 'n' Roses
Best Promotional Video　Can I Play With
　Madness, Iron Maiden
Best Retail Video　Cliff 'em All
Best Radio DJ　Tommy Vance

1989

Best Band　Aerosmith
Best Guitarist　Steve Vai
Best Male Vocalist　Steve Tyler
Best Female Vocalist　Lita Ford
Best Bassist　Steve Harris
Best Drummer　Lars Ulrich
Best Live Gig Tour　Aerosmith
Best New Band　Skid Row
Best Promotional Video　One, Metallica
Best Retail Video　Maiden England, Iron
　Maiden
Best Radio DJ　Tommy Vance

1990

Best Band　Iron Maiden
Best Guitarist　Steve Vai
Best Male Vocalist　Bruce Dickinson
Best Female Vocalist　Lita Ford
Best Bassist　Steve Harris
Best Drummer　Nicko McBrain
Best New Band　Thunder
Best Promotional Video　Holy Smoke, Iron
　Maiden
Best Retail Video　You Fat Bastards, Faith
　No More
Best Radio DJ　Tommy Vance

1991

Best Band　Metallica
Best Guitarist　Nuno Bettencourt
Best Male Vocalist　Sebastian Bach

Best Female Vocalist　Lita Ford
Best Bassist　Rachel Nolan
Best Drummer　Lars Ulrich
Best Live Gig Tour　Skid Row
Best New Band　Nirvana
Best Promotional Video　Enter Sandman,
　Metallica
Best Retail Video　Oh Say Can You
　Scream, Skid Row
Best Radio DJ　Tommy Vance

1992

Best Band　Metallica
Best Guitarist　Slash
Best Male Vocalist　James Hetfield
Best Female Vocalist　Donita Sparks
Best Bassist　Jason Newsted
Best Drummer　Lars Ulrich
Best Live Gig　Metallica
Best New Band　Ugly Kid Joe
Best Promotional Video　November Rain
　(Guns 'n' Roses)
Best Retail Video　Live At Donnington,
　AC/DC
Best Radio DJ　Tommy Vance

1993

Best Band　Metallica
Best Guitarist　Slash
Best Male Vocalist　James Hetfield
Best Female Vocalist　Lita Ford
Best Bassist　Jason Newsted
Best Drummer　Lars Ulrich
Best Live Gig Tour　Metallica
Best New Band　Wildhearts
Best Promotional Video　I Would Do
　Anything For Love (Meat Loaf)
Best Retail Video　Live At Donnington
　(Iron Maiden)
Best Radio DJ　Claire Sturgess

HARVEYS LEEDS INTERNATIONAL PIANOFORTE COMPETITION

This competition, founded in 1963 by Fanny Waterman and Marion Thorpe (who was then the Countess of Harewood), and sponsored by Harveys of Bristol Limited, is held in Leeds every three years. The first prize is the Princess Mary Gold Medal, £10,000 (donated by the Audrey and Stanley Burton Charitable Trust), the Bunkamura Orchard Hall Award of $20,000, and the Edward Boyle Prize. The other prizes include the Rachmaninov Prize of £10,000 awarded to the pianist who gives the best performances of works by the composer throughout all four stages of the competition. The last stages of the competition, when six finalists play concertos, are televised.

1963	Michael Roll	1978	Michel Dalberto	1987	Vladimir
1966	Rafael Orozco	1981	Ian Hobson		Ovchinikov
1969	Radu Lupu	1984	Jon Kimura	1990	Artur Pizarro
1972	Murray Perahia		Parker	1993	Ricardo Castro
1975	Dmitri Alexeev				

LLOYDS BANK YOUNG COMPOSER AWARDS

These awards (currently £1,000 each) were created by Lloyds Bank and the BBC to extend the range of the Young Musician of the Year competition. The award is intended to attract as wide a variety of composers as possible, including those not normally associated with the concert hall and those who do not write in the traditional 'Western Classical' music idiom. The 1993 winners were Timothy Benjamin and Oscar Bettison.

BBC YOUNG MUSICIAN OF THE YEAR

The competition is held in association with Lloyds Bank. There are a number of prizes. The overall winner receives a trophy and the Lloyds Bank Travel Award.

1978	Michael Hext (trombone)	1988	David Pyatt (horn)
1980	Nicholas Daniel (oboe)	1990	Nicola Loud (violin)
1982	Anna Markland (piano)	1992	Frederick Kempf (piano)
1984	Emma Johnson (clarinet)	1994	Natalie Clein (cello)
1986	Alan Brind (violin)		

THE BRITISH REGGAE INDUSTRY ANNUAL AWARDS

1989

Best British Male DJ Macka B
Best British Female DJ Cinderella
Best British Male Newcomer Mike Anthony
Best British Female Newcomer Sharon Marie
Best British Male Singer Barry Boom
Best British Female Singer Kofi
Best British Album *Truly Bowled Over* by John McLean
Best British Single *Raggamuffin Girl* by Tippa Irie and Peter Hunnigale
Best British Reggae Band The Instigators
Best British Producer Neil Fraser (Mad Professor)
Best British Newcomer Producer Mafia and Fluxy
Best British Radio Station Lightning FM
Best Nightclub Nightmoves Club and Restaurant
Best Album Design *Black with Sugar* by Kofi
Best International Artist Sanchez

Best International Record *Bun and Cheese* by Clement Irie and Robert French
Best International Producer Augustus Clarke
Best Radio DJ Personality Ranking Miss P
Contribution to the Reggae Industry The *Echoes* magazine
Contribution to the Reggae Industry David Rodigan
Contribution to the Reggae Industry Dub Bug

1990

Best British Male Singer Vivian Jones
Best British Female Singer Janet Lee Davis
Best British Male Newcomer Lloyd Brown
Best British Female Newcomer Wendy Walker
Best British Radio Personality (Community) D. J. Keithly
Best British Radio DJ Daddy Ernie (Choice FM)

Outstanding Achievement in the Reggae Industry Misty in Roots

(Joint winners) Best British Single 'Your Love' by Michael Prophet and Ricky Tuffy, 'More Love' by Roger Robin

Best British Album The Living Boom by Barry Boom

Best British Songwriter Philip Leo

Best British DJ Sweetie Irie

Best British Vocal Group Private Collection

Best British Producer Mafia and Fluxy

Best International Record 'Tempted to Touch' by Beres Hammond

Best International Artist Shabba Ranks

Best International Producer Donovan Germaine

1991

Best British Male Singer Peter Hunningale

Best British Female Singer Janet Lee-Davis

Best British Male DJ Macka B

Best British Female DJ no contenders

Best British Male Newcomer Apache Indian

Best British Female Newcomer no contenders

Best British Single 'Love You Down' by Lloyd Brown

Best British Vocal Group Klearview Harmonix

Best British Songwriter Philip Leo

Best British Album Strong Love by Vivian Jones

Best British Radio Personality Crucial Robbie

Best British Producer Trevor Rose/Surfa

Best British Studio Engineer Patrick Donegan

Best British Album Design Tony McDermot

Best International Band/Artist Beres Hammond

Best International Producer Donovan Germaine

Best International Record Gal Wine by Chaka Demus and Pliers

Special Contribution Jah Shaka

1992

Best British Male Singer Neville Morrison

Best British Female Singer Deborahe Glasgow

Best British DJ General Levy

Best British Newcomer China Black

Best British Single 'Heat' by General Levy

Best British Album Wickeda General by General Levy

Best British Group Misty in Roots

Best British Songwriter Mike Anthony

Best British Radio DJ Personality Trevor Sax

Best British Radio Community DJ Sugar Dread

Best British Radio Station in Support of Reggae W.N.K. Radio

Best British Reggae Producer Fashion Records

Best British Sound System Saxon

Best Reggae Video Murder She Wrote by Chaka Demus and Pliers

Best International Reggae Single Murder She Wrote by Chaka Demus and Pliers

Best International Reggae Album Mr Mention by Buju Banton

Best International Artist Shabba Ranks

Best International Newcomer Buju Banton

Best International Producer Donovan Germaine

Special Contribution to the Reggae Industry Bob Marley

BRITAIN'S SONG FOR EUROPE

An annual competition in which BBC Television viewers vote for Britain's entry in the Eurovision Song Contest (see p. 188).

1956	*no entry*	1960	'Looking High, High, High', Bryan Johnson
1957	'All', Patricia Bredin	1961	'Are You Sure?', The Allison Brothers
1958	*no entry*		
1959	'Sing Little Birdie', Teddy Johnson and Pearl Carr		

1962	'Ring-a-Ding Girl', Ronnie Carroll
1963	'Say Wonderful Things', Ronnie Carroll
1964	'I Love The Little Things', Matt Monro
1965	'I Belong', Kathy Kirby
1966	'A Man Without Love', Kenneth McKellar
1967	'Puppet On A String', Sandie Shaw
1968	'Congratulations', Cliff Richard
1969	'Boom Bang-a-Bang', Lulu
1970	'Knock Knock, Who's There?', Mary Hopkin
1971	'Jack in the Box', Clodagh Rodgers
1972	'Beg, Steal or Borrow', The New Seekers
1973	'Power to All Our Friends', Cliff Richard
1974	'Long Live Love', Olivia Newton-John
1975	'Let Me Be The One', The Shadows
1976	'Save Your Kisses For Me', Brotherhood of Man
1977	'Rock Bottom', Lynsey de Paul and Mike Moran
1978	'The Bad Old Days', Co-Co
1979	'Mary Ann', Black Lace
1980	'Love Enough for Two', Prima Donna
1981	'Making Your Mind Up', Bucks Fizz
1982	'One Step Further', Bardo
1983	'I'm Never Giving Up', Sweet Dreams
1984	'Love Games', Belle and the Devotions
1985	'Love Is', Vikki Watson
1986	'Runner in the Night', Ryder
1987	'Only the Light', Ricky Peebles
1988	'Go', Scott Fitzgerald
1989	'Why Do I Always Get It Wrong?', Live Report
1990	'Give A Little Love Back to the World', Emma Booth
1991	'A Message To Your Heart', Samantha Janus
1992	'One Step At A Time', Michael Ball
1993	'Better The Devil You Know', Sonia
1994	'We Will be Free', Frances Ruffelle

EUROVISION SONG CONTEST

A perennially popular award, the contest involves artists from all the major European countries, and attracts a huge television audience.

	Singer	Country	Song
1956	Lys Assia	Switzerland	'Refrains'
1957	Corry Brokken	Holland	'Net Als Toen'
1958	André Claveau	France	'Dors, Mon Amour'
1959	Teddy Scholten	Holland	'Een Beetje'
1960	Jacqueline Boyer	France	'Tom Pillibi'
1961	Jean Claude Pascal	Luxembourg	'Nous, Les Amoureux'
1962	Isabelle Aubret	France	'Un Premier Amour'
1963	Grethe and Jørgen Ingmann	Denmark	'Dansevise'
1964	Gigliola Cinquetti	Italy	'No Ho L'Eta per Amarti'
1965	France Gall	Luxembourg	'Poupée de Cire, Poupé de S
1966	Udo Jurgens	Austria	'Merci Chérie'
1967	Sandie Shaw	United Kingdom	'Puppet on a String'
1968	Massiel	Spain	'La, La, La'
1969	Salome	Spain	'Vivo Cantando'
	Lulu	United Kingdom	'Boom Bang-a-Bang'
	Lennie Kuhr	Holland	'De Troubadour'
	Frida Boccara	France	'Un Jour, Un Enfant'
1970	Dana	Ireland	'All Kinds of Everything'
1971	Severine	Monaco	'Un Banc, Un Arbre, Une Rue

1972	Vicky Leandros	Luxembourg	'Après Toi'
1973	Anne Marie David	Luxembourg	'Tu Te Reconnaitras'
1974	Abba	Sweden	'Waterloo'
1975	Teach-In	Holland	'Ding Ding a Dong'
1976	Brotherhood of Man	United Kingdom	'Save Your Kisses For Me'
1977	Marie Myriam	France	'L'Oiseau et L'Enfant'
1978	Izhar Cohen and the Alphabeta	Israel	'A-Ba-Ni-Bi'
1979	Milk and Honey	Israel	'Hallelujah'
1980	Johnny Logan	Ireland	'What's Another Year?'
1981	Bucks Fizz	United Kingdom	'Making Your Mind Up'
1982	Nicole	Germany	'Ein Bisschen Friden'
1983	Corinne Hermés	Luxembourg	'Si La Vie est Cadeau'
1984	Herrey's	Sweden	'Diggi-loo Diggi-ley'
1985	Bobbysocks!	Norway	'La det Swinge'
1986	Sandra Kim	Belgium	'J'aime la Vie'
1987	Johnny Logan	Ireland	'Hold Me Now'
1988	Céline Dion	Switzerland	'Ne Partez Pas Sans Moi'
1989	Riva	Yugoslavia	'Rock Me'
1990	Toto Cutugno	Italy	'Insieme 1992'
1991	Carola	Sweden	'Captured By a Love Storm'
1992	Linda Martin	Ireland	'Why Me?'
1993	Niamh Kavanagh	Ireland	'In Your Eyes'
1994	Paul Harrigan and Charlie McGettigan	Ireland	'Rock and Roll Kids'

GRAMMY AWARDS

The Grammy Award is sponsored by the National Academy of Recording Arts and Sciences of America, founded in 1957 by recording artists, composers and craftsmen to advance the arts and sciences of recording. Recordings are nominated and voted on by members of the National Academy of Recording Arts and Sciences. These members are the individuals directly and creatively involved in the making of phonograph records. Awards are announced annually on the Academy's Grammy Awards telecast over the CBS network in early spring. Below is a selection from the ninety or so categories for which awards have been made since 1958.

Record of the Year

1958	*Nel Blu Dipinto di Blu (Volare)*, Domenico Modugno
1959	*Mack the Knife*, Bobby Darin
1960	*Theme from 'A Summer Place'*, Percy Faith
1961	*Moon River*, Henry Mancini
1962	*I Left My Heart in San Francisco*, Tony Bennett
1963	*The Days of Wine and Roses*, Henry Mancini
1964	*The Girl from Ipanema*, Stan Getz and Astrud Gilberto
1965	*A Taste of Honey*, Herb Alpert and the Tijuana Brass
1966	*Strangers in the Night*, Frank Sinatra
1967	*Up, Up and Away*, 5th Dimension
1968	*Mrs Robinson*, Simon and Garfunkel
1969	*Aquarius, Let the Sunshine In*, 5th Dimension
1970	*Bridge Over Troubled Water*, Simon and Garfunkel
1971	*It's Too Late*, Carole King
1972	*The First Time Ever I Saw Your Face*, Roberta Flack
1973	*Killing Me Softly With His Song*, Roberta Flack
1974	*I Honestly Love You*, Olivia Newton-John
1975	*Love Will Keep Us Together*, Captain and Tenille

1976	*This Masquerade*, George Benson
1977	*Hotel California*, The Eagles
1978	*Just the Way You Are*, Billy Joel
1979	*What A Fool Believes*, The Doobie Brothers
1980	*Sailing*, Christopher Cross
1981	*Bette Davis Eyes*, Kim Carnes
1982	*Rosanna*, Toto
1983	*Beat It*, Michael Jackson
1984	*What's Love Got to Do With It?*, Tina Turner
1985	*We Are the World*, USA for Africa
1986	*Higher Love*, Steve Winwood
1987	*Graceland*, Paul Simon
1988	*Don't Worry, Be Happy*, Bobby McFerrin
1989	*Wind Beneath My Wings*, Bette Midler
1990	*Another Day in Paradise*, Phil Collins
1991	*Unforgettable*, Natalie Cole, with Nat 'King' Cole
1992	*Tears in Heaven*, Eric Clapton
1993	*I Will Always Love You*, Whitney Houston

Album of the Year

1958	*The Music from Peter Gunn*, Henry Mancini
1959	*Come Dance With Me*, Frank Sinatra
1960	*Button Down Mind*, Bob Newhart
1961	*Judy at Carnegie Hall*, Judy Garland
1962	*The First Family*, Vaughn Meader
1963	*The Barbra Streisand Album*, Barbra Streisand
1964	*Getz/Gilberto*, Stan Getz and Joao Gilberto
1965	*September of My Years*, Frank Sinatra
1966	*Sinatra: A Man and His Music*, Frank Sinatra
1967	*Sergeant Pepper's Lonely Hearts Club Band*, The Beatles
1968	*By the Time I Get to Phoenix*, Glen Campbell
1969	*Blood, Sweat and Tears*, Blood, Sweat and Tears
1970	*Bridge Over Troubled Water*, Simon and Garfunkel
1971	*Tapestry*, Carole King
1972	*The Concert for Bangla Desh*, George Harrison, Ravi Shankar, Bob Dylan, Leon Russell, Ringo Starr, Billy Preston, Eric Clapton and Klaus Voormann
1973	*Innervisions*, Stevie Wonder
1974	*Fulfillingness' First Finale*, Stevie Wonder
1975	*Still Crazy After All These Years*, Paul Simon
1976	*Songs in the Key of Life*, Stevie Wonder
1977	*Rumours*, Fleetwood Mac
1978	*Saturday Night Fever*, Bee Gees
1979	*52nd Street*, Billy Joel
1980	*Christopher Cross*, Christopher Cross
1981	*Double Fantasy*, John Lennon and Yoko Ono
1982	*Toto IV*, Toto
1983	*Thriller*, Michael Jackson
1984	*Can't Slow Down*, Lionel Richie
1985	*No Jacket Required*, Phil Collins
1986	*Graceland*, Paul Simon
1987	*The Joshua Tree*, U2
1988	*Faith*, George Michael
1989	*Nick of Time*, Bonnie Raitt
1990	*Back on the Block*, Quincy Jones
1991	*Unforgettable*, Natalie Cole, with Nat 'King' Cole
1992	*Unplugged*, Eric Clapton
1993	*The Bodyguard*, Whitney Houston

THE *MELODY MAKER* JAZZ AWARDS

This poll by readers of *Melody Maker* magazine was introduced in 1946, and separate British (B) and world (W) national sections were operated from 1955 until 1974 when the poll was discontinued. A special poll for jazz critics on newspapers and magazines was also held, and in 1977 *Melody Maker* organized a poll of international jazz critics to find the world's best jazz musicians and artists.

The following is just a selection of some of the winners of the *Melody Maker* readers' poll jazz awards:

Big Bands/Bandleader of the Year

1946	Geraldo
1947	Ted Heath
1952	Geraldo
1953–4	Ted Heath
1955	Ted Heath (B) and Stan Kenton (W)
1957	Johnny Dankworth (B) and Count Basie (W)
1961	Johnny Dankworth (B) and Count Basie (W)
1962	Johnny Dankworth (B) and Count Basie (W)
1963	Johnny Dankworth (B) and Count Basie (W)
1964	Johnny Dankworth (B) and Duke Ellington (W)
1965	Johnny Dankworth (B) and Duke Ellington (W)
1967	Harry South (B) and Duke Ellington (W)
1969	Mike Westbrook (B) and Duke Ellington (W)
1970	Mike Westbrook (B) and Duke Ellington (W)
1971	Mike Westbrook (B) and Sun Ra (W)
1972	Centipede (B) and Duke Ellington (W)
1973	Mike Gibbs (B) and Duke Ellington (W)
1974	Mike Gibbs (B) and Duke Ellington (W)

Musician of the Year

1949	Johnny Dankworth
1950	Johnny Dankworth
1951	Johnny Dankworth
1952	Johnny Dankworth
1953	Jack Parnell
1954	Johnny Dankworth
1955	Eric Delaney (B) and Gerry Mulligan (W)
1957	Johnny Dankworth (B) and Count Basie (W)
1961	Johnny Dankworth (B) and Miles Davis (W)
1962	Tubby Hayes (B) and Duke Ellington (W)
1963	Tubby Hayes (B) and Duke Ellington (W)
1964	Tubby Hayes (B) and Duke Ellington (W)
1965	Tubby Hayes (B) and Duke Ellington (W)
1966	Tubby Hayes (B) and Duke Ellington (W)
1967	Tubby Hayes (B) and Duke Ellington (W)
1968	Tubby Hayes (B) and Duke Ellington (W)
1969	Tubby Hayes (B) and Duke Ellington (W)
1970	John Surman (B) and Miles Davis (W)
1971	John Surman (B) and Miles Davis (W)
1972	John Surman (B) and Miles Davis (W)
1973	John McLaughlin and Mike Gibbs (B) and Miles Davis (W)
1974	Mike Gibbs (B) and Duke Ellington (W)

Other Top Bands and Small Groups

1946	Ted Heath (swing), Jack Parnell (combo) and Geraldo (sweet)
1947	Ted Heath (swing), Jack Parnell (combo) and Geraldo (sweet)
1949	Ted Heath (swing), Ray Ellington (combo), Geraldo (sweet), and Edmundo Ros (Latin American)
1950	Ted Heath (swing), Johnny Dankworth (combo), Geraldo (sweet) and Edmundo Ros (Latin American)
1951	Ted Heath (swing), Johnny Dankworth (combo), Geraldo (sweet) and Edmundo Ros (Latin American)
1952	Ted Heath (swing), Johnny Dankworth (modern), Edmundo Ros (Latin), Humphrey Lyttelton (trad)
1953	Ted Heath (swing), Johnny Dankworth (modern), Edmundo Ros (Latin), Humphrey Lyttelton (trad)

1954	Ronnie Scott (modern) and Humphrey Lyttelton (trad)
1955	Ronnie Scott (modern) (B), Humphrey Lyttelton (trad) (B) and Gerry Mulligan (modern) (W), Louis Armstrong (trad) (W)
1957	Tony Kinsey (B) and Modern Jazz Quartet (W)
1961	Tubby Hayes (B) and Modern Jazz Quartet (W)
1962	Chris Barber (trad), Tubby Hayes (B) and Dave Brubeck (W)
1963	Chris Barber (trad), Tubby Hayes (B) and Dave Brubeck (W)
1964	Tubby Hayes (B) and Modern Jazz Quartet (W)
1965	Tubby Hayes, Georgie Fame (R & B) (B) and Modern Jazz Quartet, Rolling Stones (R & B) (W)
1966	Freddy Randall (B) and Modern Jazz Quartet (W)
1967	Don Rendell/Ian Carr (B) and Modern Jazz Quartet (W)
1969	Georgie Fame (B) and Miles Davis (W)
1970	Alex Welsh (B) and Miles Davis (W)
1971	Nucleus (B) and Miles Davis (W)
1972	Nucleus (B) and Miles Davis (W)
1973	Nucleus (B) and Mahavishau Orchestra (W)
1974	Soft Machine (B) and Mahavishau Orchestra (W)

British Male Vocalist of the Year

1946	Benny Lee
1947	Benny Lee
1949	Alan Dean
1950	Alan Dean
1951	Alan Dean
1952	Alan Dean
1953	Dickie Valentine
1954	Dickie Valentine
1955	Dickie Valentine
1957	Denis Lotis
1959	George Melly (trad)
1960	George Melly (trad)
1961	George Melly (trad)
1962	George Melly (trad)
1963	George Melly (trad)
1962	Matt Monro
1963	Matt Monro
1964	Matt Monro
1965	Matt Monro
1966	Georgie Fame
1967	Georgie Fame
1968	Georgie Fame
1969	Georgie Fame
1970	Georgie Fame
1971	Georgie Fame
1972	Jack Bruce
1973	George Melly
1974	George Melly

British Female Vocalist of the Year

1946	Anne Shelton
1947	Anne Shelton
1948	Anne Shelton
1949	Terry Devon
1950	Pearl Carr
1951	Pearl Carr
1952	Lita Roza
1953	Lita Roza
1954	Lita Roza
1955	Lita Roza
1957	Cleo Laine
1961	Cleo Laine
1962	Ottilie Patterson (trad) and Cleo Laine
1963	Ottilie Patterson (trad) and Cleo Laine
1964	Cleo Laine
1965	Cleo Laine
1966	Cleo Laine
1967	Cleo Laine
1968	Cleo Laine
1969	Cleo Laine
1970	Cleo Laine
1971	Norma Winstone
1972	Norma Winstone
1973	Norma Winstone
1974	Cleo Laine

World's Top Male Singer

1955	Frank Sinatra
1956	Frank Sinatra
1957	Frank Sinatra
1958	Frank Sinatra
1959	Frank Sinatra

1960	Frank Sinatra
1961	Frank Sinatra
1962	Frank Sinatra
1963	Frank Sinatra
1964	Frank Sinatra
1965	Frank Sinatra
1966	Frank Sinatra
1967	Frank Sinatra
1968	Frank Sinatra
1969	Jon Hendricks
1970	Jon Hendricks
1971	Leon Thomas
1972	Leon Thomas
1973	Leon Thomas
1974	Leon Thomas

World's Top Female Singer

1955	Sarah Vaughan
1957	Ella Fitzgerald
1961	Ella Fitzgerald
1962	Ella Fitzgerald
1963	Ella Fitzgerald
1964	Ella Fitzgerald
1965	Ella Fitzgerald
1966	Ella Fitzgerald
1967	Ella Fitzgerald
1968	Ella Fitzgerald
1969	Ella Fitzgerald
1970	Ella Fitzgerald
1971	Norma Winstone
1972	Ella Fitzgerald
1973	Norma Winstone
1974	Ella Fitzgerald

British Vocal Group of the Year

1950	Keynotes
1951	Keynotes
1952	Stargazers
1953	Stargazers
1954	Stargazers
1955	Stargazers
1956	Stargazers
1957	Stargazers
1961	The Polka Dots
1962	The Polka Dots
1963	The Polka Dots
1964	The Polka Dots
1965	The Polka Dots
1966	Morgan James Duo
1967	Morgan James Duo

discontinued

World's Top Vocal Group

1955	Four Aces
1957	Hi-lo's
1961	Four Freshmen
1962	Four Freshmen
1963	Lambert, Hendricks and Ross
1964	Four Freshmen
1965	Swingle Singers
1966	Swingle Singers
1967	Swingle Singers

discontinued

World's Top Musicians include:

Guitar

1955	Barney Kessel
1965	Wes Montgomery

Clarinet

1955	Buddy de Franco
1965	Pee Wee Russell
1972	Benny Goodman

Saxophone

1953	Ronnie Scott
1955	Gerry Mulligan, Lee Konitz, Stan Getz
1965	Tubby Hayes, Johnny Hodges, John Coltrane and Gerry Mulligan

Top Blues Artists

1965	Jimmy Witherspoon
1966	Georgie Fame (B) and Jimmy Witherspoon
1969	John Mayall (B) and Muddy Waters
1970	John Mayall (B) and Jimmy Witherspoon
1971	John Mayall (B) and Muddy Waters
1972	John Mayall (B) and B B King
1973	John Mayall (B) and B B King
1974	John Mayall (B) and B B King

There were no Melody Maker *readers' polls after 1974*

Critics' Section

1961	***Critics' awards***
	Musician of the Year Miles Davis

Small Combo Miles Davis
New Star Ray Bryant
Big Band Duke Ellington
Male Singer Jimmy Rushing
Female Singer Ella Fitzgerald
Vocal Group Lambert,
Hendricks and Ross

1963 **Critics' section**
Musician of the Year Duke
Ellington
Big Band Duke Ellington
Combo Miles Davis
Male Singer Louis Armstrong
Female Singer Sarah Vaughan

1964 **Critics' section**
Musician of the Year Duke
Ellington
Big Band Duke Ellington
Combo Charlie Mingus
Arranger/Composer Duke
Ellington
Male Singer Louis Armstrong
Female Singer Sarah Vaughan
Blues/Gospel Marion Williams
New Star Anthony Williams

1966 **Critics' poll**
Musician of the Year Ornette
Coleman
Big Band Duke Ellington
Small Group Clark Terry/Bob
Brookmeyer

1969 **Critics' section**
Top Musician John Surman

Big Band Duke Ellington
Small Group Miles Davis
Male Singer Louis Armstrong
Female Singer Sarah Vaughan

1977 **International Jazz Critics'
Awards**
Big Band Thad Jones/Mel
Lewis
Ensemble McCoy Tyner
Composer Keith Jarrett
Arranger Gil Evans
Trumpet Dizzy Gillespie
Soprano Sax Steve Lacy
Alto Sax Anthony Braxton
Tenor Sax Sonny Rollins
Baritone Sax Gerry Mulligan
Clarinet Anthony Braxton
Flute Hubert Laws
Trombone Albert Mangelsdorff
Piano Cecil Taylor
Organ Jimmy Smith
Synthesiser Joe Zawinul
Guitar Jim Hall
Violin Jean-Luc Ponty
Acoustic Bass Niels-Henning
Orsted-Pedersen
Electric Bass Stanley Clarke
Vibes Gary Burton
Drums Elvin Jones
Percussion Airto Moreira
Misc. Instruments Roland Kirk
Male Vocal Joe Williams
Female Vocal Sarah Vaughan

THE *MELODY MAKER* READERS' POP POLL AND ANNUAL AWARDS

This annual poll by readers of the magazine was inaugurated in 1960. The separate British (B) and world (W) sections, introduced in 1963, were abandoned in 1978.

Top Male Singer of the Year

1960	Cliff Richard
1961	Cliff Richard
1962	Cliff Richard
1963	Cliff Richard (B) and Elvis Presley (W)
1964	Cliff Richard (B) and Elvis Presley (W)
1965	Cliff Richard (B) and Elvis Presley (W)
1966	Tom Jones (B) and Elvis Presley (W)
1967	Cliff Richard (B) and Otis Redding (W)
1968	Scott Walker (B) and Bob Dylan (W)
1969	Tom Jones (B) and Bob Dylan (W)
1970	Robert Plant (B) and Bob Dylan (W)
1971	Rod Stewart (B) and Neil Young (W)
1972	Rod Stewart (B) and Neil Young (W)

1973	David Bowie (B) and Robert Plant (W)
1974	Paul Rodgers (B) and David Bowie (W)
1975	Robert Plant (B and W)
1976	Jon Anderson (B) and Robert Plant (W)
1977	Jon Anderson (B and W)
1978	Jon Anderson
1979	Robert Plant
1980	Peter Gabriel
1981	David Bowie
1982	Paul Weller
1983	Boy George
1984	Bono
1985	Bono
1986	Morrissey
1987	Morrissey
1988	Morrissey
1989	Robert Smith
1990	Robert Smith
1991	Robert Smith
1992	Robert Smith
1993	Evan Dando

Female Singer of the Year

1960	Shirley Bassey
1961	Shirley Bassey
1962	Helen Shapiro
1963	Susan Maughan (B) and Brenda Lee (W)
1964	Cilla Black (B) and Mary Wells (W)
1965	Sandie Shaw (B) and Brenda Lee (W)
1966	Dusty Springfield (B and W)
1967	Dusty Springfield (B and W)
1968	Julie Driscoll (B) and Aretha Franklin (W)
1969	Christine Perfect (B) and Janis Joplin (W)
1970	Sandy Denny (B) and Joni Mitchell (W)
1971	Sandy Denny (B) and Joni Mitchell (W)
1972	Maggie Bell (B) and Joni Mitchell (W)
1973	Maggie Bell (B) and Carly Simon (W)
1974	Maggie Bell (B) and Joni Mitchell (W)

1975	Maggie Bell (B) and Joni Mitchell (W)
1976	Kiki Dee (B) and Joni Mitchell (W)
1977	Kiki Dee (B) and Joni Mitchell (W)
1978	Kate Bush
1979	Kate Bush
1980	Kate Bush
1981	Toyah
1982	Alison Moyet
1983	Annie Lennox
1984	Liz Frazer
1985	Liz Frazer
1986	Kate Bush
1987	Julianne Regan
1988	Julianne Regan
1989	Kate Bush
1990	Sinead O'Connor
1991	Toni Halliday
1992	P. J. Harvey
1993	Bjork

Brightest Hope of the Year

1960	Emile Ford
1961	The Allisons
1962	Helen Shapiro
1963	Billy J. Kramer (B) and Lesley Gore (W)
1964	Lulu and the Lovers (B) and P. J. Proby (W)
1965	Donovan (B) and Walker Bros (W)
1966	The Troggs (B) and Mama's and Papa's (W)
1967	Procul Harum (B and W)
1968	Julie Driscoll and Brian Auger Trinity (B and W)
1969	Blind Faith (B and W)
1970	Mungo Jerry (B) and Emerson, Lake and Palmer (W)
1971	Wishbone Ash (B) and Mountain (W)
1972	Roxy Music (B) and Focus (W)
1973	Nazareth (B) and Beck, Bogert and Appice (W)
1974	Bad Company (B) and Sparks (W)
1975	Camel (B and W)
1976	Thin Lizzy (B) and Peter Frampton (W)

1977	Stranglers (B) and Television (W)
1978	Kate Bush
1979	Gary Numan
1980	Saxon
1981	Altered Images
1982	Culture Club
1983	Howard Jones
1984	King
1985	The Jesus and Mary Chain
1986	The Housemartins
1987	Sugarcubes
1988	House of Love
1989	Stone Roses
1990	Ride
1991	Curve
1992	Suede
1993	Elastica

Single Disc of the Year
(World section)

1967	*Whiter Shade of Pale*, Procol Harum
1968	*US Male*, Elvis Presley
1969	*The Boxer*, Simon and Garfunkel
1970	*Bridge Over Troubled Water*, Simon and Garfunkel
1971	*My Sweet Lord*, George Harrison
1972	*American Pie*, Don McLean
1973	*Walk on the Wild Side*, Lou Reed
1974	*This Town Ain't Big Enough for Both of Us*, Sparks
1975	*I'm Not in Love*, 10cc
1976	*Bohemian Rhapsody*, Queen
1977	*Fanfare for the Common Man*, Emerson, Lake and Palmer
1978	*Baker Street*, Gerry Rafferty
1979	*I Don't Like Mondays*, Boomtown Rats
1980	*Another Brick in the Wall (Part 2)*, Pink Floyd
1981	*Ghost Town*, The Specials
1982	*Town Called Alice*, The Jam
1983	*Karma Chameleon*, Culture Club
1984	*Pride in the Name of Love*, U2
1985	*She Sells Sanctuary*, Culture Club
1986	*Panic*, The Smiths
1987	*This Corrosion*, Sisters of Mercy
1988	*Tower of Strength*, The Mission
1989	*Lullaby*, The Cure

1990	*Only One I Know*, Charlatans
1991	*Smells Like Teen Spirit*, Nirvana
1992	*The Drowners*, Suede
1993	*Creep*, Radiohead

LP/Album of the Year (World section)

1967	*Sergeant Pepper's Lonely Hearts Club Band*, The Beatles
1968	*John Wesley Harding*, Bob Dylan
1969	*Nashville Skyline*, Bob Dylan
1970	*Hot Rats*, Frank Zappa
1971	*After the Gold Rush*, Neil Young
1972	*Harvest*, Neil Young
1973	*Dark Side of the Moon*, Pink Floyd
1974	*Tubular Bells*, Mike Oldfield
1975	*Physical Graffiti*, Led Zeppelin
1976	*A Trick of the Tail*, Genesis
1977	*Works*, Emerson, Lake and Palmer
1978	*Live and Dangerous*, Thin Lizzy
1979	*In Through the Out Door*, Led Zeppelin
1980	*The Wall*, Pink Floyd
1981	*Dare*, Human League
1982	*The Gift*, Jam
1983	*Seven and the Ragged Tiger*, Duran Duran
1984	*The Unforgettable Fire*, U2
1985	*Head on the Door*, The Cure
1986	*The Queen is Dead*, The Smiths
1987	*Kiss Me, Kiss Me, Kiss Me*, The Cure
1988	*Children*, The Mission
1989	*Doolittle*, Pixies
1990	*Nowhere*, Ride
1991	*Nevermind*, Nirvana
1992	*Automatic For The People*, REM
1993	*Siamese Dream*, Smashing Pumpkins

Top Live Act

1973	Alice Cooper
1974	Emerson, Lake and Palmer
1975	Led Zeppelin
1976	Genesis
1977	Genesis
1978	Genesis
1979	Led Zeppelin
1980	Genesis
1981	Bruce Springsteen and the East Street Band

1982	Jam		1977	Yes
1983	Duran Duran		1978	Genesis
1984	U2		1979	Led Zeppelin
1985	U2		1980	Genesis
1986	The Smiths		1981	Genesis
1987	The Cure		1982	Jam
1988	The Mission		1983	Duran Duran
1989	The Cure		1984	The Smiths
1990	Pixies		1985	U2
1991	Carter USM		1986	The Smiths
1992	The Cure		1987	The Smiths
1993	Blur		1988	The Mission
			1989	Pixies

Top Band

1973	Yes		1990	Pixies
1974	Yes		1991	Wonder Stuff
1975	Led Zeppelin		1992	The Cure
1976	Yes		1993	Suede

MELODY MAKER'S CHARTS

Charts for 1993 were:

Top 10 Independent Singles

1. *'Eject'*, Senser/Ultimate
2. *'Open Up'*, Leftfield & Lydon/Hard Hands
3. *'Enough is Enough'*, Chumbawamba/One Little Indian
4. *'Cannonball'*, The Breeders/4AD
5. *'Belaruse'*, The Levellers/China
6. *'The Key'*, Senser/Ultimate
7. *'Electric Mainline EP'*, Spiritualized/Dedicated
8. *'So Young'*, Suede/Nude
9. *'This Garden'*, The Levellers/China
10. *'On EP'*, Aphex Twin/Warp

Top 10 UK Singles

1. *'I'd Do Anything for Love'*, Meat Loaf/Virgin
2. *'All That She Wants'*, Ace of Base/Virgin
3. *'(I Can't Help) Falling in Love With You'*, UB40/DEP
4. *'Mr Blobby'*, Mr Blobby/Destiny
5. *'No Limit'*, 2 Unlimited/PWL Continental
6. *'Babe'*, Take That/RCA
7. *'Mr Vain'*, Culture Beat/Epic
8. *'Pray'*, Take That/RCA
9. *'Five Live EP'*, George Michael/Queen/Lisa Stansfield/Parlophone
10. *'I Will Always Love You'*, Whitney Houston/Arista

Top 10 Independent Albums

1. *Début*, Björk/One Little Indian
2. *Siamese Dream*, Smashing Pumpkins/Hut
3. *In On The Killtaker*, Fugazi/Dischord
4. *Levellers*, The Levellers/China
5. *Orbital II*, Orbital/Internal
6. *Tindersticks*, Tindersticks/This Way Up
7. *Madder Rose*, Madder Rose/Seed
8. *The Last Splash*, The Breeders/4AD
9. *Suede*, Suede/Nude
10. *Sabresonic*, Sabres of Paradise/Warp

Top 10 UK Albums

1. *Bat Out of Hell II – Back Into Hell*, Meat Loaf/Virgin
2. *Original Soundtrack – 'The Bodyguard'*, Various Artists/Arista
3. *Automatic for the People*, REM/Warner Brothers
4. *So Close*, Dina Carroll/A&M
5. *One Woman – The Ultimate Collection*, Diana Ross/EMI
6. *So Far So Good*, Bryan Adams/A&M
7. *Both Sides*, Phil Collins/Virgin

8. *Promises and Lies*, UB40/DEP International
9. *Unplugged*, Eric Clapton/Duck
10. *Everything Changes*, Take That/RCA

Top 10 Solid Grooves

1. *Underworld*, Rez/Cowgirl (Junior Boy's Own)
2. *Slam*, Positive Education (Soma)
3. *Leftfield and Lydon*, Open Up (Hard Hands)

4. *Underworld*, Mmmm . . . Skyscraper, I Love You! (Junior Boy's Own)
5. *Jam and Spoon*, Follow Me (Dance Pool/Sony)
6. *Ege Bam Yasi*, I Want More (Finiflex)
7. *CJ Bolland*, Mantra (R&S)
8. *Underground Resistance*, Galaxy 2 Galaxy (Underground Resistance)
9. *Robert Armani*, Circus Bells (D-Jax Up Beats)
10. *The Joy*, Shine (Playground)

NME ANNUAL CRITICS' POLL RECORDS OF THE YEAR

Singles

1976	Thin Lizzy, *'The Boys Are Back In Town'*
1977	Sex Pistols, *'Pretty Vacant'*
1978	Buzzcocks, *'Ever Fallen In Love'*
1979	The Jam, *'Eton Rifles'*
1980	Joy Division, *'Love Will Tear Us Apart'*
1981	The Specials, *'Ghost Town'*
1982	Grandmaster Flash and The Furious Five, *'The Message'*
1983	Michael Jackson, *'Billie Jean'*
1984	Womack and Womack, *'Love Wars'*
1985	The Jesus and Mary Chain, *'Never Understand'*
1986	Prince and The Revolution, *'Kiss'*
1987	Prince and The Revolution, *'Sign O'The Times'*
1988	Nick Cave, *'The Mercy Seat'*
1989	The Stone Roses, *'She Bangs The Drum'*
1990	Deee-Lite, *'Groove Is In the Heart'*
1991	Primal Scream, *'Higher Than The Sun'*
1992	Suede, *'The Drowners'*
1993	The Breeders, *'Cannonball'*

Albums

1976	Bob Dylan, *Desire*
1977	David Bowie, *Heroes*
1978	Bruce Springsteen, *Darkness On The Edge Of Town*
1979	Talking Heads, *Fear Of Music*
1980	Joy Division, *Closer*
1981	Grace Jones, *Night Clubbin*
1982	Marvin Gaye, *Midnight Love*
1983	Elvis Costello, *Punch The Clock*
1984	Bobby Womack, *The Poet II*
1985	Tom Waits, *Raindogs* / The Jesus and Mary Chain, *Psychocandy*
1986	Prince, *Parade*
1987	Public Enemy, *Yo! Bum Rush The Show*
1988	Public Enemy, *It Takes a Nation of Millions to Hold us Back*
1989	De La Soul, *3 Feet High and Rising*
1990	Happy Mondays, *Pills and Thrills and Bellyaches*
1991	Nirvana, *Nevermind*
1992	Sugar, *Copper Blue*
1993	Bjork, *Debut*

THE _NME_ BRATS AWARDS

In 1994, the old *New Musical Express* Poll Winners Awards were relaunched, 21 years after the last *NME* party in 1973. The awards, which are being revitalized as the Brats in answer to the widely criticized and largely conservative Brits, were held on 25 January at London's New Empire venue in Tottenham Court Road. Vic Reeves and Bob Mortimer hosted the evening. The awards are voted for by *NME* readers.

Best Band

1. Suede

2. New Order
3. Smashing Pumpkins

4. REM
5. Blur
6. The Lemonheads
7. Nirvana
8. The Fall
9. Manic Street Preachers
10. Pet Shop Boys

Best Single

1. Radiohead, *'Creep'*
2. The Breeders, *'Cannonball'*
3. New Order, *'Regret'*
4. Leftfield/Lydon, *'Open Up'*
5. Suede, *'Animal Nitrate'*
6. Rage Against the Machine, *'Killing in the Name of'*
7. Pet Shop Boys, *'Go West'*
8. Credit to the Nation, *'Call It What You Want'*
9. Senser, *'Eject'*
10. Smashing Pumpkins, *'Today'*

Best LP

1. The Boo Radleys, *Giant Steps*
2. Smashing Pumpkins, *Siamese Dreams*
3. Bjork, *Debut*
4. Blur, *Modern Life is Rubbish*
5. Suede, *Suede*
6. PJ Harvey, *Dry*
7. Nirvana, *In Utero*
8. The Lemonheads, *Come on Feel the Lemonheads*
9. New Order, *Republic*
10. Teenage Fanclub, *Thirteen*

Best Rap Act

Cypress Hill

Worst Record

1. Meat Loaf, *I Would Do Anything For Love*
2. Mr Blobby, *Mr Blobby*
3. 2 Unlimited, *No Limit*
4. Whitney Houston, *I Will Always Love You*
5. 4 Non Blondes, *What's Up*
6. Culture Beat, *Mr Vain*
7. Take That and Lulu, *Relight My Fire*
8. Jazzy Jeff and The Fresh Prince, *Boom! Shake the Room*
9. The Spin Doctors, *Two Princes*
10. Bryan Adams, *Please Forgive Me*

Best Club/Venue

1. The Forum, London
2. Brixton Academy
3. Sheffield Leadmill
4. Nottingham Rock City
5. Glasgow Barrowlands
6. The Garage, London
7. Manchester Academy
8. Brighton Zap Club
9. Leeds Town and County Club
10. Club Dog

Best Solo Artist

1. Bjork
2. Morrissey
3. Paul Weller
4. PJ Harvey
5. Neil Young
6. Julian Cope
7. The Aphex Twin
8. Frank Black
9. Kate Bush
10. Juliana Hatfield

The Philip Hall/ON Award for Best New Act (Voted by *NME*)

Credit to the Nation

The Godlike Genius Award for Unique Services to Music (Voted by *NME*)

John Peel

Vibes Award for Best Dance Act (Voted by *NME*)

Orbital

Best New Band

1. Elastica
2. Rage Against the Machine
3. Tindersticks
4. Senser
5. Radiohead
6. Madder Rose
7. Credit to the Nation
8. Grant Lee Buffalo
9. One Dove
10. Belly

NME/XD Premium Lager Live Event

Megadog

JOHN PEEL'S FESTIVE 50

Voted for by listeners to John Peel's BBC Radio 1 programme, who nominate 3 tracks in order of preference. Since 1982 only tracks released as recordings or broadcast in live sessions in the current year are eligible. The tracks which receive most votes are compiled into the top 50 chart and broadcast over the Christmas period.

1980	Sex Pistols, 'Anarchy in the UK'	1987	Sugarcubes, 'Birthday'
1981	Joy Division, 'Atmosphere'	1988	House of Love, 'Destroy the Heart'
1982	New Order, 'Temptation'		
1983	New Order, 'Blue Monday'	1989	The Sundays, 'Can't Be Sure'
1984	The Smiths, 'How Soon Is Now'	1990	The Fall, 'Bill is Dead'
1985	Jesus and Mary Chain, 'Never Understand'	1991	Nirvana, 'Smells Like Teen Spirit'
		1992	Bang Bang Machine, 'Geek Love'
1986	The Smiths, 'There is a Light That Never Goes Out'	1993	Chumbawamba and Credit to the Nation, 'Enough is Enough'

To celebrate 25 years of Radio 1, listeners were invited to vote for their 3 favourite records of all time. A top 100 was broadcast throughout the day on August bank hoiday, 1992:

1. Queen, *Bohemian Rhapsody*
2. Led Zeppelin, *Stairway to Heaven*
3. Bryan Adams, *Everything I Do, I Do It For You*
4. John Lennon, *Imagine*
5. Gerry Rafferty, *Baker Street*
6. Derek and The Dominoes, *Layla*
7. George Michael, *Careless Whisper*
8. 10cc, *I'm Not In Love*
9. The Beatles, *Hey Jude*
10. Meat Loaf, *Bat Out of Hell*

In 1993 a similar poll to establish listeners' all time favourite LPs was held:

1. Simply Red, *Stars*
2. The Beatles, *Sergeant Pepper's Lonely Hearts Club Band*
3. U2, *The Joshua Tree*
4. Meat Loaf, *Bat Out Of Hell*
5. Pink Floyd, *Dark Side of the Moon*
6. REM, *Out of Time*
7. Michael Jackson, *Thriller*
8. Dire Straits, *Brothers In Arms*
9. REM, *Automatic For The People*
10. Nirvana, *Nevermind*

THE *Q* AWARDS

The annual *Q* awards (from the magazine *Q*, the popular modern guide to music) constitute one of the major events of the rock 'n' roll calendar. First awarded in 1990, the fourth annual awards were presented at the Café Royal, London, in November 1993.

Best Compilation (or Reissue) Album (voted by the judging panel)

1990	The Beach Boys, *Pet Sounds*
1991	Bob Dylan, *The Bootleg Series Vols 1–3*
1992	Bob Marley, *Songs of Freedom*
1993	The Beach Boys, *Good Vibrations*

Best Production (voted by the judging panel)

1990	Paul Oakenfold and Steve Osborne, *Pills 'n' Thrills* Happy Mondays, *Bellyaches*
1991	Trevor Horn, *Seal*
1992	Peter Gabriel and Daniel Lanois, *Us* The Orb, *UF Orb*
1993	Flood, Eno and The Edge, *Zooropa*

Best New Act
(voted by the Q readership)

1990	They Might Be Giants
1991	Seal
1992	Tori Amos
1993	Suede

The *Q* Inspiration Award
(voted by Q magazine)

| 1992 | BB King |
| 1993 | Donald Fagen |

Best Act in the World Today
(voted by the Q readership)

1990	U2
1991	REM
1992	U2
1993	U2

Best Album
(voted by the Q readership)

1990	World Party Goodbye Jumbo
1991	REM Out of Time
1992	REM Automatic For The People
1993	Sting Ten Summoner's Tales

Best Songwriter
(voted by the judging panel)

| 1990 | Prince |
| 1991 | Richard Thompson |

| 1992 | U2 |
| 1993 | Neil Finn (of Crowded House, for 'Together Alone') |

Best Live Act

1990	The Rolling Stones
1991	Simple Minds
1992	Crowded House
1993	Neil Young

The *Q* Merit Award

1990	Paul McCartney
1991	Lou Reed
1992	Led Zeppelin
1993	Elton John

Q's Best Albums of 1993
(Top Ten out of Fifty)

The Auteurs, *New Wave*
Nirvana, *In Utero*
Cypress Hill, *Black Sunday*
The Spin Doctors, *Pocket Full of Kryptonite*
Aimee Mann, *Whatever*
Sting, *Ten Summoner's Tales*
Meat Loaf, *Bat Out Of Hell II: Back Into Hell*
UB40, *Promises and Lies*
New Order, *Republic*
Neil Young, *Unplugged*

SELECT MAGAZINE'S POLL

The 1994 results were:

Band of the Year

1. Suede
2. Blur
3. New Order
4. Lemonheads
5. Rage Against the Machine
6. Pet Shop Boys
7. U2
8. REM
9. Nirvana
10. Levellers

Dance Tune of the Year

1. Leftfield Lydon, 'Open Up'
2. Sub Sub, 'Ain't No Love (Ain't No Use)'
3. Orb, 'Little Fluffy Clouds'
4. Bjork, 'Big Time Sensuality'
5. Capella, 'U Got 2 Let The Music'
6. Cypress Hill, 'Insane in the Brain'
7. M-People, 'One Night in Heaven'
8. Orbital, 'Lush 3.1/3.2'
9. Moby, 'Move'
10. M-People, 'Movin' on Up'

Live Act of the Year

1. U2
2. Orb
3. Levellers
4. Blur
5. Suede
6. Smashing Pumpkins
7. Rage Against the Machine
8. Pulp
9. Carter USM
10. Lemonheads

Single of the Year

1. *'Animal Nitrate'*, Suede
2. *'Creep'*, Radiohead
3. *'Open Up'*, Lydon Leftfield
4. *'Lipgloss'*, Pulp
5. *'Bullet In The Head'*, Ratm
6. *'Regret'*, New Order
7. *'Today'*, Smashing Pumpkins
8. *'Killing in the Name'*, Ratm
9. *'Cannonball'*, Breeders
10. *'For Tomorrow'*, Blur

Album of the Year

1. *Suede*, Suede
2. *Debut*, Bjork
3. *Modern Life is Rubbish*, Blur
4. *Siamese Dream*, Smashing Pumpkins
5. *Black Sunday*, Cypress Hill
6. *Giant Steps*, Boo Radleys

7. *In Utero*, Nirvana
8. *Zooropa*, U2
9. *Come On Feel the Lemonheads*, Lemonheads
10. *Construction for the Modern Idiot*, Wonder Stuff

TV Show of the Year

1. *The Smell of Reeves and Mortimer*
2. *Sean's Show*
3. *Big Breakfast*
4. *Have I Got News For You*
5. *The Beat*
6. *Red Dwarf*
7. *Northern Exposure*
8. *Newman and Baddiel in Pieces*
9. *Naked City*
10. *Later with Jools Holland*

SMASH HITS POLL

The 1993 results were:

Best Album

1. *Everything Changes*, Take That
2. *Take That and Party*, Take That
3. *Walthamstow*, East 17
4. *Erotica*, Madonna
5. *The Bodyguard*, Whitney Houston
6. *Joey Lawrence*, Joey Lawrence
7. *Promises and Lies*, UB40
8. *Keep the Faith*, Bon Jovi
9. *Dangerous*, Michael Jackson
10. *Very*, Pet Shop Boys

Best Dancer in Pop

1. Jason Orange
2. Mark Owen
3. Howard Donald
4. Michael Jackson
5. Madonna
6. Fresh Prince
7. Terry Coldwell
8. Janet Jackson
9. Brian Harvey
10. Kylie

Best-dressed Person

1. Mark Owen
2. Robbie Williams
3. Gary Barlow
4. Jordan Knight
5. Howard Donald
6. Joey Lawrence
7. Jason Orange
8. Sean Maguire
9. Andi Peters
10. Dina Carrol

Best British Group

1. Take That
2. East 17
3. BBI
4. Pet Shop Boys
5. Worlds Apart
6. Eternal
7. M People
8. Wet Wet Wet
9. UB40
10. Suede

Best Group in the World

1. Take That
2. NKOTB
3. East 17
4. BBI
5. Bon Jovi
6. U2

7. 2 Unlimited
8. Guns 'n' Roses
9. Pet Shop Boys
10. REM

Best Film Actor

1. Tom Cruise
2. Keanu Reeves
3. Christian Slater
4. Kevin Costner
5. Johnny Depp
6. Mel Gibson
7. Brad Pitt
8. Eddie Murphy
9. Harrison Ford
10. Tom Hanks

Best Pop Video

1. *Pray*, Take That
2. *Relight My Fire*, Take That
3. *I'd Do Anything For Love*, Meat Loaf
4. *Go West*, Pet Shop Boys
5. *Boom! Shake the Room*, Jazzy Jeff and The Fresh Prince
6. *Rain*, Madonna
7. *Nothin' My Love Can't Fix*, Joey Lawrence
8. *Boom Shak-A-Lak*, Apache Indian
9. *Stay*, Eternal
10. *Mr Vain*, Culture Beat

Best Dance Act

1. 2 Unlimited
2. Jazzy Jeff and The Fresh Prince
3. M People
4. Culture Beat
5. Eternal
6. Michael Jackson
7. Urban Cookie
8. Apache Indian
9. Chaka Demus and Pliers
10. Marky Mark

Best Male Solo Singer

1. Michael Jackson
2. Haddaway
3. Prince
4. Joey Lawrence
5. Shaggy
6. Apache Indian
7. Kenny Thomas
8. Jamiroquai

9. Terence Trent D'Arby
10. George Michael

Best Radio DJ

1. Neil Fox
2. Bruno Brooks
3. Simon Mayo
4. Steve Wright
5. Mark Goodier
6. Chris Tarrant
7. Pat Sharp
8. Simon Bates
9. Jakki Brambles
10. Chris Evans

Best Female Solo Singer

1. Whitney Houston
2. Madonna
3. Dina Carroll
4. Gabrielle
5. Mariah Carey
6. Janet Jackson
7. Dannii
8. Kylie
9. Lulu
10. Michelle Gayle

Best Alternative/Indie Type Band

1. Nirvana
2. Apache Indian
3. The Farm
4. The Lemonheads
5. Suede
6. Spin Doctors
7. REM
8. Manic Street Preachers
9. Stereo MCs
10. Radiohead

Best Rock Outfit

1. Meat Loaf
2. Guns 'n' Roses
3. Bon Jovi
4. Nirvana
5. Extreme
6. U2
7. Take That
8. Def Leppard
9. Manic Street Preachers
10. Iron Maiden

Best Single

1. *'Boom! Shake the Room'*, Jazzy Jeff and The Fresh Prince
2. *'Pray'*, Take That
3. *'Relight My Fire'*, Take That
4. *'Why Can't I Wake Up With You?'*, Take That
5. *'I'd Do Anything For Love'*, Meat Loaf
6. *'Dreams'*, Gabrielle
7. *'Mr Vain'*, Culture Beat
8. *'I Will Always Love You'*, Whitney Houston
9. *'No Limit'*, 2 Unlimited
10. *'Deep'*, East 17

Smash Hits/Radio One FM – Best New Act

1. Eternal
2. Bad Boys Inc
3. The Lemonheads
4. Jamiroquai
5. Joey Lawrence
6. Worlds Apart
7. Culture Beat
8. M People
9. Gabrielle
10. Spin Doctors

Worst TV Programme

1. *Emmerdale*
2. *Neighbours*
3. *Brookside*
4. *Home and Away*
5. *Coronation Street*
6. *GMTV*
7. *Blue Peter*
8. *The Nine O'Clock News*
9. *World in Action*
10. *Eastenders*

Worst Male Singer

1. Jason Donovan
2. Joey Lawrence
3. Michael Jackson
4. Jamiroquai

5. Apache Indian
6. Tony Mortimer
7. Jordan Knight
8. Gary Barlow
9. Terence Trent D'Arby
10. Prince

Worst Single

1. *'Don't Talk About Love'*, Bad Boys Inc.
2. *'Go West'*, Pet Shop Boys
3. *'Relight My Fire'*, Take That
4. *'West End Girls'*, East 17
5. *'This Is It'*, Dannii
6. *'No Limit'*, 2 Unlimited
7. *'Suntan'*, Stan
8. *'Deep'*, East 17
9. *'Heaven Must Be Missing an Angel'*, Worlds Apart
10. *'Living On My Own'*, Freddie Mercury

Worst Group

1. Bad Boys Inc
2. East 17
3. NKOTB
4. Worlds Apart
5. Take That
6. Suede
7. The Lemonheads
8. Pet Shop Boys
9. Girlfriend
10. Guns 'n' Roses

Worst Female Singer

1. Madonna
2. Kylie
3. Dannii
4. Gabrielle
5. Michelle Gayle
6. Cilla Black
7. Bjork
8. Whitney Houston
9. Lulu
10. Sonia

TOP TEN OF MUSIC

Compiled by Russell Ash, these list the bestselling albums and singles.

Top Albums in the UK

1960	*South Pacific*, Soundtrack	1962	*West Side Story*, Soundtrack
1961	*G.I. Blues*, Elvis Presley	1963	*With the Beatles*, Beatles
		1964	*Beatles for Sale*, Beatles

1965	*Sound of Music*, Soundtrack	1953	'I Believe', Frankie Laine
1966	*Sound of Music*, Soundtrack	1954	'Secret Love', Doris Day
1967	*Sergeant Pepper's Lonely Hearts Club Band*, Beatles	1955	'Rose Marie', Slim Whitman
		1956	'I'll Be Home', Pat Boone
1968	*Sound of Music*, Soundtrack	1957	'Diana', Paul Anka
1969	*Abbey Road*, Beatles	1958	'Jailhouse Rock', Elvis Presley
1970	*Bridge Over Troubled Water*, Simon and Garfunkel	1959	'Living Doll', Cliff Richard
		1960	'It's Now or Never', Elvis Presley
1971	*Bridge Over Troubled Water*, Simon and Garfunkel	1961	'Are You Lonesome Tonight', Elvis Presley
1972	*20 Dynamic Hits*, Various	1962	'I Remember You', Frank Ifield
1973	*Don't Shoot Me, I'm Only the Piano Player*, Elton John	1963	'She Loves You', Beatles
		1964	'Can't Buy Me Love', Beatles
		1965	'Tears', Ken Dodd
1974	*The Singles 1969–1973*, Carpenters	1966	'Green Green Grass of Home', Tom Jones
1975	*The Best of the Stylistics*, Stylistics	1967	'Release Me', Engelbert Humperdinck
1976	*Greatest Hits*, Abba	1968	'Hey Jude', Beatles
1977	*Arrival*, Abba	1969	'Sugar Sugar', Archies
1978	*Saturday Night Fever*, Soundtrack	1970	'The Wonder of You', Elvis Presley
		1971	'My Sweet Lord', George Harrison
1979	*Parallel Lines*, Blondie	1972	'I'd Like to Teach the World to Sing', New Seekers
1980	*Super Trouper*, Abba		
1981	*King of the Wild Frontier*, Adam and the Ants	1973	'I Love You Love Me Love', Gary Glitter
1982	*Love Songs*, Barbra Streisand	1974	'You Won't Find Another Fool Like Me', New Seekers
1983	*Thriller*, Michael Jackson		
1984	*Can't Slow Down*, Lionel Richie	1975	'Bohemian Rhapsody', Queen
1985	*Brothers in Arms*, Dire Straits	1976	'Save Your Kisses for Me', Brotherhood of Man
1986	*True Blue*, Madonna		
1987	*Bad*, Michael Jackson	1977	'Mull of Kintyre', Wings
1988	*Kylie*, Kylie Minogue	1978	'Rivers of Babylon', 'Brown Girl in the Ring', Boney M
1989	*Ten Good Reasons*, Jason Donovan		
		1979	'YMCA', Village People
1990	*But Seriously*, Phil Collins	1980	'Don't Stand So Close to Me', Police
1991	*Stars*, Simply Red	1981	'Don't You Want Me', Human League
1992	*Stars*, Simply Red		
		1982	'Come On Eileen', Dexy's Midnight Runners

Top Albums of all Times

UK	*Sergeant Pepper's Lonely Hearts Club Band*, Beatles
USA	*Thriller*, Michael Jackson
Worldwide	*Thriller*, Michael Jackson

Children's Albums (UK)

1. *The Muppet Show*, Muppets
2. *Mary Poppins*, Original Soundtrack
3. *Oliver!*, Original Soundtrack

Top Singles in the UK

1952	'Auf Wiedersehen (Sweetheart)', Vera Lynn
1983	'Karma Chameleon', Culture Club
1984	'Do They Know It's Christmas?', Band Aid
1985	'The Power of Love', Jennifer Rush
1986	'Every Loser Wins', Nick Berry
1987	'Never Gonna Give You Up', Rick Astley
1988	'Mistletoe and Wine', Cliff Richard
1989	'Ride on Time', Black Box

1990	*'Unchained Melody'*, Righteous Brothers
1991	*'(Everything I do) I Do It For You'*, Bryan Adams
1992	*'I Will Always Love You'*, Whitney Houston

Top Singles in the UK (by decade)

1950s	*'Rock Around The Clock'*, Bill Haley and His Comets
1960s	*'She Loves You'*, Beatles
1970s	*'Mull of Kintyre'*, Wings
1980s	*'Do They Know It's Christmas?'*, Band Aid

Favourite Singles of All Time

Both Capital Radio and BBC Radio 1 have conducted polls in recent years. The winners have been:

| 1988 | Capital Radio, *'Careless Whisper'*, George Michael |

	BBC Radio 1,*'I Owe You Nothing'*, Bros
1992	Capital Radio, *'(Everything I Do) I Do It For You'*, Bryan Adams
	BBC Radio 1, *'Bohemian Rhapsody'*, Queen

Top Singles in the USA (by decade)

1950s	*'Hound Dog/Don't Be Cruel'*, Elvis Presley
1960s	*'I Want to Hold Your Hand'*, Beatles
1970s	*'You Light Up My Life'*, Debby Boone
1980s	*'We Are the World'*, USA For Africa

Top Singles of all Time

| Worldwide | *White Christmas*, Bing Crosby |
| UK | *Do They Know It's Christmas*, Band Aid |

NOBEL PRIZES

The Nobel Foundation was established at the beginning of the century to give effect to the wishes expressed by Alfred Nobel in his will. Alfred B. Nobel (1833–96) was the inventor of dynamite and bequeathed $9,000,000 to the Foundation.

The award of a Nobel Prize is accepted as the highest form of international recognition in the fields in which it is given: physics, chemistry, medicine, literature, peace and, since 1969, economics.

The Royal Academy of Science in Sweden picks the prizewinners in physics, chemistry and economics. The medical faculty of Stockholm's Caroline Institute chooses the winner in the field of physiology or medicine. The Swedish Academy of Literature names the winner in the field of literature. The Norwegian parliament elects a committee of five persons to select the winner of the prize for peace.

Currently the value of the prize is around £687,000. The prizewinners are listed separately under subject headings.

OFFICES

OFFICE OF THE YEAR

Begun in the 1970s, the nationwide search for the best working offices in Britain is now a well-established event.

The Office of the Year Awards are currently sponsored by the contract flooring division of international fibre manufacturer, Du Pont. Du Pont's sponsorship is based on the promotion of ANTRON Excel, its flagship nylon 6.6 fibre for the contract carpet market. The competition plays an increasingly important role in helping to raise awareness and standards in British office design.

Now (1994) in its twenty-second year, the competition, organized and run by the Institute of Facilities Management, is aimed at recognizing excellence and encouraging the provision of effective, comfortable and healthy working environments in an increasingly complex and demanding economic climate. Any British business which has invested time and resources to ensure a better working environment for its staff is eligible to enter.

The recent winners (in 3 categories) have been:

Purpose Built

1992	Standard Life Assurance, Edinburgh
1993	Pearl Assurance, Peterborough

Existing Buildings

1992	Glaxo Pharmaceuticals, Stockley Park, Middx.
1993	British Council, Medlock Street, Manchester

Smaller Offices

1992	Hannah Reed & Associates, Cambridge Camden Graphics, London
1993	Levitt Bernstein Associates, Kingsland Passage, London

OXFORD UNIVERSITY

THE NORRINGTON TABLE

Calculating for the academic league for Oxford University has been an exercise undertaken recently by the *Daily Telegraph*'s Brian Fenner.

The results for the top six in the Norrington Table since 1990 have been published as follows by the *Telegraph*.

1990

1. Merton
2. Queen's
3. Corpus Christi
4. St John's
5. Balliol
6. Jesus

1991

1. St John's
2. Balliol
3. Wadham
4. Magdalen
5. University
6. Merton

1992

1. Merton
2. St John's
3. Corpus Christi
4. Jesus
5. Balliol
6. Lady Margaret Hall

1993

1. Merton
2. St John's
3. Balliol
4. University
5. Queen's
6. Magdalen

PARLIAMENT

HIGHLAND PARK/*SPECTATOR* PARLIAMENTARIAN OF THE YEAR

Since 1984, awards for parliamentary performance and skills have been presented at the Highland Park/*Spectator* Parliamentarian of the Year annual luncheon. The list of winners is an entertaining one.

1984

Parliamentarian of the Year   Rt. Hon. Dr David Owen MP
Backbencher of the Year   Nicholas Budgen MP
Debater of the Year   John Cunningham MP
Troublemaker of the Year   Tam Dalyell MP
Member to Watch   Malcolm Rifkind MP

1985

Parliamentarian of the Year   Rt. Hon. John Biffen MP
Backbencher of the Year   Rt. Hon. James Callaghan MP
Constituency Member of the Year   Frank Field MP
Questioner of the Year   Terence Higgins MP
Member to Watch   Simon Hughes MP

1986

Parliamentarian of the Year   John Smith MP
Backbencher of the Year   Rt. Hon. Roy Jenkins MP
Inquisitor of the Year   Dr John Gilbert MP
Member to Watch   John MacGregor MP
Special Award   Rt. Hon. Norman St John-Stevas MP

1987

Parliamentarian of the Year   Rt. Hon. Nigel Lawson MP
Backbencher of the Year   Jonathan Aitken MP, Richard Shepherd MP
New Member of the Year   John Redwood MP
Member to Watch   Gordon Brown MP
Special Award   Enoch Powell MP

1988

Parliamentarian of the Year   Rt. Hon. Edward Heath MP
Member of the Year   Tony Blair MP
Backbencher of the Year   Sir George Young, Bart, MP
Whip of the Year   Rt. Hon. The Lord Denham
Debater of the Year   Robin Cook MP
Personal Award   Ken Maginnis MP

1989

Parliamentarian of the Year   Rt. Hon. John Smith MP
Member to Watch   Charles Kennedy MP
Backbencher of the Year   Eric Heffer MP
Wit of the Year   Neil Hamilton MP
Debater of the Year   John Prescott MP
Speech of the Year   Rt. Hon. Nigel Lawson MP

1990

Parliamentarian of the Year   Rt. Hon. Douglas Hurd MP
Member to Watch   Brian Wilson MP
Backbencher of the Year   Anthony Benn MP
Campaigner of the Year   Clare Short MP
Party Leader of the Year   Paddy Ashdown MP
Speech of the Year   Rt. Hon. Sir Geoffrey Howe MP

1991

Parliamentarian of the Year   Rt. Hon. Robin Cook MP
Member to Watch   Rt. Hon. David Mellor MP
Backbencher of the Year   David Nellist MP
Campaigner of the Year   William Cash MP
Special Award   Rt. Hon. Michael Foot MP

1992

Parliamentarian of the Year   Dame Betty
  Boothroyd MP
Member to Watch   Michael Forsyth MP
New Member   Iain Duncan-Smith MP
Campaigner of the Year   Elizabeth
  Peacock MP
Special Awards   Lord Cledwyn of
  Penrhos and Richard Ryder MP

1993

Parliamentarian of the Year   George
  Robertson MP, Geoffrey Hoon MP
Member to Watch   Nicholas Soames MP
Backbencher of the Year   Sir Peter
  Tapsell MP

In delivering the judges' citations for the 1993 awards at the presentation luncheon at the Savoy Hotel, London, Mr Dominic Lawson, Editor of the *Spectator*, said of the award to Mr Hoon:

> The principal task of an opposition is to defeat the Government. In July a combination of the opposition parties and Conservative rebels did just that, on the question of the opt-out from the Social Chapter of the Maastricht Treaty. A backbench Labour lawyer, Mr Geoffrey Hoon, and Labour's European spokesman, Mr George Robertson, between them constructed the trap that forced the Government to allow a vote on this question. When the Government lost, only a vote of confidence tied to the question saved the Prime Minister's skin. This rare humiliation was regarded by the judges as a skilful and ingenious use of parliamentary procedures.

The awards were presented by the Rt Hon. Lord Callaghan of Cardiff, the Guest of Honour. Mr Robertson and Mr Hoon were presented with the perpetual trophy, an Orkney silver quaich (a traditional Scottish drinking vessel). All winners received miniature silver quaichs engraved with their names.

The awards and the luncheon were sponsored by Highland Park 12-Year-Old Single Malt Whisky.

PEACE

NOBEL PRIZE FOR PEACE

The first Nobel Peace Prize was awarded in 1901, five years after the death of Alfred Nobel, to Jean Henri Dunant, the Swiss founder of the Red Cross, and Frederic Passy, a French advocate of international arbitration. For further details on the range of Nobel Prizes, see p. 206.

The awards since 1945 have been as follows:

1945	Cordell Hull (USA)	1950	Ralph J. Bunche (USA)
1946	Emily G. Balch (USA)	1951	Léon Jouhaux (Fra)
	John R. Mott (USA)	1952	Albert Schweitzer (Fra, German-
1947	Friends Service Council (GB)		born)
	American Friends Service	1953	George C. Marshall (USA)
	Committee (USA)	1954	Office of UN High Commissioner
1948	*no award*		for Refugees
1949	Lord John Boyd Orr (GB)	1955	*no award*

1956	*no award*
1957	Lester B. Pearson (Can)
1958	Georges Pire (Bel)
1959	Philip J. Noel-Baker (GB)
1960	Albert J. Luthuli (SAf)
1961	Dag Hammarskjöld (Swe) (posthumous)
1962	Linus C. Pauling (USA)
1963	International Committee of the Red Cross / Red Cross Societies League
1964	Martin Luther King Jr (USA)
1965	United Nations Childrens Fund (UNICEF)
1966	*no award*
1967	*no award*
1968	René Cassin (Fra)
1969	International Labour Organization (ILO)
1970	Norman E. Borlaug (USA)
1971	Willy Brandt (FRG)
1972	*no award*
1973	Henry A. Kissinger (USA, German-born) / Le Duc Tho (NViet)
1974	Eisaku Sato (Jap) / Sean MacBride (Ire)

1975	Andrei D. Sakharov (USSR)
1976	Betty Williams (GB) / Mairead Corrigan (GB)
1977	Amnesty International
1978	Anwar el Sadat (Egy) / Menachem Begin (Isr)
1979	Mother Teresa of Calcutta (Alb)
1980	Adolfo Pérez Esquivel (Arg)
1981	Office of the UN High Commission for Refugees
1982	Alva Myrtal (Swe) / Alfonso Garcia Robles (Mex)
1983	Lech Walesa (Pol)
1984	Archbishop Desmond Tutu (SAf)
1985	International Physicians for the Prevention of Nuclear War
1986	Elie Wiesel (USA, Romanian-born)
1987	President Oscar Arias Sanchez (CoR)
1988	UN Peacekeeping Forces
1989	Dalai Lama (Tib)
1990	Mikhail Gorbachev (USSR)
1991	Aung San Suu Kyi (Mya)
1992	Rigoberta Menchu (Gua)
1993	F. W. de Klerk (SAf) / Nelson Mandela (SAf)

PETS

PET SLIMMER OF THE YEAR

This new event, the *Weight Watchers* Magazine/Hill's Pet Slimmer of the Year, was first held in 1993, when 20 finalists from over 2,000 entrants gathered in West London. The judges were headed by renowned animal lover and novelist, Jilly Cooper. At stake was a fabulous holiday in Aspen, Colorado, courtesy of Aspen Reservations. For the winning pet there is a special Animal Auntie to look after them at home while their owners are away and a year's supply of the appropriate Hill's pet food.

The winner was Candy. *Weight Watchers* reported that Candy is nearly half the dog she was – and all the better for it. Previously a grumpy 25.5kg/57lb canine couch potato, Candy shed a staggering 42 per cent of her bodyweight, a massive loss of 11kg/24lb, in just nine months on Hill's Prescription Diet.

Candy's vital statistics:

Age	6
Was	25.5kg/57lb
Now	15kg/33lb
Lost	11kg/24lb

Hardest struggle Giving up pork pies and doughnuts
Biggest lifestyle change No longer grumpy and loves long walks

PHONES

WHAT? MOBILE AND CELLPHONE MAGAZINE AWARDS

The first ever awards in this category were made as 1994 opened – partly reflecting the massive increase in the popularity of mobile phones. The inaugural winners were:

Phone of the Year   Ericsson EH237
Most Technologically Advanced   Sony CM-R111
Best Emergency Phone   Motorola Traveller

Best Value   NEC
Best GSM   Orbitel 902
Best Accessory Message Pager   Hutchinson
Best Carkit   Motorola

PHOTOGRAPHY

AMATEUR PHOTOGRAPHER OF THE YEAR

The Dixons–Kodak Amateur Photographer of the Year is one of the top competitions of the photographic calendar. The competition, which is sponsored by *Amateur Photographer*, Dixons and Kodak is launched in April each year for all UK amateur photographers. As well as the title of Amateur Photographer of the Year, the winner receives £1000 cash, camera and lens equipment and a gold and silver trophy, donated by Haking International.

1991   Julie Durn (Havant, Hants)
1992   Julie Durn (Havant, Hants)
1993   John Watkins (Woodford Bridge)

The category winners for 1992 were:

Chinon People Award   David Johnston, *Under 16*   Julie Roper (15)
Nikon Sport/Action Award   Julie Durn (Havant, Hants) (also the top prizewinning shot), *Under 16*   Mark McNamee (14) (Merseyside)
Minolta Transport Award   Mike Heath (Manchester), *Under 16*   Darren Heath (10) (son of Mike Heath)
Pentax Landscape/Cityscape Award   William Roscoe (Bournemouth and Poole College), *Under 16*   Claire Thomas (13)
Canon Wildlife/Environment Award   Rob Hartley, *Under 16*   Rob Hartley (14) (winner of senior award as well)

Category Winners (1993)

Sport and Action   John Taylor
Wildlife (under 16)   Becky Thomas (11)
Royalty   Steve Guscott
Landscape   John Parkhouse, *Under 16*   Claire Thomas (14, sister of Becky, above)
Hobbies   Khalid Ghani, *Under 16*   Julie Roper (15)
People   Ian Brockbank, *Under 16*   Emma Grant (7)

The 1993 overall winner's shot took John Watkins two years to achieve. The idea came when he spotted an old tap in a friend's garden. He built a similar one in his own garden, grew the ivy alongside it and set up a bird table 1.5m/5ft away.

Young Amateur Photographer of the Year

1991   Julie Roper (14)
1992   Rob Hartley (14)
1993   Mark McNamee (15)

Camera Club of the Year

Amateur Photographer, in association with Konica, also organizes an annual competition for the top Camera Club. The 1993 winner was Solihull Photographic.

PHYSICAL STRENGTH

WORLD'S STRONGEST MAN

The annual contest which began in 1978 to bestow the accolade of 'the world's strongest man' was held in August 1993 in the 2000-year-old Roman amphitheatre in Orange in Provence, France. The previous year it had been held in Iceland.

In this trial of strength and endurance, spread over 2 days, the 8 competitors in the final battled it out for the coveted title, the £10,000 prize money and the Tonka Trophy. Each competitor weighs around 133kg/21 stones on average, having spent about £1200 a month on food alone in training. The 1993 results were:

1. Gary Taylor (GB)
2. Magnus Ver Magnusson (Ice, 1991 winner)
3. Riku Kiri (Fin)

PHYSICS

NOBEL PRIZE FOR PHYSICS

The first Nobel Prize for Physics was awarded in 1901 to Wilhelm C. Roentgen of Germany. Among the British recipients to be awarded the honour before 1945 were:

1904	Lord Rayleigh (John W. Strutt)
1906	Sir Joseph John Thomson
1915	Sir William H. Bragg
1917	Charles G. Barkla
1927	Charles T. R. Wilson (*joint award*)
1928	Owen W. Richardson
1933	Paul A. M. Dirac (*joint award*)
1935	Sir James Chadwick
1937	George P. Thomson (*joint award*)

The full list of winners since 1945 is:

1945	Wolfgang Pauli (USA)
1946	Percy Williams Bridgman (USA)
1947	Sir Edward V. Appleton (GB)
1948	Patrick M. S. Blackett (GB)
1949	Hideki Yukawa (Jap)
1950	Cecil F. Powell (GB)
1951	Sir John D. Cockcroft (GB)
	Ernest T. S. Walton (Ire)
1952	Felix Block (USA, Swiss-born)
	Edward Purcell (USA)

1953	Fritz Zernike (Hol)	1974	Antony Hewish (GB)
1954	Max Born (GB, German-born)		Sir Martin Ryle (GB)
	Walther Bothe (FRG)	1975	L. James Rainwater (USA)
1955	Polykarp Kusch (USA, German-born)		Aage Bohr (Den)
	Willis E. Lamb (USA)		Ben Roy Mottelson (Den, USA-born)
1956	John Bardeen (USA)	1976	Burton Richter (USA)
	Walter H. Brattain (USA)		Samuel C. C. Ting (USA)
	William Shockley (USA)	1977	John H. Van Vleck (USA)
1957	Tsung-Dao Lee (USA, Chinese-born)		Philip W. Anderson (USA)
	Chen Ning Yang (USA, Chinese-born)		Sir Nevill F. Mott (GB)
1958	Paval A. Cherenkov (USSR)	1978	Piotr Leontevich Kapitsa (USSR)
	Ilya M. Frank (USSR)		Arno A. Penzias (USA, German-born)
	Igor J. Tamm (USSR)		Robert W. Wilson (USA)
1959	Owen Chamberlain (USA)	1979	Abdus Salam (GB)
	Emilio G. Segrè (USA, Italian-born)		Sheldon Glashow (USA)
1960	Donald A. Glaser (USA)		Steven Weinberg (USA)
1961	Robert Hofstadter (USA)	1980	James W. Cronin (USA)
	Rudolf L. Mössbauer (FRG)		Val Fitch (USA)
1962	Lev D. Landau (USSR)	1981	Nicolaas Bloemergern (USA)
1963	Maria Goeppert-Mayer (USA)		Arthur Schawlow (USA)
	J. Hans D. Jensen (FRG)	1982	Kenneth Wilson (USA)
	Eugene P. Wigner (USA)	1983	Subrahmanyan Chandrasekhar (USA)
1964	Nikolai G. Basov (USSR)		William Fowler (USA)
	Aleksandr M. Prokhorov (USSR)	1984	Carlo Rubbia (Ita)
	Charles H. Townes (USA)		Simon van der Meer (Hol)
1965	Richard P. Feynman (USA)	1985	Klaus von Klitzing (Ger)
	Julian S. Schwinger (USA)	1986	Erns Ruska (Ger)
	Sin-itiro Tomonaga (Jap)		Gerd Binnig (Ger)
1966	Alfred Kastler (Fra)		Heinrich Rohrer (Swi)
1967	Hans A. Bethe (USA, German-born)	1987	Georg Bednorz (Ger)
			Alex Müller (Swi)
1968	Luis W. Alvarez (USA)	1988	Leon M. Lederman (USA)
1969	Murray Gell-Man (USA)		Melvin Schwartz (USA)
1970	Hannes O. G. Alfven (Swe)		Jack Steinberger (Ger)
	Louis E. F. Néel (Fra)	1989	Norman Ramsey (USA)
1971	Dennis Gabor (GB, Hungarian-born)		Hans Dehmelt (USA)
			Wolfgang Paul (Ger)
1972	John Bardeen (USA)	1990	Jerome Friedman (USA)
	Leon N. Cooper (USA)		Henry Kendall (USA)
	John R. Schrieffer (USA)		Richard Taylor (Can)
1973	Ivar Giaever (USA, Norwegian-born)	1991	Pierre-Giles de Gennes (Fra)
	Leo Esaki (Jap)	1992	Georges Charpak (Fra)
	Brian D. Josephson (GB)	1993	Russell Hulse (USA)
			Joseph Taylor (USA)

PIPESMOKING

PIPESMOKER OF THE YEAR

The award was first instituted in 1964 to honour distinguished pipesmokers in the UK. The first Pipesmoker of the Year was Rupert Davies, then playing 'Maigret' in a television series. Only one man has been elected to the title twice: Harold Wilson (Lord Wilson) in 1965 and 1976; in 1976 he was elected Pipeman of the Decade. The oldest Pipesmoker of the Year was Lord Shinwell, elected in his eighties, who lived to over a hundred, having smoked a pipe since he was fourteen. The award consists of a silver pipe trophy, and in recent years a craftsman of the British pipe industry has carved a special presentation pipe reflecting the trade, sport or profession of the individual honoured, which is kept by the recipient. Installation is at a charity luncheon at the Savoy Hotel in January each year.

1964	Rupert Davies	1980	Edward Fox
1965	Rt Hon. Harold Wilson	1981	James Galway
1966	Andrew Cruickshank	1982	Dave Lee Travis
1967	Warren Mitchell	1983	Patrick Moore
1968	Peter Cushing	1984	Henry Cooper
1969	Jack Hargreaves	1985	Jimmy Greaves
1970	Eric Morecambe	1986	David Bryant
1971	Rt Hon. The Lord Shinwell	1987	Barry Norman
1972	*not held*	1988	Ian Botham
1973	Frank Muir	1989	Jeremy Brett
1974	Fred Trueman	1990	Laurence Marks
1975	Campbell Adamson	1991	Sir John Harvey-Jones
1976	Rt Hon. Harold Wilson	1992	Tony Benn
1977	Brian Barnes	1993	Rod Hull
1978	Magnus Magnusson	1994	Sir Ranulph Fiennes
1979	J. B. Priestley		

PIZZA AND PASTA

PIZZA AND PASTA ASSOCIATION AWARDS

The Pizza and Pasta Association awards, launched in 1987, are designed to acknowledge high standards of skill and enterprise in the pizza and pasta industry. Open to anyone working in the industry, from managers and restaurateurs to suppliers and manufacturers, the awards are presented annually at a gala dinner held in London. Entries for the awards can come from individuals wishing to put forward their own businesses or from others wishing to nominate customers or outlets they know. Every entry is thoroughly examined on its merits by independent assessors and those considered the best are submitted to a panel of judges for final adjudication. Four final nominations are made in each category and the finalists receive an invitation to attend the gala dinner at which the awards are announced.

Pizza and Pasta Operator of the Year

This is the top award given to an individual or company whom the judges consider to have made an outstanding contribution to the growth, development, reputation and prosperity of the pizza and pasta industry. The 1993 winner was Peter Gross, of the Gourmet Pizza Company.

Other category awards included:

Pasta Restaurant of the Year Vito's Trattoria, Chester; Nuvoli, New Malden, Surrey; Pizza Margherita, Lancaster
Pizza Restaurant of the Year Casa Italia, Southport, Mersey

Pizza Take-Away/Delivery Operator of the Year Pizzaline, Clacton-on-Sea, Essex
Most Innovative Pasta Store Rea's Bakery, Cumbria
Most Innovative Pizza Store Sainsbury's

The 1994 overall award for Pizza and Pasta Operator of the Year went to Pizza Express. Other category awards included:

Pizza Restaurant of the Year California Pizza Factory
Pasta Restaurant of the Year Gianni's Pizzeria and Restaurant, Harrogate
Pizza Take-Away/Home Delivery Operator of the Year Pizza Pan

Pizza and Pasta Writer/Broadcaster of the Year Antonio Carluccio
Pizza and Pasta Store of the Year William Morrison Supermarkets

PLAIN ENGLISH

THE GOLDEN BULL AWARD

The Plain English Campaign each year awards its booby prize (the Golden Bull) to the most confused and bureaucratic gobbledygook example of English usage that has come to its attention. Among the winners in 1993 was the 163-word definition of a hospital bed sent to the Welsh Office by the Value For Money Unit of the NHS Directorate. Its definition was:

Bed: A device or arrangement that may be used to permit a patient to lie down when the need to do so is a consequence of the patient's condition rather than a need for active intervention such as examination, diagnostic investigation, manipulative treatment, obstetric delivery or transport. Beds, couches or trolleys are also counted as hospital beds where: (a) used regularly to permit a patient to lie down rather than for merely examination or transport (e.g. in a day surgery ward); (b) used whilst attending for a specific short procedure taking an hour or less such as endoscopy, provided that such devices are used only because of the active intervention and not because of the patient's condition; (c) used regularly as a means of support for patients needing a lengthy procedure such as renal dialysis (includes special chairs etc.); (d) used regularly to allow patients to lie down after sedation. NB: A device specifically and solely for the purpose of delivery should not be counted as a bed.

NO NONSENSE AWARD

This new award, for the most baffling remark of the year, was won by former chairman of the England cricket selectors, Ted Dexter, for his 'explanation' of England's defeat by Australia in the June 1993 second test:

> Maybe we are in the wrong sign. Maybe Venus is in the wrong juxtaposition with something else. I don't know.

PLOUGHING

The British National Ploughing Championships, which are held in a different part of Britain each year, are organized by the Society of Ploughmen Ltd. Until 1988 there was only a British champion in Conventional Ploughing. From 1989 onwards there was a British champion in Conventional Ploughing (C) and also one in Reversible Ploughing (R). Ploughmen compete on the first day of the championships and qualifiers go on to compete on the second day in the 'Plough-Offs', from which the champions are found.

BRITISH NATIONAL CHAMPION PLOUGHMAN

1980	T. Raymond Goodwin	1990	Graeme Witty (C)
1981	David W. J. Bonning		John P. Hill (R)
1982	Frank H. Millington	1991	Graeme Witty (C)
1983	John P. Hill		John P. Hill (R)
1984	Vivien E. Samuel	1992	Graeme Witty (C)
1985	John P. Hill		John P. Hill (R)
1986	John P. Hill	1993	Adrian J. Brewer (C)
1987	T. Raymond Goodwin		John P. Hill (R)
1988	Graeme Witty		
1989	Graeme Witty (C)		
	Ian R. Wilson (R)		

Vivien Samuel was World Champion Ploughman (Conventional Ploughing) in 1980, winning the World Ploughing Contest in New Zealand.

Graeme Witty has been World Champion Ploughman (Conventional) three times, winning in the USA in 1988, Holland in 1990 and Spain in 1992.

John Hill has been World Champion Ploughman (Reversible) twice, winning in Spain in 1992 and Sweden in 1993. (The reversible section has only been included since 1992.)

POETRY

THE QUEEN'S GOLD MEDAL FOR POETRY

The Gold Medal for Poetry was instituted by King George V in 1933 at the suggestion of the then Poet Laureate, John Masefield. Recommendations for the award of the medal are made by a committee under the chairmanship of the Poet Laureate. The medal is normally given for a book of verse published by a British subject in the English language.

1934	Laurence Whistler	1967	Charles Causley
1936	W. H. Auden	1968	Robert Graves
1940	Michael Thwaites	1969	Stevie Smith
1952	Andrew Young	1970	Roy Fuller
1953	Arthur Waley	1971	Sir Stephen Spender
1954	Ralph Hodgson	1973	John Heath-Stubbs
1955	Ruth Pitter	1974	Ted Hughes
1956	Edmund Blunden	1977	Norman Nicholson
1957	Siegfried Sassoon	1981	D. J. Enright
1959	Francis Cornford	1986	Norman MacCaig
1960	John Betjeman	1988	Derek Walcott
1962	Christopher Fry	1989	Allen Curnow
1963	William Plomer	1990	Sorley Maclean
1964	The Reverend Ronald Thomas (R. S. Thomas)	1991	Judith Wright
		1992	Kathleen Raine
1965	Philip Larkin		

POLO

BRITISH OPEN

1956	Los Indios	1969	Windsor Park	1982	Southfield
1957	Windsor Park	1970	Boca Raton	1983	Falcons
1958	Cowdray Park	1971	Pimms	1984	Southfield
1959	Casarejo	1972	Pimms	1985	Maple Leafs
1960	Casarejo	1973	Stowell Park	1986	Tramontana
1961	Cowdray Park	1974	Stowell Park	1987	Tramontana
1962	Cowdray Park	1975	Greenhill Farm	1988	Tramontana
1963	La Vulci	1976	Stowell Park	1989	Tramontana
1964	Jersey Lilies	1977	Foxcote	1990	Hildon
1965	Jersey Lilies	1978	Stowell Park	1991	Tramontana
1966	Windsor Park	1979	Songhai	1992	Black Bears
1967	Woolmer's Park	1980	Stowell Park	1993	Alcatel
1968	Pimms	1981	Falcons		

POPULARITY

MADAME TUSSAUD'S

Each year Madame Tussaud's, one of London's favourite tourist attractions, hands out questionnaires to all their visitors to discover their heroes and heroines. The lists (given here since 1984) make fascinating reading.

1984

Politics
1. Margaret Thatcher
2. Ken Livingstone
3. Ronald Reagan
4. Bob Hawke
5. Neil Kinnock

Sport
1. John McEnroe
2. Daley Thompson
3. Pelé (Edson Arantes do Nascimento)
4. Jayne Torvill and Christopher Dean
5. Bjorn Borg

Entertainment
1. Boy George
2. Michael Jackson
3. David Bowie
4. Liza Minnelli
5. Frank Sinatra

The Arts
1. Pablo Picasso
2. Vincent Van Gogh
3. Agatha Christie
4. { Wolfgang Amadeus Mozart / André Previn

Beauty
1. HRH The Princess of Wales
2. { Joan Collins / Victoria Principal
4. Marilyn Monroe
5. Sophia Loren

Hate and Fear
1. Adolf Hitler
2. Arthur Scargill
3. Colonel Gadaffi
4. Margaret Thatcher
5. Ronald Reagan

Hero or Heroine of All Time
1. Winston Churchill
2. Superman
3. Harrison Ford
4. { Mahatma Gandhi / Horatio Nelson

Favourite Hero or Heroine in Madame Tussaud's
1. Boy George
2. David Bowie
3. Henry VIII
4. Mahatma Gandhi
5. The Royal Family

1985

Politics
1. Margaret Thatcher
2. Sir Winston Churchill
3. Neil Kinnock
4. Bob Hawke
5. Ronald Reagan

Sport
1. Daley Thompson
2. John McEnroe
3. Ian Botham
4. Jayne Torvill and Christopher Dean
5. Sebastian Coe

Entertainment
1. David Bowie
2. { Joan Collins / Michael Jackson
4. { John Cleese / Cliff Richard

The Arts
1. Pablo Picasso
2. Vincent Van Gogh
3. { Ludwig van Beethoven / Salvador Dali / Rembrandt Harmenszoon van Rijn

Beauty and Glamour
1. Joan Collins
2. Marilyn Monroe
3. { Linda Evans / Victoria Principal
5. Dolly Parton

Hate and Fear
1. Adolf Hitler
2. Margaret Thatcher
3. Ronald Reagan
4. { Colonel Gadaffi / Jack the Ripper

Hero or Heroine of All Time
1. { James Dean
   { Superman
3. Roger Moore
4. { Bob Geldof
   { Rambo

Favourite Person
1. David Bowie
2. Michael Jackson
3. Boy George
4. The Royal Family
5. Joan Collins

1986

Politics
1. Margaret Thatcher
2. Ronald Reagan
3. John F. Kennedy
4. Sir Winston Churchill
5. Norman Tebbit

Sport
1. Daley Thompson
2. John McEnroe
3. Ian Botham
4. Pelé (Edson Arantes do Nascimento)
5. Boris Becker

Entertainment
1. Benny Hill
2. David Bowie
3. JR
4. { Elvis Presley
   { Meryl Streep

The Arts
1. Pablo Picasso
2. Ludwig van Beethoven
3. { Vincent Van Gogh
   { David Hockney
   { William Shakespeare

Beauty and Glamour
1. Joan Collins
2. HRH The Princess of Wales
3. Marilyn Monroe
4. Samantha Fox
5. Nastassja Kinski

Hate and Fear
1. Adolf Hitler

2. Colonel Gadaffi
3. Ronald Reagan
4. Margaret Thatcher
5. Jack the Ripper

Hero or Heroine
1. Superman
2. James Dean
3. Winston Churchill
4. { Joan of Arc
   { Horatio Nelson

Favourite Person
1. David Bowie
2. Bob Geldof
3. Michael Jackson
4. The Royal Family
5. Ian Botham

1987

Politics
1. { Mikhail Gorbachev
   { Margaret Thatcher
3. Ronald Reagan
4. Mahatma Gandhi
5. John F. Kennedy

Sport
1. Daley Thompson
2. Boris Becker
3. Nelly Cooman
4. Johann Cruyff
5. Bjorn Borg

Entertainment
1. { Benny Hill
   { Madonna
3. { Michael Jackson
   { Rob Lowe
5. Dame Edna Everage

The Arts
1. { Pablo Picasso
   { Rembrandt Harmenszoon van Rijn
3. Vincent Van Gogh
4. Salvador Dali
5. Rolf Harris

Beauty
1. { Joan Collins
   { HRH The Princess of Wales
3. Marilyn Monroe

4. Madonna
5. Jane Seymour

Hate and Fear
1. Adolf Hitler
2. Ronald Reagan
3. Colonel Gadaffi
4. Ayatollah Khomeini
5. Margaret Thatcher

Hero or Heroine
1. James Dean
2. { Batman
   Indiana Jones
   Elvis Presley
   Sylvester Stallone }

Favourite Person
1. David Bowie
2. Bob Geldof
3. Michael Jackson
4. Grace Jones
5. Benny Hill

1988
Politics
1. Margaret Thatcher
2. { Neil Kinnock
   Ronald Reagan }
4. Mikhail Gorbachev
5. George Bush

Sport
1. Daley Thompson
2. Boris Becker
3. Steve Davis
4. Carl Lewis
5. Ian Botham

Entertainment
1. Michael Jackson
2. David Bowie
3. Cliff Richard
4. { Kylie Minogue
   Eddie Murphy }

The Arts
1. Pablo Picasso
2. Henry Moore

3. Charles Dickens
4. { Ludwig van Beethoven
   Wolfgang Amadeus Mozart }

Beauty
1. Joan Collins
2. HRH The Princess of Wales
3. Marilyn Monroe
4. Natassja Kinski
5. Anneka Rice

Hate and Fear
1. Adolf Hitler
2. Margaret Thatcher
3. Colonel Gadaffi
4. { Edwina Currie
   Charles Manson }

Hero or Heroine
1. Superman
2. John Wayne
3. { Winston Churchill
   Clint Eastwood }
5. Sylvester Stallone

Favourite Person
1. Bob Geldof
2. Michael Jackson
3. HRH The Duchess of York
4. { Richard Branson
   Michael Caine }

1989
Politics
1. Margaret Thatcher
2. Mikhail Gorbachev
3. Mahatma Gandhi
4. Neil Kinnock
5. Benazir Bhutto

Sport
1. Boris Becker
2. Daley Thompson
3. Frank Bruno
4. Steffi Graff
5. Ian Botham

Entertainment
1. { Eddie Murphy
   Cliff Richard }

3. Lenny Henry
4. ⎰ Jason Donovan
   ⎱ Michael Jackson

The Arts
1. Pablo Picasso
2. Ludwig van Beethoven
3. ⎰ Wolfgang Amadeus Mozart
   ⎱ Vincent Van Gogh
5. Jason Donovan

Beauty
1. Marilyn Monroe
2. Joan Collins
3. Kylie Minogue
4. HRH The Princess of Wales
5. Jerry Hall

Hate and Fear
1. Adolf Hitler
2. Margaret Thatcher
3. Colonel Gadaffi
4. ⎰ Jack the Ripper
   ⎱ Nicolai Ceausescu

Hero or Heroine
1. James Dean
2. Elvis Presley
3. Winston Churchill
4. Superman
5. Jason Donovan

Favourite Person
1. Paul Hogan
2. Kylie Minogue
3. Elvis Presley
4. Eddie Murphy
5. Archbishop Tutu

1990
Politics
1. Margaret Thatcher
2. Mikhail Gorbachev
3. John Major
4. ⎰ Neil Kinnock
   ⎱ Michael Heseltine

Sport
1. Boris Becker
2. Peter Shilton
3. Paul Gascoigne

4. Gary Lineker
5. Stefen Edberg

Entertainment
1. Eddie Murphy
2. Benny Hill
3. Michael Jackson
4. Lenny Henry
5. Dame Edna Everage

The Arts
1. Pablo Picasso
2. Wolfgang Amadeus Mozart
3. ⎰ Vincent Van Gogh
   ⎱ Luciano Pavarotti
5. William Shakespeare

Beauty
1. Jerry Hall
2. Cher
3. Marilyn Monroe
4. Madonna
5. Joan Collins

Hate and Fear
1. Saddam Hussein
2. Adolf Hitler
3. Margaret Thatcher
4. Jack the Ripper
5. Freddie Kruger

Hero or Heroine
1. Superman
2. James Bond
3. Robin Hood
4. James Dean
5. John Wayne

Favourite Person
1. Eddie Murphy
2. Michael Jackson
3. Benny Hill
4. ⎰ Bob Geldof
   ⎱ James Bond

1991
Politics
1. John Major
2. Margaret Thatcher
3. ⎰ George Bush
   ⎱ Mikhail Gorbachev
5. Paddy Ashdown

Sport
1. Boris Becker
2. Gary Lineker
3. Paul Gascoigne
4. Daley Thompson
5. John McEnroe

Entertainment
1. Benny Hill
2. { Cher / Sylvester Stallone
4. Eddie Murphy
5. Lenny Henry

The Arts
1. Pablo Picasso
2. Luciano Pavarotti
3. Salvador Dali
4. { Vincent Van Gogh / William Shakespeare

Beauty
1. Jerry Hall
2. Cher
3. Marilyn Monroe
4. HRH The Princess of Wales
5. Joan Collins

Hate and Fear
1. Adolf Hitler
2. Saddam Hussein
3. Margaret Thatcher
4. Colonel Gadaffi
5. Freddie Kruger

Hero or Heroine
1. Superman
2. { Marilyn Monroe / Mahatma Gandhi
4. { John Wayne / Mikhail Gorbachev

Favourite Person
1. Michael Jackson
2. { Cher / HRH The Princess of Wales
4. John Major
5. Eddie Murphy

1992

Politics
1. Margaret Thatcher
2. Mikhail Gorbachev
3. John Major
4. Bill Clinton
5. George Bush

Sport
1. Paul Gascoigne
2. Boris Becker
3. Gary Lineker
4. { Daley Thompson / Nigel Mansell

Entertainment
1. Michael Jackson
2. Eddie Murphy
3. Madonna
4. Gerard Depardieu
5. Dame Edna Everage

The Arts
1. Vincent Van Gogh
2. Pablo Picasso
3. Luciano Pavarotti
4. Gerard Depardieu
5. Wolgang Amadeus Mozart

Beauty
1. Cindy Crawford
2. Cher
3. Joan Collins
4. HRH The Princess of Wales
5. Jerry Hall

Hate and Fear
1. Saddam Hussein
2. Adolf Hitler
3. Margaret Thatcher
4. Colonel Gadaffi
5. Jack the Ripper

Hero or Heroine
1. Superman
2. Marilyn Monroe
3. Arnold Schwarzenegger
4. Winston Churchill
5. Sylvester Stallone

Favourite Person
1. Michael Jackson
2. Eddie Murphy
3. Cher
4. Henry VIII
5. John F. Kennedy

POSTMAN/POSTWOMAN

RADIO 2/ROYAL MAIL POSTIE OF THE YEAR

The annual search for the Postie of the Year is currently organized by the Royal Mail in association with BBC Radio 2. The competition organizers look for 'the postman or woman who contributes that special extra something to their local community'. Top prize for the national Postie of the Year is a £1,000 travel voucher. The winner's nominee will get a £500 travel voucher, plus a free letter a day for a year and a leather-bound writing kit.

The 1993 winner was Phil Bell, forty-six, from Paddington, West London, who reads the mail for a blind woman on his round and takes her washing to the launderette.

PRESS

BRITISH PRESS AWARDS

These began in 1963 as the Hannen Swaffer National Press Awards, sponsored by Odhams Press in memory of Hannen Swaffer. The title was changed to the IPC Press Awards in 1967 when the International Publishing Corporation took over Odhams, and a further change was made in 1975 when the present name was adopted. These long-standing awards (which reached their 30th year in 1993 and attracted 567 entries for the 14 categories) are sponsored by the Post Office in conjunction with *UK Press Gazette*. Widely regarded as the 'Oscars' of the British newspaper industry, they are voted by some 350 of the editors of Britain's national and provincial press. Recent winners were:

1991

Journalist of the Year   Martin Woollacott, The Guardian
Reporter of the Year   The BCCI report team, *Financial Times*
Cecil Harmsworth King Young Journalist of the Year   Jay Rayner, freelance contributor for *The Guardian*
David Blundy Award   Victoria Clark, *The Observer*
Provincial Journalist of the Year   Mike Hildrey and Ally McLaws, *Glasgow Evening News*
Arthur Sandles Award   Alex Frater, *The Observer*
David Holden International Reporter of the Year   Jonathan Steele, *The Guardian*
Photographer of the Year   Steve Wood, *Daily Express*
Columnist of the Year   Matthew Parris, *The Times*

Feature Writer of the Year   James Dalrymple, *Sunday Times*
Graphic Artist of the Year   James Ferguson, *Financial Times*, and Alan Gilliland, *Daily Telegraph*
Specialist Writer of the Year   City team, *Mail on Sunday*
Magazine Writer of the Year   Robert Chesshyre, *Telegraph* magazine
Chairman's Awards   Tom Bower, writer, and W. F. Deedes, *Daily Telegraph*

1992

Journalist of the Year   Maggie O'Kane, The Guardian
Reporter of the Year   David Hencke, *The Guardian*
David Holden International Reporter   Maggie O'Kane and Ed Vulliamy, *The Guardian*
David Blundy Award   Allister Sparks, *The Observer*

Provincial Journalist of the Year Steve Davies, *Southampton Advertiser*

Reporting Team of the Year *Financial Times* Maxwell Investigation Team

Columnist of the Year Simon Jenkins, *The Times*

Critic of the Year Allison Pearson, *Independent on Sunday*

Magazine Writer of the Year Russell Miller, *Sunday Times*

Sports Journalist of the Year Hugh McIlvanney, *The Observer*

Cecil King Young Journalist of the Year Andrew Malone, *Scotland on Sunday*

Feature Writer of the Year Lynda Lee-Potter, *Daily Mail*

Specialist Writer of the Year Anatole Kaletsky, *The Times*

Arthur Sandies Travel and Leisure Writer of the Year Alexander Frater, *The Observer*

Chairman's Awards Andrew Morton and Raymond Snoddy, *Financial Times*

1993

Newspaper of the Year *The Daily Telegraph*

Journalist of the Year Mark Rossiter, Editor, *Warrington Guardian*

Reporter of the Year Tina Weaver, *Today*

Foreign Journalist of the Year Shyam Bhatia, *The Observer*

Foreign Stringer of the Year Anthony Loyd, *The Times*

Regional Journalist of the Year Helen Weathers, *Wales on Sunday*

Sports Journalist of the Year Harry Harris, *Daily Mirror*

Young Journalist of the Year Esther Oxford, *The Independent*

Feature Writer of the Year Fiammetta Rocco, *Independent on Sunday*

Columnist of the Year Matthew Parris, *The Times*

Arts and Leisure Journalist Brian Sewell, *Evening Standard*

Exclusive of the Year *The Observer* (on the Government's secret talks with the IRA leadership)

Image of the Year Mike Boden, *Warrington Guardian*

Team Journalism *Warrington Guardian* (on the IRA bombing)

Regional Newspaper of the Year *Evening Times*, Glasgow

NEWSPAPER INDUSTRY AWARDS

These awards, first begun in 1990, are organized by Haymarket's *Newspaper Focus* magazine. The 1994 winners were:

National Newspaper of the Year Guardian

Regional Colour Supplement Guardian (for *The Guide*)

National Colour Supplement *The Sunday Review*/*Independent on Sunday*

Community Newspaper Northamptonshire *Evening Telegraph*

Production Management Birmingham *Post and Mail*

National Newspaper Editor Andrew Jaspan, *Scotland on Sunday*

Regional Newspaper Editor Neil Fowler, *The Journal* (Newcastle)

Marketing and Promotion Daily Star

Best Use of Colour Scotland on Sunday

Newspaper Presswork Yorkshire Post

Best Use of Photography *The Sunday Review*/*Independent on Sunday*

Sunday Newspaper Scotland on Sunday

Free Newspaper Bognor Regis Observer

Regional Newspaper *The Journal* (Newcastle)

Outstanding Achievements Alan Graham, director, Midland News Association

Miss Beautiful Eyes 1994, Jennie Aucote   Miss Pears 1993, Candice Carpenter

Participants in a recent Children's Society Sponsored Knitathlon

Holly Hunter, Best Leading Film Actress (*The Piano*) and Sir Anthony Hopkins, Best Leading Actor (*The Remains of the Day*) at the 1994 BAFTA Awards

Robert Stephens, winner of the 1993 Laurence Olivier Award for Best Actor in *Henry IV Part I*

above Charlie McGettigan and Paul Harrigan (Ireland), winners of the 1994 Eurovision Song Contest; *right* Natalie Clein, 1994 BBC Young Musician of the Year

below Nick Park's film, *The Wrong Trousers*, was named as Best Short Animated Film at the 1994 BAFTA Awards

above Ribblehead
Viaduct, 1993 winner of
the Public and
Commercial Sector
Award of the Ian Allan
Railway Heritage
Awards; *left* Woodlea
Primary School, Borden,
winner of the 1993
RIBA Building of the
Year Award

opposite Haddon Hall,
Derbyshire, 1993
Garden of the Year

left Pragna Patel, winner of the 1993 *Cosmopolitan* Achievement Award; *below* Dr Richard Roberts, co-winner of the 1993 Nobel Prize for Medicine

Headmistress Mary Cameron celebrates being voted Britain's
1994 Teacher of the Year

above Staff of the Blue Boar (Motorways) Ltd, Watford Gap, winner of the 1993 Motorways Best Cup of Tea Award; *left* Willie Rushton with the manager of the Phoenix and Firkin, *Evening Standard* 1993 Pub of the Year; *below* Ford Mondeo, 1994 European Car of the Year

'WHAT THE PAPERS SAY' AWARDS

Winners of the latest 'What the Papers Say' Awards, announced in February 1994:

Newspaper of the Year Observer

Scoop of the Year Clare Henderson, Grimsby Evening Telegraph (for revealing that Norman Lamont had resigned)

Columnist of the Year Suzanne Moore (*Guardian*)

Editor of the Year Richard Stott (*Today*)

Cartoonist of the Year Steve Bell (*Guardian*)

Investigation of the Year Robert Peston (*Financial Times*)

Gerald Berry Award Jill Tweedie (*Guardian*) (posthumously) for her services to journalism

PUBS

Many breweries organize their own 'Pub of the Year' awards, but there is no higher accolade than to win recognition from an independent body. For real ale fans, CAMRA's stamp of approval means such a pub is a must.

CAMRA NATIONAL PUB OF THE YEAR

Most of CAMRA's branches run annual Pub of the Year competitions. Nominations from branches for the national awards (inaugurated in 1989) produce both regional winners and a national winner. In 1993 the award was split.

1989	Boar's Head, Kinmuck, near Aberdeen	1992	Great Western, Wolverhampton
1990	Cap and Feathers, Tillingham, Essex	1993	Fisherman's Tavern, Broughty Ferry, Scotland Three Kings, Hanley Castle, Hereford & Worcester
1991	The Bell, Aldworth, Berks		

CAMRA REAL ALE CLUB OF THE YEAR

1991	St Teresa's Parish Centre, Penwortham, Lancs	1993	Galleywood Sports and Social Club, Galleywood, Essex
1992	ICI Club, Huddersfield, Yorks	1994	Beamish Mary Inn, near Stanley, Durham

GOOD PUB GUIDE AWARDS

An equally prized accolade is to achieve this award in the *Good Pub Guide*. The 1994 guide gives the following winners:

Cellarman of the Year Graham Titcombe, Blackwood Arms, Littleworth Common, Bucks

Own-Brew Pub of the Year The Rising Sun, Shraleybrook, Staffs

Whisky Pub of the Year Wight Mouse Bar, Clarendon Hotel, Chale, Isle of Wight

Wine Pub of the Year The Fox, Lower Oddington, Glos

Dining Pub of the Year   The Blue Lion, Witton, Yorks

Outstanding Good Value Cheap Food Pub   The Admiral, St Helier, Jersey

Fish Pub of the Year   The Half Moon, Kirdford, Sussex

Best Vegetarian Pub Cooking   Royal Oak, Barrington, Cambs

Top Yorkshire Pudding Pub   Half Moon, Skidby, Humberside

Best Traditional English Cooking   Green Man, Gosfield, Essex

Best Home-made Puddings   Duke of York, Berrow, Hereford & Worcester

Cheese Pub of the Year   Royal Oak, Didsbury, Manchester

Warmest Welcome of the Year   Lathkil, Over Haddon, Derbyshire

Landlord of the Year   Stephen Waring, Wenlock Edge Inn, Shropshire

Unspoilt Pub of the Year   The Bell, Aldworth, Berks

Overall Winner: Pub of the Year   Royal Oak, Appleby, Cumbria

EGON RONAY/HEINEKEN PUB OF THE YEAR

The popular Egon Ronay/Heineken *Pub and Inn Guide* gives a variety of annual awards to pubs in such categories as Family Pub, Bed and Breakfast Pub, etc. The Pub of the Year Award is made to the pub which combines a high standard of food and good accommodation with a warm, welcoming atmosphere. The first award, back in 1980, went to Wendy and Peter Amey of The Fox, Ansty, Dorset.

Among the 1993–4 winners of the respective awards were:

Pub of the Year   The Lamb, Great Rissington, Glos

Family Pub of the Year   Bridge Inn, Ratho, Scotland

Bed and Breakfast Pub of the Year   Chequers Inn, Froggatt Edge, Calver Bridge, Derbyshire

Newcomers of the Year   Five Arrows Hotel, High Street, Waddesdon, Bucks, and Fox Inn, Lower Oddington, Glos

British Cheese Pub of the Year   Shepherds Inn, Melmerby, near Penrith, Cumbria

THE *EVENING STANDARD* PUB OF THE YEAR AWARD

The London *Evening Standard* has organized this annual competition since 1967 to find the best pub in London. The judges are sent to inspect all the pubs nominated by readers, and the winning landlord, his wife and the nominator all get a free holiday. Winners since 1991 (brewers' names in brackets) were as follows:

1991	The Ship, Wandsworth (Youngs)	1993	The Phoenix and Firkin, Denmark Hill (Firkins Brewery, now part of Allied Lyons)
1992	The Tavern, Westminster (Youngs)		

Of the different breweries, Young's have been the most successful of all the brewers. Even though Young's houses make up only three per cent of the total number of pubs in Greater London, seven of them have come first in the competition since 1970, three have been awarded second place and dozens have been named as finalists.

BREWERY PUB CHAIN OF THE YEAR

Won in 1994 by the East Midland Mansfield Brewery – a Nottinghamshire brewery which, only two weeks earlier, picked up the Champion of Champions trophy for its Riding Bitter.

QUIZZES

MASTERMIND

This competition has been organized each year since 1972 by BBC Television. The entrants answer detailed questions on a special subject of their own choice, and then face further questions on general knowledge. If unsure of an answer the competitor may 'pass', rather than lose time whilst the compère Magnus Magnusson corrects a mistake. The top scorers in each round go forward to the semi-finals and finals, and the eventual winner is awarded the Mastermind trophy.

1972	Nancy Wilkinson (part-time lecturer)	1984	Margaret Harris (deputy headmistress)
1973	Patricia Owen (lecturer in English)	1985	Ian Meadows (hospital driver)
1974	Elizabeth Horrocks (housewife)	1986	Jennifer Keaveney (careers information officer)
1975	John Hart (schoolmaster)	1987	Jeremy Bradbrooke (general practitioner)
1976	Roger Prichard (civil servant)		
1977	Sir David Hunt (retired ambassador)	1988	David Beamish (House of Lords clerk)
1978	Rosemary James (teacher)	1989	Mary-Elizabeth Raw (veterinary surgeon)
1979	Philip Jenkins (research assistant)		
1980	Fred Housego (licensed taxi-driver)	1990	David Edwards (schoolmaster)
		1991	Stephen Allen (actor, stage name Stephen Tomlin)
1981	Leslie Grout (schoolmaster)		
1982	Sir David Hunt (Champion of Champions)	1992	Steve Williams (computer programmer)
1983	Christopher Hughes (underground train-driver)	1993	Gavin Fuller (historian/archivist)

The 1993 winner, Gavin Fuller, a part-time naval archivist, became the youngest Mastermind champion. He chose the Crusades, 1095–1154, as his final specialist subject, winning 32 points. The 1994 final, from Coventry Cathedral, will mark the 400th programme. Out of the 2,000 who wish to enter each year, 300 are auditioned and eventually 48 make it to the heats.

BRAIN OF BRITAIN

BBC Radio 4 organizes this annual nationwide general quiz. The first winner, in 1953–54, was Martin Dakin. Winners (since 1980) and their region have been:

1980	Tim Paxton, Scotland	1987	Ian Sutton, Midlands
1981	Peter Barlow, Home Counties	1988	Paul Monaghan, North
1982	John Pusey, South	1989	Barbara Thompson, North
1983	Sue Marshall, North	1990	Jim Eccleston, North
1984	Peter Bates, West	1991	Chris Wright, Wales
1985	Richard Fife, Midlands	1992	Mike Billson, South
1986	Stephen Gore, South	1993	Geoff Colton, Home Counties

RADIO

SONY RADIO AWARDS

The 1993 winners of the top award for radio were:

Outstanding Sports Broadcast: Barcelona Olympics, BBC Radio 5

Outstanding Special Event: Coca Cola National Music Day, MCM Networking (UK) Ltd for Independent Radio

Magazine/Special Interest Programme: Punters, BBC Radio 4

Sports Reporter of the Year: Jonathan Agnew, BBC Radio 3 and 5

Breakfast Show – Contemporary Music: Tony Blackburn Breakfast Show, Capital Gold

Breakfast Show – Non-Contemporary Music: Nick Bailey, Classic FM; Sarah Lucas, Classic FM

Response to a News Event: Ayodhya, BBC Radio Leicester

News and Current Affairs Sequence: Good Morning Ulster, BBC Radio Ulster

Breakfast Show – Speech Based: Mike Carlton's Morning Report, LBC Newstalk 97.3 FM

News and Current Affairs Programme: File on 4 – Feltham Remand Centre, BBC Radio 4

Local Broadcaster of the Year: David Dunseith, BBC Radio Ulster

Phone-in: Hayes Over Britain, BBC Badio 2

Documentary/Feature: Soundtrack: Jason and the Thunderbirds, BBC Radio 4

Specialist Music Programme: Scotland's Music, BBC Radio Scotland

Art Programme or Feature: Larks Ascending, BBC Radio 4

Popular Music Programme: Unsung Heroes, Unique Broadcasting for BBC Radio One FM

Use of Comedy/Comedy Show: Knowing Me, Knowing You, BBC Radio 4

Music Programming: Friel's Fancy, BBC Radio Ulster

Outstanding Service to the Community: Year of Action, BBC Radio Nottingham

Newcomer: Tom Bright, Radio Wave 96.5

News Reporter of the Year: Malcolm Brabant, BBC Radio 4

Best Actor: Keith Clifford, *Randle's Scandals*, BBC Radio 4

Best Actress: Miriam Margolyes, *The Queen and I*, BBC Radio 4

Society of Authors Award for Best Dramatization/Adaptation: Weir of Hermiston, BBC Radio Scotland/Radio 4

MELODY MAKER RADIO SHOW OF THE YEAR

1964	Saturday Club	1979	Friday Rock Show
1965	Saturday Club	1980	Friday Rock Show
1966	Saturday Club	1981	John Peel
1967	Radio London Fab 40	1982	John Peel
1968	Top Gear, John Peel	1983	David Jenson
1969	Top Gear, John Peel	1984	John Peel
1970	Top Gear, John Peel	1985	John Peel
1971	John Peel's In Concert Sunday Show	1986	John Peel
1972	Sounds of the Seventies	1987	John Peel
1973	Sounds of the Seventies	1988	John Peel
1974	Alan Freeman's Saturday Show	1989	John Peel
1975	Alan Freeman's Saturday Show	1990	John Peel
1976	Alan Freeman's Saturday Show	1991	John Peel
1977	Alan Freeman's Saturday Show	1992	John Peel
1978	Alan Freeman's Saturday Show	1993	John Peel

RAILWAYS

LONDON UNDERGROUND – BEST STATION GARDEN

One of the more unusual annual competitions, first run in 1977, currently sponsored by Sainsbury's Homebase, is the Underground Station Garden Competition. Judging is for three categories – gardens, best-cultivated gardens and hanging baskets/tubs. Recent winners were:

Garden Preston Road (1991, 1992), Chesham (1993)

Best Cultivated Garden Stanmore (1992),

Best Hanging Basket West Hampstead (1992)

BEST-KEPT BRITISH RAIL TERMINUS

The 1993 award sponsored by London Regional Passenger Committee and Cartner Engineering Ltd went to Liverpool Street, London, two years after the 119-year-old station had received a multi-million-pound transformation. Liverpool Street was voted best kept of British Rail's sixteen London termini, with marks given in categories that included litter control, clarity of information, helpfulness and presentation of staff.

IAN ALLAN RAILWAY HERITAGE AWARDS

The Best Restored Station Competition started in 1979 for Restored Railway Buildings in Private Ownership. In 1985 the competition became the Ian Allan Railway Heritage Awards and it was extended to public-sector-owned property. Any restored railway structures may be entered, both large and small, and also new structures built in traditional style and workmanship.

In 1991 the dates of the competition were changed so that from 1992 the complete competition would take place in one year; previously it had run over into the next year.

A money prize was offered from 1989 for both the winners and runners up. The total prizes now available amount to £5,000 per year. The competition is sponsored by Ian Allan Ltd, British Rail, The Railway Heritage Trust and Westinghouse Signals Ltd.

Private Sector Premier Award

1979	Oakworth Station, Keighley and Worth Valley Railway
1980	Staverton Station, Dart Valley Railway
1981	Ropley Station, Mid-Hants Railway
1982	Highley Station, Severn Valley Railway
1983	Arley Station, Severn Valley Railway
1984	Damems Station, Keighley and Worth Valley Railway
1985	Bo'Ness Station, Scottish Railway Preservation Society
1986	Haven Street Station, Isle of Wight Steam Railway
1987	Kidderminster Town, Severn Valley Railway
1988	Rowden Mill Station House, The Wilkinson Family
1989	Ingrow Station, Keighley and Worth Valley Railway
1990/1	Errol Station, Errol Station Trust
1992	Bowes-Lyon Bridge, Crich, Tramway Museum Society
1993	Scotscalder Station House, D. Brittain-Catlin

Public and Commercial Sector Award

1985	North Woolwich Station, Passmore Edwards Museum
1986	Wellingborough Station, BR London Midland Region
1987	St Denys Station, BR Southern Region
1988	Glasgow Central, ScotRail Architects
1989	Lewes Station, BR Department of Architecture & Design
1990/1	Wicker Arch, Sheffield, BR Regional Civil Engineers, York
1992	Cathedral Arches, Salford, BR Property Board and Craft-Kind Ltd
1993	Ribblehead Viaduct, Regional Railways North East (et al)

REFUSE COLLECTION

WORLD REFUSE COLLECTION CHAMPIONSHIPS

This annual contest to find the top dustmen of the year tests the competitors' skills in driving, running and loading over a specially timed race. Defending their title in 1993 at Worthing, Sussex, were the sextet of Wayne Moore, Adrian Smith, Stuart Archer, Kevin Blurton, Haiden Wragg and Stuart Dilley from Hinckley in Leicestershire.

RESTAURANTS

EGON RONAY RESTAURANT OF THE YEAR

Of the many restaurant awards, one of the most impressive is the Egon Ronay award. The award is made to the restaurant whose consistent excellence or enterprise is found to be outstanding. The winner receives, and keeps for a year, an engraved Wedgwood plate. The first winner, in 1969, was the Thornbury Castle, in Thornbury, Avon. Among famous early winners in London were Le Gavroche (1972), Wilton's (1975) and Carrier's (1977). Recent winners were:

1987	Walnut Tree Inn, Abergavenny, Wales
1988	Morels, Haslemere, Surrey
1989	L'Arlequin, London
1990	Waterside Inn, Bray-on-Thames, Berks
1991	L'Ortolan, Shinfield, nr Reading, Berks
1992	Bibendum, London
1993	The Carved Angel, Dartmouth, Devon
1994	Le Soufflé Restaurant, Inter-Continental Hotel, London

Within its restaurant category, Egon Ronay makes awards for chefs, cellars, cheeseboards and desserts. Here are some recent awards in these categories.

Egon Ronay Cellar of the Year

1988	Champany Inn, Linlithgow, Scotland
1989	Old Bridge Hotel, Huntingdon
1990	La Potinière, Gullane, Scotland
1991	White Horse Inn, Chilgrove, W. Sussex
1992	The Cross, Kingussie, Scotland
1993	Croque-en-Bouche, Malvern
1994	Gravetye Manor, East Grinstead, W. Sussex

Egon Ronay California Cellar of the Year

1990	Gidleigh Park, Chagford, Devon
1991	Croque-en-Bouche, Malvern, Hereford & Worcester
1992	190 Queen's Gate, London
1993	Gravetye Manor, East Grinstead, W. Sussex
1994	Lower Slaughter Manor, Lower Slaughter, Glos

Egon Ronay Chef of the Year

1992	Marco Pierre White, Harveys, London
1993	Shaun Hill, Gidleigh Park, Chagford, Devon
1994	Paul Heathcote, Paul Heathcote Restaurant, Longridge, Lancs

Egon Ronay Dessert of the Year

1992	Roger Pizey, Harveys, London
1993	Jean-Christophe Novelli, Le Provence at Gordleton Mill, Lymington, Hants
1994	John Burton-Race, L'Ortolan, Shinfield, nr Reading, Berks

Egon Ronay British Cheeseboard of the Year

1993	Old Vicarage, Witherslack, Cumbria
1994	The Lygon Arms, Broadway, Hereford & Worcester

Egon Ronay's Duboeuf Guide Just a Bite Awards

This award is for the less expensive quicker snack or 'just a bite' category. 1993 winners were:

London Restaurant of the Year Osteria Antica Bologna, Northcote Road, London

England Restaurant of the Year California Pizza Factory, High Street, Harborne, Birmingham

Scotland Restaurant of the Year The Laigh, Hanover Street, Edinburgh

Wales Restaurant of the Year Jodie's, Telford Road, Menai Bridge, Anglesey

Tea Place of the Year Hudson's Coffee House, City Plaza Shopping Centre, Cannon Street, Birmingham

The 1994 winners were:

London Restaurant of the Year Patisserie Valerie, Brompton Road, London

England Restaurant of the Year Magpie Café, Pier Road, Whitby N. Yorks

Scotland Restaurant of the Year Brambles, College Street, St Andrew, Fife

Wales Restaurant of the Year Hive on the Quay, Cadwgan Place, Aberaeron, Dyfed

Coffee Place of the Year Monmouth Coffee House, Monmouth Street, London

---

THE *TIME OUT* EATING AND DRINKING AWARDS

The popular *Time Out* magazine also gives its awards (in 1994 in their sixth year) to a variety of restaurants in the capital. Awards in 1993 were made in eight categories:

Michelob Best Bar The Dog House
Best Chinese Restaurant Vegetarian Cottage
Best New Restaurant Granita
Best Budget Meal Wagamama
Best Service Ransome's Dock
Sunday Best Frocks
Best Vegetarian Meal The Gate
Best Modern British The Square

The 1994 Winners were:

Michelob Best Bar The Crown and Goose, NW1
Best Budget Meal Jigsaw, W12
Sunday Best Christopher's, WC2
Best Modern British Fifth Floor, SW1
Best Turkish Restaurant Mangal, E8
Best Vegetarian Meal Mantanah, SE25
Best Service The Oak Room, W1
Best New Restaurant Quaglino's, SW1

ROWING

OLYMPIC GAMES

Men's Single Sculls

1900	Henri Barrelet (Fra)
1904	Frank Greer (USA)
1908	Harry Blackstaffe (GB)
1912	William Kinnear (GB)
1920	John Kelly Snr (USA)
1924	Jack Beresford Jr (GB)
1928	Henry Pearce (Aus)
1932	Henry Pearce (Aus)
1936	Gustav Schäfer (Ger)
1948	Mervyn Wood (Aus)
1952	Yuriy Tyukalov (USSR)
1956	Vyacheslav Ivanov (USSR)
1960	Vyacheslav Ivanov (USSR)
1964	Vyacheslav Ivanov (USSR)
1968	Henri Jan Wienese (Hol)
1972	Yuriy Malishev (USSR)
1976	Pertti Karppinen (Fin)
1980	Pertti Karppinen (Fin)
1984	Pertti Karppinen (Fin)
1988	Thomas Lange (GDR)
1992	Thomas Lange (Ger)

Men's Double Sculls

1904	John Mulcahy/William Varley (USA)
1920	Paul Costello/John Kelly (USA)
1924	Paul Costello/John Kelly (USA)
1928	Paul Costello/Charles McIlvaine (USA)
1932	William Garrett Gilmore/Kenneth Myers (USA)
1936	Jack Beresford/Leslie Southwood (GB)
1948	Richard Burnell/Herbert Bushnell (GB)
1952	Tranquilo Capozzo/Eduardo Guerrero (Arg)
1956	Aleksandr Berkutov/Yuriy Tyukalov (USSR)
1960	Vaclav Kozak/Pavel Schmidt (Cze)
1964	Boris Dubrovsky/Oleg Tyurin (USSR)

1968	Anatoliy Sass/Aleksandr Timoshinin (USSR)
1972	Gennadiy Korshikov/Aleksandr Timoshinin (USSR)
1976	Alf Hansen/Frank Hansen (Nor)
1980	Joachim Dreifke/Klaus Kroppelien (GDR)
1984	Bradley Lewis/Paul Enquist (USA)
1988	Ronald Florijn/Nicolaas Rienks (Hol)
1992	Peter Antonie/Mark Hawkins (Aus)

Men's Coxless Pairs

1904	Robert Farnam/Joseph Ryan (USA)
1908	John Fenning/Gordon Thomson (GB)
1924	Antonie Beijnen/Wilhelm Rosingh (Hol)
1928	Kurt Moeschter/Bruno Muller (Ger)
1932	Lewis Clive/Arthur Edwards (GB)
1936	Willie Eichorn/Hugo Strauss (Ger)
1948	George Laurie/John Wilson (GB)
1952	Charles Logg/Thomas Price (USA)
1956	James Fifer/Duvall Hecht (USA)
1960	Valentin Boreyko/Oleg Golovanov (USSR)
1964	George Hungerford/Roger Jackson (Can)
1968	Heinz-Jürgen Bothe/Jorg Lucke (GDR)
1972	Siegfried Brietzke/Wolfgang Mager (GDR)
1976	Bernd Landvoigt/Jorg Landvoigt (GDR)
1980	Petru Losub/Valer Toma (Rom)
1988	Andrew Holmes/Steven Redgrave (GB)
1992	Matthew Pinsent/Steven Redgrave (GB)

Men's Coxed Pairs

1900	Holland
1906	Italy
1920	Italy
1924	Switzerland
1928	Switzerland
1932	USA
1936	Germany
1948	Denmark
1952	France
1956	USA
1960	West Germany
1964	USA
1968	Italy
1972	East Germany
1976	East Germany
1980	East Germany
1984	Italy
1988	Italy
1992	Great Britain

Men's Quadruple Sculls

1976	East Germany
1980	East Germany
1984	West Germany
1988	Italy
1992	Germany

Men's Coxless Fours

1904	USA
1908	Great Britain
1924	Great Britain
1928	Great Britain
1932	Great Britain
1936	Germany
1948	Italy
1952	Yugoslavia
1956	Canada
1960	USA
1964	Denmark
1968	East Germany
1972	East Germany
1976	East Germany
1980	East Germany
1984	New Zealand
1988	East Germany
1992	Australia

Men's Coxed Fours

1900	{ Germany { France

1912	Germany
1920	Switzerland
1924	Switzerland
1928	Italy
1932	Germany
1936	Germany
1948	USA
1952	Czechoslovakia
1956	Italy
1960	Germany
1964	Germany
1968	New Zealand
1972	West Germany
1976	USSR
1980	East Germany
1984	Great Britain
1988	East Germany
1992	Romania

Men's Eights

1900	USA
1904	USA
1908	Great Britain
1912	Great Britain
1920	USA
1924	USA
1928	USA
1932	USA
1936	USA
1948	USA
1952	USA
1956	USA
1960	West Germany
1964	USA
1968	West Germany
1972	New Zealand
1976	East Germany
1980	East Germany
1984	Canada
1988	West Germany
1992	Canada

Women's Single Sculls

1976	Christine Scheiblich (GDR)
1980	Sanda Toma (Rom)
1984	Valeria Racila (Rom)
1988	Jutta Behrendt (GDR)
1992	Elisabeta Lipa (Rom)

Women's Double Sculls

1976	Svetla Otzetova/Zdravka Yordanova (Bul)
1980	Yelena Khlopsteva/Larisa Popova (USSR)
1984	Marioara Popescu/Elisabeta Oleniuc (Rom)
1988	Birgit Peter/Martina Schroeter (GDR)
1992	Kerstin Koppen/Kathrin Boron (Ger)

Women's Coxless Pairs

1976	Stoyanka Grouitcheva/Siika Kelbetcheva (Bul)
1980	Cornelia Klier/Ute Steindorf (GDR)
1984	Rodica Arba/Elena Horvat (Rom)
1988	Rodica Arba/Olga Homeghi (Rom)
1992	Marnie McBean/Kathleen Heddle (Can)

Women's Quadruple Sculls

1976	East Germany
1980	East Germany
1984	Romania
1988	East Germany
1992	Germany

Women's Coxless Fours

| 1992 | Canada |

Women's Eights

1976	East Germany
1980	East Germany
1984	USA
1988	East Germany

UNIVERSITY BOAT RACE

1946	Oxford	1971	Cambridge
1947	Cambridge	1972	Cambridge
1948	Cambridge	1973	Cambridge
1949	Cambridge	1974	Oxford
1950	Cambridge	1975	Cambridge
1951	Cambridge	1976	Oxford
1952	Oxford	1977	Oxford
1953	Cambridge	1978	Oxford
1954	Oxford	1979	Oxford
1955	Cambridge	1980	Oxford
1956	Cambridge	1981	Oxford
1957	Cambridge	1982	Oxford
1958	Cambridge	1983	Oxford
1959	Oxford	1984	Oxford
1960	Oxford	1985	Oxford
1961	Cambridge	1986	Cambridge
1962	Cambridge	1987	Oxford
1963	Oxford	1988	Oxford
1964	Cambridge	1989	Oxford
1965	Oxford	1990	Oxford
1966	Oxford	1991	Oxford
1967	Oxford	1992	Oxford
1968	Cambridge	1993	Cambridge
1969	Cambridge	1994	Cambridge
1970	Cambridge		

RUGBY LEAGUE

WORLD CUP/INTERNATIONAL CHAMPIONS

1954	Great Britain	1972	Great Britain
1957	Australia	1975	Australia
1960	Great Britain	1977	Australia
1968	Australia	1988	Australia
1970	Australia	1992	Australia

CHALLENGE CUP

1897	Batley	1938	Salford
1898	Batley	1939	Halifax
1899	Oldham	1941	Leeds
1900	Swinton	1942	Leeds
1901	Batley	1943	Dewsbury
1902	Broughton Rangers	1944	Bradford Northern
1903	Halifax	1945	Huddersfield
1904	Halifax	1946	Wakefield Trinity
1905	Warrington	1947	Bradford Northern
1906	Bradford	1948	Wigan
1907	Warrington	1949	Bradford Northern
1908	Hunslet	1950	Warrington
1909	Wakefield Trinity	1951	Wigan
1910	Leeds	1952	Workington Town
1911	Broughton Rangers	1953	Huddersfield
1912	Dewsbury	1954	Warrington
1913	Huddersfield	1955	Barrow
1914	Hull	1956	St Helens
1915	Huddersfield	1957	Leeds
1920	Huddersfield	1958	Wigan
1921	Leigh	1959	Wigan
1922	Rochdale Hornets	1960	Wakefield Trinity
1923	Leeds	1961	St Helens
1924	Wigan	1962	Wakefield Trinity
1925	Oldham	1963	Wakefield Trinity
1926	Swinton	1964	Widnes
1927	Oldham	1965	Wigan
1928	Swinton	1966	St Helens
1929	Wigan	1967	Featherstone Rovers
1930	Widnes	1968	Leeds
1931	Halifax	1969	Castleford
1932	Leeds	1970	Castleford
1933	Huddersfield	1971	Leigh
1934	Hunslet	1972	St Helens
1935	Castleford	1973	Featherstone Rovers
1936	Leeds	1974	Warrington
1937	Widnes	1975	Widnes

1976	St Helens	1986	Castleford
1977	Leeds	1987	Halifax
1978	Leeds	1988	Wigan
1979	Widnes	1989	Wigan
1980	Hull Kingston Rovers	1990	Wigan
1981	Widnes	1991	Wigan
1982	Hull	1992	Wigan
1983	Featherstone Rovers	1993	Wigan
1984	Widnes	1994	Wigan
1985	Wigan		

PREMIERSHIP TROPHY

1975	Leeds	1985	St Helens
1976	St Helens	1986	Warrington
1977	St Helens	1987	Wigan
1978	Bradford Northern	1988	Widnes
1979	Leeds	1989	Widnes
1980	Widnes	1990	Widnes
1981	Hull Kingston Rovers	1991	Hull
1982	Widnes	1992	Wigan
1983	Widnes	1993	St Helens
1984	Hull Kingston Rovers	1994	Wigan

KNOCKOUT TROPHY

1972	Halifax	1984	Leeds
1973	Leeds	1985	Hull Kingston Rovers
1974	Warrington	1986	Wigan
1975	Bradford Northern	1987	Wigan
1976	Widnes	1988	St Helens
1977	Castleford	1989	Wigan
1978	Warrington	1990	Wigan
1979	Widnes	1991	Warrington
1980	Bradford Northern	1992	Widnes
1981	Warrington	1993	Wigan
1982	Hull	1994	Wigan
1983	Wigan		

ENGLISH LEAGUE

1906	Leigh	1920	Hull
1907	Halifax	1921	Hull
1908	Hunslet	1922	Wigan
1909	Wigan	1923	Hull Kingston Rovers
1910	Oldham	1924	Batley
1911	Oldham	1925	Hull Kingston Rovers
1912	Huddersfield	1926	Wigan
1913	Huddersfield	1927	Swinton
1914	Salford	1928	Swinton
1915	Huddersfield	1929	Huddersfield

1930	Huddersfield	1965	Halifax
1931	Swinton	1966	St Helens
1932	St Helens	1967	Wakefield Trinity
1933	Salford	1968	Wakefield Trinity
1934	Wigan	1969	Leeds
1935	Swinton	1970	St Helens
1936	Hull	1971	St Helens
1937	Salford	1972	Leeds
1938	Hunslet	1973	Dewsbury
1939	Salford	1974	Salford
1946	Wigan	1975	St Helens
1947	Wigan	1976	Salford
1948	Warrington	1977	Featherstone Rovers
1949	Huddersfield	1978	Widnes
1950	Wigan	1979	Hull Kingston Rovers
1951	Workington Town	1980	Bradford Northern
1952	Wigan	1981	Bradford Northern
1953	St Helens	1982	Leigh
1954	Warrington	1983	Hull
1955	Warrington	1984	Hull Kingston Rovers
1956	Hull	1985	Hull Kingston Rovers
1957	Oldham	1986	Halifax
1958	Hull	1987	Wigan
1959	St Helens	1988	Widnes
1960	Wigan	1989	Widnes
1961	Leeds	1990	Wigan
1962	Huddersfield	1991	Wigan
1963	Swinton / Hunslet	1992	Wigan
1964	Swinton / Oldham	1993	Wigan
		1994	Wigan

RUGBY UNION

WORLD CUP

1987	New Zealand
1991	Australia

FIVE NATIONS CHAMPIONSHIP

1883	England	1890	England / Scotland	1897	—
1884	England			1898	—
1885	—	1891	Scotland	1899	Ireland
1886	England / Scotland	1892	England	1900	Wales
1887	Scotland	1893	Wales	1901	Scotland
1888	—	1894	Ireland	1902	Wales
1889	—	1895	Scotland	1903	Scotland
		1896	Ireland	1904	Scotland

1905	Wales	1936	Wales	1970	{ Wales
1906	{ Ireland	1937	England		France
	Wales	1938	Scotland	1971	Wales
1907	Scotland		{ England	1972	—
1908	Wales	1939	{ Wales		{ Ireland
1909	Wales		Ireland		France
1910	England	1947	{ Wales	1973	{ Scotland
1911	Wales		England		Wales
1912	{ England	1948	Ireland		England
	Ireland	1949	Ireland	1974	Ireland
1913	England	1950	Wales	1975	Wales
1914	England	1951	Ireland	1976	Wales
	{ England	1952	Wales	1977	France
1920	{ Scotland	1953	England	1978	Wales
	Wales		{ England	1979	Wales
1921	England	1954	{ Wales	1980	England
1922	Wales		France	1981	France
1923	England	1955	{ Wales	1982	Ireland
1924	England		France	1983	{ France
1925	Scotland	1956	Wales		Ireland
1926	{ Scotland	1958	England	1984	Scotland
	Ireland	1959	France	1985	Ireland
1927	{ Scotland	1960	{ France	1986	{ France
	Ireland		England		Scotland
1928	England	1961	France	1987	France
1929	Scotland	1962	France	1988	{ Wales
1930	England	1963	England		France
1931	Wales	1964	{ Scotland	1989	France
	{ England		Wales	1990	Scotland
1932	{ Wales	1965	Wales	1991	England
	Ireland	1966	Wales	1992	England
1933	Scotland	1967	France	1993	France
1934	England	1968	France	1994	Wales
1935	Ireland	1969	Wales		

ENGLISH COUNTY CHAMPIONSHIP

1889	Yorkshire	1902	Durham	1914	Midlands
1890	Yorkshire	1903	Durham	1915	*not held*
1891	Lancashire	1904	Kent	1916	*not held*
1892	Yorkshire	1905	Durham	1917	*not held*
1893	Yorkshire	1906	Devon	1918	*not held*
1894	Yorkshire	1907	{ Devon	1919	*not held*
1895	Yorkshire		Durham	1920	Gloucestershire
1896	Yorkshire	1908	Cornwall	1921	Gloucestershire
1897	Kent	1909	Durham	1922	Gloucestershire
1898	Northumberland	1910	Gloucestershire	1923	Somerset
1899	Devon	1911	Devon	1924	Cumberland
1900	Durham	1912	Devon	1925	Leicestershire
1901	Devon	1913	Gloucestershire	1926	Yorkshire

1927	Kent	1950	Cheshire	1972	Gloucestershire
1928	Yorkshire	1951	East Midlands	1973	Lancashire
1929	Middlesex	1952	Middlesex	1974	Gloucestershire
1930	Gloucestershire	1953	Yorkshire	1975	Gloucestershire
1931	Gloucestershire	1954	Middlesex	1976	Gloucestershire
1932	Gloucestershire	1955	Lancashire	1977	Lancashire
1933	Hampshire	1956	Middlesex	1978	North Midlands
1934	East Midlands	1957	Devon	1979	Middlesex
1935	Lancashire	1958	Warwickshire	1980	Lancashire
1936	Hampshire	1959	Warwickshire	1981	Northumberland
1937	Gloucestershire	1960	Warwickshire	1982	Lancashire
1938	Lancashire	1961	Cheshire	1983	Gloucestershire
1939	Warwickshire	1962	Warwickshire	1984	Gloucestershire
1940	*not held*	1963	Warwickshire	1985	Middlesex
1941	*not held*	1964	Warwickshire	1986	Warwickshire
1942	*not held*	1965	Warwickshire	1987	Yorkshire
1943	*not held*	1966	Middlesex	1988	Lancashire
1944	*not held*	1967	Surrey	1989	Durham
1945	*not held*	1967	Durham	1990	Lancashire
1946	*not held*	1968	Middlesex	1991	Cornwall
1947	Lancashire	1969	Lancashire	1992	Lancashire
1948	Lancashire	1970	Staffordshire	1993	Lancashire
1949	Lancashire	1971	Surrey	1994	Yorkshire

PILKINGTON CUP

1972	Gloucester	1980	Leicester	1988	Harlequins
1973	Coventry	1981	Leicester	1989	Bath
1974	Coventry	1982	Gloucester	1990	Bath
1975	Bedford	1983	Bristol	1991	Harlequins
1976	Gosforth	1984	Bath	1992	Bath
1977	Gosforth	1985	Bath	1993	Leicester
1978	Gloucester	1986	Bath	1994	Bath
1979	Leicester	1987	Bath		

COURAGE ENGLISH LEAGUE

1987/8	Leicester	1990/1	Bath	1993/4	Bath
1988/9	Bath	1991/2	Bath		
1989/90	Wasps	1992/3	Bath		

SCHWEPPES WELSH CUP

1972	Neath	1980	Bridgend	1988	Llanelli
1973	Llanelli	1981	Cardiff	1989	Neath
1974	Llanelli	1982	Cardiff	1990	Neath
1975	Llanelli	1983	Pontypool	1991	Llanelli
1976	Llanelli	1984	Cardiff	1992	Llanelli
1977	Newport	1985	Llanelli	1993	Cardiff
1978	Swansea	1986	Cardiff		
1979	Bridgend	1987	Cardiff		

HEINEKEN WELSH LEAGUE

1990/1	Neath	1992/3	Llanelli
1991/2	Swansea	1993/4	Swansea

McEWANS SCOTTISH LEAGUE

1974	Hawick	1981	Gala	1988	Kelso
1975	Hawick	1982	Hawick	1989	Kelso
1976	Hawick	1983	Gala	1990	Melrose
1977	Hawick	1984	Hawick	1991	Boroughmuir
1978	Hawick	1985	Hawick	1992	Melrose
1979	Heriot's FP	1986	Hawick	1993	Melrose
1980	Gala	1987	Hawick	1994	Melrose

IRISH LEAGUE

1991	Cork Constitution	1993	Young Munster
1992	Garryowen	1994	Garryowen

SALESMEN

SALESMAN OF THE YEAR

This new award, organized by Mitchell Marketing Associates, was instituted in 1993. Sponsored by *The Times*, it was the principal prize of the British and European Sales and Marketing Awards 1993, for the best sales campaign of the year. The award was designed to recognize sales people as the key to economic recovery.

The inaugural winner was Richard Branson, Chairman of the Virgin Group. The award followed the long legal battle between British Airways and Virgin Atlantic and the launch of the commercial radio station Virgin 1215.

SANDWICHES

BRITISH SANDWICH ASSOCIATION AWARDS

The annual search to find Britain's top sandwich makers and retailers is organized by the British Sandwich Association. Awards are presented at a special gala dinner in London each spring. The 1993 winners were:

BSA Award   Marks & Spencer
Sandwich Manufacturer of the Year   Breadwinners Foods

The company, which was founded in 1979 by Peter Bartlett, operates from Park Royal in London, supplying sandwiches to many of London's banks and accountancy firms.

Sandwich Bar of the Year   Upper Crust Brasserie, Liverpool

Located in a Victorian building which is believed to be the world's first purpose-built office block – built in 1852 – Upper Crust has been designed by partner Gary Morris to recreate the atmosphere of that time. Decorated with gas lanterns, an electronic pianola and bric-à-brac from the last century, this gives outstanding character to this popular Liverpool sandwich bar.

Sandwich Retailer of the Year Award Marks & Spencer, Moorgate

Sandwich Buyer of the Year Mike Fraser

Sandwich Photographer of the Year Patrice de Villiers

Sandwich Journalist of the Year Richard Cawley, Jackie Giles

Supplier New Product Award Cherry Valley Farms

Sandwich Server of the Year Sergine Alder, Pret à Manger, St Martin's Lane, London

Most Innovative Sandwich Ditty's Home Bakery

Meat Sandwich Bar Murray's, Alderley Edge, Cheshire

The 1994 winners were:

Sandwich Bar of the Year Pret À Manger

BSA Award Shell UK

Sandwich Manufacturer of the Year Green Meadow Foods Ltd

Baker/Sandwich Maker of the Year Miss Maude's Coffee Shop and Patisserie, Kirkcaldy, Scotland

Sandwich Retailer of the Year Award Littlewoods Chain Stores Ltd

Sandwich Buyer of the Year Richard Cushing, Shell Oil UK

New Product of the Year Food for Thought's, Square Omelette and Breakfast Omelette

Sandwich Photographer of the Year Joanna Trobe, Trobe Studios Ltd

SAUSAGES

SAUSAGE OF THE YEAR TROPHY

The traditional British sausage clearly still has a large following. With a membership of over 8,000, the British Sausage Appreciation Society awards its various Sausage of the Year trophies at its annual Sausage Convention.

Among the 1993 winners was Walker and Son, the Leicester pork pie and sausage manufacturers, who carried off the top award for producing the Sausage of the Year sold through a multiple retailer. The firm makes and supplies the Cumberland Ring sausage sold at Tesco stores throughout the country. The sausage is made to an old Walker's family recipe using only natural ingredients of prime pork blended with herbs and seasoning and contained within a natural hog casing.

CHAMPION OF CHAMPIONS SAUSAGE MAKER

Early in 1994 Alan Woodward, a 54-year-old butcher from Henfield in W. Sussex, received the 'Champion of Champions' accolade – for a winning entry that was made of pork with a dash of gin!

SCHOOLS

In November 1993 the first published league tables for the performance of schools and colleges at 'A' level appeared. The most successful school was King Edward's, an independent boys' school in Birmingham, which registered the best score of 37.4. It was followed by: 33.4 per cent King Edward VI High School for Girls, Birmingham; 30.5 per cent King's School, Cheshire (boys); 30 per cent Merchant Taylors' Boys, Sefton (boys); 29.9 per cent Wolverhampton Grammar School (mixed); 29.5 per cent Queen's School, Cheshire (girls); 29.4 per cent Hampton School, Richmond-upon-Thames (boys); 29.1 per cent Eton College, Berks (boys).

In the competition to be best sixth-form college the top college for 'A' level was Hills Road Sixth Form College in Cambridge, where 357 candidates achieved an average A and AS level points score of 21.4 – the equivalent of two B grades and one C – compared with the national average of 14.7.

Its nearest rivals were Sir John Deane's College, Northwich, Cheshire 21.0 per cent; Woodhouse College, Finchley 19.2 per cent; King George V College, Southport 19.1 per cent; Shrewsbury Sixth Form College 18.8 per cent; and York Sixth Form College 18.2 per cent.

SCIENCE

YOUNG SCIENCE WRITER AWARDS

The Young Science Writer Awards, which reached their sixth year in 1993, are backed by the British Association for the Advancement of Science and the *Daily Telegraph*. The awards are in two age-group bands: 16–21 and 22–28. The 1993 winners were:

16–21 group

1. Emily Beardall, St Aidan's High School, Harrogate, Yorks
2. Richard Wade-Martins, Cambridge University

22–28 group

1. Robert Ward, Manchester University
2. Harriet Coles, University College, London

The winners were presented with their awards by Sir David Weatherall, president of the British Association, at its annual meeting at Keele University in August. As well as having their entries published and winning £500 each, they each visited America, expenses paid, to attend the association's sister conference in San Francisco.

SCRABBLE

BRITISH NATIONAL CHAMPIONSHIPS

These were inaugurated in 1971. Anyone of any age can enter. The contestants play qualifying games and regional finals, the top 100 players going through to the grand finals. Here the contestants play three games against different opponents, very strict word rules apply and only two minutes are allowed for each move. The player with the highest aggregate score becomes the champion. Recent winners were:

1992	Philip Nelkon
1993	Alan Saldanha

The 1993 winner, 15-year-old Alan Saldanha from South Kensington, was the youngest person to make the final in the competition's 23-year history. He beat 38-year-old Manchester mathematics lecturer Dr Karl Khoshnaw by 407 points to 369 with words like 'reasted' (rancid) and 'aneroid' (without liquids). He received his prize, an engraved trophy and gold-plated Scrabble set, from writer and Tory MP Gyles Brandreth at the New Connaught Rooms, Holborn.

WORLD CHAMPIONSHIP

The first World Championship took place in London in 1992. The winner was Peter Morris (USA) who took the $10,000 first prize. The winner at the 1993 competition was Britain's Mark Nyman, 26, who finally vanquished his opponent, Joel Wapnick of Montreal, with a score of 417 to 369, with such winning words as 'dojo' (a judo hall), 'velours' (felt-like fabric) and 'quint' (a sequence of five cards in piquet). His winning word was 'wet'.

The championship attracted 64 top players from 22 countries.

SECRETARIES

SECRETARY OF THE YEAR

A highly prestigious award, the United Kingdom Top Secretary is that sponsored by the London Chamber of Commerce and Industry. The 1993 winner, Jennifer Pothecary, 23, of Lytham St Anne's, beat a total of 500 other contestants to win the award.

The winner listed the main requirements for the job as 'initiative, common sense and the ability to forward-plan; a flexible, enthusiastic approach and a good sense of humour'.

In the contest, sponsored by *The Times*, to find the Professional Secretary of the Year, the 1994 winner was Leanne Middleton.

SHEEPDOGS

ONE MAN AND HIS DOG AWARDS

The ever-popular *One Man and His Dog* TV series has produced the following winners.

Brace

1980	Glyn Jones with Gel and Bracken
1981	Thomas Longton with Bess and Lassie
1982	Geoff Billingham with Jed and Trim
1983	Tim Longton with Tweed and Clun Roy

1984	John Campbell with Roy and Moss
1985	John MacLeod with Cap and Ben
1986	Meirion Jones with Bill and Cap
1987	Colin Gordon with Robbie and Nell
1988	Jim Cropper with Cap 1 and Cap 2
1989	Harford Logan with Mickey and Jim
1990	Glyn Jones with Taff and Cap
1991	Colin Gordon with Cap and Meg
1992	Ian Jones with Roy and Mac
1993	Aled Owen with Ben and Craig

Singles

1980	Bob Shennan with Mirk
1981	Raymond Macpherson with Tweed
1982	Stuart Davidson with Ben
1983	Dick Nicholls with Rod
1984	Evan Hopkins with Fly
1985	John Wilson with Peg

1986	Maurice Collin with Shep
1987	Alex McCuish with Hemp
1988	Jim Grierson with Mark
1989	Gwyn Jones with Queen
1990	Katy Cropper with Trim
1991	Colin Gordon with Meg
1992	Trevor Evans with Nap
1993	Paddy Byrne with Nip

Young Handlers Championship

1981	David Bristow with Tweed
1982	Merion Owen with Jill
1983	Liam Marley with Glen
1984	Jane McDonald with Roy
1985	Mark France with Flash
1986	Mark Owen with Silver
1987	James Gill with Ben
1988	Janet Mason with Slade
1989	Graham Powell with Jill
1990	Donal O'Sullivan with Bin
1991	Robert Ellis with Roy
1992	Vanessa Reed with Jen
1993	Martin Doherty with Moss

SHIRE HORSES

The Shire Horse Society runs two major events each year, the National Shire Horse Show and the Shire Horse of the Year Championship.

NATIONAL SHIRE HORSE SHOW

The National Shire Horse Show is held annually on the third Saturday in March, and the following Championships are judged: Champion Stallion, Champion Mare, Champion Gelding, Champion Turnout.

Champion Stallion

	Winning animal	*Exhibitor*
1980	Ladbrook Aristocrat	A. W. Lewis
1981	Metheringham Joseph	T. E. Moss
1982	Cubley Charlie	J. and E. Salt
1983	Cubley Charlie	J. and E. Salt
1984	Cubley Charlie	J. and E. Salt
1985	Tremoelgoch Enterprise	G. Lloyd Owen
1986	Cubley Charlie	J. and E. Salt
1987	Hillmoor Prince Charles	A. Bull
1988	Herswell Premier	J. D. Joseph
1989	Deighton Bomber	P. and W. Bedford

	Winning animal	Exhibitor
1990	Gronant Charlie	C. J. and S. Leverett
	Winning animal	Exhibitor
1991	Gronant Charlie	C. J. and S. Leverett
1992	Deighton Commodore	P. and W. Bedford
1993	Deighton Commodore	P. and W. Bedford

Champion Mare

	Winning animal	Exhibitor
1980	Jim's Lucky Charm	J. B. Cooke Ltd
1981	Jim's Lucky Charm	J. B. Cooke Ltd
1982	Saredon Pure Gold	J. and E. Salt
1983	Earnshaw Ruby	R. T. Mortimer
1984	Landcliffe Laura	P. and W. Bedford
1985	Landcliffe Laura	P. and W. Bedford
1986	Landcliffe Laura	P. and W. Bedford
1987	Greenhaulme Country Girl	K. M. Jones
1988	Landcliffe Laura	P. and W. Bedford
1989	Stanley House Duchess	R. Hull
1990	Bewholme Wendy	P. and W. Bedford
1991	Bewholme Wendy	P. and W. Bedford
1992	Deighton Starlight	P. and W. Bedford
1993	Bewholme Wendy	P. and W. Bedford

Champion Gelding

	Winning animal	Exhibitor
1980	Ty Fry Hiawatha	W. S. Innes
1981	Cowerslane Lord	T. J. Yates
1982	Cowerslane Lord	T. J. Yates
1983	Whitley Statesman	A. W. Wright
1984	Manitou Ben	P. Ball
1985	Ben	G. Hunter
1986	St Vincents Chieftain	E. Coward Ltd
1987	St Vincents Royale	E. Coward Ltd
1988	St Vincents Royale	E. Coward Ltd
1989	St Vincents Royale	E. Coward Ltd
1990	Bay View Bandit	H. Pollard
1991	Quixhill Sir James	J. and E. Salt
1992	Redhouse Charles	J. Levitt
1993	Deighton Albion	P. and W. Bedford

Champion Turnout

	Exhibitor
1987	Bass Museum
1988	Whitbread & Co plc
1989	Young & Co plc
1990	Coalite
1991	Coalite
1992	Coalite
1993	Whitbread & Co plc

STARMIN SHIRE HORSE OF THE YEAR CHAMPIONSHIP

The Shire Horse of the Year Championship is a series of Qualifying Shows where a Champion and Reserve are selected, and the Champion from each of these Shows goes forward for a final at the Horse of the Year Show in Wembley each year.

	Winning animal	*Exhibitor*
1974	Lillingstone Again	H. Eady Robinson
1975	Cowerslane Gem	T. Yates
1977	Cowerslane Trueman	T. Yates
1978	Cowerslane Gem	T. Yates
1979	Jim's Lucky Charm	J. B. Cooke Ltd
1980	Decoy Royal Surprise	G. T. Ward & Son Ltd
1981	Jim's Lucky Charm	J. B. Cooke Ltd
1982	Jim's Lucky Charm	J. B. Cooke Ltd
1983	Tremoelgoch Miss Fashion	G. Lloyd Owen
1984	Jim's Chance	W. H. Griffith
1985	Landcliffe Laura	P. and W. Bedford
1986	Landcliffe Laura	P. and W. Bedford
1987	Landcliffe Laura	P. and W. Bedford
1988	Landcliffe Laura	P. and W. Bedford
1989	St Vincents Royale	R. Coward Ltd
1990	High Bank Heaths Hendy	D. Worthington
1991	Gronant Charlie	C. J. and S. Leverett
1992	Bewholme Wendy	P. and W. Bedford
1993	Bewholme Wendy	P. and W. Bedford

SHOOTING

OLYMPIC GAMES

Men's Free Pistol

1896	Sumner Paine (USA)
1900	Conrad Roderer (Swi)
1908	Paul von Asbroeck (Bel)
1912	Alfred Lane (USA)
1920	Karl Frederick (USA)
1936	Torsten Ullmann (Swe)
1948	Edwin Vazquez Cam (Per)
1952	Huelet Benner (USA)
1956	Pentti Linnosvuo (Fin)
1960	Aleksey Gushchin (USSR)
1964	Vaino Markkanen (Fin)
1968	Grigory Kossykh (USSR)
1972	Ragner Skanakar (Swe)
1976	Uwe Potteck (GDR)
1980	Aleksandr Melentyev (USSR)
1984	Xu Haifeng (Chn)
1988	Sorin Babii (Rom)
1992	Konstantin Koukachik (CIS)

Men's Rapid Fire Pistol

1896	Jean Phrangoudis (Gre)
1900	Maurice Larrouy (Fra)
1912	Alfred Lane (USA)
1920	Guilherme Paraense (Bra)
1924	Henry Bailey (USA)
1932	Renzo Morigi (Ita)
1936	Cornelius van Oyen (Ger)
1948	Karoly Takacs (Hun)
1952	Karoly Takacs (Hun)
1956	Stefan Petrescu (Rom)
1960	William McMilliam (USA)
1964	Pentti Linnosvuo (Fin)
1968	Jozef Zapedzki (Pol)
1972	Jozef Zapedzki (Pol)
1976	Norbert Klaar (GDR)

1980	Corneliu Ion (Rom)
1984	Takeo Kamachi (Jap)
1988	Afanasi Kouzmine (USSR)
1992	Ralf Schumann (Ger)

Men's Small Bore Rifle (Prone)

1908	A. A. Carnell (GB)
1912	Frederick Hird (USA)
1920	Lawrence Nuesslein (USA)
1924	Pierre Coquelin de Lisle (Fra)
1932	Bertil Ronnmark (Swe)
1936	Willy Rogeberg (Nor)
1948	Arthur Cook (USA)
1952	Iosif Sarbu (Rom)
1956	Gerald Ouellette (Can)
1960	Peter Kohnke (FRG)
1964	Kaszlo Hammerl (Hun)
1968	Jan Kurka (Cze)
1972	Jo-Jun Li (NKo)
1976	Karl Heinz Smieszek (FRG)
1980	Karoly Varga (Hun)
1984	Edward Etzel (USA)
1988	Miroslav Varga (Cze)
1992	Lee Eun-chui (SKo)

Men's Small Bore Rifle (Three Position)

1952	Erling Kongshaug (Nor)
1956	Anatoliy Bogdanov (USSR)
1960	Viktor Shamburkin (USSR)
1964	Lones Wigger (USA)
1968	Bernd Klingner (FRG)
1972	John Writer (USA)
1976	Lanny Bassham (USA)
1980	Viktor Vlasov (USSR)
1984	Malcolm Cooper (GB)
1988	Malcolm Cooper (GB)

1992	Grachy Petikiane (CIS)

Men's Running Game Target

1900	Louis Debray (Fra)
1972	Yokov Zheleznial (USSR)
1976	Aleksandr Gazov (USSR)
1980	Igor Sokolov (USSR)
1984	Li Yuwei (Chn)
1988	Tor Heiestad (Nor)
1992	Michael Jakosits (Ger)

Men's Air Rifle

1984	Philippe Heberle (Fra)
1988	Goran Maksimovic (Yug)
1992	Yuriy Fedkin (CIS)

Men's Air Pistol

1988	Taniou Kiriakov (Bul)
1992	Wang Yifu (Chn)

Women's Sport Pistol

1984	Linda Thom (Can)
1988	Nino Saluokvadze (USSR)
1992	Marina Logvinenko (CIS)

Women's Small Bore Rifle

1984	Wu Xiaoxuan (Chn)
1988	Silvia Sperber (FRG)
1992	Launi Melli (USA)

Women's Air Rifle

1984	Pat Spurgin (USA)
1988	Irina Chilova (USSR)
1992	Yeo Kab Soon (SKo)

Women's Air Pistol

1988	Jasna Sekaric (Yug)
1992	Marina Logvinenko (CIS)

OPEN

Men's Trap

1900	Roger de Barbarian (Fra)
1908	Walter Ewing (Can)
1912	James Graham (USA)
1920	Mark Arie (USA)
1924	Gyula Halasy (Hun)
1952	George Genereux (Can)
1956	Galliano Rossini (Ita)
1960	Ion Dumitrescu (Rom)
1964	Ennio Mattarelli (Ita)
1968	Bob Braithwaite (GB)
1972	Angelo Scalzone (Ita)
1976	Don Haldeman (USA)

1980	Luciano Giovanetti (Ita)
1984	Luciano Giovanetti (Ita)
1988	Dmitri Monakov (USSR)
1992	Petr Hrdlicka (Cze)

Men's Skeet

1968	Yevgeniy Petrov (USSR)
1972	Konrad Wirnhier (FRG)
1976	Josef Panacek (Cze)
1980	Jans Kjeld Rasmussen (Den)
1984	Matthew Dryke (USA)
1988	Axel Wegner (GDR)
1992	Zhang Shan (Chn)

SKIING

OLYMPIC GAMES: ALPINE

Men's Alpine Combination (Downhill and Slalom)

1936	Franz Pfnür (Ger)
1948	Henri Oreiller (Fra)
1988	Hubert Stroiz (Aut)
1992	Josef Polig (Ita)
1994	Lasse Kjus (Nor)

Men's Downhill

1948	Henri Oreiller (Fra)
1952	Zeno Colò (Ita)
1956	Toni Sailer (Aut)
1960	Jean Vuarnet (Fra)
1964	Egon Zimmermann (Aut)
1968	Jean-Claud Killy (Fra)
1972	Bernhard Russi (Swi)
1976	Franz Klammer (Aut)
1980	Leonhard Stock (Aut)
1984	William Johnson (USA)
1988	Pirmin Zurbriggen (Swi)
1992	Patrick Ortlieb (Aut)
1994	Tommy Moe (USA)

Men's Slalom

1948	Edy Reinalter (Swi)
1952	Othmar Schneider (Aut)
1956	Toni Sailer (Aut)
1960	Ernst Hinterseer (Aut)
1964	Josef Stiegler (Aut)
1968	Jean-Claude Killy (Fra)
1972	Francisco Fernandez Ochoa (Spa)
1976	Piero Gros (Ita)
1980	Ingemar Stenmark (Swe)
1984	Phil Mahre (USA)
1988	Alberto Tomba (Ita)
1992	Finn-Christian Jagge (Nor)
1994	Thomas Stangassinger (Aut)

Men's Giant Slalom

1952	Stein Eriksen (Nor)
1956	Toni Sailer (Aut)
1960	Roger Staub (Swi)
1964	François Boulieu (Fra)
1968	Jean-Claude Killy (Fra)
1972	Gustavo Thoeni (Ita)
1976	Heini Hemmi (Swi)
1980	Ingemar Stenmark (Swe)
1984	Max Julen (Swi)
1988	Alberto Tomba (Ita)
1992	Alberto Tomba (Ita)
1994	Markus Wasmeier (Ger)

Men's Super Giant Slalom

1988	Franck Riccard (Fra)
1992	Kjetil Andre Aamodt (Nor)
1994	Markus Wasmeier (Ger)

Women's Alpine Combination (Downhill and Slalom)

1936	Christel Cranz (Ger)
1948	Trude Beiser (Aut)
1988	Anita Wachter (Aut)
1992	Petra Kronberger (Aut)
1994	Pernilla Wiberg (Swe)

Women's Downhill

1948	Hedy Schlunegger (Swi)
1952	Trude Jochum (née Beiser) (Aut)
1956	Madeleine Berthod (Swi)
1960	Heidi Biebl (FRG)
1964	Christl Haas (Aut)
1968	Olga Pall (Aut)
1972	Marie-Thérèse Nadig (Swi)
1976	Rosi Mittermaier (FRG)
1980	Annemarie Moser-Pröll (Aut)
1984	Michela Figini (Swi)
1988	Marina Kiehl (FRG)
1992	Kerrin Lee-Gartner (Can)
1994	Katja Seizinger (Ger)

Women's Slalom

1948	Gretchen Fraser (USA)
1952	Andrea Mead-Lawrence (USA)
1956	Renée Colliard (Swi)
1960	Anne Heggtveit (Can)
1964	Christine Goitschel (Fra)
1968	Marielle Goitschel (Fra)
1972	Barbara Cochran (USA)
1976	Rosi Mittermaier (FRG)

1980	Hanni Wenzel (Lie)
1984	Paoletta Magoni (Ita)
1988	Vreni Schneider (Swi)
1992	Petra Kronberger (Aut)
1994	Vreni Schneider (Swi)

Women's Giant Slalom

1952	Andrea Mead-Lawrence (USA)
1956	Ossi Reichert (FRG)
1960	Yvonne Rüegg (Swi)
1964	Marielle Goitschel (Fra)
1968	Nancy Greene (Can)

1972	Marie-Thérèse Nadig (Swi)
1976	Kathy Kreiner (Can)
1980	Hanni Wenzel (Lie)
1984	Debbie Armstrong (USA)
1988	Vreni Schneider (Swi)
1992	Pernilla Wiberg (Swe)
1994	Deborah Compagnoni

Women's Super Giant Slalom

1988	Sigrid Wolf (Aut)
1992	Deborah Compagnoni (Ita)
1994	Diann Roffe (USA)

OLYMPIC GAMES: NORDIC

Men's 10km Cross-country (Classical)

| 1992 | Vegard Ulvang (Nor) |
| 1994 | Bjon Daelie (Nor) |

Men's Pursuit Start

| 1994 | Bjørn Daelie (Nor) |

Men's 30km Cross-country (Classical)

1956	Veikko Hakulinen (Fin)
1960	Sixten Jernberg (Swe)
1964	Eero Mäntyranta (Fin)
1968	Franco Nones (Ita)
1972	Vyacheslav Vedenin (USSR)
1976	Sergey Savelyev (USSR)
1980	Nikolay Zimyatov (USSR)
1984	Nikolay Zimyatov (USSR)
1988	Aleksey Prokurakov (USSR)
1992	Vegard Ulvang (Nor)
1994	Thomas Alsgaard (Nor)

Men's 50km Cross-country

1924	Thorleif Haug (Nor)
1928	Per-Erik Hedlund (Swe)
1932	Veli Saarinen (Fin)
1936	Elis Wiklund (Swe)
1948	Nils Karlsson (Swe)
1952	Veikko Hakulinen (Fin)
1956	Sixten Jernberg (Swe)
1960	Kalevi Hämäläinen (Fin)
1964	Sixten Jernberg (Swe)
1968	Ole Ellefsaeter (Nor)
1972	Pål Tyldum (Nor)
1976	Ivar Formo (Nor)
1980	Nikolay Zimyatov (USSR)

1984	Thomas Wassberg (Swe)
1988	Gunde Svan (Swe)
1992	Bjørn Daelie (Nor)
1994	Vladimir Smirnov (Kaz)

Men's 4 × 10km Cross-country Relay

1936	Finland
1948	Sweden
1952	Finland
1956	USSR
1960	Finland
1964	Sweden
1968	Norway
1972	USSR
1976	Finland
1980	USSR
1984	Sweden
1988	Sweden
1992	Norway
1994	Italy

Men's Team Ski Jumping

1988	Finland
1992	Finland
1994	Germany

Men's Nordic Combined – Skiing and Jumping

1924	Thorleif Haug (Nor)
1928	Johan Grøttumsbraaten (Nor)
1932	Johan Grøttumsbraaten (Nor)
1936	Oddbjørn Hagen (Nor)
1948	Heikki Hasu (Fin)
1952	Simon Slåtvik (Nor)
1956	Sverre Stenersen (Nor)

1960	Georg Thoma (FRG)
1964	Tormod Knutsen (Nor)
1968	Franz Keller (FRG)
1972	Ulrich Wehling (GDR)
1976	Ulrich Wehling (GDR)
1980	Ulrich Wehling (GDR)
1984	Tom Sandberg (Nor)
1988	Hippolyt Kempf (Swi)
1992	Fabrice Guy (Fra)
1994	Fred Borre Lundberg (Nor)

Men's Team Nordic Combined

1988	West Germany
1992	Japan
1994	Japan

Men's Ski Jumping – Normal Hill

1924	Jacob Tullin Thams (Nor)
1928	Alf Andersen (Nor)
1932	Birger Ruud (Nor)
1936	Birger Ruud (Nor)
1948	Petter Hugstedt (Nor)
1952	Arnfinn Bergmann (Nor)
1956	Anti Hyvärinen (Fin)
1960	Helmut Recknagel (GDR)
1964	Viekko Kankkänen (Fin)
1968	Jiri Raska (Cze)
1972	Yukio Kasaya (Jap)
1976	Hans-Georg Aschenbach (GDR)
1980	Toni Innauer (Aut)
1984	Jens Weissflog (GDR)
1988	Matti Nykänen (Fin)
1992	Ernst Vettori (Aut)
1994	Espen Bredesen (Nor)

Men's Ski Jumping – Large Hill

1964	Toralf Engan (Nor)
1968	Vladimir Byeloussov (USSR)
1972	Wojciech Fortuna (Pol)
1976	Karl Schnabl (Aut)
1980	Jouko Törmänen (Fin)
1984	Matti Nykänen (Fin)
1988	Matti Nykänen (Fin)

1992	Toni Nieminen (Fin)
1994	Jens Weissflog (Ger)

Women's 5km Cross-country

1964	Klaudia Boyarskikh (USSR)
1968	Toini Gustafsson (Swe)
1972	Galina Kulakova (USSR)
1976	Helena Takalo (Fin)
1980	Raisa Smetanina (USSR)
1984	Marja-Liisa Hämäläinen (Fin)
1988	Marjo Matikainen (Fin)
1992	Marjat Lukkarinen (Fin)
1994	Ljubov Egorova (Rus)

Women's Pursuit Start

1994	Ljubov Egorova (Rus)

Women's 15km Cross-country (Classical) (freestyle 1994)

1992	Ljubov Egorova (CIS)
1994	Manuela Di Centa (Ita)

Women's 20km Cross-country (Freestyle)

1984	Marja-Liisa Hämäläinen (Fin)
1988	Tamara Tikhonova (USSR)

Women's 30km Cross-country

1992	Stefania Belmondo (Ita)
1994	Manuela Di Centa (Ita)

Women's 4 × 5km Cross-country Relay

1956	Finland
1960	Sweden
1964	USSR
1968	Norway
1972	USSR
1976	USSR
1980	East Germany
1984	Norway
1988	USSR
1992	CIS
1994	Russia

SLIMMING

SLIMMER OF THE YEAR

Slimmer Magazine's 'Slimmer of the Year' contest was established in 1971. The contest winner is announced each year at a press reception held in September.

The winner is selected on the basis of physical weight-loss achieved to reach target weight and, in the view of the judges, a story which will be an inspiration to others. The first winner was Jeannette Chappell from Stoke-on-Trent (losing 41kg/6½ stone). In 1979, Valerie Thorpe, of Belper in Derbyshire, recorded an incredible 114kg/18-stone weight loss.

The 1993 winner was Eileen Mennear.

SMILES

BRIGHTEST SMILE OF THE YEAR

The Brightest Smile of the Year accolade, awarded by the British Safety Council, is designed to highlight the destructive effects of stress. The award for 1993 went to 25-year-old Diane Jarvis, a model from Chesterfield. The British Safety Council also recognizes the Miss Beautiful Eyes competition (to highlight the importance of eye safety). The 1994 winner was sixteen-year-old Jennie Aucote from Atherstone, Warwickshire.

SNOOKER

EMBASSY WORLD PROFESSIONAL CHAMPIONSHIP

1976	Ray Reardon (Wal)	1986	Joe Johnson (Eng)
1977	John Spencer (Eng)	1987	Steve Davis (Eng)
1978	Ray Reardon (Wal)	1988	Steve Davis (Eng)
1979	Terry Griffiths (Wal)	1989	Steve Davis (Eng)
1980	Cliff Thorburn (Can)	1990	Stephen Hendry (Sco)
1981	Steve Davis (Eng)	1991	John Parrott (Eng)
1982	Alex Higgins (NIre)	1992	Stephen Hendry (Sco)
1983	Steve Davis (Eng)	1993	Stephen Hendry (Sco)
1984	Steve Davis (Eng)	1994	Stephen Hendry (Sco)
1985	Dennis Taylor (NIre)		

SNUFF-TAKING

UNITED KINGDOM CHAMPIONSHIP

The rules for this championship are clear. The contestants edge along a long table, snorting as they go. Behind this table sit 25 official servers, holding in their hands two spoons containing a pinch of snuff – so, in all, 50 brands are represented.

As a competitor moves along the line of servers, snuff is placed upon the back of his hand. The snuff is to be cleared as far as possible; every grain must go up the nose, and not drop on the table.

The UK Championships are synonymous with the Pope family. Jack Pope was 5 times champion (1980–4), his son Larry 6 times champion (1985–90) and then Jack Pope's younger son, Roderick, took over the title in 1991 when Larry retired.

SPEEDWAY

WORLD CHAMPIONSHIP

1949	Tommy Price (Eng)	1972	Ivan Mauger (NZ)
1950	Freddie Williams (Wal)	1973	Jerry Szczakiel (Pol)
1951	Jack Young (Aus)	1974	Anders Michanek (Swe)
1952	Jack Young (Aus)	1975	Ole Olsen (Den)
1953	Freddie Williams (Wal)	1976	Peter Collins (Eng)
1954	Ronnie Moore (NZ)	1977	Ivan Mauger (NZ)
1955	Peter Craven (Eng)	1978	Ole Olsen (Den)
1956	Ove Fundin (Swe)	1979	Ivan Mauger (NZ)
1957	Barry Briggs (NZ)	1980	Michael Lee (Eng)
1958	Barry Briggs (NZ)	1981	Bruce Penhall (USA)
1959	Ronnie Moore (NZ)	1982	Bruce Penhall (USA)
1960	Ove Fundin (Swe)	1983	Egon Muller (FRG)
1961	Ove Fundin (Swe)	1984	Erik Gundersen (Den)
1962	Peter Craven (Eng)	1985	Erik Gundersen (Den)
1963	Ove Fundin (Swe)	1986	Hans Nielsen (Den)
1964	Barry Briggs (NZ)	1987	Hans Nielsen (Den)
1965	Bjorn Knutsson (Swe)	1988	Erik Gundersen (Den)
1966	Barry Briggs (NZ)	1989	Hans Nielsen (Den)
1967	Ove Fundin (Swe)	1990	Per Jonsson (Swe)
1968	Ivan Mauger (NZ)	1991	Jan Pedersen (Den)
1969	Ivan Mauger (NZ)	1992	Gary Havelock (Eng)
1970	Ivan Mauger (NZ)	1993	Sam Ermolenko (USA)
1971	Ole Olsen (Den)		

SQUASH

WORLD CHAMPIONSHIP

Men's		1981	Jahangir Khan (Pak)
1976	Geoff Hunt (Aus)	1982	Jahangir Khan (Pak)
1977	Geoff Hunt (Aus)	1983	Jahangir Khan (Pak)
1979	Geoff Hunt (Aus)	1984	Jahangir Khan (Pak)
1980	Geoff Hunt (Aus)	1985	Jahangir Khan (Pak)

1986	Ross Norman (NZ)	1979	Heather McKay (Aus)
1987	Jansher Khan (Pak)	1981	Rhonda Thorne (Aus)
1988	Jahangir Khan (Pak)	1983	Vicki Cardwell (Aus)
1989	Jansher Khan (Pak)	1985	Susan Devoy (NZ)
1990	Jansher Khan (Pak)	1987	Susan Devoy (NZ)
1991	Rodney Martin (Aus)	1989	Martine Le Moignan (UK)
1992	Jansher Khan (Pak)	1990	Susan Devoy (NZ)
1993	Jansher Khan (Pak)	1991	Susan Devoy (NZ)
		1992	Susan Devoy (NZ)

Women's

1976	Heather McKay (Aus)

1993	Michelle Martin (Aus)

BRITISH OPEN

Men's

1930	Don Butcher (UK)
1931	Don Butcher (UK)
1932	Abdelfattah Amr Bey (Egy)
1933	Abdelfattah Amr Bey (Egy)
1934	Abdelfattah Amr Bey (Egy)
1935	Abdelfattah Amr Bey (Egy)
1936	Abdelfattah Amr Bey (Egy)
1937	Abdelfattah Amr Bey (Egy)
1938	James Dear (UK)
1946	Mahmoud Karim (Egy)
1947	Mahmoud Karim (Egy)
1948	Mahmoud Karim (Egy)
1949	Mahmoud Karim (Egy)
1950	Hashim Khan (Pak)
1951	Hashim Khan (Pak)
1952	Hashim Khan (Pak)
1953	Hashim Khan (Pak)
1954	Hashim Khan (Pak)
1955	Hashim Khan (Pak)
1956	Roshan Khan (Pak)
1957	Hashim Khan (Pak)
1958	Azam Khan (Pak)
1959	Azam Khan (Pak)
1960	Azam Khan (Pak)
1961	Azam Khan (Pak)
1962	Mohibullah Khan (Pak)
1963	Abdelfattah Abou Taleb (Egy)
1964	Abdelfattah Abou Taleb (Egy)
1965	Abdelfattah Abou Taleb (Egy)
1966	Abdelfattah Abou Taleb (Egy)
1967	Jonah Barrington (UK)
1968	Jonah Barrington (UK)
1969	Geoff Hunt (Aus)
1970	Jonah Barrington (UK)
1971	Jonah Barrington (UK)
1972	Jonah Barrington (UK)
1973	Jonah Barrington (UK)

1974	Geoff Hunt (Aus)
1975	Qamar Zaman (Pak)
1976	Geoff Hunt (Aus)
1977	Geoff Hunt (Aus)
1978	Geoff Hunt (Aus)
1979	Geoff Hunt (Aus)
1980	Geoff Hunt (Aus)
1981	Geoff Hunt (Aus)
1982	Jahangir Khan (Pak)
1983	Jahangir Khan (Pak)
1984	Jahangir Khan (Pak)
1985	Jahangir Khan (Pak)
1986	Jahangir Khan (Pak)
1987	Jahangir Khan (Pak)
1988	Jahangir Khan (Pak)
1989	Jahangir Khan (Pak)
1990	Jahangir Khan (Pak)
1991	Jahangir Khan (Pak)
1992	Jansher Khan (Pak)
1993	Jansher Khan (Pak)

Women's

1922	Joyce Cave (UK)
1923	Nancy Cave (UK)
1924	Joyce Cave (UK)
1925	Cecily Fenwick (UK)
1926	Cecily Fenwick (UK)
1928	Joyce Cave (UK)
1929	Nancy Cave (UK)
1930	Nancy Cave (UK)
1931	Cecily Fenwick (UK)
1932	Susan Noel (UK)
1933	Susan Noel (UK)
1934	Susan Noel (UK)
1935	Margot Lumb (UK)
1936	Margot Lumb (UK)
1937	Margot Lumb (UK)
1938	Margot Lumb (UK)

1939	Margot Lumb (UK)
1947	Joan Curry (UK)
1948	Joan Curry (UK)
1949	Joan Curry (UK)
1950	Janet Morgan (UK)
1951	Janet Morgan (UK)
1952	Janet Morgan (UK)
1953	Janet Morgan (UK)
1954	Janet Morgan (UK)
1955	Janet Morgan (UK)
1956	Janet Morgan (UK)
1957	Janet Morgan (UK)
1958	Janet Morgan (UK)
1959	Janet Morgan (UK)
1960	Sheila Macintosh (UK)
1961	Fran Marshall (UK)
1962	Heather Blundell (Aus)
1963	Heather Blundell (Aus)
1964	Heather Blundell (Aus)
1965	Heather Blundell (Aus)
1966	Heather McKay (née Blundell) (Aus)
1967	Heather McKay (Aus)
1968	Heather McKay (Aus)
1969	Heather McKay (Aus)
1970	Heather McKay (Aus)
1971	Heather McKay (Aus)
1972	Heather McKay (Aus)
1973	Heather McKay (Aus)
1974	Heather McKay (Aus)
1975	Heather McKay (Aus)
1976	Heather McKay (Aus)
1977	Heather McKay (Aus)
1978	Susan Newman (Aus)
1979	Barbara Wall (Aus)
1980	Vicki Hoffman (Aus)
1981	Vicki Hoffman (Aus)
1982	Vicki Cardwell (née Hoffman) (Aus)
1983	Vicki Cardwell (Aus)
1984	Susan Devoy (NZ)
1985	Susan Devoy (NZ)
1986	Susan Devoy (NZ)
1987	Susan Devoy (NZ)
1988	Susan Devoy (NZ)
1989	Susan Devoy (NZ)
1990	Susan Devoy (NZ)
1991	Lisa Opie (UK)
1992	Susan Devoy (NZ)
1993	Michelle Martin (Aus)

SWIMMING

OLYMPIC GAMES

Men's 50m Freestyle

1988	Matt Biondi (USA)
1992	Aleksandr Popov (Rus)

Men's 100m Freestyle

1896	Alfréd Hajós (Hun)
1904	Zoltán von Halmay (Hun)
1906	Charles Daniels (USA)
1908	Charles Daniels (USA)
1912	Duke Kahanamoku (USA)
1920	Duke Kahanamoku (USA)
1924	Johnny Weissmuller (USA)
1928	Johnny Weissmuller (USA)
1932	Yasuji Miyazaki (Jap)
1936	Ferenc Csik (Hun)
1948	Walter Ris (USA)
1952	Clarke Scholes (USA)
1956	Jon Henricks (Aus)
1960	John Devitt (Aus)
1964	Don Schollander (USA)
1968	Mike Wenden (Aus)
1972	Mark Spitz (USA)
1976	Jim Montgomery (USA)
1980	Jorg Woithe (GDR)
1984	Howdy Gaines (USA)
1988	Matt Biondi (USA)
1992	Aleksandr Popov (CIS)

Men's 400m Freestyle

1896	Paul Neumann (Aut)
1904	Charles Daniels (USA)
1906	Otto Scheff (Aut)
1908	Henry Taylor (UK)
1912	George Hodgson (Can)
1920	Norman Ross (USA)
1924	Johnny Weissmuller (USA)

1928	Albeto Zorilla (Arg)
1932	Buster Crabbe (USA)
1936	Jack Medica (USA)
1948	William Smith (USA)
1952	Jean Boiteux (Fra)
1956	Murray Rose (Aus)
1960	Murray Rose (Aus)
1964	Don Schollander (USA)
1968	Mike Burton (USA)
1972	Brad Cooper (Aus)
1976	Brian Goodell (USA)
1980	Vladimir Salnikov (USSR)
1984	George DiCarlo (USA)
1988	Uwe Dassler (GDR)
1992	Yevgeniy Sadoviy (CIS)

Men's 200m Freestyle

1900	Frederick Lane (Aus)
1904	Charles Daniels (USA)
1968	Mike Wenden (Aus)
1972	Mark Spitz (USA)
1976	Bruce Furniss (USA)
1980	Sergey Koplyakov (USSR)
1984	Michael Gross (FRG)
1988	Duncan Armstrong (Aus)

Men's 1500m Freestyle

1896	Alfréd Hajós (Hun)
1900	John Jarvis (UK)
1904	Emil Rausch (Ger)
1906	Henry Taylor (UK)
1908	Henry Taylor (UK)
1912	George Hodgson (Can)
1920	Norman Ross (USA)
1924	Andrew Charlton (Aus)
1928	Arne Borg (Swe)
1932	Kusuo Kitamura (Jap)
1936	Noboru Terada (Jap)
1948	James McLane (USA)
1952	Ford Konno (USA)
1956	Murray Rose (Aus)
1960	John Konrads (Aus)
1964	Bob Windle (Aus)
1968	Mike Burton (USA)
1972	Mike Burton (USA)
1976	Brian Goodell (USA)
1980	Vladimir Salnikov (USSR)
1984	Michael O'Brien (USA)
1988	Vladimir Salnikov (USSR)
1992	Kieren Perkins (Aus)

Men's 100m Backstroke

1904	Walter Brack (Ger)
1908	Arno Bieberstein (Ger)
1912	Harry Hebuer (USA)
1920	Warren Kealoha (USA)
1924	Warren Kealoha (USA)
1928	George Kojac (USA)
1932	Masaji Kiyokawa (Jap)
1936	Adolf Kiefer (USA)
1948	Allen Stack (USA)
1952	Yoshinobu Oyakawa (USA)
1956	David Theile (Aus)
1960	David Theile (Aus)
1968	Roland Matthes (GDR)
1972	Roland Matthes (GDR)
1976	John Naber (USA)
1980	Bengt Baron (Swe)
1984	Rick Carey (USA)
1988	Daichi Suzuki (Jap)
1992	Mark Tewksbury (Can)

Men's 200m Backstroke

1900	Ernst Hoppenberg (Ger)
1964	Jed Graef (USA)
1968	Roland Matthes (GDR)
1972	Roland Matthes (GDR)
1976	John Naber (USA)
1980	Sándor Wladár (Hun)
1984	Rick Carey (USA)
1988	Igor Polyanskiy (USSR)
1992	Martin López-Zubero (Spa)

Men's 100m Breaststroke

1968	Don McKenzie (USA)
1972	Nobutaka Taguchi (Jap)
1976	John Hencken (USA)
1980	Duncan Goodhew (UK)
1984	Steve Lundquist (USA)
1988	Adrian Moorhouse (UK)
1992	Nelson Diebel (USA)

Men's 200m Breaststroke

1908	Frederick Holman (UK)
1912	Walter Bathe (Ger)
1920	Håken Malmroth (Swe)
1924	Robert Skelton (USA)
1928	Yoshiyuki Tsuruta (Jap)
1932	Yoshiyuki Tsuruta (Jap)
1936	Tetsuo Hamuro (Jap)
1948	Joseph Verdeur (USA)
1952	John Davies (Aus)

1956	Masaru Furukawa (Jap)
1960	William Mulliken (USA)
1964	Ian O'Brien (Aus)
1968	Felipe Munoz (Mex)
1972	John Hencken (USA)
1976	David Wilkie (UK)
1980	Robertas Zhulpa (USSR)
1984	Victor Davis (Can)
1988	József Szabó (Hun)
1992	Mike Barrowman (USA)

Men's 100m Butterfly

1968	Doug Russell (USA)
1972	Mark Spitz (USA)
1976	Matt Vogel (USA)
1980	Pär Arvidsson (Swe)
1984	Michael Gross (FRG)
1988	Anthony Nesty (Sur)
1992	Pablo Morales (USA)

Men's 200m Butterfly

1956	William Yorzyk (USA)
1960	Mike Troy (USA)
1964	Kevin Berry (Aus)
1968	Carl Robie (USA)
1972	Mark Spitz (USA)
1976	Mike Bruner (USA)
1980	Sergey Fesenko (USSR)
1984	Jon Sieben (Aus)
1988	Michael Gross (FRG)
1992	Melvin Stewart (USA)

Men's 200m Individual Medley

1968	Charles Hickcox (USA)
1972	Gunnar Larsson (Swe)
1984	Alex Baumann (Can)
1988	Tamás Darnyi (Hun)
1992	Tamás Darnyi (Hun)

Men's 400m Individual Medley

1964	Richard Roth (USA)
1968	Charles Hickcox (USA)
1972	Gunnar Larsson (Swe)
1976	Rod Strachan (USA)
1980	Aleksandr Sidorenko (USSR)
1984	Alex Baumann (Can)
1988	Tamás Darnyi (Hun)
1992	Tamás Darnyi (Hun)

Men's 4 × 100m Freestyle Relay

| 1964 | USA |
| 1968 | USA |

1972	USA
1984	USA
1988	USA
1992	USA

Men's 4 × 200m Freestyle Relay

1906	Hungary
1908	United Kingdom
1912	Australasia
1920	USA
1924	USA
1928	USA
1932	Japan
1936	Japan
1948	USA
1952	USA
1956	Australia
1960	USA
1964	USA
1968	USA
1972	USA
1976	USA
1980	USSR
1984	USA
1988	USA
1992	CIS

Men's 4 × 100m Medley Relay

1960	USA
1964	USA
1968	USA
1972	USA
1976	USA
1980	Australia
1984	USA
1988	USA
1992	USA

Men's Springboard Diving

1908	Albert Zürner (Ger)
1912	Paul Günther (Ger)
1920	Louis Kuehn (USA)
1924	Albert White (USA)
1928	Peter Desjardins (USA)
1932	Michael Galitzen (USA)
1936	Richard Degener (USA)
1948	Bruce Harlan (USA)
1952	David Browning (USA)
1956	Robert Clotworthy (USA)
1960	Gary Tobian (USA)
1964	Kenneth Sitzberger (USA)

1968	Bernard Wrightson (USA)
1972	Vladimir Vasin (USSR)
1976	Philip Boggs (USA)
1980	Aleksandr Portnov (USSR)
1984	Greg Louganis (USA)
1988	Greg Louganis (USA)
1992	Mark Lenzi (USA)

Men's Highboard Platform Diving

1904	George Sheldon (USA)
1906	Gottlob Walz (Ger)
1908	Hjalmar Johansson (Swe)
1912	Erik Adlerz (Swe)
1920	Clarence Pinkston (USA)
1924	Albert White (USA)
1928	Peter Desjardins (USA)
1932	Harold Smith (USA)
1936	Marshall Wayne (USA)
1948	Samuel Lee (USA)
1952	Samuel Lee (USA)
1956	Joaquin Capilla (Mex)
1960	Robert Webster (USA)
1964	Robert Webster (USA)
1968	Klaus Dibiasi (Ita)
1972	Klaus Dibiasi (Ita)
1976	Klaus Dibiasi (Ita)
1980	Falk Hoffmann (GDR)
1984	Greg Louganis (USA)
1988	Greg Louganis (USA)
1992	Sun Shuwei (Chn)

Women's 50m Freestyle

1988	Kristin Otto (GDR)
1992	Yang Wenyi (Chn)

Women's 100m Freestyle

1912	Fanny Durack (Aus)
1920	Ethelda Bleibtrey (USA)
1924	Ethel Lackie (USA)
1928	Albina Osipowich (USA)
1932	Helene Madison (USA)
1936	Hendrika Mastenbroek (Hol)
1948	Greta Andersen (Den)
1952	Katalin Szöke (Hun)
1956	Dawn Fraser (Aus)
1960	Dawn Fraser (Aus)
1964	Dawn Fraser (Aus)
1968	Jan Henne (USA)
1972	Sandra Neilson (USA)
1976	Kornelia Ender (GDR)
1980	Barbara Krause (GDR)

1984	{ Nancy Hogshead (USA) / Carrie Steinseifer (USA) }
1988	Kristin Otto (GDR)
1992	Zhuang Yong (Chn)

Women's 200m Freestyle

1968	Debbie Meyer (USA)
1972	Shane Gould (Aus)
1976	Kornelia Ender (GDR)
1980	Barbara Krause (GDR)
1984	Mary Wayte (USA)
1988	Heike Friedrich (GDR)
1992	Nicole Haislett (USA)

Women's 400m Freestyle

1920	Ethelda Bleibtrey (USA)
1924	Martha Norelius (USA)
1928	Martha Norelius (USA)
1932	Helene Madison (USA)
1936	Hendrika Mastenbroek (Hol)
1948	Ann Curtis (USA)
1952	Valéria Gyenge (Hun)
1956	Lorraine Crapp (Aus)
1960	Chris Von Saltza (USA)
1964	Virginia Duenkel (USA)
1968	Debbie Meyer (USA)
1972	Shane Gould (Aus)
1976	Petra Thümer (GDR)
1980	Ines Diers (GDR)
1984	Tiffany Cohen (USA)
1988	Janet Evans (USA)
1992	Dagmar Hase (Ger)

Women's 800m Freestyle

1968	Debbie Meyer (USA)
1972	Keena Rothhammer (USA)
1976	Petra Thümer (GDR)
1980	Michelle Ford (Aus)
1984	Tiffany Cohen (USA)
1988	Janet Evans (USA)
1992	Janet Evans (USA)

Women's 100m Backstroke

1924	Sybil Bauer (USA)
1928	Maria Braun (Hol)
1932	Eleanor Holm (USA)
1936	Nida Senff (Hol)
1948	Karen Harup (Den)
1952	Joan Harrison (SAf)
1956	Judy Grinham (UK)
1960	Lynn Burke (USA)
1964	Cathy Ferguson (USA)

1968	Kaye Hall (USA)
1972	Melissa Belote (USA)
1976	Ulrike Richter (GDR)
1980	Rica Reinisch (GDR)
1984	Theresa Andrews (USA)
1988	Kristin Otto (GDR)
1992	Krisztina Egerszegi (Hun)

Women's 200m Backstroke

1968	Pokey Watson (USA)
1972	Melissa Belote (USA)
1976	Ulrike Richter (GDR)
1980	Rica Reinisch (GDR)
1984	Jolanda de Rover (Hol)
1988	Krisztina Egerszegi (Hun)
1992	Krisztina Egerszegi (Hun)

Women's 100m Breaststroke

1968	Djurdjica Bjedov (Yug)
1972	Catherine Carr (USA)
1976	Hannelore Anke (GDR)
1980	Ute Geweniger (GDR)
1984	Petra Van Staveren (Hol)
1988	Tania Dangalakova (Bul)
1992	Yelena Rudkovskaya (CIS/Bls)

Women's 200m Breaststroke

1924	Lucy Morton (UK)
1928	Hilde Schrader (Ger)
1932	Claire Dennis (Aus)
1936	Hideko Maehata (Jap)
1948	Petronella van Vliet (Hol)
1952	Eva Székely (Hun)
1956	Ursula Happe (FRG)
1960	Anita Lonsbrough (UK)
1964	Galina Prozumenshchikova (USSR)
1968	Sharon Wichman (USA)
1972	Beverley Whitfield (Aus)
1976	Marina Koshevaya (USSR)
1980	Lina Kachushite (USSR)
1984	Anne Ottenbrite (Can)
1988	Silke Hörner (GDR)
1992	Kyoko Iwasaki (Jap)

Women's 100m Butterfly

1956	Shelley Mann (USA)
1960	Carolyn Schuler (USA)
1964	Sharon Stouder (USA)
1968	Lynette McClements (Aus)
1972	Mayumi Aoki (Jap)
1976	Kornelia Ender (GDR)

1980	Caren Metschuck (GDR)
1984	Mary T. Meagher (USA)
1988	Kristin Otto (GDR)
1992	Qian Hong (Chn)

Women's 200m Butterfly

1968	Ada Kok (Hol)
1972	Karen Moe (USA)
1976	Andrea Pollack (GDR)
1980	Ines Geissler (GDR)
1984	Mary T. Meagher (USA)
1988	Kathleen Nord (GDR)
1992	Summer Sanders (USA)

Women's 200m Individual Medley

1968	Claudia Kolb (USA)
1972	Sharon Gould (Aus)
1984	Tracy Caulkins (USA)
1988	Daniela Hunger (GDR)
1992	Lin Li (Chn)

Women's 400m Individual Medley

1964	Donna De Varona (USA)
1968	Claudia Kolb (USA)
1972	Gail Neall (Aus)
1976	Ulrike Tauber (GDR)
1980	Petra Schneider (GDR)
1984	Tracy Caulkins (USA)
1988	Janet Evans (USA)
1992	Krisztina Egerszegi (Hun)

Women's 4 × 100m Freestyle Medley

1912	United Kingdom
1920	USA
1924	USA
1928	USA
1932	USA
1936	Holland
1948	USA
1952	Hungary
1956	Australia
1960	USA
1964	USA
1968	USA
1972	USA
1976	USA
1980	East Germany
1984	USA
1988	East Germany
1992	USA

Women's 4 × 100m Medley Relay

1960	USA
1964	USA
1968	USA
1972	USA
1976	East Germany
1980	East Germany
1984	USA
1988	East Germany
1992	USA

Women's Synchronized Swimming

Solo

1984	Tracie Ruiz (USA)
1988	Carolyn Waldo (Can)
1992	Kristen Babb-Sprague (USA)

Duet

1984	Candy Costie and Tracie Ruiz (USA)
1988	Michelle Cameron and Carolyn Waldo (Can)
1992	Karen and Sarah Josephson (USA)

Women's Springboard Diving

1920	Aileen Riggin (USA)
1924	Elizabeth Becker (USA)
1928	Helen Meany (USA)
1932	Georgia Coleman (USA)
1936	Marjorie Gestring (USA)
1948	Victoria Draves (USA)
1952	Pat McCormick (USA)

1956	Pat McCormick (USA)
1960	Ingrid Krämer (GDR)
1964	Ingrid Engel (*née* Krämer) (GDR)
1968	Sue Gossick (USA)
1972	Micki King (USA)
1976	Jennifer Chandler (USA)
1980	Irina Kalinina (USSR)
1984	Sylvie Bernier (Can)
1988	Gao Min (Chn)
1992	Gao Min (Chn)

Women's Highboard Platform Diving

1912	Greta Johansson (Swe)
1920	Stefani Fryland-Clausen (Den)
1924	Caroline Smith (USA)
1928	Elizabeth Pinkston (USA)
1932	Dorothy Poynton (USA)
1936	Dorothy Hill (*née* Poynton) (USA)
1948	Victoria Draves (USA)
1952	Pat McCormick (USA)
1956	Pat McCormick (USA)
1960	Ingrid Krämer (GDR)
1964	Lesley Bush (USA)
1968	Milena Duchkova (Cze)
1972	Ulrika Knape (Swe)
1976	Elena Vaytsekhovskaya (USSR)
1980	Martina Jäschke (GDR)
1984	Zhou Jihong (Chn)
1988	Xu Yanmei (Chn)
1992	Fu Mingxia (Chn)

WORLD CHAMPIONSHIPS

Men's 50m Freestyle

1986	Tom Jager (USA)
1991	Tom Jager (USA)

Men's 100m Freestyle

1973	Jim Montgomery (USA)
1975	Andrew Coan (USA)
1978	David McCagg (USA)
1982	Jörg Woithe (GDR)
1986	Matt Biondi (USA)
1991	Matt Biondi (USA)

Men's 200m Freestyle

1973	Jim Montgomery (USA)
1975	Tim Shaw (USA)
1978	William Forrester (USA)
1982	Michael Gross (FRG)
1986	Michael Gross (FRG)
1991	Giorgio Lamberti (Ita)

Men's 400m Freestyle

1973	Rick DeMont (USA)
1975	Tim Shaw (USA)
1978	Vladimir Salnikov (USSR)
1982	Vladimir Salnikov (USSR)
1986	Rainer Henkel (FRG)
1991	Jörg Hoffmann (Ger)

Men's 1500m Freestyle

1973	Steve Holland (Aus)
1975	Tim Shaw (USA)
1978	Vladimir Salnikov (USSR)
1982	Vladimir Salnikov (USSR)

| 1986 | Rainer Henkel (FRG) |
| 1991 | Jörg Hoffmann (Ger) |

Men's 4 × 100m Freestyle

1973	USA
1975	USA
1978	USA
1982	USA
1986	USA
1991	USA

Men's 4 × 200m Freestyle Relay

1973	USA
1975	West Germany
1978	USA
1982	USA
1986	East Germany
1991	Germany

Men's 100m Backstroke

1973	Roland Matthes (GDR)
1975	Roland Matthes (GDR)
1978	Robert Jackson (USA)
1982	Dirk Richter (GDR)
1986	Igor Polyanski (USSR)
1991	Jeff Rouse (USA)

Men's 200m Backstroke

1973	Roland Matthes (GDR)
1975	Zoltan Verraszto (Hun)
1978	Jesse Vassallo (USA)
1982	Rick Carey (USA)
1986	Igor Polyanski (USSR)
1991	Martin López Zubera (Spa)

Men's 100m Breaststroke

1973	John Hencken (USA)
1975	David Wilkie (UK)
1978	Walter Kusch (GDR)
1982	Steve Lundquist (USA)
1986	Victor Davis (Can)
1991	Norbert Rosza (Hun)

Men's 200m Breaststroke

1973	David Wilkie (UK)
1975	David Wilkie (UK)
1978	Nick Nevid (USA)
1982	Victor Davis (Can)
1986	József Szabó (Hun)
1991	Mike Barrowman (USA)

Men's 100m Butterfly

1973	Bruce Robertson (Can)
1975	Greg Jagenburg (USA)
1978	Joe Bottom (USA)
1982	Matt Gribble (USA)
1986	Pablo Morales (USA)
1991	Anthony Nesty (Sur)

Men's 200m Butterfly

1973	Robin Backhaus (USA)
1975	William Forrester (USA)
1978	Michael Bruner (USA)
1982	Michael Gross (FRG)
1986	Michael Gross (FRG)
1991	Melvin Stewart (USA)

Men's 200m Individual Medley

1973	Gunnar Larsson (Swe)
1975	András Hargitay (Hun)
1978	Graham Smith (Can)
1982	Aleksey Sidorenko (USSR)
1986	Tamás Darnyi (Hun)
1991	Tamás Darnyi (Hun)

Men's 400m Individual Medley

1973	András Hargitay (Hun)
1975	András Hargitay (Hun)
1978	Jesse Vassallo (USA)
1982	Ricardo Prado (Bra)
1986	Tamás Darnyi (Hun)
1991	Tamás Darnyi (Hun)

Men's 4 × 100m Medley Relay

1973	USA
1975	USA
1978	USA
1982	USA
1986	USA
1991	USA

Men's 25km River Swim

| 1991 | Chad Hundeby (USA) |

Men's 1m Springboard Diving

| 1991 | Edwin Jongejans (Hol) |

Men's Springboard Diving (3m from 1991)

1973	Phil Boggs (USA)
1975	Phil Boggs (USA)
1978	Phil Boggs (USA)
1982	Greg Louganis (USA)

1986	Greg Louganis (USA)
1991	Kent Ferguson (USA)

Men's Highboard (Platform) Diving

1973	Klaus Dibiasi (Ita)
1975	Klaus Dibiasi (Ita)
1978	Greg Louganis (USA)
1982	Greg Louganis (USA)
1986	Greg Louganis (USA)
1991	Sun Shuwei (Chn)

Women's 50m Freestyle

1986	Tamara Costache (Rom)
1991	Zuang Yong (Chn)

Women's 100m Freestyle

1973	Kornelia Ender (GDR)
1975	Kornelia Ender (GDR)
1978	Barbara Krause (GDR)
1982	Birgit Meineke (GDR)
1986	Kristin Otto (GDR)
1991	Nicole Haislett (USA)

Women's 200m Freestyle

1973	Keena Rothhammer (USA)
1975	Shirley Babashoff (USA)
1978	Cynthia Woodhead (USA)
1982	Annemarie Verstappen (Hol)
1986	Heike Friedrich (GDR)
1991	Hayley Lewis (Aus)

Women's 400m Freestyle

1973	Heather Greenwood (USA)
1975	Shirley Babashoff (USA)
1978	Tracey Wickham (Aus)
1982	Carmela Schmidt (GDR)
1986	Heike Friedrich (GDR)
1991	Janet Evans (USA)

Women's 800m Freestyle

1973	Noveila Calligaris (Ita)
1975	Jenny Turrall (Aus)
1978	Tracey Wickham (Aus)
1982	Kim Lineham (USA)
1986	Astrid Strauss (GDR)
1991	Janet Evans (USA)

Women's 4 × 100m Freestyle Relay

1973	East Germany
1975	East Germany
1978	USA
1982	East Germany
1986	East Germany
1991	USA

Women's 4 × 200m Freestyle Relay

1986	East Germany
1991	Germany

Women's 100m Backstroke

1973	Ulrike Richter (GDR)
1975	Ulrike Richter (GDR)
1978	Linda Jezek (USA)
1982	Kristin Otto (GDR)
1986	Betsy Mitchell (USA)
1991	Krisztina Egerszegi (Hun)

Women's 200m Backstroke

1973	Melissa Belote (USA)
1975	Birgit Treiber (GDR)
1978	Linda Jezek (USA)
1982	Cornelia Sirch (GDR)
1986	Cornelia Sirch (GDR)
1991	Krisztina Egerszegi (Hun)

Women's 100m Breaststroke

1973	Renate Vogel (GDR)
1975	Hannelore Anke (GDR)
1978	Yulia Bogdanova (USSR)
1982	Ute Geweniger (GDR)
1986	Sylvia Gerasch (GDR)
1991	Linley Frame (Aus)

Women's 200m Breaststroke

1973	Renate Vogel (GDR)
1975	Hannelore Anke (GDR)
1978	Lina Kachushite (USSR)
1982	Svetlana Varganova (USSR)
1986	Silke Horner (GDR)
1991	Yelena Volkova (USSR)

Women's 100m Butterfly

1973	Kornelia Ender (GDR)
1975	Kornelia Ender (GDR)
1978	Mary-Joan Pennington (USA)
1982	Mary T. Meagher (USA)
1986	Kornelia Gressler (GDR)
1991	Qian Hong (Chn)

Women's 200m Butterfly

1973	Rosemarie Kother (GDR)
1975	Rosemarie Kother (GDR)
1978	Tracy Caulkins (USA)
1982	Ines Geissler (GDR)
1986	Mary T. Meagher (USA)
1991	Summer Sanders (USA)

Women's 200m Individual Medley

1973	Angela Hübner (GDR)
1975	Kathy Heddy (USA)
1978	Tracy Caulkins (USA)
1982	Petra Schneider (GDR)
1986	Kristin Otto (GDR)
1991	Lin Li (Chn)

Women's 400m Individual Medley

1973	Gudrun Wegner (GDR)
1975	Ulrike Tauber (GDR)
1978	Tracy Caulkins (USA)
1982	Petra Schneider (GDR)
1986	Kathleen Nord (GDR)
1991	Lin Li (Chn)

Women's 4 × 100m Medley Relay

1973	East Germany
1975	East Germany
1978	USA
1982	East Germany
1986	East Germany
1991	USA

Women's 25km River Swim

1991	Shelley Taylor-Smith (Aus)

Women's 1m Springboard Diving

1991	Gao Min (Chn)

Women's Springboard Diving (3m from 1991)

1973	Christine Kohler (GDR)
1975	Irina Kalinina (USSR)
1978	Irina Kalinina (USSR)
1982	Megan Neyer (USA)
1986	Gao Min (Chn)
1991	Gao Min (Chn)

Women's Highboard (Platform) Diving

1973	Ulrike Knape (Swe)
1975	Janet Ely (USA)
1978	Irina Kalinina (USSR)
1982	Wendy Wyland (USA)
1986	Lin Chen (Chn)
1991	Fu Mingxia (Chn)

Women's Synchronized Swimming
Solo

1973	Teresa Andersen (USA)
1975	Gail Buzonas (USA)
1978	Helen Vanderburg (Can)
1982	Tracie Ruiz (USA)
1986	Carolyn Waldo (Can)
1991	Sylvie Frechette (Can)

Duet

1973	Teresa Andersen and Gail Johnson (USA)
1975	Robin Curren and Amanda Norrish (USA)
1978	Michele Calkins and Helen Vanderburg (Can)
1982	Kelly Kryczka and Sharon Hambrook (Can)
1986	Carolyn Waldo and Michelle Cameron (Can)
1991	Karen and Sarah Josephson (USA)

Women's Synchronized Swimming Team

1973	USA
1975	USA
1978	USA
1982	Canada
1986	Canada
1991	USA

TABLE TENNIS

OLYMPIC GAMES

Men's Singles

1988	Yoo Nam-kyu (SKo)
1992	Jan-Ove Waldner (Swe)

Men's Doubles

1988	Chen Longcan and Wei Qingguang (Chn)
1992	Lu Lin and Wang Tao (Chn)

Women's Singles

1988   Chen Jing (Chn)

1992   Deng Yaping (Chn)

Women's Doubles

1988   Hyun Jung-hwa and Yang
        Young-ja (SKo)

1992   Qiao Hong and Deng Yaping
        (Chn)

TEA

TOP TEA PLACE OF THE YEAR

This prestigious award is presented annually by the Tea Council, who send out a team of undercover professional teatasters to judge a whole string of outlets nationwide. The 1993 winner was Betty's Café Tea Rooms, Ilkley, W. Yorks.

A similar award is given by the Egon Ronay organization (see Restaurants, p. 231).

The Tea Council also gives an award for what was once the most unlikely of events – a perfect 'cuppa' on a motorway. In 1993 the *Motorways Cup of Tea* award was won by the Blue Boar, at Watford Gap on the M1 – Britain's oldest motorway service station, which opened in 1958.

TEACHERS

TEACHER OF THE YEAR

The annual search for Britain's Teacher of the Year culminates at a ceremony sponsored by *Woman* magazine and the *Encyclopaedia Britannica*. The winner (from 12 finalists) is presented with a cheque for £5,000 for his or her school and a crystal apple trophy.

The 1994 winner was Mary Cameron (Kilchoan Primary School). Mary Cameron, 58, has taught two generations of local people in the remote Gaelic-speaking Highland community of Kilchoan, on the Ardnamurchan peninsula. A crofter's daughter, she expected to stay for only a couple of days when she stood in for a sick teacher thirty-five years ago. But she never left, and became headmistress and sole full-time teacher at the nine-pupil school.

LONDON TEACHER OF THE YEAR

The 1994 winner was Elizabeth Wilson, 24, of Hacton Primary School, Hornchurch.

TELEVISION

BRITISH ACADEMY OF FILM AND TELEVISION ARTS AWARDS

Formerly the Society of Film and TV Arts and the Guild of Television Producers and Directors, the Academy gives one of Britain's most prestigious show business awards.

A selection of the awards is given here.

Best Drama Production (in 1982 the Single Play was changed to Single Drama)

1954	Christian Simpson
1955	Gill Calder
1956	Joy Harrington
1957	*Play:* Rudolph Cartier
1958	*Play:* Silvio Narizzano
1959	*Play:* William Kotcheff
1960	*Play:* Peter Dews
1961	*Play:* Andrew Osborn
1962	*Play:* David Rose and Charles Jarrott
1963	*Play:* John Jacobs *Series:* Philip Mackie
1964	*Play:* Philip Saville *Series:* Rex Firkin
1965	*Play:* Cyril Coke and Peter Hammond *Series:* Philip Mackie and Silvio Narizzano
1966	*Play:* Kenneth Loach *Series:* Peter Graham Scott
1967	*Play:* Kenneth Loach
1968	Anthony Page, *Parachute*
1969	*Play:* Christopher Morahan, *The Letter; Nora You've Made Your Bed Now Lie on It* *Series:* Verity Lambert, Somerset Maugham series
1970	Alan Bridges
1971	*Play:* Ted Kotcheff, *Edna, The Inebriate Woman* *Series:* John Hawkesworth, *Upstairs Downstairs*
1972	*Single Play:* Jack Gold *Series:* Derek Granger
1973	*Single Play:* Michael Apted *Series:* John Hawkesworth, *Upstairs Downstairs*
1974	*Single Play:* Jon Scoffield, *Antony and Cleopatra* *Series:* James Ormerod, *South Riding*
1975	*Single Play:* Alan Parker, *The Evacuees* *Series:* Cecil Clarke and John Gorrie, *Edward VII*
1976	*Single Play:* Michael Tuchner, *Bar Mitzvah Boy*
	Series: Andrew Brown, *Rock Follies*
1977	*Single Play:* John Goldschmidt, *Spend Spend Spend* *Series:* Peter Goodchild and John Glenister, *Marie Curie*
1978	*Single Play:* David Hare, *Licking Hitler* *Series:* Andrew Brown and Waris Hussein, *Edward and Mrs Simpson*
1979	*Single Play:* Brian Gibson, *Blue Remembered Hills* *Series:* Jonathan Powell and Moira Armstrong, *Testament of Youth*
1980	*Single Play:* Peter Duffell, *Caught on a Train* *Series:* Peter Goodchild and Barry Davis, *Oppenheimer*
1981	*Single Play:* Stephen Frears, *Going Gently* *Series:* Derek Granger etc. *Brideshead Revisited*
1982	*Single Drama:* Pat O'Connor, *The Ballroom of Romance* *Series:* Michael Wearing and Philip Saville, *Boys from the Blackstuff*
1983	*Single Drama:* John Schlesinger, *An Englishman Abroad* *Series:* Andrew Brown and Jim Goddard, *Kennedy*
1984	*Single Drama:* Mick Jackson, *Threads* *Series:* Christopher Morahan and Jim O'Brien, *The Jewel in the Crown*
1985	*Single Drama:* Norman Stone and David Thompson, *Shadowlands* *Series:* Michael Wearing and Martin Campbell, *Edge of Darkness*
1986	*Single Drama:* Giles Foster and Sue Birtwistle, *Hotel Du Lac* *Series:* Sally Head and Philip Saville, *The Life and Loves of a She Devil*

1987	Single Drama: Life Story
	Series: Tutti Frutti
1988	Single Drama: Tumbledown
	Series: A Very British Coup
1989	Single Drama: The Accountant
	Series: Traffik
1990	Single Drama: News Hounds
	Series: Oranges Are Not the Only Fruit
1991	Single Drama: A Question of Attribution
	Series: Prime Suspect
1992	Single Drama: An Ungentlemanly Act
	Series: Inspector Morse (Deirdre Keir)
1993	Single Drama: Safe
	Series: Between the Lines

Best Factual Production

1957	Donald Baverstock and the Production Team of Tonight
1958	The Production Team of Tonight
1959	Denis Mitchell
1960	Michael Redington
	Current Affairs: Sportsview Unit
1961	Tim Hewat
	Current Affairs: Bill Allenby
1962	Richard Cawston
1963	Peter Morley and Cyril Bennett
	Documentary: Anthony de Lotbiniere
1964	The Production Team of World in Action
	Documentary: Jack Gold
1965	Jeremy Isaacs and the Production Team of This Week
	Documentary: Charles Squires
1966	The Production Team of 24 Hours
	Documentary: Kevin Billington
1967	Desmond Wilcox and Bill Morton
	Documentary: Kevin Billington
1968	Documentary: Michael Darlow and Mike Wooller
	Current Affairs: Phillip Whitehead and Production Team
1969	Documentary: Paul Watson, A Year in the Life
	Current Affairs: ITN Production Team

1970	Adrian Cowell
1971	Jeremy Wallington and Production Team, World in Action
1972	Series: Peter Goodchild and Production Team
1973	Series: Gus MacDonald
1974	Series: Peter Goodchild/Bruce Norman, Horizon
1975	Series: Brian Moser, Disappearing World
1976	Series: John Purdie/Roger Mills, Sailor
1977	Documentary: Tim King, Casualty
	Series: Antony Thomas, The South African Experience
1978	Documentary: Adrian Cavell, The Opium Warlords
	Series: Christopher Ralling, The Voyage of Charles Darwin
1979	Documentary: Don Haworth, Fred Dibnah, Steeplejack
	Series: Mark Anderson, Circuit 11, Miami
1980	Documentary: Rex Bloomstein, Christmas (Strangeways)
	Series: Rex Bloomstein, Strangeways
1981	Series: Ireland: A Television History
1982	Series: Roger Graef and Charles Stewart, Police
1983	Series: Roger Mills, 40 Minutes
1984	Series: Roger Laughton and David Wallace, River Journeys
1985	Series: Edward Mirzoeff and Roger Mills, 40 Minutes
1986	Series: Ray Fitzwalter, World in Action
1987	Series: The Duty Men
1988	Series: Arena
1989	Series: 40 Minutes
1990	Series: The Trials of Life
1991	Series: Naked Hollywood
1992	Series: Noel's House Party
1993	Series: The Ark

Best Light Entertainment Production/Programme

| 1957 | Brian Tesler |
| 1958 | Joan Kemp-Welch |

1959	Bill Ward
1960	James Gilbert
1961	George Inns
1962	Duncan Wood
1963	Colin Clews
1964	Francis Essex
	Situation Comedy: Joe McGrath
1965	Joe McGrath
	Situation Comedy: Michael Mills
1966	Ned Sherrin
	Situation Comedy: Dick Clement
1967	James Gilbert
	Situation Comedy: Michael Mills
1968	Dennis Main Wilson
1969	*Musical:* Yvonne Littlewood, *Just Pet*
	Situation Comedy: Mark Stuart
1970	David Croft and Team
1971	John Robins and David Bell, *The Benny Hill Show*
1972	*Programme:* Ian McNaughton and Production team
	Situation Comedy: Graeme Muir
1973	*Programme:* David Bell
	Situation Comedy: James Gilbert, *Whatever Happened to the Likely Lads?*
1974	*Programme:* David Bell
	Situation Comedy: Sydney Lotterby
1975	*Programme:* Terry Hughes, *The Two Ronnies*
	Situation Comedy: John Howard Davies, *Fawlty Towers*
1976	*Programme: The Muppet Show* Production Team
	Situation Comedy: Sydney Lotterby, *Porridge*
1977	*Programme:* Ernest Maxin, *Morecambe and Wise Christmas Show*
	Situation Comedy: Ronnie Baxter, *Rising Damp*
1978	*Programme:* David Mallet, *The Kenny Everett Video Show*
	Situation Comedy: Sydney Lotterby, *Going Straight*
1979	*Programme:* Alan Bell and Jim Franklin, *Ripping Yarns*
	Situation Comedy: Douglas

	Argent and Bob Spiers, *Fawlty Towers*
1980	*Programme:* John Lloyd, Sean Hardie and Bill Wilson, *Not the Nine O'Clock News*
	Situation Comedy: Sydney Lotterby, *Yes Minister*

Light Entertainment Programme

1981	*The Stanley Baxter Series*, David Bell and John Kaye Cooper
1982	*Three of a Kind*, Paul Jackson
1983	*Carrott's Lib*, Geoff Posner
1984	*Another Audience with Dame Edna Everage*, Richard Drewett
1985	*Victoria Wood as seen on TV*, Geoff Posner
1986	*Victoria Wood as seen on TV*, Geoff Posner
1987	*Victoria Wood as seen on TV*
1988	*An Audience with Victoria Wood*
1989	*Clive James on the '80s*
1990	*Whose Line is it Anyway?*
1991	*Have I Got News For You*

Best Specialized Production

1963	Margaret Dale
1964	Ned Sherrin
1965	Peter Watkins
1966	Ken Russell
1967	Basil Coleman
1968	Jack Gold
1969	Biddy Baxter, Edward Barnes and Rosemary Gill: Fred Burnley
1970	Christopher Burstall
1971	Norman Swallow
1972	*Programme:* Mai Zetterling and Team
	Series: Michael Dibb
1973	*Programme:* Colin Nears
	Series: Patrick Dowling
1974	*Programme:* Brian Gibson
	Series: Humphrey Burton
1975	*Programme:* David Cobham
	Series: Michael Latham
1976	*Programme:* David Hargreaves
	Outside Broadcast Programme: FA Cup Final Production Team

Discontinued

Other Award

1979	Melvyn Bragg, *The South Bank Show* (LWT)
1980	Leslie Megahey, *Omnibus*

Special Awards

1964	*The Great War*
1965	Joy Whitby
1966	BBC-ITV World Cup Consortium
1967	Donald Wilson and Team for *The Forsyte Saga* David Nicholas and John Phillips for *Home is the Sailor*
1968	ITN's *News at Ten* Bryan Cowgill, David Coleman and the Olympics Production Team
1969	*Monty Python's Flying Circus* Michael Gill and Peter Montagnon
1970	Ronald Travers and Mark Shivas
1971	Jenny Barraclough
Discontinued	

Most Original Programme

1978	*Pennies from Heaven*, produced by Kenith Trodd
Discontinued	

Best Actuality Coverage/News/ Outside Broadcasts

1977	Antony Craxton
1978	*The Open Golf Championship*, produced by A. P. Wilkinson
1979	Ian Engelmann, *Last Night of the Proms*
1980	David Goldsmith and Production Team, *Iranian Embassy Siege*
1981	ITN Production Team (coverage of Poland)
1982	BBC TV News Team (Falklands War)
1983	ITN Production Team (the Lebanon Crisis)
1984	Michael Buerk and Mohamed Amin (*Nine O'clock News*, Ethiopian Famine)
1985	BBC1 & 2 Production Team, *Live Aid for Africa*
1986	Stewart Purvis, *Channel 4 News*
1987	Channel 4 News (coverage of Zeebrugge disaster)
1988	Channel 4 Production Team
1989	Tiananmen Square Massacre (BBC News)
1990	Channel 4 News Team
1991	ITN (coverage of the Gulf War)
1993	ITN (coverage of Russia, the storming of the Moscow White House, Georgia civil war)

Best Actor

1954	Paul Rogers
1955	Peter Cushing
1956	Michael Gough
1957	Michael Hordern
1958	Donald Pleasence
1959	Patrick McGoohan
1960	Lee Montague
1961	Rupert Davies
1962	Harry H. Corbett
1963	Alan Badel
1964	Patrick Wymark
1965	Alan Badel
1966	Warren Mitchell
1967	Eric Porter
1968	Roy Dotrice, *Brief Lives*
1969	Edward Woodward, *Callan; A Dream Divided* (*Omnibus* series); *A Bit of a Holiday*
1970	Keith Michell, *The Six Wives of Henry VIII; An Ideal Husband*
1971	John Le Mesurier, *Traitor*
1972	Anthony Hopkins, *War and Peace*
1973	Frank Finlay, *Adventures of Don Quixote; The Death of Adolf Hitler; Candide*
1974	Peter Barkworth, *Crown Matrimonial*
1975	John Hurt, *Naked Civil Servant*
1976	Derek Jacobi, *I Claudius*
1977	Peter Barkworth, *Professional Foul, The Country Party*
1978	Edward Fox, *Edward and Mrs Simpson*
1979	Alec Guinness, *Tinker, Tailor, Soldier, Spy*
1980	Denholm Elliott, *Gentle Folk; In Hiding; Blade on the Feather; The Stinker*

1981	Anthony Andrews, *Brideshead Revisited*
1982	Alec Guinness, *Smiley's People*
1983	Alan Bates, *An Englishman Abroad*
1984	Tim Pigott-Smith, *The Jewel in the Crown*
1985	Bob Peck, *The Edge of Darkness*
1986	Michael Gambon *The Singing Detective*
1987	David Jason *Porterhouse Blue*
1988	Ray McAnnally *A Very British Coup*
1990	Ian Richardson, *House of Cards*
1991	Robert Lindsay, *G.B.H.*
1992	John Thaw, *Inspector Morse*
1993	Robbie Coltrane, *Cracker*

Best Actress

1954	Googie Withers
1955	Virginia McKenna
1956	Rosalie Crutchley
1957	Heather Sears
1958	Gwen Watford
1959	Catherine Lacey
1960	Billie Whitelaw
1961	Ruth Dunning
1962	Brenda Bruce
1963	Vivien Merchant
1964	Katherine Blake
1965	Gwen Watford
1966	Vanessa Redgrave
1967	Judi Dench
1968	Wendy Craig, *Not in Front of the Children*
1969	Margaret Tyzack, *The First Churchills*
1970	Annette Crosbie, *Catherine of Aragon* (from *The Six Wives of Henry VIII*)
1971	Patricia Hayes, *Edna, the Inebriate Woman*
1972	Billie Whitelaw, *The Sextet* (series of 8 plays)
1973	Celia Johnson, *Mrs Palfrey at the Claremont*
1974	Lee Remick, *Jennie*
1975	Annette Crosbie, *Edward the Seventh*
1976	Sian Phillips, *I Claudius*; *How Green Was My Valley*
1977	Penelope Keith, *Norman Conquests*; *Saving it from Albie*
1978	Francesca Annis, *Lillie*

1979	Cheryl Campbell, *Testament of Youth*
1980	Dame Peggy Ashcroft, *Cream in my Coffee*; *Caught on a Train*
1981	Judi Dench *Going Gently*, *A Fine Romance*, and *The Cherry Orchard*
1982	Beryl Reid, *Smiley's People*
1983	Coral Browne, *An Englishman Abroad*
1984	Peggy Ashcroft, *The Jewel in the Crown*
1985	Claire Bloom, *Shadowlands*
1986	Anna Massey, *Hotel Du Lac*
1987	Emma Thompson, *Tutti Frutti* and *Fortunes of War*
1988	Thora Hird, *Talking Heads: A Cream Cracker Under The Settee*
1990	Geraldine McEwan, *Oranges Are Not the Only Fruit*
1991	Helen Mirren, *Prime Suspect*
1992	Helen Mirren, *Prime Suspect 2*
1993	Helen Mirren, *Prime Suspect*

Best Light Entertainment Performance

1957	Tony Hancock
1958	Alan Melville
1959	Tony Hancock
1960	Stanley Baxter
1961	Eric Sykes
1962	Michael Bentine
1963	Morecambe and Wise
1964	Millicent Martin
1965	Peter Cook and Dudley Moore
1966	John Bird
1967	Alan Bennett
1968	Marty Feldman
1969	Eric Morecambe and Ernie Wise
1970	Eric Morecambe and Ernie Wise
1971	Ronnie Corbett and Ronnie Barker
1972	Eric Morecambe and Ernie Wise
1973	Eric Morecambe and Ernie Wise
1974	Stanley Baxter
1975	Ronnie Barker, *Porridge*
1976	Penelope Keith, *The Good Life*
1977	Ronnie Barker, *Porridge*
1978	Ronnie Barker, *Going Straight* and *The Two Ronnies*

1979	John Cleese, *Fawlty Towers*
1980	Rowan Atkinson, *Not the Nine O'Clock News*
1981	Nigel Hawthorne, *Yes Minister*
1982	Nigel Hawthorne, *Yes Minister*
1983	Tracy Ullman, *Three of a Kind*
1984	Judi Dench, *A Fine Romance*
1985	Victoria Wood, *Victoria Wood as seen on TV*
1986	Nigel Hawthorne, *Yes Minister*
1987	Nigel Hawthorne, *Yes Prime Minister*
1988	Victoria Wood, *An Audience with Victoria Wood*
1990	David Jason, *Only Fools and Horses*
1991	Richard Wilson, *One Foot in the Grave*
1992	Joanna Lumley, *Absolutely Fabulous*
1993	Richard Wilson, *One Foot in the Grave, One Foot in the Algarve*

Best Comedy Series

1964	Joe McGrath
1965	Michael Mills
1966	Dick Clement
1967	Michael Mills

1969	*Please Sir*, Mark Stuart
1972	*My Wife Next Door*, Graeme Muir
1973	*Whatever Happened to the Likely Lads*, James Gilbert
1974	*Porridge*, Sydney Lotterby
1975	*Fawlty Towers*, John Howard Davies
1976	*Porridge (Special)*, Sydney Lotterby
1977	*Rising Damp*, Ronnie Barker
1978	*Going Straight*, Sydney Lotterby
1979	*Fawlty Towers*, Douglas Argent and Bob Spiers
1980	*Yes Minister*, Sydney Lotterby
1981	*Yes Minister*, Peter Whitmore
1982	*Yes Minister*, Peter Whitmore
1983	*Hi-De-Hi*, John Kilby
1984	*The Young Ones*, Paul Jackson
1985	*Only Fools and Horses*, Ray Butt
1986	*Just Good Friends*, Ray Butt and Sue Bysh
1987	*Blackadder III*
1988	*Only Fools and Horses (Christmas Special)*
1989	*Blackadder Goes Forth*
1990	*The New Statesman*
1991	*One Foot in the Grave*
1992	*Absolutely Fabulous*
1993	*Who Else?*, Rory Bremner

THE *MELODY MAKER* POLLS

TV Show of the Year

1960	*Boy Meets Girl* (ITV)
1961	*Juke Box Jury* (BBC)
1962	*Thank Your Lucky Stars* (ITV)
1963	*Lucky Stars – Summer Spin* (ITV)
1964	*Ready Steady Go* (ITV)
1965	*Ready Steady Go* (ITV)
1966	*Top of the Pops* (BBC)
1967	*Top of the Pops* (BBC)
1968	*Top of the Pops* (BBC)
1969	*Colour Me Pop*
1970	*Disco 2*
1971	*Disco 2*
1972	*The Old Grey Whistle Test* (BBC 2)
1973	*The Old Grey Whistle Test* (BBC 2)
1974	*The Old Grey Whistle Test* (BBC 2)
1975	*The Old Grey Whistle Test* (BBC 2)
1976	*The Old Grey Whistle Test* (BBC 2)

1977	*The Old Grey Whistle Test* (BBC 2)
1978	*Revolver*
1979	*The Old Grey Whistle Test* (BBC 2)
1980	*The Old Grey Whistle Test* (BBC 2)
1981	*Tiswas*
1982	*The Young Ones*
1983	*The Tube*
1984	*The Tube*
1985	*Eastenders*
1986	*Brookside*
1987	*Blackadder III*
1988	*Brookside*
1989	*Blackadder IV*
1990	*Twin Peaks*
1991	*Twin Peaks*
1992	*Have I Got News For You?*
1993	*Red Dwarf*

Male TV Artist of the Year		**Female TV Artist of the Year**	
1960	Bruce Forsyth	1960	Alma Cogan
1961	Anthony Newley	1961	Alma Cogan
1962	Bruce Forsyth	1962	Helen Shapiro
1963	Norman Vaughan	1963	Millicent Martin
1964	Cliff Richard	1964	Kathy Kirby
1965	Cliff Richard	1965	Cathy McGowan
1966	Barry Fantoni	1966	Cathy McGowan
1967	Simon Dee	1967	Lulu
1968	Simon Dee	1968	Lulu
1969	Tom Jones	1969	Lulu
Discontinued		*Discontinued*	

THE BRITISH COMEDY AWARDS

The fourth annual awards, hosted by Jonathan Ross, took place on 12 December 1993. The winners were:

Top TV Comedy Actor Rik Mayall

Top TV Comedy Actress Joanna Lumley (*Absolutely Fabulous*)

Best ITV Sitcom Watching

Top ITV Entertainment Presenter Michael Barrymore

Top Channel 4 Entertainment Presenter Chris Evans

Best BBC Sitcom One Foot in the Grave

Best Radio Comedy Knowing Me Knowing You with Alan Partridge

Best New Television Comedy Absolutely Fabulous

BBC Top Entertainment Presenter Noel Edmonds

Top TV Comedy Newcomer Steve Coogan

Top Male Comedy Performer Dave Allen

Best TV Comedy Drama The Snapper

Best Comedy Film Groundhog Day

Best Live Stand-up Comedian Eddie Lizard

Best Channel 4 Sitcom Drop the Dead Donkey

Top Female Comedy Performers Dawn French and Jennifer Saunders

Top British Comedy Writer (Writers Guild Award) Richard Curtis

Top Variety Performer (Writers Guild Award) Ken Dodd

Top TV Comedy Personality Joanna Lumley

Best Comedy Series 1993 The Smell of Reeves and Mortimer

Best Entertainment Series Barrymore

BBC SPORTS PERSONALITY OF THE YEAR

1954	Chris Chataway (athletics)	1968	David Hemery (athletics)
1955	Gordon Pirie (athletics)	1969	Ann Jones (tennis)
1956	Jim Laker (cricket)	1970	Henry Cooper (boxing)
1957	Dai Rees (golf)	1971	Princess Anne (equestrianism)
1958	Ian Black (swimming)	1972	Mary Peters (athletics)
1959	John Surtees (motorcycling)	1973	Jackie Stewart (motor racing)
1960	David Broome (showjumping)	1974	Brendan Foster (athletics)
1961	Stirling Moss (motor racing)	1975	David Steele (cricket)
1962	Anita Lonsbrough (swimming)	1976	John Curry (ice skating)
1963	Dorothy Hyman (athletics)	1977	Virginia Wade (tennis)
1964	Mary Rand (athletics)	1978	Steve Ovett (athletics)
1965	Tommy Simpson (cycling)	1979	Sebastian Coe (athletics)
1966	Bobby Moore (football)	1980	Robin Cousins (ice skating)
1967	Henry Cooper (boxing)	1981	Ian Botham (cricket)

1982	Daley Thompson (athletics)	1988	Steve Davis (snooker)
1983	Steve Cram (athletics)	1989	Nick Faldo (golf)
1984	Jayne Torvill and Christopher	1990	Paul Gascoigne (football)
	Dean (ice dancing)	1991	Liz McColgan (athletics)
1985	Barry McGuigan (boxing)	1992	Nigel Mansell (motor racing)
1986	Nigel Mansell (motor racing)	1993	Linford Christie (athletics)
1987	Fatima Whitbread (athletics)		

PANASONIC/ITV SPORTS PERSONALITY OF THE YEAR

The 1993 Panasonic/ITV Sports Personality of the Year was won in November 1993 by Sally Gunnell – she beat off Linford Christie, Colin Jackson, Nigel Mansell and Lennox Lewis.

ROYAL TELEVISION SOCIETY AWARDS

1993

Entertainment Victoria Wood's All Day Breakfast Show (BBC)

Situation comedy: One Foot in the Grave (BBC)

Single documentary Katie & Eilish – Siamese Twins (Yorkshire Television)

Documentary series Pandora's Box – The League of Gentleman (BBC)

Team award The Big Breakfast (Planet 24 for Channel 4)

Arts Bookmark – Miss Pym's Day Out (BBC)

Outside Broadcast Last Night of the Proms (BBC)

Technique Lee Eynon for the videotape editing of the Barcelona Olympics, British medals sequence (BBC)

Regional programme The Snow Show (Gallus Besom Productions for BBC Scotland)

Regional Documentary Tuesday Special: Caution – Our Hands Are Tied (Central Independent Television)

Children's Factual Newsround Special – SOS: The Suffering of Somalia (BBC)

Children's Entertainment What's That Noise! (BBC)

Children's drama The Borrowers (Working Title Production for BBC)

Performance awards David Jason "for the range, depth . . . and sheer volume of his work"; Julia Sawalha, Absolutely Fabulous

Writer's award Andy Hamilton and Guy Jenkin, Drop the Dead Donkey

Drama serial Goodbye Cruel World (BBC)

Drama Series Between the Lines – Out of the Game (BBC in association with Island World Productions)

Single drama Hedd Wyn (Pendefig production for Channel 4 Wales)

Judges' award Anna Home, head of children's programmes, BBC Television, and Lewis Rudd, controller, young people's programmes, Central Productions

Cyril Bennett award (for outstanding contribution to television programming): Charles Wheeler

Gold medal Sir Michael Checkland, "for his achievements in ensuring the survival and success of . . . the BBC"

OBSERVER MOST POPULAR TV PROGRAMMES

According to *The Observer* the most popular television programmes in the 40 years from 1953 have been:

1953	The Coronation	1955	Sunday Night at the London Palladium
1954	Christmas Party		

1956	*The Gang Show*		1977	*Mike Yarwood's Christmas*
1957	*Take Your Pick*		1978	*Sale of the Century*
1958	*Take Your Pick*		1979	*To the Manor Born*
1959	*Wagon Train*		1980	*Dallas*
1960	*Royal Variety Performance*		1981	*The Benny Hill Show*
1961	*Royal Variety Performance*		1982	*Coronation Street*
1962	*Royal Variety Performance*		1983	*Coronation Street*
1963	*Royal Variety Performance*		1984	*Coronation Street*
1964	*Steptoe and Son*		1985	*Coronation Street*
1965	*Royal Variety Performance*		1986	*EastEnders*
1966	*Miss World*		1987	*EastEnders*
1967	*Royal Variety Performance*		1988	*EastEnders*
1968	*Special Royal Performance*		1989	*Coronation Street*
1969	*Miss World*		1990	*Coronation Street*
1970	*Miss World*		1991	*Coronation Street*
1971	*Benny Hill Show*		1992	*EastEnders*
1972	*Eurovision Song Contest*			
1973	*Eurovision Song Contest*			
1974	*This is Your Life*			
1975	*Royal Variety Performance*			
1976	*Generation Game*			

THE *TV TIMES* POPULARITY POLL

The survey of *TV Times* readers, published in August 1993, produced the following results:

Top TV soap operas

1. *Coronation Street*
2. *Home and Away*
3. *EastEnders*
4. *Emmerdale*
5. *Brookside*

Funniest Man

1. David Jason
2. Eric Morecambe
3. Richard Wilson
4. Ronnie Barker
5. Michael Crawford

Best Comedy

1. *Only Fools and Horses*
2. *One Foot in the Grave*
3. *Keeping Up Appearances*
4. *Morecambe and Wise*
5. *Steptoe and Son*

Funniest Woman

1. Patricia Routledge
2. Victoria Wood
3. Dawn French
4. Penelope Keith
5. Stephanie Cole

TENNIS

WIMBLEDON CHAMPIONSHIP

Men's Singles

1877	Spencer Gore (UK)		1881	William Renshaw (UK)
1878	Frank Hadow (UK)		1882	William Renshaw (UK)
1879	Revd John Hartley (UK)		1883	William Renshaw (UK)
1880	Revd John Hartley (UK)		1884	William Renshaw (UK)
			1885	William Renshaw (UK)

1886	William Renshaw (UK)
1887	Herbert Lawford (UK)
1888	Ernest Renshaw (UK)
1889	William Renshaw (UK)
1890	Willoughby Hamilton (UK)
1891	Wilfred Baddeley (UK)
1892	Wilfred Baddeley (UK)
1893	Joshua Pim (UK)
1894	Joshua Pim (UK)
1895	Wilfred Baddeley (UK)
1896	Harold Mahoney (UK)
1897	Reginald Doherty (UK)
1898	Reginald Doherty (UK)
1899	Reginald Doherty (UK)
1900	Reginald Doherty (UK)
1901	Arthur Gore (UK)
1902	Lawrence Doherty (UK)
1903	Lawrence Doherty (UK)
1904	Lawrence Doherty (UK)
1905	Lawrence Doherty (UK)
1906	Lawrence Doherty (UK)
1907	Norman Brookes (Aus)
1908	Arthur Gore (UK)
1909	Arthur Gore (UK)
1910	Tony Wilding (NZ)
1911	Tony Wilding (NZ)
1912	Tony Wilding (NZ)
1913	Tony Wilding (NZ)
1914	Norman Brookes (Aus)
1919	Gerald Patterson (Aus)
1920	Bill Tilden (USA)
1921	Bill Tilden (USA)
1922	Gerald Patterson (Aus)
1923	William Johnston (USA)
1924	Jean Borotra (Fra)
1925	René Lacoste (Fra)
1926	Jean Borotra (Fra)
1927	Henri Cochet (Fra)
1928	René Lacoste (Fra)
1929	Henri Cochet (Fra)
1930	Bill Tilden (USA)
1931	Sidney Wood (USA)
1932	Ellsworth Vines (USA)
1933	Jack Crawford (Aus)
1934	Fred Perry (UK)
1935	Fred Perry (UK)
1936	Fred Perry (UK)
1937	Donald Budge (USA)
1938	Donald Budge (USA)
1939	Bobby Riggs (USA)
1946	Yvon Petra (Fra)
1947	Jack Kramer (USA)
1948	Bob Falkenburg (USA)
1949	Ted Schroeder (USA)
1950	Budge Patty (USA)
1951	Dick Savitt (USA)
1952	Frank Sedgman (Aus)
1953	Vic Seixas (USA)
1954	Jaroslav Drobny (Egy)
1955	Tony Trabert (USA)
1956	Lew Hoad (Aus)
1957	Lew Hoad (Aus)
1958	Ashley Cooper (Aus)
1959	Alex Olmedo (USA)
1960	Neale Fraser (Aus)
1961	Rod Laver (Aus)
1962	Rod Laver (Aus)
1963	Chuck McKinley (USA)
1964	Roy Emerson (Aus)
1965	Roy Emerson (Aus)
1966	Manuel Santana (Spa)
1967	John Newcombe (Aus)
1968	Rod Laver (Aus)
1969	Rod Laver (Aus)
1970	John Newcombe (Aus)
1971	John Newcombe (Aus)
1972	Stan Smith (USA)
1973	Jan Kodes (Cze)
1974	Jimmy Connors (USA)
1975	Arthur Ashe (USA)
1976	Björn Borg (Swe)
1977	Björn Borg (Swe)
1978	Björn Borg (Swe)
1979	Björn Borg (Swe)
1980	Björn Borg (Swe)
1981	John McEnroe (USA)
1982	Jimmy Connors (USA)
1983	John McEnroe (USA)
1984	John McEnroe (USA)
1985	Boris Becker (FRG)
1986	Boris Becker (FRG)
1987	Pat Cash (Aus)
1988	Stefan Edberg (Swe)
1989	Boris Becker (FRG)
1990	Stefan Edberg (Swe)
1991	Michael Stich (Ger)
1992	André Agassi (USA)
1993	Pete Sampras (USA)
1994	Pete Sampras (USA)

Women's Singles

1884	Maud Watson (UK)
1885	Maud Watson (UK)
1886	Blanche Bingley (UK)

1887	Lottie Dod (UK)
1888	Lottie Dod (UK)
1889	Blanche Hillyard (UK)
1890	Helene Rice (UK)
1891	Lottie Dod (UK)
1892	Lottie Dod (UK)
1893	Lottie Dod (UK)
1894	Blanche Hillyard (UK)
1895	Charlotte Cooper (UK)
1896	Charlotte Cooper (UK)
1897	Blanche Hillyard (UK)
1898	Charlotte Cooper (UK)
1899	Blanche Hillyard (UK)
1900	Blanche Hillyard (UK)
1901	Charlotte Sterry (UK)
1902	Muriel Robb (UK)
1903	Dorothea Douglass (UK)
1904	Dorothea Douglass (UK)
1905	May Sutton (USA)
1906	Dorothea Douglass (UK)
1907	May Sutton (USA)
1908	Charlotte Sterry (UK)
1909	Dora Boothby (UK)
1910	Dorothea Lambert Chambers (UK)
1911	Dorothea Lambert Chambers (UK)
1912	Ethel Larcombe (UK)
1913	Dorothea Lambert Chambers (UK)
1914	Dorothea Lambert Chambers (UK)
1919	Suzanne Lenglen (Fra)
1920	Suzanne Lenglen (Fra)
1921	Suzanne Lenglen (Fra)
1922	Suzanne Lenglen (Fra)
1923	Suzanne Lenglen (Fra)
1924	Kathleen McKane (UK)
1925	Suzanne Lenglen (Fra)
1926	Kathleen Godfree (UK)
1927	Helen Wills (USA)
1928	Helen Wills (USA)
1929	Helen Wills (USA)
1930	Helen Moody (USA)
1931	Cilly Aussem (Ger)
1932	Helen Moody (USA)
1933	Helen Moody (USA)
1934	Dorothy Round (UK)
1935	Helen Moody (USA)
1936	Helen Jacobs (USA)
1937	Dorothy Round (UK)
1938	Helen Moody (USA)
1939	Alice Marble (USA)
1946	Pauline Betz (USA)
1947	Margaret Osborne (USA)
1948	Louise Brough (USA)
1949	Louise Brough (USA)
1950	Louise Brough (USA)
1951	Doris Hart (USA)
1952	Maureen Connolly (USA)
1953	Maureen Connolly (USA)
1954	Maureen Connolly (USA)
1955	Louise Brough (USA)
1956	Shirley Fry (USA)
1957	Althea Gibson (USA)
1958	Althea Gibson (USA)
1959	Maria Bueno (Bra)
1960	Maria Bueno (Bra)
1961	Angela Mortimer (UK)
1962	Karen Susman (USA)
1963	Margaret Smith (Aus)
1964	Maria Bueno (Bra)
1965	Margaret Smith (Aus)
1966	Billie Jean King (USA)
1967	Billie Jean King (USA)
1968	Billie Jean King (USA)
1969	Ann Jones (UK)
1970	Margaret Court (Aus)
1971	Evonne Goolagong (Aus)
1972	Billie Jean King (USA)
1973	Billie Jean King (USA)
1974	Chris Evert (USA)
1975	Billie Jean King (USA)
1976	Chris Evert (USA)
1977	Virginia Wade (UK)
1978	Martina Navratilova (USA)
1979	Martina Navratilova (USA)
1980	Evonne Cawley (Aus)
1981	Chris Evert Lloyd (USA)
1982	Martina Navratilova (USA)
1983	Martina Navratilova (USA)
1984	Martina Navratilova (USA)
1985	Martina Navratilova (USA)
1986	Martina Navratilova (USA)
1987	Martina Navratilova (USA)
1988	Steffi Graf (FRG)
1989	Steffi Graf (FRG)
1990	Martina Navratilova (USA)
1991	Steffi Graf (Ger)
1992	Steffi Graf (Ger)
1993	Steffi Graf (Ger)
1994	Conchita Martinez (Spa)

Men's Doubles

1879   L. R. Erskine and Herbert Lawford (UK)
1880   Ernest Renshaw and William Renshaw (UK)
1881   Ernest Renshaw and William Renshaw (UK)
1882   Revd John Hartley and R. T. Richardson (UK)
1883   C. W. Grinstead and C. E. Welldon (UK)
1884   Ernest Renshaw and William Renshaw (UK)
1885   Ernest Renshaw and William Renshaw (UK)
1886   Ernest Renshaw and William Renshaw (UK)
1887   Patrick Bowes-Lyon and Herbert Wilberforce (UK)
1888   Ernest Renshaw and William Renshaw (UK)
1889   Ernest Renshaw and William Renshaw (UK)
1890   Joshua Pim and Frank Stoker (UK)
1891   Herbert Baddeley and Wilfred Baddeley (UK)
1892   Harry Barlow and Ernest Lewis (UK)
1893   Joshua Pim and Frank Stoker (UK)
1894   Herbert Baddeley and Wilfred Baddeley (UK)
1895   Herbert Baddeley and Wilfred Baddeley (UK)
1896   Herbert Baddeley and Wilfred Baddeley (UK)
1897   Lawrence Doherty and Reginald Doherty (UK)
1898   Lawrence Doherty and Reginald Doherty (UK)
1899   Lawrence Doherty and Reginald Doherty (UK)
1900   Lawrence Doherty and Reginald Doherty (UK)
1901   Lawrence Doherty and Reginald Doherty (UK)
1902   Frank Riseley and Sidney Smith (UK)
1903   Lawrence Doherty and Reginald Doherty (UK)
1904   Lawrence Doherty and Reginald Doherty (UK)
1905   Lawrence Doherty and Reginald Doherty (UK)
1906   Frank Riseley and Sidney Smith (UK)
1907   Norman Brookes (Aus) and Anthony Wilding (NZ)
1908   Major Ritchie (UK) and Anthony Wilding (NZ)
1909   Arthur Gore and Roper Barrett (UK)
1910   Major Ritchie (UK) and Anthony Wilding (NZ)
1911   Max Decugis and André Gobert (Fra)
1912   Charles Dixon and Roper Barrett (UK)
1913   Charles Dixon and Roper Barrett (UK)
1914   Norman Brookes (Aus) and Anthony Wilding (NZ)
1919   Pat O'Hara Wood and Ronald Thomas (Aus)
1920   Charles Garland and Richard Williams (USA)
1921   Randolph Lycett and Max Woosnam (UK)
1922   James Anderson (Aus) and Randolph Lycett (UK)
1923   Leslie Godfree and Randolph Lycett (UK)
1924   Frank Hunter and Vincent Richards (USA)
1925   Jean Borotra and René Lacoste (Fra)
1926   Jacques Brugnon and Henri Cochet (Fra)
1927   Frank Hunter and Bill Tilden (USA)
1928   Jacques Brugnon and Henri Cochet (Fra)
1929   William Allison and John Van Ryn (USA)
1930   William Allison and John Van Ryn (USA)
1931   George Lott and John Van Ryn (USA)
1932   Jean Borotra and Jacques Brugnon (Fra)
1933   Jean Borotra and Jacques Brugnon (Fra)

1934	George Lott and Lester Stoefen (USA)
1935	Jack Crawford and Adrian Quist (Aus)
1936	Pat Hughes and Raymond Tuckey (UK)
1937	Don Budge and Gene Mako (USA)
1938	Don Budge and Gene Mako (USA)
1939	Ellwood Cooke and Bobby Riggs (USA)
1946	Tom Brown and Jack Kramer (USA)
1947	Bob Falkenburg and Jack Kramer (USA)
1948	John Bromwich and Frank Sedgman (Aus)
1949	Ricardo Gonzales and Frank Parker (USA)
1950	John Bromwich and Adrian Quist (Aus)
1951	Ken McGregor and Frank Sedgman (Aus)
1952	Ken McGregor and Frank Sedgman (Aus)
1953	Lew Hoad and Ken Rosewall (Aus)
1954	Rex Hartwig and Mervyn Rose (Aus)
1955	Rex Hartwig and Lew Hoad (Aus)
1956	Lew Hoad and Ken Rosewall (Aus)
1957	Gardnar Mulloy and Budge Patty (USA)
1958	Sven Davidson and Ulf Schmidt (Swe)
1959	Roy Emerson and Neale Fraser (Aus)
1960	Rafael Osuna (Mex) and Dennis Ralston (USA)
1961	Roy Emerson and Neale Fraser (Aus)
1962	Bob Hewitt and Fred Stolle (Aus)
1963	Rafael Osuna and Antonio Palafox (Mex)
1964	Bob Hewitt and Fred Stolle (Aus)
1965	John Newcombe and Tony Roche (Aus)
1966	Ken Fletcher and John Newcombe (Aus)
1967	Bob Hewitt and Frew McMillan (SAf)
1968	John Newcombe and Tony Roche (Aus)
1969	John Newcombe and Tony Roche (Aus)
1970	John Newcombe and Tony Roche (Aus)
1971	Roy Emerson and Rod Laver (Aus)
1972	Bob Hewitt and Frew McMillan (SAf)
1973	Jimmy Connors (USA) and Ilie Nastase (Rom)
1974	John Newcombe and Tony Roche (Aus)
1975	Vitas Gerulaitis and Sandy Mayer (USA)
1976	Brian Gottfried (USA) and Raúl Ramirez (Mex)
1977	Ross Case and Geoff Masters (Aus)
1978	Bob Hewitt and Frew McMillan (SAf)
1979	Peter Fleming and John McEnroe (USA)
1980	Peter McNamara and Paul McNamee (Aus)
1981	Peter Fleming and John McEnroe (USA)
1982	Peter McNamara and Paul McNamee (Aus)
1983	Peter Fleming and John McEnroe (USA)
1984	Peter Fleming and John McEnroe (USA)
1985	Heinz Günthardt (Swi) and Balázs Taróczy (Hun)
1986	Joakim Nyström and Mats Wilander (Swe)
1987	Ken Flach and Robert Seguso (USA)
1988	Ken Flach and Robert Seguso (USA)
1989	John Fitzgerald (Aus) and Anders Järryd (Swe)
1990	Rick Leach and Jim Pugh (USA)
1991	John Fitzgerald (Aus) and Anders Järryd (Swe)
1992	John McEnroe (USA) and Michael Stich (Ger)

1993	Todd Woodbridge and Mark Woodforde (Aus)
1994	Todd Woodbridge and Mark Woodforde (Aus)

Women's Doubles

1913	Winifred McNair and Dora Boothby (UK)
1914	Agnes Morton (UK) and Elizabeth Ryan (USA)
1919	Suzanne Lenglen (Fra) and Elizabeth Ryan (USA)
1920	Suzanne Lenglen (Fra) and Elizabeth Ryan (USA)
1921	Suzanne Lenglen (Fra) and Elizabeth Ryan (USA)
1922	Suzanne Lenglen (Fra) and Elizabeth Ryan (USA)
1923	Suzanne Lenglen (Fra) and Elizabeth Ryan (USA)
1924	Hazel Wightman and Helen Wills (USA)
1925	Suzanne Lenglen (Fra) and Elizabeth Ryan (USA)
1926	Mary Browne and Elizabeth Ryan (USA)
1927	Helen Wills and Elizabeth Ryan (USA)
1928	Peggy Saunders and Phyllis Watson (UK)
1929	Peggy Michell and Phyllis Watson (UK)
1930	Helen Moody (née Wills) and Elizabeth Ryan (USA)
1931	Dorothy Barron and Phyllis Mudford (UK)
1932	Doris Metaxa (Fra) and Josane Sigart (Bel)
1933	Simone Mathieu (Fra) and Elizabeth Ryan (USA)
1934	Simone Mathieu (Fra) and Elizabeth Ryan (USA)
1935	Freda James and Kay Stammers (UK)
1936	Freda James and Kay Stammers (UK)
1937	Simone Mathieu (Fra) and Billie Yorke (UK)
1938	Sarah Fabyan and Alice Marble (USA)
1939	Sarah Fabyan and Alice Marble (USA)
1946	Louise Brough and Margaret Osborne (USA)
1947	Doris Hart and Pat Todd (USA)
1948	Louise Brough and Margaret Du Pont (USA)
1949	Louise Brough and Margaret Du Pont (USA)
1950	Louise Brough and Margaret Du Pont (USA)
1951	Shirley Fry and Doris Hart (USA)
1952	Shirley Fry and Doris Hart (USA)
1953	Shirley Fry and Doris Hart (USA)
1954	Louise Brough and Margaret Du Pont (USA)
1955	Angela Mortimer and Anne Shilcock (UK)
1956	Angela Buxton (UK) and Althea Gibson (USA)
1957	Althea Gibson and Darlene Hard (USA)
1958	Maria Bueno (Bra) and Althea Gibson (USA)
1959	Jean Arth and Darlene Hard (USA)
1960	Maria Bueno (Bra) and Darlene Hard (USA)
1961	Karen Hantze and Billie Jean Moffitt (USA)
1962	Billie Jean Moffitt and Karen Susman (USA)
1963	Maria Bueno (Bra) and Darlene Hard (USA)
1964	Margaret Smith and Lesley Turner (Aus)
1965	Maria Bueno (Bra) and Billie Jean Moffitt (USA)
1966	Maria Bueno (Bra) and Nancy Richey (USA)
1967	Rosemary Casals and Billie Jean King (USA)
1968	Rosemary Casals and Billie Jean King (USA)
1969	Margaret Court and Judy Tegart (Aus)
1970	Rosemary Casals and Billie Jean King (USA)
1971	Rosemary Casals and Billie Jean King (USA)
1972	Billie Jean King (USA) and Betty Stove (Hol)
1973	Rosemary Casals and Billie Jean King (USA)

1974	Evonne Goolagong (Aus) and Peggy Michel (USA)	1921	Randolph Lycett (UK) and Elizabeth Ryan (USA)
1975	Ann Kiyomura (USA) and Kazuko Sawamatsu (Jap)	1922	Pat O'Hara Wood (USA) and Suzanne Lenglen (Fra)
1976	Chris Evert (USA) and Martina Navratilova (Cze)	1923	Randolph Lycett (UK) and Elizabeth Ryan (USA)
1977	Helen Cawley (Aus) and Joanne Russell (USA)	1924	Brian Gilbert and Kathleen McKane (UK)
1978	Kerry Reid and Wendy Turnbull (Aus)	1925	Jean Borotra and Suzanne Lenglen (Fra)
1979	Billie Jean King (USA) and Martina Navratilova (Cze)	1926	Leslie Godfree and Kathleen Godfree (UK)
1980	Kathy Jordan and Anne Smith (USA)	1927	Frank Hunter and Elizabeth Ryan (USA)
1981	Martina Navratilova and Pam Shriver (USA)	1928	Pat Spence (SAf) and Elizabeth Ryan (USA)
1982	Martina Navratilova and Pam Shriver (USA)	1929	Frank Hunter and Helen Wills (USA)
1983	Martina Navratilova and Pam Shriver (USA)	1930	Jack Crawford (Aus) and Elizabeth Ryan (USA)
1984	Martina Navratilova and Pam Shriver (USA)	1931	George Lott and Anna Harper (USA)
1985	Kathy Jordan (USA) and Elizabeth Smylie (Aus)	1932	Enrique Maier (Spa) and Elizabeth Ryan (USA)
1986	Martina Navratilova and Pam Shriver (USA)	1933	Gottfried von Cramm and Hilda Krahwinkel (Ger)
1987	Claudia Kohde-Kilsch (FRG) and Helena Sukova (Cze)	1934	Ryuki Miki (Jap) and Dorothy Round (UK)
1988	Steffi Graf (FRG) and Gabriela Sabatini (Arg)	1935	Fred Perry and Dorothy Round (UK)
1989	Jana Novotna and Helena Sukova (Cze)	1936	Fred Perry and Dorothy Round (UK)
1990	Jana Novotna and Helena Sukova (Cze)	1937	Don Budge and Alice Marble (USA)
1991	Larisa Savchenko and Natalya Zvereva (USSR)	1938	Don Budge and Alice Marble (USA)
1992	Gigi Fernandez (USA) and Natalya Zvereva (Bls)	1939	Bobby Riggs and Alice Marble (USA)
1994	Gigi Fernandez (USA) and Natalya Zvereva (Bls)	1946	Tom Brown and Louise Brough (USA)
1993	Gigi Fernandez (USA) and Natalya Zvereva (Bls)	1947	John Bromwich (Aus) and Louise Brough (USA)
		1948	John Bromwich (Aus) and Louise Brough (USA)

Mixed Doubles

1913	Hope Crisp and Agnes Tuckey (UK)	1949	Eric Sturgess and Sheila Summers (SAf)
1914	Cecil Parke and Ethel Larcombe (UK)	1950	Eric Sturgess (SAf) and Louise Brough (USA)
1919	Randolph Lycett (UK) and Elizabeth Ryan (USA)	1951	Frank Sedgman (Aus) and Doris Hart (USA)
1920	Gerald Patterson (Aus) and Suzanne Lenglen (Fra)	1952	Frank Sedgman (Aus) and Doris Hart (USA)

1953	Vic Seixas and Doris Hart (USA)
1954	Vic Seixas and Doris Hart (USA)
1955	Vic Seixas and Doris Hart (USA)
1956	Vic Seixas and Shirley Fry (USA)
1957	Mervyn Rose (Aus) and Darlene Hard (USA)
1958	Bob Howe and Lorraine Coghlan (Aus)
1959	Rod Laver (Aus) and Darlene Hard (USA)
1960	Rod Laver (Aus) and Darlene Hard (USA)
1961	Fred Stolle and Lesley Turner (Aus)
1962	Neale Fraser (Aus) and Margaret Du Pont (USA)
1963	Ken Fletcher and Margaret Smith (Aus)
1964	Fred Stolle and Lesley Turner (Aus)
1965	Ken Fletcher and Margaret Smith (Aus)
1966	Ken Fletcher and Margaret Smith (Aus)
1967	Owen Davidson (Aus) and Billie Jean King (USA)
1968	Ken Fletcher and Margaret Court (Aus)
1969	Fred Stolle (Aus) and Ann Jones (UK)
1970	Ilie Nastase (Rom) and Rosemary Casals (USA)
1971	Owen Davidson (Aus) and Billie Jean King (USA)
1972	Ilie Nastase (Rom) and Rosemary Casals (USA)
1973	Owen Davidson (Aus) and Billie Jean King (USA)
1974	Owen Davidson (Aus) and Billie Jean King (USA)
1975	Marty Riessen (USA) and Margaret Court (Aus)
1976	Tony Roche (Aus) and Françoise Durr (Fra)
1977	Bob Hewitt and Greer Stevens (SAf)
1978	Frew McMillan (SAf) and Betty Stove (Hol)
1979	Bob Hewitt and Greer Stevens (SAf)
1980	John Austin and Tracy Austin (USA)
1981	Frew McMillan (SAf) and Betty Stove (Hol)
1982	Kevin Curren (SAf) and Anne Smith (USA)
1983	John Lloyd (UK) and Wendy Turnbull (Aus)
1984	John Lloyd (UK) and Wendy Turnbull (Aus)
1985	Paul McNamee (Aus) and Martina Navratilova (USA)
1986	Ken Flach and Kathy Jordan (USA)
1987	Jeremy Bates and Jo Durie (UK)
1988	Sherwood Stewart and Zina Garrison (USA)
1989	Jim Pugh (USA) and Jana Novotná (Cze)
1990	Rick Leach and Zina Garrison (USA)
1991	John Fitzgerald and Elizabeth Smylie (Aus)
1992	Cyril Suk (Cze) and Larisa Savchenko (Lat)
1993	Mark Woodforde (Aus) and Martina Navratilova (USA)
1994	Todd Woodbridge (Aus) and Helena Sukova (Cze)

US OPEN

Men's Singles

1881	Richard Sears (USA)
1882	Richard Sears (USA)
1883	Richard Sears (USA)
1884	Richard Sears (USA)
1885	Richard Sears (USA)
1886	Richard Sears (USA)
1887	Richard Sears (USA)
1888	Henry Slocum Jr (USA)
1889	Henry Slocum Jr (USA)
1890	Oliver Campbell (USA)
1891	Oliver Campbell (USA)
1892	Oliver Campbell (USA)
1893	Robert Wrenn (USA)
1894	Robert Wrenn (USA)
1895	Fred Hovey (USA)

1896	Robert Wrenn (USA)
1897	Robert Wrenn (USA)
1898	Malcolm Whitman (USA)
1899	Malcolm Whitman (USA)
1900	Malcolm Whitman (USA)
1901	William Larned (USA)
1902	William Larned (USA)
1903	Lawrence Doherty (UK)
1904	Holcombe Ward (USA)
1905	Beals Wright (USA)
1906	William Clothier (USA)
1907	William Larned (USA)
1908	William Larned (USA)
1909	William Larned (USA)
1910	William Larned (USA)
1911	William Larned (USA)
1912	Maurice McLoughlin (USA)
1913	Maurice McLoughlin (USA)
1914	Norris Williams (USA)
1915	William Johnston (USA)
1916	Norris Williams (USA)
1917	Lindley Murray (USA)
1918	Lindley Murray (USA)
1919	William Johnston (USA)
1920	Bill Tilden (USA)
1921	Bill Tilden (USA)
1922	Bill Tilden (USA)
1923	Bill Tilden (USA)
1924	Bill Tilden (USA)
1925	Bill Tilden (USA)
1926	René Lacoste (Fra)
1927	René Lacoste (Fra)
1928	Henri Cochet (Fra)
1929	Bill Tilden (USA)
1930	John Doeg (USA)
1931	Ellsworth Vines (USA)
1932	Ellsworth Vines (USA)
1933	Fred Perry (UK)
1934	Fred Perry (UK)
1935	Wilmer Allison (USA)
1936	Fred Perry (UK)
1937	Donald Budge (USA)
1938	Donald Budge (USA)
1939	Bobby Riggs (USA)
1940	Donald McNeil (USA)
1941	Bobby Riggs (USA)
1942	Ted Schroeder (USA)
1943	Joseph Hunt (USA)
1944	Frank Parker (USA)
1945	Frank Parker (USA)
1946	Jack Kramer (USA)

1947	Jack Kramer (USA)
1948	Ricardo Gonzales (USA)
1949	Ricardo Gonzales (USA)
1950	Arthur Larsen (USA)
1951	Frank Sedgman (USA)
1952	Frank Sedgman (USA)
1953	Tony Trabert (USA)
1954	Vic Seixas (USA)
1955	Tony Trabert (USA)
1956	Ken Rosewall (Aus)
1957	Malcolm Anderson (Aus)
1958	Ashley Cooper (Aus)
1959	Neale Fraser (Aus)
1960	Neale Fraser (Aus)
1961	Roy Emerson (Aus)
1962	Rod Laver (Aus)
1963	Raphael Osuna (Mex)
1964	Roy Emerson (Aus)
1965	Manuel Santana (Spa)
1966	Fred Stolle (Aus)
1967	John Newcombe (Aus)
1968	Arthur Ashe (USA)
1969	Rod Laver (Aus)
1970	Ken Rosewall (Aus)
1971	Stan Smith (USA)
1972	Ilie Nastase (Rom)
1973	John Newcombe (Aus)
1974	Jimmy Connors (USA)
1975	Manuel Orantes (Spa)
1976	Jimmy Connors (USA)
1977	Guillermo Vilas (Arg)
1978	Jimmy Connors (USA)
1979	John McEnroe (USA)
1980	John McEnroe (USA)
1981	John McEnroe (USA)
1982	Jimmy Connors (USA)
1983	Jimmy Connors (USA)
1984	John McEnroe (USA)
1985	Ivan Lendl (Cze)
1986	Ivan Lendl (Cze)
1987	Ivan Lendl (Cze)
1988	Mats Wilander (Swe)
1989	Boris Becker (FRG)
1990	Pete Sampras (USA)
1991	Stefan Edberg (Swe)
1992	Stefan Edberg (Swe)
1993	Pete Sampras (USA)

Women's Singles

| 1887 | Ellen Hansell (USA) |
| 1888 | Bertha Townsend (USA) |

1889	Bertha Townsend (USA)	1938	Alice Marble (USA)
1890	Ellen Roosevelt (USA)	1939	Alice Marble (USA)
1891	Mabel Cahill (USA)	1940	Alice Marble (USA)
1892	Mabel Cahill (USA)	1941	Sarah Cooke (USA)
1893	Aline Terry (USA)	1942	Pauline Betz (USA)
1894	Helen Helwig (USA)	1943	Pauline Betz (USA)
1895	Juliette Atkinson (USA)	1944	Pauline Betz (USA)
1896	Elisabeth Moore (USA)	1945	Sarah Cooke (USA)
1897	Juliette Atkinson (USA)	1946	Pauline Betz (USA)
1898	Juliette Atkinson (USA)	1947	Louise Brough (USA)
1899	Marion Jones (USA)	1948	Margaret Du Pont (USA)
1900	Myrtle McAteer (USA)	1949	Margaret Du Pont (USA)
1901	Elisabeth Moore (USA)	1950	Margaret Du Pont (USA)
1902	Marion Jones (USA)	1951	Maureen Connolly (USA)
1903	Elisabeth Moore (USA)	1952	Maureen Connolly (USA)
1904	May Sutton (USA)	1953	Maureen Connolly (USA)
1905	Elisabeth Moore (USA)	1954	Doris Hart (USA)
1906	Helen Homans (USA)	1955	Doris Hart (USA)
1907	Evelyn Sears (USA)	1956	Shirley Fry (USA)
1908	Maud Bargar-Wallach (USA)	1957	Althea Gibson (USA)
1909	Hazel Hotchkiss (USA)	1958	Althea Gibson (USA)
1910	Hazel Hotchkiss (USA)	1959	Maria Bueno (Bra)
1911	Hazel Hotchkiss (USA)	1960	Darlene Hard (USA)
1912	Mary Browne (USA)	1961	Darlene Hard (USA)
1913	Mary Browne (USA)	1962	Margaret Smith (Aus)
1914	Mary Browne (USA)	1963	Maria Bueno (Bra)
1915	Molla Bjurstedt (USA)	1964	Maria Bueno (Bra)
1916	Molla Bjurstedt (USA)	1965	Margaret Smith (Aus)
1917	Molla Bjurstedt (USA)	1966	Maria Bueno (Bra)
1918	Molla Bjurstedt (USA)	1967	Billie Jean King (USA)
1919	Hazel Wightman (née Hotchkiss) (USA)	1968	Virginia Wade (UK)
		1969	Margaret Court (Aus)
1920	Molla Mallory (née Bjurstedt) (USA)	1970	Margaret Court (Aus)
		1971	Billie Jean King (USA)
1921	Molla Mallory (USA)	1972	Billie Jean King (USA)
1922	Molla Mallory (USA)	1973	Margaret Court (Aus)
1923	Helen Wills (USA)	1974	Billie Jean King (USA)
1924	Helen Wills (USA)	1975	Chris Evert (USA)
1925	Helen Wills (USA)	1976	Chris Evert (USA)
1926	Molla Mallory (USA)	1977	Chris Evert (USA)
1927	Helen Wills (USA)	1978	Chris Evert (USA)
1928	Helen Wills (USA)	1979	Tracy Austin (USA)
1929	Helen Wills (USA)	1980	Chris Evert Lloyd (USA)
1930	Betty Nuthall (UK)	1981	Tracy Austin (USA)
1931	Helen Moody (née Wills)	1982	Chris Evert Lloyd (USA)
1932	Helen Jacobs (USA)	1983	Martina Navratilova (USA)
1933	Helen Jacobs (USA)	1984	Martina Navratilova (USA)
1934	Helen Jacobs (USA)	1985	Hanna Mandlikova (Cze)
1935	Helen Jacobs (USA)	1986	Martina Navratilova (USA)
1936	Alice Marble (USA)	1987	Martina Navratilova (USA)
1937	Anita Lizana (Chi)	1988	Steffi Graf (FRG)

1989	Steffi Graf (FRG)	1992	Monica Seles (Yug)
1990	Gabriela Sabatini (Arg)	1993	Steffi Graf (Ger)
1991	Monica Seles (Yug)		

FRENCH CHAMPIONSHIPS

Men's Singles

1925	René Lacoste (Fra)
1926	Henri Cochet (Fra)
1927	René Lacoste (Fra)
1928	Henri Cochet (Fra)
1929	René Lacoste (Fra)
1930	Henri Cochet (Fra)
1931	Jean Borotra (Fra)
1932	Henri Cochet (Fra)
1933	Jack Crawford (Aus)
1934	Gottfried Von Cramm (Ger)
1935	Fred Perry (UK)
1936	Gottfried Von Cramm (Ger)
1937	Henner Henkel (Ger)
1938	Donald Budge (USA)
1939	Donald McNeill (USA)
1946	Marcel Bernard (Fra)
1947	József Asboth (Hun)
1948	Frank Parker (USA)
1949	Frank Parker (USA)
1950	Budge Patty (USA)
1951	Jaroslav Drobny (Egy)
1952	Jaroslav Drobny (Egy)
1953	Ken Rosewall (Aus)
1954	Tony Trabert (USA)
1955	Tony Trabert (USA)
1956	Lew Hoad (Aus)
1957	Sven Davidson (Swe)
1958	Mervyn Rose (Aus)
1959	Nicola Pietrangeli (Ita)
1960	Nicola Pietrangeli (Ita)
1961	Manuel Santana (Spa)
1962	Rod Laver (Aus)
1963	Roy Emerson (Aus)
1964	Manuel Santana (Spa)
1965	Fred Stolle (Aus)
1966	Tony Roche (Aus)
1967	Roy Emerson (Aus)
1968	Ken Rosewall (Aus)
1969	Rod Laver (Aus)
1970	Jan Kodes (Cze)
1971	Jan Kodes (Cze)
1972	Andres Gimeno (Spa)
1973	Ilie Nastase (Rom)
1974	Björn Borg (Swe)

1975	Björn Borg (Swe)
1976	Adriano Panatta (Ita)
1977	Guillermo Vilas (Arg)
1978	Björn Borg (Swe)
1979	Björn Borg (Swe)
1980	Björn Borg (Swe)
1981	Björn Borg (Swe)
1982	Mats Wilander (Swe)
1983	Yannick Noah (Fra)
1984	Ivan Lendl (Cze)
1985	Mats Wilander (Swe)
1986	Ivan Lendl (Cze)
1987	Ivan Lendl (Cze)
1988	Mats Wilander (Swe)
1989	Michael Chang (USA)
1990	Andrés Gómez (Ecu)
1991	Jim Courier (USA)
1992	Jim Courier (USA)
1993	Sergei Bruguera (Spa)
1994	Sergei Bruguera (Spa)

Women's Singles

1925	Suzanne Lenglen (Fra)
1926	Suzanne Lenglen (Fra)
1927	Kea Bouman (Hol)
1928	Helen Wills Moody (USA)
1929	Helen Wills Moody (USA)
1930	Helen Wills Moody (USA)
1931	Cilly Aussem (Ger)
1932	Helen Moody (USA)
1933	Margaret Scriven (UK)
1934	Margaret Scriven (UK)
1935	Hilde Sperling (Ger)
1936	Hilde Sperling (Ger)
1937	Hilde Sperling (Ger)
1938	Simone Mathieu (Fra)
1939	Simone Mathieu (Fra)
1946	Margaret Osborne (USA)
1947	Pat Todd (USA)
1948	Nelly Landry (Fra)
1949	Margaret Du Pont (USA)
1950	Doris Hart (USA)
1951	Shirley Fry (USA)
1952	Doris Hart (USA)
1953	Maureen Connolly (USA)

1954	Maureen Connolly (USA)	1974	Chris Evert (USA)
1955	Angela Mortimer (UK)	1975	Chris Evert (USA)
1956	Althea Gibson (USA)	1976	Sue Barker (UK)
1957	Shirley Bloomer (UK)	1977	Mimi Jausovec (Yug)
1958	Zsuzsi Körmöczy (Hun)	1978	Virginia Ruzici (Rom)
1959	Christine Truman (UK)	1979	Chris Evert Lloyd (USA)
1960	Darlene Hard (USA)	1980	Chris Evert Lloyd (USA)
1961	Ann Haydon (UK)	1981	Hana Mandlikova (Cze)
1962	Margaret Smith (Aus)	1982	Martina Navratilova (USA)
1963	Lesley Turner (Aus)	1983	Chris Evert Lloyd (USA)
1964	Margaret Smith (Aus)	1984	Martina Navratilova (USA)
1965	Lesley Turner (Aus)	1985	Chris Evert Lloyd (USA)
1966	Ann Jones (UK)	1986	Chris Evert Lloyd (USA)
1967	Françoise Durr (Fra)	1987	Steffi Graf (FRG)
1968	Nancy Richey (USA)	1988	Steffi Graf (FRG)
1969	Margaret Court (née Smith) (Aus)	1989	Arantxa Sánchez (Spa)
1970	Margaret Court (Aus)	1990	Monica Seles (Yug)
1971	Evonne Goolagong (Aus)	1991	Monica Seles (Yug)
1972	Billie Jean King (USA)	1992	Monica Seles (Yug)
1973	Margaret Court (Aus)	1993	Steffi Graf (Ger)
		1994	Arantxa Sánchez (Spa)

OLYMPIC GAMES

Men's Singles

1896	John Boland (UK/Ire)
1900	Hugh Doherty (UK)
1904	Beals Wright (USA)
1906	Max Decugis (Fra)
1908	Josiah Ritchie (UK)
1912	Charles Winslow (SAf)
1920	Louis Raymond (SAf)
1924	Vince Richards (USA)
1988	Miloslav Mecir (Cze)
1992	Marc Rosset (Swi)

Women's Singles

1900	Charlotte Cooper (UK)
1906	Esmée Simiriotou (Gre)
1908	Dorothea Lambert Chambers (UK)
1912	Marguerite Broquedis (Fra)
1920	Suzanne Lenglen (Fra)
1924	Helen Wills (USA)
1988	Steffi Graf (FRG)
1992	Jennifer Capriatti (USA)

Men's Doubles

1896	John Boland (Ire) and Fritz Traun (Ger)
1900	Reginald and Hugh Doherty (UK)
1904	Beals Wright and Edgar Leonard (USA)
1906	Max Decugis and Maurice Germot (Fra)
1908	George Hillyard and Reginald Doherty (UK)
1912	Charles Winslow and Harold Kitson (SAf)
1920	Oswald Turnbull and Max Woosnam (UK)
1924	Vince Richards and Frank Hunter (UK)
1988	Ken Flach and Robert Seguso (USA)
1992	Boris Becker and Michael Stich (Ger)

Women's Doubles

1920	Winifred McNair and Kathleen McKane (UK)
1924	Hazel Wightman and Helen Wills (USA)
1988	Pam Shriver and Zina Garrison (USA)
1992	Gigi Fernandez and Mary Joe Fernandez (USA)

Mixed Doubles

1900	Reginald Doherty and Charlotte Cooper (UK)
1906	Max and Marie Decugis (Fra)
1912	(a) Heinrich Schomburg and Dora König (Ger)
1912	(b) Percy Dixon and Edith Hannam (UK)
1920	Max Decugis and Suzanne Lenglen (Fra)
1924	Norris Williams and Hazel Wightman (USA)

DAVIS CUP

Year	Winner	Year	Winner	Year	Winner
1900	USA	1934	Great Britain	1968	USA
1902	USA	1935	Great Britain	1969	USA
1903	British Isles	1936	Great Britain	1970	USA
1904	British Isles	1937	USA	1971	USA
1905	British Isles	1938	USA	1972	USA
1906	British Isles	1939	Australia	1973	Australia
1907	Australasia	1946	USA	1974	South Africa
1908	Australasia	1947	USA	1975	Sweden
1909	Australasia	1948	USA	1976	Italy
1911	Australasia	1949	USA	1977	Australia
1912	British Isles	1950	Australia	1978	USA
1913	USA	1951	Australia	1979	USA
1914	Australasia	1952	Australia	1980	Czechoslovakia
1919	Australasia	1953	Australia	1981	USA
1920	USA	1954	USA	1982	USA
1921	USA	1955	Australia	1983	Australia
1922	USA	1956	Australia	1984	Sweden
1923	USA	1957	Australia	1985	Sweden
1924	USA	1958	USA	1986	Australia
1925	USA	1959	Australia	1987	Sweden
1926	USA	1960	Australia	1988	West Germany
1927	France	1961	Australia	1989	West Germany
1928	France	1962	Australia	1990	USA
1929	France	1963	USA	1991	France
1930	France	1964	Australia	1992	USA
1931	France	1965	Australia	1993	Germany
1932	France	1966	Australia		
1933	Great Britain	1967	Australia		

THEATRE

LAURENCE OLIVIER AWARDS

These awards, established in 1976 as the Society of West End Theatre (SWET) Awards, were renamed in 1984 after one of the most famous twentieth-century actors. The bronze awards, specially commissioned by the Society from the sculptor Harry Franchetti, represent the young Laurence Olivier as King Henry V at the Old Vic, London, in 1937.

They are annually presented by SWET, in association with American Express, under the patronage of the *Observer*.

Designer of the Year

1976	Farrah for *Henry IV Parts 1 and 2* and *Henry V*
1977	John Napier for *King Lear*
1978	Ralph Koltai for *Brand*
1979	William Dudley for *Undiscovered Country*
1980	John Napier and Dermot Hayes for *Nicholas Nickleby*
1981	Carl Toms for *The Provok'd Wife*
1982	John Gunter for *Guys and Dolls*
1983	Ralph Koltai for *Cyrano de Bergerac*
1984	John Gunter for *Wild Honey*
1985	William Dudley for *The Mysteries* and *The Critics*
1986	William Dudley for *Futurists*, *Kafka's Dick* and *The Merry Wives of Windsor*
1987	Lucio Fanti (with Design Team) for *The Hairy Ape*
1988	Richard Hudson for his season at the Old Vic
1989–90	Bob Crowley for *Ma Rainey's Black Bottom*, *Hedda Gabler*, *Ghetto* and *The Plantagenets*

Best Set Designer

1991	Mark Thompson for *The Wind in the Willows*
1992	Mark Thompson for *The Comedy of Errors*
1993	Ian MacNeil for *An Inspector Calls*
1994	Mark Thompson for *Hysteria*

Best Lighting Designer

1991	Jean Kalman for *Richard III* and *White Chameleon*
1992	Mark Henderson for *Murmuring Judges* and *Long Day's Journey into Night*
1993	Howell Binkley for *Kiss of the Spider Woman*
1994	Rick Fisher for *Hysteria*, *Machines* and *Moonlight*

Best Costume Designer

| 1991 | Jasper Conran for *The Rehearsal* |
| 1992 | Mark Thompson for *The Comedy of Errors* |

| 1993 | William Dudley for *Heartbreak House* etc |
| 1994 | Gerald Scarfe for *An Absolute Turkey* |

Director of the Year

1976	Jonathan Miller for *The Three Sisters*
1977	Clifford Williams for *Wild Oats*
1978	Terry Hands for *Henry VI*
1979	Michael Bogdanov for *The Taming of the Shrew*
1980	Trevor Nunn and John Caird for *Nicholas Nickleby*
1981	Peter Wood for *On The Razzle*
1982	Richard Eyre for *Guys and Dolls*
1983	Terry Hands for *Cyrano de Bergerac*
1984	Christopher Morahan for *Wild Honey*
1985	Bill Bryden for *The Mysteries*
1986	Bill Alexander for *The Merry Wives of Windsor*
1987	Declan Donnellan for *The Cid*, *Twelfth Night* and *Macbeth*
1988	Deborah Warner for *Titus Andronicus*
1989–90	Michael Bogdanov for *The Wars of the Roses*

Best Director of a Play

1991	David Thacker for *Pericles*
1992	Deborah Warner for *Hedda Gabler*
1993	Stephen Daldry for *An Inspector Calls*

Best Director of a Musical

1991	Richard Jones for *Into the Woods*
1992	Simon Callow for *Carmen Jones*
1993	Nicholas Hytner for *Carousel*

Best Choreographer

1991	Charles Augins for *Five Guys Named Moe*
1992	Rafael Aguila for *Matador*
1993	Susan Stroman for *Crazy for You*

Actor of the Year in a Revival

1976	Alan Howard for *Henry IV Parts 1 and 2* and *Henry V*
1977	Ian McKellen for *Pillars of the Community*
1978	Alan Howard for *Coriolanus*
1979	Warren Mitchell for *Death of a Salesman*
1980	Jonathan Pryce for *Hamlet*
1981	Daniel Massey for *Man and Superman*
1982	Stephen Moore for *A Doll's House*
1983	Derek Jacobi for *Cyrano de Bergerac*
1984	Ian McKellen for *Wild Honey*
1988	Brian Cox for *Titus Andronicus*

Actress of the Year in a Revival

1976	Dorothy Tutin for *A Month in the Country*
1977	Judi Dench for *Macbeth*
1978	Dorothy Tutin for *The Double Dealer*
1979	Zoë Wanamaker for *Once in a Lifetime*
1980	Judi Dench for *Juno and the Paycock*
1981	Margaret Tyzack for *Who's Afraid of Virginia Woolf?*
1982	Cheryl Campbell for *A Doll's House*
1983	Frances de la Tour for *A Moon for the Misbegotten*
1984	Vanessa Redgrave for *The Aspern Papers*
1988	Harriet Walter for *Twelfth Night* and *Three Sisters*

Actor of the Year in a New Play

1976	Paul Copley for *King and Country*
1977	Michael Bryant for *State of Revolution*
1978	Tom Conti for *Whose Life is it Anyway?*
1979	Ian McKellen for *Bent*
1980	Roger Rees for *Nicholas Nickleby*
1981	Trevor Eve for *Children of a Lesser God*

1982	Ian McDiarmid for *Insignificance*
1983	Jack Shepherd for *Glengarry Glen Ross*
1984	Brian Cox for *Rat in the Skull*
1988	David Haig for *Our Country's Good*

Actress of the Year in a New Play

1976	Peggy Ashcroft for *Old World*
1977	Alison Fiske for *Dusa, Fish, Stas and Vi*
1978	Joan Plowright for *Filumena*
1979	Jane Lapotaire for *Piaf*
1980	Frances de la Tour for *Duet for One*
1981	Elizabeth Quinn for *Children of a Lesser God*
1982	Rosemary Leach for *84 Charing Cross Road*
1983	Judi Dench for *Pack of Lies*
1984	Thuli Dumakude for *Poppie Nongena*
1988	Pauline Collins for *Shirley Valentine*

Best Actor

1985	Antony Sher for *Richard III* and *Torch Song Trilogy*
1986	Albert Finney for *Orphans*
1987	Michael Gambon for *A View From the Bridge*
1989–90	Oliver Ford-Davies for *Racing Demon*
1991	Nigel Hawthorne for *The Madness of George III*
1993	Robert Stephens for *Henry IV Parts 1 and 2*
1994	Mark Rylance for *Much Ado About Nothing*

Best Actress

1985	Yvonne Bryceland for *The Road to Mecca*
1986	Lindsay Duncan for *Les Liaisons Dangereuses*
1987	Judi Dench for *Antony and Cleopatra*
1989–90	Fiona Shaw for *Electra, As You Like It* and *The Good Person of Sichuan*
1991	Kathryn Hunter for *The Visit*

1992	Juliet Stevenson for *Death and The Maiden*
1993	Alison Steadman for *The Rise and Fall of Little Voice*
1994	Fiona Shaw for *Machinal*

Best Comedy Performance

1976	Penelope Keith for *Donkey's Years*
1977	Denis Quilley for *Privates on Parade*
1978	Ian McKellen for *The Alchemist*
1979	Barry Humphries for *A Night with Dame Edna*
1980	Beryl Reid for *Born in the Gardens*
1981	Rowan Atkinson for *Rowan Atkinson in Revue*
1982	Geoffrey Hutchings for *Poppy*
1983	Griff Rhys Jones for *Charley's Aunt*
1984	Maureen Lipman for *See How They Run*
1988	Alex Jennings for *Too Clever by Half*
1989–90	Michael Gambon for *Man of the Moment*
1991	Alan Cumming for *Accidental Death of an Anarchist*
1992	Desmond Barrit for *The Comedy of Errors*
1993	Simon Cadell for *Travels With My Aunt*
1994	Griff Rhys Jones for *An Absolute Turkey*

Best Actor in a Supporting Role

1977	Nigel Hawthorne for *Privates on Parade*
1978	Robert Eddison for *Twelfth Night*
1979	Patrick Stewart for *Antony and Cleopatra*
1980	David Threlfall for *Nicholas Nickleby*
1981	Joe Melia for *Good*
1982	David Healy for *Guys and Dolls*
1983	Alan Devlin for *A Moon for the Misbegotten*
1984	Edward Petherbridge for *Strange Interlude*
1991	David Bradley for *King Lear*
1992	Oleg Menshikov for *When She Danced*

1993	Julian Glover for *Henry IV Parts 1 and 2*
1994	Joseph Mydell for *Perestroika*

Best Actress in a Supporting Role

1977	Mona Washbourne for *Stevie*
1978	Elizabeth Spriggs for *Love Letters on Blue Paper*
1979	Doreen Mantle for *Death of a Salesman*
1980	Suzanne Bertish for *Nicholas Nickleby*
1981	Gwen Watford for *Present Laughter*
1982	Anna Massey for *The Importance of Being Earnest*
1983	Abigail McKern for *As You Like It*
1984	Marcia Warren for *Stepping Out*
1991	Sara Crowe for *Private Lives*
1992	Frances de la Tour for *When She Danced*
1993	Barbara Leigh-Hunt for *An Inspector Calls*
1994	Helen Burns for *The Last Yankee*

Outstanding Performance of the Year in a Supporting Role

1976	Margaret Courtenay for *Separate Tables*
1985	Imelda Staunton for *A Chorus of Disapproval* and *The Corn is Green*
1986	Paul Jesson for *The Norman Heart*
1987	Michael Bryant for *King Lear* and *Antony and Cleopatra*
1988	Eileen Atkins for *Cymbeline*, *The Winter's Tale* and *Mountain Language*
1989–90	Michael Bryant for *Hamlet*, *The Voysey Inheritance* and *Racing Demon*

Performance of the Year in a Musical

1977	Ann Sharkey for *Maggie*
1978	Elaine Paige for *Evita*

Best Actor in a Musical or Entertainment

1979	Anton Rodgers for *Songbook*

1980	Denis Quilley for *Sweeney Todd*
1981	Michael Crawford for *Barnum*
1982	Roy Hudd for *Underneath the Arches*
1983	Denis Lawson for *Mr Cinders*
1984	Paul Clarkson for *The Hired Man*
1985	Robert Lindsay for *Me and My Girl*
1986	Michael Crawford for *The Phantom of the Opera*
1987	John Bardon and Emil Wolk for *Kiss Me Kate*
1988	Con O'Neill for *Blood Brothers*
1989–90	Jonathan Pryce for *Miss Saigon*
1991	Philip Quast for *Sunday in the Park with George*
1992	Alan Bennett for *Talking Heads*
1993	Henry Goodman for *Assassins*
1994	Alun Armstrong for *Sweeney Todd*

Best Actress in a Musical or Entertainment

1979	Virginia McKenna for *The King and I*
1980	Gemma Craven for *They're Playing Our Song*
1981	Carlin Glynn for *The Best Little Whorehouse in Texas*
1982	Julia McKenzie for *Guys and Dolls*
1983	Barbara Dickson for *Blood Brothers*
1984	Natalia Makarova for *On Your Toes*
1985	Patti Lupone for *Les Misérables* and *The Cradle Will Rock*
1986	Lesley Mackie for *Judy*
1987	Nichola McAuliffe for *Kiss Me Kate*
1988	Patricia Routledge for *Candide*
1989–90	Lea Salonga for *Miss Saigon*
1991	Imelda Staunton for *Into the Woods*
1992	Wilhelmena Fernandez for *Carmen Jones*
1993	Joanna Riding for *Carousel*
1994	Julia Mckenzie for *Sweeney Todd*

Best Supporting Performance in a Musical

1991	Karla Burns for *Show Boat*
1992	Jenny Galloway for *The Boys from Syracuse*
1993	Janie Dee for *Carousel*
1994	Sara Kestelman for *Cabaret*

Outstanding Achievement of the Year in Musicals

1981	Gillian Lynne, choreographer of *Cats*
1982	*Guys and Dolls*
1984	Ned Sherrin for the conception of *The Ratepayers' Iolanthe*

Most Promising Newcomer of the Year in Theatre

1980	Edward Duke for the creation, adaptation and performance in *Jeeves Takes Charge*
1981	Alice Krige for *Arms and the Man*
1982	Kenneth Branagh for *Another Country*
1983	John Retallack for directing *Quixote* and *The Provok'd Wife*
1984	Tim Flavin for *On Your Toes*
1985	Cheek by Jowl Company for *Andromache*, *Pericles* and *Vanity Fair*
1986	Sally Dexter for *Dalliance*
1987	Suzan Sylvester for *A View From the Bridge*
1988	Richard Jones for *Too Clever by Half*
1989–90	Jeremy Northam for *The Voysey Inheritance*

Most Outstanding Achievement in Opera

1977	Glyndebourne Festival Opera's *Don Giovanni*
1978	English National Opera for their enterprising repertoire
1979	The Royal Opera's *The Rake's Progress*
1980	English National Opera's *Cosi Fan Tutte*
1981	The Royal Opera's *Les Contes D'Hoffmann*

1982	English National Opera's *Rigoletto*
1986	English National Opera's *Doctor Faust*, Graham Clark and Thomas Allen specially commended
1987	English National Opera's *Lady Macbeth of Mtsensk*
1988	Leontina Vaduva for her performance in *Manon* (Royal Opera)
1989–90	The Komische Oper's *Orpheus and Eurydice*
1991	Mark Elder for conducting English National Opera's *Duke Bluebeard's Castle*, *Macbeth*, *Pelléas and Mélisande*, and *Wozzeck*
1992	The Royal Opera's *Mitridate, Rè Di Ponto*
1993	Sir Edward Downes for *The Fiery Angel and Stiffelio* at the Royal Opera House
1994	Orchestra of English National Opera for *Lohengrin* and *Inquest of Love* at the Coliseum

Additional Opera Awards

1978	The Royal Opera's *Lohengrin*
1980	Rosalind Plowright for *The Turn of the Screw* (English National Opera)
1981	Anne Mackay for *The Gypsy Princess* (Sadler's Wells Theatre production)
1982	Jeffrey Tate for *La Clemenza di Tito* (Royal Opera)
1983	The Cologne Opera's *Il Matrimonio Segreto*
1983	Valerie Masterson for *Semele* (Royal Opera)
1984	The Welsh National Opera's *From the House of the Dead*
1984	Philip Langridge for *Osud* (English National Opera)
1985	English National Opera's *Xerxes*
1985	Kathleen Battle for *Ariadne Auf Naxos* (Royal Opera)

Most Outstanding Achievement in Dance

1977	London Festival Ballet's *Romeo and Juliet*

1978	Robert Cohan, Artistic Director, London Contemporary Dance Theatre
1979	Peter Schaufuss for *La Sylphide*
1980	The Royal Ballet's *Gloria*
1981	Stuttgart Ballet's *Forgotten Lane*
1982	Le Ballet de L'Opéra de Paris's *Le Songe d'Une Nuit d'Eté*
1986	The Ballet Rambert for their sixtieth anniversary season
1987	Trisha Brown for her season at Sadler's Wells
1988	The Dancers of the Kirov Ballet for their London season
1989–90	London Contemporary Dance Theatre for their production of Kim Brandstrup's *Orfeo*
1991	Twyla Tharp and Jennifer Tipton for choreography and lighting of the American Ballet Theatre's *In the Upper Room*
1992	*In the Middle, Somewhat Elevated* for William Forsythe's choreography and performance by the Royal Ballet
1993	Siobhan Davies for choreography of *Winnsboro Cotton Mill Blues* at the Royalty
1994	Dancers of London Contemporary Dance Theatre for their season at Saddler's Wells

Additional Dance Awards

1978	The Royal Ballet's *A Month in the Country*
1981	Bryony Brind for *Dances of Albion* (Royal Ballet)
1982	Elisabeth Platel for *La Sylphide* (Le Ballet de L'Opéra de Paris)
1983	The Royal Ballet's *Requiem*
1983	Alessandra Ferri for *Valley of Shadows* (Royal Ballet)
1984	The Dance Theatre of Harlem's *Giselle*
	David Bintley for *Petrushka* (Sadler's Wells Royal Ballet)
1985	Merce Cunningham Dance Company's *Pictures*
	Yoko Morishita for *Giselle* (Matsuyama Ballet Company)

Best Comedy

1976	*Donkey's Years* by Michael Frayn

1977   *Privates on Parade* by Peter Nichols

1978   *Filumena* by Eduardo de Filippo adapted by Keith Waterhouse and Willis Hall

1979   *Middle Age Spread* by Roger Hall

1980   *Educating Rita* by Willy Russell

1981   *Steaming* by Nell Dunn

1982   *Noises Off* by Michael Frayn

1983   *Daisy Pulls it Off* by Denise Deegan

1984   *Up 'n' Under* by John Godber

1985   *A Chorus of Disapproval* by Alan Ayckbourn

1986   *When We Are Married* by J. B. Priestley

1987   *Three Men on a Horse* by John Cecil Holm and George Abbott

1988   *Shirley Valentine* by Willy Russell

1989–90 *Single Spies* by Alan Bennett

1991   *Out of Order* by Ray Cooney

1992   *La Bête* by David Hirson

1993   *The Rise and Fall of Little Voice* by Jim Cartwright

1994   *Hysteria* by Terry Johnson

Musical of the Year

1976   *A Chorus Line* – book by James Kirkwood and Nicholas Dante; music by Marvin Hamlisch; lyrics by Edward Kleban

1977   *The Comedy of Errors* by William Shakespeare; music by Guy Woolfenden

1978   *Evita* – lyrics by Tim Rice; music by Andrew Lloyd Webber

1979   *Songbook* – music by Monty Norman; lyrics by Julian More; book by Monty Norman and Julian More

1980   *Sweeney Todd* – music and lyrics by Stephen Sondheim; book by Hugh Wheeler; based on the play by Christopher Bond

1981   *Cats* – music by Andrew Lloyd Webber based on *Old Possum's Book of Practical Cats* by T. S. Eliot

1982   *Poppy* – book and lyrics by Peter Nichols; music by Monty Norman

1983   *Blood Brothers* by Willy Russell

1984   *42nd Street* – music by Harry Warren; lyrics by Al Dubin; book by Michael Stewart and Mark Bramble; based on a novel by Bradford Ropes

1985   *Me and My Girl* – book and lyrics by L. Arthur Rose and Douglas Furber; music by Noel Gay

1986   *The Phantom of the Opera* – music by Andrew Lloyd Webber; lyrics by Charles Hart; additional lyrics by Richard Stilgoe

1987   *Follies* – music and lyrics by Stephen Sondheim; book by John Goldman

1988   *Candide* – book adapted from Voltaire by Hugh Wheeler; music by Leonard Bernstein; lyrics by Richard Wilbur

1989–90 *Return to the Forbidden Planet* by Bob Carlton

The American Express Award for Best Musical

1991   *Sunday in the Park with George* – music and lyrics by Stephen Sondheim; book by James Lapine

1992   *Carmen Jones* by Oscar Hammerstein II, based on Meilhac and Halévy's adaptation of Prosper Merimée's *Carmen* with original music by Bizet

1993   *Crazy for You* – music and lyrics by George Gershwin and Ira Gershwin, book by Ken Ludwig, at the Prince Edward

1994   *City of Angels* – book by Larry Gelbart, music by Cy Coleman, lyrics by David Zippel

Best Musical Revival

1991   *Show Boat* – book and lyrics by Oscar Hammerstein II: music by Jerome Kern

1992   *The Boys from Syracuse* – music by Richard Rodgers; lyrics by Lorenz Hart; book by George Abbott

1993   *Carousel* – music by Richard Rodgers; book and lyrics by Oscar Hammerstein II

1994   *Sweeney Todd* – music and lyrics by Stephen Sondheim, book by Hugh Wheeler

The BBC Award for Best Play

1976   *Dear Daddy* by Denis Cannan
1977   *The Fire That Consumes* by Henry de Montherlant; English version by Vivian Cox with Bernard Miles
1978   *Whose Life is it Anyway?* by Brian Clark
1979   *Betrayal* by Harold Pinter
1980   *The Life and Adventures of Nicholas Nickleby* by Charles Dickens; adapted by David Edgar
1981   *Children of a Lesser God* by Mark Medoff
1982   *Another Country* by Julian Mitchell
1983   *Glengarry Glen Ross* by David Mamet
1984   *Benefactors* by Michael Frayn
1985   *Red Noses* by Peter Barnes
1986   *Les Liaisons Dangereuses* by Christopher Hampton
1987   *Serious Money* by Caryl Churchill
1988   *Our Country's Good* by Timberlake Wertenbaker
1989–90   *Racing Demon* by David Hare
1991   *Dancing at Lughnasa* by Brian Friel
1992   *Death and the Maiden* by Ariel Dorfman
1993   *Six Degrees of Separation* by John Guare
1994   *Arcadia* by Tom Stoppard

Best Revival

1991   *Pericles* by William Shakespeare
1992   *Hedda Gabler* by Henrik Ibsen
1993   *An Inspector Calls* by J. B. Priestley
1994   *Machinal* by Sophie Treadwell

Best Entertainment

1991   *Five Guys Named Moe* by Clarke Peters
1992   *Talking Heads* by Alan Bennett
1993   *Travels With My Aunt* by Graham Greene, adapted and directed by Giles Havergal
1994   *A Christmas Carol* by Charles Dickens, adapted and staged by Patrick Stewart

The *Observer* Award for Outstanding Achievement (in Memory of Kenneth Tynan)

1985   Anthony Hopkins for *Pravda*
1986   The Lyric Theatre, Hammersmith for *The House of Bernarda Alba*
1987   Thelma Holt for producing the International Festival at the National Theatre
1988   Maly Theatre of Leningrad for *Stars in the Morning Sky*
1989–90   Declan Donnellan for *Fuente Ovejuna*
1991   Cameron Mackintosh
1992   The Gate Theatre, Notting Hill for *A Season of Classics from the Spanish Golden Age*
1993   The Almeida, Islington

Society of London Theatres' Special Award for Lifetime Achievement

1994   Sam Wanamaker

EVENING STANDARD DRAMA AWARDS

These have been awarded annually since 1955 by the London evening newspaper. The award for Best Director is named after the late Sydney Edwards, the former Arts Editor of the paper.

1984

Best Performance by an Actor   Ian McKellen
Best Performance by an Actress   Maggie Smith

Best Play   *Benefactors* by Michael Frayn
Best Comedy   *Stepping Out* by Richard Harris
Best Musical   *42nd Street*

*The Sydney Edwards Award for Best
Director*   Christopher Morahan for *Wild
Honey*
Most Promising Playwright   Sharman
MacDonald for *When I Was A Girl, I
Used to Scream and Shout*
*Most Outstanding Achievement in
Opera*   Sir Georg Solti
*Most Outstanding Achievement in
Ballet*   Wayne Eagling

1985

Best Performance by an Actor   Antony
Sher
Best Performance by an Actress   Vanessa
Redgrave
Best Play   *Pravda* by David Hare and
Howard Brenton
Best Comedy   *A Chorus of Disapproval*
by Alan Ayckbourn
Best Musical   *Are You Lonesome
Tonight?*
*The Sydney Edwards Award for Best
Director*   Bill Bryden for *The Mysteries*
Most Promising Playwright   Billy Hamon
for *Grafters*
*Most Outstanding Achievement in
Opera*   Nicholas Hytner
Opera Award-Special Award   Lord
Harewood
*Most Outstanding Achievement in
Ballet*   Natalia Makarova

1986

Best Performance by an Actor   Albert
Finney
Best Performance by an Actress   Julia
McKenzie
Best Play   *Les Liaisons Dangereuses* by
Christopher Hampton
Best Comedy   *A Month of Sundays* by
Bob Larbey
Best Musical   *The Phantom of the Opera*
*The Sydney Edwards Award for Best
Director*   Nuria Espert for *The House of
Bernarda Alba*
Most Promising Playwright   Frank
McGuinness for *Observe the Sons of
Ulster Marching to the Somme*
*Most Outstanding Achievement in
Opera*   Harrison Birtwistle

*Most Outstanding Achievement in
Ballet*   Ludmila Semenyaka

1987

Best Performance by an Actor   Michael
Gambon
Best Performance by an Actress   Judi
Dench
Best Play   *A Small Family Business* by
Alan Ayckbourn
Best Comedy   *Serious Money* by Caryl
Churchill
Best Musical   *Follies*
*The Sydney Edwards Award for Best
Director*   Peter Hall for *Antony and
Cleopatra*
Most Promising Playwright   Stephen Bill
for *Curtains*
*Most Outstanding Achievement in
Opera*   English National Opera
*Most Outstanding Achievement in
Ballet*   Lesley Collier

1988

Best Performance by an Actor   Eric
Porter
Best Performance by an Actress   Lindsay
Duncan
Best Play   *Aristocrats* by Brian Friel
Best Comedy   *Lettice and Lovage* by
Peter Shaffer
*The Sydney Edwards Award for Best
Director*   Deborah Warner for *Titus
Andronicus*
Most Promising Playwright   Timberlake
Wertenbaker for *Our Country's Good*
Special Award   National Theatre
*Most Outstanding Achievement in
Opera*   London Philharmonic and
South Bank Centre
*Most Outstanding Achievement in
Ballet*   DV8

1989

Best Performance by an Actor   Ian
McKellen
Best Performance by an Actress   Felicity
Kendal
Best Play   *Ghetto* by Joshua Sobol
Best Comedy   *Henceforward* by Alan
Ayckbourn

Best Musical   Miss Saigon
The Sydney Edwards Award for Best
    Director   Nicholas Hytner for Ghetto
    and Miss Saigon
Most Promising Playwright   Stephen
    Jeffreys for Valued Friends
Special Award   Stephen Sondheim
Most Outstanding Achievement in
    Opera   Luciano Berio
Most Outstanding Achievement in
    Ballet   Viviana Durante

1990

Best Performance by an Actor   Richard
    Harris
Best Performance by an Actress   Josette
    Simon
Best Play   Shadowlands by William
    Nicholson
Best Comedy   Man of the Moment by
    Alan Ayckbourn and Jeffrey Bernard is
    Unwell by Keith Waterhouse
Best Musical   Into the Woods
The Sydney Edwards Award for Best
    Director   Clare McIntyre for My Heart's
    a Suitcase
Most Outstanding Achievement in
    Opera   Edward Downes
Most Outstanding Achievement in
    Ballet   Darcey Bussell

1991

Best Performance by an Actor   John
    Wood
Best Performance by an Actress   Vanessa
    Redgrave
Best Play   Dancing at Lughnasa by Brian
    Friel
Best Comedy   Kvetch by Steven Berkoff
Best Musical   Carmen Jones by Oscar
    Hammerstein II

The Sydney Edwards Award for Best
    Director   Trevor Nunn for Timon of
    Athens
Most Promising Playwright   Rona Munro
    for Bold Girls
Most Outstanding Achievement in
    Opera   Sir Harrison Birtwistle
Most Outstanding Achievement in
    Ballet   Sir Kenneth Macmillan

1992

Best Actor   Nigel Hawthorne
Best Actress   Diana Rigg
Best Play   Angels in America by Tony
    Kushner
Best Comedy   The Rise and Fall of Little
    Voice by Jim Cartwright
Best Musical   Kiss of the Spider Woman
Most Promising Playwright   Philip Ridley
    for The Fastest Clock in the Universe
The Sydney Edwards Award for Best
    Director   Stephen Daldry for An
    Inspector Calls

1993

Best Play   Arcadia by Tom Stoppard
Best Actor   Ian Holm for Moonlight
Best Actress   Fiona Shaw for Machinal
Best Musical   City of Angels
Best Comedy   Jamais Vu by Ken
    Campbell
The Sydney Edwards Award for Best
    Director   Terry Hands for Tamburlaine
    the Great
Most Promising Playwright   Brad Fraser
    for Unidentified Human Remains and
    Simon Donald for The Life of Stuff
The Patricia Rothermere Award   Diana
    Rigg is honoured for services to the
    theatre and a scholarship goes to
    drama student Matthew Evans

THE 'TONY' AWARDS

The top winners in 1994 of these prestigious American awards were:

Best Play   Tony Kushner's Perestroika
Best Musical   Stephen Sondheim's
    Passion
Best Musical Revival   Carousel
Best Play Revival   An Inspector Calls

Best Actor in a Play   Steven Spinella,
    Perestroika
Best Actress in a Play   Diana Rigg, Medea
Best Director of a Play   Stephen Daldry,
    An Inspector Calls

Best Actor in a Musical Boyd Gaines, *She Loves Me*

Best Actress in a Musical Donna Murphy, *Passion*

Best Director of a Musical Nicholas Hytner, *Carousel*

Best Choreography Award Sir Kenneth Macmillan, *Carousel*

Best Featured Actress in a Play Jane Adams, *An Inspector Calls*

Best Costume Design Beauty and the Beast

Lifetime Achievement Hume Cronyn and Jessica Tandy

TIDDLYWINKS

While the children's game of tiddlywinks became popularized in late Victorian times, the adult game only came into being in 1955. In the adult game, much of the time is spent trying to cover up enemy counters with your own, effectively capturing them, rather than attempting to flick the counters into a cup. This leads to a game in which strategy and tactics play a crucial role, as well as the skill and manual dexterity needed to play a counter to where you want it to go. The English Tiddlywinks Association (ETwA) was formed in 1958 to coordinate promotional and tournament activities. In the 1960s the adult game spread across the Atlantic to America, where it took firm hold.

Tiddlywinks, like tennis, can be played as either a pairs game or a singles game. Thus there is a National Singles championship and a National Pairs championship, both of which date from the early 1970s. There are also World Singles and World Pairs titles.

WORLD CHAMPIONSHIPS

There have been 39 World Singles (WS) contests to date:

Jun 1973–Nov 1974	WS1	Bill Renke (USA)
Nov 1974–Aug 1978	WS2–WS5	Severin Drix (USA)
Aug 1978–Feb 1983	WS6–WS14	David Lockwood (USA)
Feb 1983–Feb 1985	WS15–WS19	Larry Kahn (USA)
Feb 1985–Nov 1985	WS20–WS21	Arye Gittelman (USA)
Nov 1985–Dec 1985	WS22	Alan Dean (GB)
Dec 1985–Nov 1986	WS23	Larry Kahn (USA)
Nov 1986–Sep 1988	WS24–WS27	Jonathan Mapley (GB)
Sep 1988–Nov 1990	WS28–WS31	Larry Kahn (USA)
Nov 1990–Nov 1990	WS32–WS33	Andy Purvis (GB)
Nov 1990–Sep 1992	WS34–WS35	Larry Kahn (USA)
Sep 1992–	WS36–WS39	Geoffrey Myers (GB)

There have been 13 World Pairs (WP) contests to date:

Jul 1978–Jun 1983	WP1–WP2	Severin Drix (USA) and Larry Kahn (USA)
Jun 1983–Feb 1984	WP3	Josef Sachs (USA) and Charles Frankston (USA)
Feb 1984–Nov 1988	WP4–WP5	Larry Kahn (USA) and Arye Gittelman (USA)
Nov 1988–Jul 1989	WP6	David Lockwood (USA) and Jim Marlin (USA)
Jul 1989–Jul 1989	WP7	Larry Kahn (USA) and Charles Relle (GB)
Jul 1989–Sep 1990	WP8	David Lockwood (USA) and Jim Marlin (USA)
Sep 1990–	WP9–WP13	Geoffrey Myers and Andy Purvis (GB)

NATIONAL CHAMPIONSHIPS

British Singles

1980	Jonathan Mapley
1981	Charles Relle
1982	David Lockwood (USA)
1983	Jonathan Mapley
1984	Larry Kahn (USA)
1985	Larry Kahn (USA)
1986	Alan Dean
1987	Larry Kahn (USA)
1988	David Lockwood (USA)
1989	Larry Kahn (USA)
1990	David Lockwood (USA)
1991	Geoffrey Myers
1992	Andy Purvis
1993	Patrick Barrie

British Pairs

1980	Jonathan Mapley and David Rose
1981	Nigel Knowles and Charles Relle
1982	Nigel Knowles and Charles Relle
1983	Jonathan Mapley and Alan Dean
1984	Jonathan Mapley and Alan Dean
1985	David Lockwood (USA) and Alan Boyce
1986	Charles Relle and Mike Surridge
1987	Jonathan Mapley and Tony Brennan
1988	Alan Dean and Mike Surridge
1989	Larry Kahn (USA) and Charles Relle
1990	Geoffrey Myers and Andy Purvis
1991	Geoffrey Myers and Andy Purvis
1992	Geoffrey Myers and Andy Purvis
1993	Richard Moore and Patrick Barrie (English Pairs)
	Richard Moore and Julian Wiseman (Scottish Pairs)

TOASTMASTERS

GUILD OF PROFESSIONAL TOASTMASTERS AFTER-DINNER AWARD

This award was the idea of Ivor Spencer, President and Founder of the Guild, to give an incentive to speakers to improve the quality of their speeches. The award was first made in 1967 to Lord Redcliffe-Maud, and the following year to Harold Wilson. Other early winners included Alfred Marks (1970), Clement Freud (1972) and Tommy Trinder (1974). Recent winners were:

1987	Bob Monkhouse (TV presenter)
1988	Lord Tonypandy (former Speaker, House of Commons)
1989	Margaret Thatcher (Prime Minister)
1990	Sir Peter Ustinov (actor)
1991	Denis Norden (TV presenter and scriptwriter)
1992	Bob Monkhouse (the first speaker to win the award a second time)

The founder of the awards, Ivor Spencer, has officiated as a professional Toastmaster at over 1,000 Royal events since his career commenced 39 years ago. It was documented in the House of Commons on 3 February 1992. On 16 February 1994 the Guild of Professional Toastmasters presented him with an award to mark this special achievement.

TOURISM

ENGLAND FOR EXCELLENCE AWARDS

The England for Excellence Awards were created in 1988 by the English Tourist Board to recognize and reward the highest standards of excellence in all major sectors of tourism in England. The coveted Leo statuette, presented each year to winners, has become firmly established as the ultimate accolade in the English tourist industry.

Up to 1994 there had been 72 winners of an England for Excellence Award. Only 3 organizations had won awards on more than one occasion: Bournemouth – Resort of the Year 1989 and 1992; Center Parcs – Tourism Destination Award 1988 and Green Tourism Award 1990; and Butlins – English Travel Company of the Year 1990 and 1992.

Resort of the Year

1988	Torbay
1989	Bournemouth
1990	Eastbourne
1991	*no award*
1992	Bournemouth

Holiday/Travel Company of the Year

1988	English Country Cottages
1989	Warner Holidays
1990	Butlins Holiday Worlds
1991	Alvechurch Boat Centres Ltd

Bed and Breakfast of the Year

1991	Prospect Cottage, Cheltenham, Glos
1992	The Old Rectory, Ripon, N. Yorks
1993	Halfway House, Crayke, York

Caravan Holiday Park of the Year

1991	Merley Court Touring Park, Wimborne, Dorset
1992	Foxhunter Park, Monkton, Kent
1993	New Forest Country Holidays, Godshill, Fordingbridge, Hants

Holiday Destination of the Year

1988	Center Parcs, Notts
1989	Lancaster
1990	Gloucester
1991	South Somerset
1993	Nottingham

Hotel of the Year

1991	Chewton Glen Hotel, New Milton, Hants
1992	The Lanesborough, London
1993	Swallow Hotel, Five Ways, Birmingham

Tourism and the Environment Award

1991	Pensthorpe Waterfowl Park and Nature Reserve, Fakenham, Norfolk
1992	Losehill Hall, Peak National Park Centre, Castleton, Derbyshire
1993	Eco-Hull, British Waterways and Alvechurch Boat Centres Ltd, Scarfield Wharf, Alvechurch, Birmingham

Self-Catering Holiday of the Year

1991	Beacon Hill Farm Holidays, Morpeth, Northumberland
1992	Anglers' Paradise Holidays, Devon
1993	Longlands at Cartmel, Cartmel, Cumbria

Tourism For All Award

1990	Dobwells Family Adventure Park, Cornwall
1991	Yorkshire Mining Museum, Wakefield, W. Yorks
1992	Museum of Science and Industry, Manchester
1993	Plymouth Dome, The Hoe, Plymouth, Devon

Tourism Training Award

1992	Lucketts Travel
1993	White Rose Line, The Boatyard, Lendal Bridge, York

Tourist Information Centre of the Year Award

1988	Sheffield
1989	Somerset Visitor Centre
1990	Norwich
1991	Pickering, N. Yorks
1992	Fontwell, West Sussex
1993	Pickering, N. Yorks

Visitor Attraction of the Year Award

1991	White Cliffs Experience, Dover, Kent

1992	National Fishing Heritage Centre, Great Grimsby, Humberside
1993	Eureka! The Museum for Children, Halifax, W. Yorks

Outstanding/Long Term Contribution to Tourism

1988	Sidney De Haan
1989	Lord Montagu of Beaulieu
1990	Lord Forte
1991	Lord King of Wartnaby
1992	Sir Andrew Lloyd Webber
1993	Sir Bob Scott

TOYS

TOY OF THE YEAR

The original Toy of the Year competition began in 1965 when the first Toy of the Year was won by Mettoy's 007 Aston Martin – a die-cast version of James Bond's car.

1966	Action Man	1980	Rubik's Cube
1967	Spirograph	1981	Rubik's Cube
1968	Sindy	1982	Star Wars figures and vehicles
1969	Hot Wheels	1983	Star Wars figures and vehicles
1970	Sindy	1984	Master of the Universe figures etc
1971	Katie Copycat		
1972	Plasticraft	1985	Transformers
1973	Mastermind (board game)	1986	Transformers
1974	Lego Family kit	1987	Sylvanian Families
1975	Lego Basic kit	1988	Sylvanian Families
1976	Peter Powell Kites	1989	Sylvanian Families
1977	Playpeople	1990	Teenage Hero Turtles
1978	Combine Harvester (Britains)	1991	Nintendo Gameboy
1979	Legoland Space sets	1992	WWF Wrestlers

GOOD TOY GUIDE TOY OF THE YEAR

More recently, the *Good Toy Guide* evaluates toys for children under eight for play and learning potential, good safety standards and durability. Toys are tested by children and parents through the National Association of Toy and Leisure Libraries. The 1993 overall winner was the flip-track rail and road set by Fisher-Price.

TRAVEL

YOUNG TRAVEL WRITER OF THE YEAR

Inaugurated in 1992, the *Daily Telegraph*/Cathay Pacific Airways Young Travel Writer of the Year award provides a great opportunity for budding travel writers to have their work in print. In the 1993 competition, the 6 national finalists, chosen from 450 entries, travelled to Vietnam in March 1993. Each wrote a 1,000-word description of the trip. The judges – Bernice Davison (the *Daily Telegraph*'s Travel Editor), Jim Dunn (on behalf of Cathay Pacific), and Deputy Travel Editor Nigel Richardson – voted Roderick Mackenzie, 25, of Marylebone, London, the overall winner. His article appeared in the paper and he also received commissions for at least three more articles.

The six 1994 finalists travelled to Hong Kong and China. The winner was Richard Young, 22, of Cheltenham.

TRIATHLON

WORLD CHAMPIONSHIPS

Men

1989	Mark Allen (USA)
1990	Greg Welch (Aus)
1991	Miles Stewart (Aus)
1992	Simon Lessing (GB)
1993	Spencer Smith (GB)

Women

1989	Erin Baker (NZ)
1990	Karen Smyers (USA)
1991	Jo-Anne Richie (Can)
1992	Michellie Jones (Aus)
1993	Michellie Jones (Aus)

VIDEOS AND HOME CINEMA

WHAT VIDEO? AWARDS

The annual *What Video?* awards, published in December 1993, reflected the types of video equipment that had landed on the *What Video?* test bench. The following came out with flying colours:

Best Value Camcorder   Panasonic NV-S20

Best Value VCR   Samsung V1375

Best Family Camcorder   JVC GR-AX55

Best VideoPlus VCR   Ferguson FV74LVX

Best Luxury VCR   Mitsubishi HS-M1000

Best Nicam VCR   Toshiba V-813B

Best Luxury Camcorder   Panasonic NV-S85

Best VCR of the Year   Toshiba V813B

Best Camcorder of the Year   Panasonic NV-S85

Pro-Logic Amplifier of the Year   Yamaha DSP-A2070

Best Centre Channel Speaker   Jamo Centre 200

Best Home Cinema Speaker System   Polk Home Cinema Package

VOLLEYBALL

OLYMPIC GAMES

Men

1964	USSR
1968	USSR
1972	Japan
1976	Poland
1980	USSR
1984	USA
1988	USA
1992	Brazil

Women

1964	Japan
1968	USSR
1972	USSR
1976	Japan
1980	USSR
1984	China
1988	USSR
1992	Cuba

WORLD CHAMPIONSHIPS

Men

1949	USSR
1952	USSR
1956	Czechoslovakia
1960	USSR
1962	USSR
1966	Czechoslovakia
1970	East Germany
1974	Poland
1978	USSR
1982	USSR
1986	USA
1990	Italy

Women

1952	USSR
1956	USSR
1960	USSR
1962	Japan
1966	Japan
1970	USSR
1974	Japan
1978	Cuba
1982	China
1986	China
1990	USSR

WATER POLO

OLYMPIC GAMES

1900	Great Britain		1956	Hungary
1904	United States		1960	Italy
1908	Great Britain		1964	Hungary
1912	Great Britain		1968	Yugoslavia
1920	Great Britain		1972	Soviet Union
1924	France		1976	Hungary
1928	Germany		1980	Soviet Union
1932	Hungary		1984	Yugoslavia
1936	Hungary		1988	Yugoslavia
1948	Italy		1992	Italy
1952	Hungary			

WATER SKIING

WORLD CHAMPIONSHIPS

Men

1949	Christian Jourdan (Fra) and Guy de Clerk (Bel)
1950	Dick Pope Jr (USA)
1953	Alfredo Mendoza (USA)
1955	Alfredo Mendoza (USA)
1957	Joe Cash (USA)
1959	Chuck Stearns (USA)
1961	Bruno Zaccardi (Ita)
1963	Billy Spencer (USA)
1965	Roland Hillier (USA)
1967	Mike Suyderhoud (USA)
1969	Mike Suyderhoud (USA)
1971	George Athans (Can)
1973	George Athans (Can)
1975	Carlos Suarez (Ven)
1977	Mike Hazelwood (UK)
1979	Joel McClintock (Can)
1981	Sammy Duvall (USA)
1983	Sammy Duvall (USA)
1985	Sammy Duvall (USA)
1987	Sammy Duvall (USA)
1989	Patrice Martin (Fra)
1991	Patrice Martin (Fra)
1993	Patrice Martin (Fra)

Women

1949	Willa Worthington (USA)
1950	Willa McGuire (USA)
1953	Leah Marie Rawls (USA)
1955	Willa McGuire (USA)
1957	Marina Doria (Swi)
1959	Vickie Van Hook (USA)
1961	Sylvie Hulsemann (Lux)
1963	Jeanette Brown (USA)
1965	Liz Allan (USA)
1967	Jeanette Stewart-Wood (UK)
1969	Liz Allan (USA)
1971	Christy Weir (USA)
1973	Lisa St John (USA)
1975	Liz Shetter (née Allan) (USA)
1977	Cindy Todd (USA)
1979	Cindy Todd (USA)
1981	Karin Roberge (USA)
1983	Ana Maria Carrasco (Ven)
1985	Karen Neville (Aus)
1987	Deena Brush (USA)
1989	Deena Mapple (née Brush) (USA)
1991	Karen Neville (Aus)
1993	Nataly Rumiantseva (Rom)

WEIGHTLIFTING

OLYMPIC GAMES

Flyweight (up to 52kg)

1972	Zygmunt Smalacerz (Pol)
1976	Aleksandr Voronin (USSR)
1980	Kanybek Osmonoliev (USSR)
1984	Zeng Guoqiang (Chn)
1988	Sevdalim Marinov (Bul)
1992	Ivan Ivanov (Bul)

Bantamweight (up to 56kg)

1948	Joseph de Pietro (USA)
1952	Ivan Udodov (USSR)
1956	Charles Vinci (USA)
1960	Charles Vinci (USA)
1964	Aleksey Vakhonin (USSR)
1968	Mohammad Nassiri (Irn)
1972	Imre Foldi (Hun)
1976	Norair Nurikyan (Bul)
1980	Daniel Nunez (Cub)
1984	Wu Shude (Chn)
1988	Oleg Mirzoian (USSR)
1992	Chun Byung-Kwan (SKo)

Featherweight (up to 60kg)

1920	Frans de Haes (Bel)
1924	Pierino Gabetti (Ita)
1928	Franz Andrysek (Aut)
1932	Raymond Suvigny (Fra)
1936	Anthony Terlazzo (USA)
1948	Mohmoud Fayad (Egy)
1952	Rafael Chimishkyan (USSR)
1956	Isaac Berger (USA)
1960	Yevgeniy Minayev (USSR)
1964	Yoshinobu Miyake (Jap)
1968	Yoshinobu Miyake (Jap)
1972	Norair Nurikyan (Bul)
1976	Nikolai Kolesnikov (USSR)
1980	Viktor Mazin (USSR)
1984	Chen Weiquiang (Chn)
1988	Naim Suleymanoglu (Tur)
1992	Naim Suleymanoglu (Tur)

Lightweight (up to 67.5kg)

1920	Alfred Neuland (Est)
1924	Edmond Decottignies (Fra)
1928	Kurt Helbig (Ger) / Hans Haas (Aut)
1932	René Duverger (Fra)
1936	Anwar M. Meshbah (Egy) / Robert Fein (Aut)
1948	Ibrahim Shams (Egy)
1952	Tommy Kono (USA)
1956	Igor Rybak (USSR)
1960	Viktor Bushuyev (USSR)
1964	Waldemar Baszanowski (Pol)
1968	Waldemar Baszanowski (Pol)
1972	Mukharbi Kirzhinov (USSR)
1976	Pyotr Korol (USSR)
1980	Yanko Rusev (Bul)
1984	Jing Yuan Yao (Chn)
1988	Joachim Kunz (GDR)
1992	Israil Militosian (CIS)

Middleweight (up to 75kg)

1920	Henri Gance (Fra)
1924	Carlo Galimberti (Ita)
1928	Roger François (Fra)
1932	Rudolf Ismayr (Ger)
1936	Khadr El Thouni (Egy)
1948	Frank Spellman (USA)
1952	Peter George (USA)
1956	Fyodor Bogdanovski (USSR)
1960	Aleksandr Kurinov (USSR)
1964	Hans Zdrazila (Cze)
1968	Viktor Kurentsov (USSR)

1972	Yordan Bikov (Bul)
1976	Yordan Bikov (Bul)
1980	Asen Zlatev (Bul)
1984	Karl-Heinz Radschinsky (FRG)
1988	Borislav Guidikov (Bul)
1992	Fyodor Kassapu (CIS)

Light-heavyweight (up to 82.5kg)

1920	Ernest Cadine (Fra)
1924	Charles Rigoulot (Fra)
1928	Said Nosseir (Egy)
1932	Louis Hostin (Fra)
1936	Louis Hostin (Fra)
1948	Stanley Stanczyk (USA)
1952	Trofim Lomakin (USSR)
1956	Tommy Kono (USA)
1960	Ireneusz Palinski (Pol)
1964	Rudolf Plyukfelder (USSR)
1968	Boris Selitsky (USSR)
1972	Leif Jenssen (Nor)
1976	Valeriy Shary (USSR)
1980	Yurik Vardanyan (USSR)
1984	Petre Becheru (Rom)
1988	Israil Arsamakov (USSR)
1992	Pyrros Dimas (Gre)

Middle-heavyweight (up to 90kg)

1952	Norbert Schemansky (USA)
1956	Arkadiy Vorobyev (USSR)
1960	Arkadiy Vorobyev (USSR)
1964	Vladimir Golovanov (USSR)
1968	Kaarlo Kangasniemi (Fin)
1972	Andom Nikolov (Bul)
1976	David Rigert (USSR)
1980	Peter Baczako (Hun)
1984	Nicu Vlad (Rom)
1988	Anatoliy Khrapatu (USSR)
1992	Kakhi Kakhiashvili (CIS)

Middle-heavyweight (up to 100kg)

1980	Ota Zaremba (Cze)
1984	Rolf Milser (FRG)
1988	Pavel Kouznetsov (USSR)
1992	Viktor Tregubov (CIS)

Heavyweight (up to 110kg)

1920	Filippo Bottino (Ita)
1924	Giuseppe Tonani (Ita)
1928	Josef Strassberger (Ger)
1932	Jaroslav Skobla (Cze)
1936	Josef Manger (Aut)
1948	John Davis (USA)

1952	John Davis (USA)	1988	Yuri Zakharevich (USSR)
1956	Paul Anderson (USA)	1992	Ronny Weller (Ger)
1960	Yuriy Vlasov (USSR)		
1964	Leonid Zhabotinsky (USSR)		**Super-heavyweight (over 110kg)**
1968	Leonid Zhabotinsky (USSR)	1972	Vasiliy Alexeyev (USSR)
1972	Jan Talts (USSR)	1976	Vasiliy Alexeyev (USSR)
1976	Yuriy Zaitsev (USSR)	1980	Sultan Rakhmanov (USSR)
1980	Leonid Taranenko (USSR)	1984	Dino Lukin (Aus)
1984	Norberto Oberburger (Ita)	1988	Alexander Kurlovich (USSR)
		1992	Alexander Kurlovich (CIS)

WINE

ENGLISH WINE OF THE YEAR

Since the 1970s, the English Vineyards Association has organized and administered this competition. The competition was initiated in 1974 with the Gore Browne Trophy (a memorial to a pioneer in the revived English viticulture) as its prestigious supreme trophy awarded to the English Wine of the Year. Winning wines (and producers in brackets) since 1980 were:

1980	Magdelen Rivaner '79 (P. Cook, Norfolk)	1987	Biddenden Ortega '86 (R. Barnes, Kent)
1981	Tenterden Seyval '80 (S. Skelton, Kent)	1988	Chiltern Valley Old Luxters '87 (D. Ealand, Oxon)
1982	Wootton, Schonburger '81 (C. L. B. Gillespie, Somerset)	1989	Carr Taylor Reichensteiner '88 (D. Carr Taylor, Sussex)
1983	Lamberhurst Huxelrebe '82 (K. McAlpine, Kent)	1990	Lamberhurst Schonburger '88 (K. McAlpine, Kent)
1984	Barton Manor Dry '83 (A. H. Goddard, Isle of Wight)	1991	Tenterden Special Reserve '89 (M. Kay, Kent)
1985	Lamberhurst Schonburger '84 (K. McAlpine, Kent)	1992	Thames Valley Botrytis '91 (J. Leighton, Berks)
1986	Wootton Seyval '85 (C. L. B. Gillespie, Somerset)	1993	Thames Valley Fumé '91 (J. Leighton, Berks)

WINE BAR OF THE YEAR

Organized, along with the London Pub of the Year, by the *Evening Standard*, is the annual competition to find the capital's wine bar of the year. The 1993 winner was the Fire Station, Waterloo (a refurbished old LCC Fire Station, originally built in 1910, now run by Michael Richards).

WHICH WINE GUIDE SPECIALIST WINE MERCHANT OF THE YEAR

The 1993 winners were:

| *Bordeaux* | Justerini and Brooks | *Rhône* | Croque-en-Bouche |
| *Burgundy* | Adam Bancroft | *Italian* | Valvolla and Crolla |

German Adnam	*High Street Chain* Thresher
Spanish Moreno	*Best Mail Order Merchant* Lay and
Australian Oddbins	Wheeler
Fine Wines Farr Vintners	*Best Independent Merchant* D. Byrne & Co
Best Supermarket Waitrose	*Best Out of Town* B. H. Wines

WINE-TASTING

THE DAILY TELEGRAPH/THRESHERS WINE TASTER OF THE YEAR

The 1993 contest for this prestige title, which is sponsored by Threshers, was held at the Whitbread Brewery in the City of London. The victor, Jonathan Lane of Shrewsbury, beat 23 other finalists.

The 24 finalists sat in the galleried Smeatons Hall at the brewery to taste wines ranging from Ernest and Julio Gallo White Grenache, retailing at about £3.59, to Marques d'Grinon, an acclaimed Cabernet Sauvignon selling at about £10.49.

The judges were Oz Clarke, *Daily Telegraph* wine correspondent, Robert Joseph, *Sunday Telegraph* wine correspondent, Miss Jo Standen, a master of wine and buyer for Thresher, and Mr Kim Tidy, Thresher's head buyer.

The winner receives a two-week trip to New Zealand plus £500 of wines from Threshers. Mr Lane defeated second-placed Jacqui Dewdney – literally by a nose!

WOMEN

WOMEN OF ACHIEVEMENT AWARD

Each year, *Cosmopolitan* magazine organizes prestigious awards for its Women of Achievement. The winner of the top award receives a prize of £5,000. The awards are for women whose commitment and hard work make them shine in their chosen field. Among the finalists in 1993 were a helicopter instructor, the director of a record company, the owner of a vegetarian café and a harpsichordist. The judges included Dr Mary Archer, Baroness Blackstone, Helena Kennedy QC and Sue MacGregor (presenter with BBC Radio 4's *Today*).

For the overall winner the judges' overwhelming vote went to Pragna Patel, 33, of Southall Black Sisters for her campaigning work for women's rights.

The category winners were:

Creative Arts	Sandy Powell (33)	Costume Designer
The Professions	Sian Griffiths (33)	Sub Officer, London Fire Brigade
Voluntary Work	Charlotte Fadipe (29)	Founder, The Black Network
Communication	Penny Marshall (31)	Reporter, ITN
Education	Alison Laver (28)	Senior Lecturer, Canterbury Christchurch College

Entrepreneurship	Diane Harding (30)	Managing Director, Wilson Wilcox Furnishings
Sport {	Alison Kevin (26)	Rugby Football Union
	Rebecca Stephens (32)	Mountaineer
Performing Arts {	Tilda Swinton (32)	Actress
	Meera Syal ((32)	Writer and Actress
Science and Technology	Helen Sharman (30)	Astronaut
Sales, Marketing and Retail	Caroline Gilby (30)	Senior Buyer, Augustus Barnett
Industry	Lorna Marie Tucker (29)	Project Manager, Westland Helicopters

EUROPEAN WOMEN OF ACHIEVEMENT AWARDS

These awards are presented at an annual lunch in Piccadilly organized by the European Union of Women. They recognize an outstanding achievement by women in a variety of areas, including business.

1991

Fiona Colquhoun　Director of Personnel for Cable and Wireless PLC

Patricia Grant　Managing Director of Nurforst Ltd

Kathleen O'Donovan　Finance Director BTR

1992

Jullet Lodge　Professor of European Politics, University of Hull

Maureen Tomison　Chairman, Decision Makers Ltd

Ann Gloag　Managing Director, Stage Coach Holdings PLC

1993

Helen Bamber (68)　Charity Director, for a lifetime's work with the victims of torture from Belsen concentration camp to Bosnia. Founder, 1985, Medical Foundation for the Care of Victims of Torture

Elizabeth Vann (34)　Managing Director, Baby Organix. Ms Vann, who is based in Poole, Dorset, won the category for smaller businesses for her gourmet baby food company, which she started in 1991

Anke Harris (47)　Managing Director, Mapline Engineering Gundy Harris, an engineering design company. Mrs Harris, who was born in Germany, launched her company 6 years ago and the number of her staff has grown from 40 to 111. Winner of the large business category

Rebecca Stephens (31)　Collecting a special award for 'scaling new heights for women' was Miss Rebecca Stephens, who became the first British woman to reach the summit of Mount Everest in May 1993

WORKING WOMEN MEAN BUSINESS

Sponsored by *Options* magazine and Hutchison Telecom, these annual awards reward the achievement of women in the business world. Awards are given in two categories – those women who work within a business organization and those women who run their own businesses.

The 1993 joint winners were:

Rebecca Jenkins (32)　A former lorry driver from Bristol who is now managing director of the Bristol-based Lane Group, a distribution and logistics company. She won in the category for women who work within an organization

Fiona Price (33)   Managing director of Fiona Price & Partners, a firm of independent financial advisers based in Covent Garden. She won in the class for women who run their own business

---

THE TIMES/VEUVE CLICQUOT BUSINESSWOMAN OF THE YEAR

This award, founded in 1973, is sponsored by *The Times* Newspaper Ltd and Veuve Clicquot Champagne as an accolade for those, often unknown, women who have reached the top in British business. Until 1978 the award was entitled *The Times* Veuve Clicquot Champagne Award for A Woman in a Man's World. The first winner of the award was Stella Brumell, Managing Director, Benford Ltd. manufacturers of concrete mixers. The 1994 winner was Jan Fletcher, 38, who runs The Fletcher Group, a motor franchise group based in Leeds.

WRESTLING

OLYMPIC GAMES FREESTYLE

Light-flyweight (up to 48kg)

1904	Robert Curry (USA)
1972	Roman Dmitriyev (USSR)
1976	Hassan Issaev (Bul)
1980	Claudio Pollio (Ita)
1984	Robert Weaver (USA)
1988	Takashi Kobayashi (Jap)
1992	Kil Il (NKo)

Flyweight (up to 52kg)

1904	George Mehnert (USA)
1948	Lennart Viitala (Fin)
1952	Hasan Gamici (Tur)
1956	Mirian Tsalkalamanidze (USSR)
1960	Ahmet Bilek (Tur)
1964	Yoshikatsu Yoshida (Jap)
1968	Shigeo Nakata (Jap)
1972	Kiyomi Kato (Jap)
1976	Kiyomi Kato (Jap)
1980	Anatoliy Beloglazov (USSR)
1984	Saban Trstena (Yug)
1988	Mitsuru Sato (Jap)
1992	Li Hak-Son (NKo)

Bantamweight (up to 57kg)

1904	Isidor Niflot (USA)
1908	George Mehnert (USA)
1924	Kustaa Pihlajamaki (Fin)
1928	Kaarlo Makinen (Fin)
1932	Robert Pearce (USA)
1936	Odon Zombori (Hun)
1948	Nasuh Akar (Tur)
1952	Shohachi Ishii (Jap)
1956	Mustafa Dagistanli (Tur)
1960	Terrence McCann (USA)
1964	Yojiro Uetake (Jap)
1968	Yojiro Uetake (Jap)
1972	Hideaki Yanagida (Jap)
1976	Vladimir Yumin (USSR)
1980	Sergey Beloglazov (USSR)
1984	Hideaki Tomiyama (Jap)
1988	Sergey Beloglazov (USSR)
1992	Alejandro Diaz (Cub)

Featherweight (up to 62kg)

1904	Benjamin Bradshaw (USA)
1908	George Dole (USA)
1920	Charles Ackerly (USA)
1924	Robin Reed (USA)
1928	Allie Morrison (USA)
1932	Hermanni Pihlajamaki (Fin)
1936	Kustaa Pihlajamaki (Fin)
1948	Gazanfer Bilge (Tur)
1952	Bayram Sit (Tur)
1956	Shozo Sasahara (Jap)
1960	Mustafa Dagistanli (Tur)
1964	Osamu Watanabe (Jap)
1968	Musaaki Kaneko (Jap)
1972	Zagalav Abdulbekov (USSR)
1976	Jung-Mo Yang (SKo)

1980	Magomedgasan Abushev (USSR)
1984	Randy Lewis (USA)
1988	John Smith (USA)
1992	John Smith (USA)

Lightweight (up to 68kg)

1904	Otto Roehm (USA)
1908	George de Relwyskow (GB)
1920	Kalle Anttila (Fin)
1924	Russell Vis (USA)
1928	Osvald Kapp (Est)
1932	Charles Pacome (Fra)
1936	Károly Kárpáti (Hun)
1948	Celál Atik (Tur)
1952	Olle Anderberg (Swe)
1956	Emamali Habibi (Iran)
1960	Shelby Wilson (USA)
1964	Enyu Valchev (Bul)
1968	Abdollah Movahed Ardabili (Irn)
1972	Dan Gable (USA)
1976	Pavel Pinigin (USSR)
1980	Saipulla Absaidov (USSR)
1984	In-Tak You (SKo)
1988	Arsen Fadzeyev (USSR)
1992	Arsen Fadzeyev (CIS)

Welterweight (up to 74kg)

1904	Charles Erickson (USA)
1924	Hermann Gehri (Swi)
1928	Arvo Haavisto (Fin)
1932	Jack Van Bebber (USA)
1936	Frank Lewis (USA)
1948	Yasar Dogu (Tur)
1952	William Smith (USA)
1956	Mitsuo Ikeda (Jap)
1960	Douglas Blubaugh (USA)
1964	Ismail Ogan (Tur)
1968	Mahmut Atalay (Tur)
1972	Wayne Wells (USA)
1976	Jiichiro Date (Jap)
1980	Valentin Raitchev (Bul)
1984	David Schulz (USA)
1988	Kenneth Monday (USA)
1992	Park Joon-Scon (SKo)

Middleweight (up to 82kg)

1908	Stanley Bacon (GB)
1920	Eino Leino (Fin)
1924	Fritz Hagmann (Swi)
1928	Ernst Kyburz (Swi)
1932	Ivar Johansson (Swe)
1936	Emile Poilvé (Fra)
1948	Glen Brand (USA)
1952	David Tsimakuridze (USSR)
1956	Nikola Stanchev (Bul)
1960	Hasan Gungor (Tur)
1964	Prodan Gardschev (Bul)
1968	Boris Gurevich (USSR)
1972	Levan Tediashvili (USSR)
1976	John Peterson (USA)
1980	Ismail Abilov (Bul)
1984	Mark Schultz (USA)
1988	Han Myung-Woo (SKo)
1992	Kevin Jackson (USA)

Light-heavyweight (up to 90kg)

1920	Anders Larsson (Swe)
1924	John Spellman (USA)
1928	Thure Sjostedt (Swe)
1932	Peter Mehringer (USA)
1936	Knut Fridell (Swe)
1948	Henry Wittenberg (USA)
1952	Wiking Palm (Swe)
1956	Gholam Takhti Reza (Irn)
1960	Ismet Atli (Tur)
1964	Aleksandr Medved (USSR)
1968	Ahmet Ayik (Tur)
1972	Ben Peterson (USA)
1976	Levan Tediashvili (USSR)
1980	Sanasar Oganesyan (USSR)
1984	Ed Banach (USA)
1988	Makharbek Khadartsev (USSR)
1992	Makharbek Khadartsev (CIS)

Mid-heavyweight (up to 100kg)

1904	Bernhuff Hansen (USA)
1908	George O'Kelly (GB)
1920	Robert Roth (Swi)
1924	Harry Steel (USA)
1928	Johan Richthoff (Swe)
1932	Johan Richthoff (Swe)
1936	Kristjan Palusalu (Est)
1948	Gyula Bóbis (Hun)
1952	Arsen Mekokishvili (USSR)
1956	Hamit Kaplan (Tur)
1960	Wilfried Dietrich (Ger)
1964	Aleksandr Ivanitskiy (USSR)
1968	Aleksandr Medved (USSR)
1972	Ivan Yarygin (USSR)
1976	Ivan Yarygin (USSR)
1980	Ilya Mate (USSR)
1984	Lou Banach (USA)
1988	Vasile Puscasu (Rom)
1992	Leri Khabelov (CIS)

Super-heavyweight (over 100kg)

1972	Aleksandr Medved (USSR)
1976	Soslan Andiyev (USSR)
1980	Soslan Andiyev (USSR)
1984	Bruce Baumgartner (USA)
1988	David Gobedzhishvili (USSR)
1992	Bruce Baumgartner (USA)

OLYMPIC GAMES GRECO–ROMAN

Light-flyweight (up to 48kg)

1972	Gheorghe Berceanu (Rom)
1976	Aleksey Schumakov (USSR)
1980	Zaksylik Ushkempirov (USSR)
1984	Vincenzo Maenza (Ita)
1988	Vincenzo Maenza (Ita)
1992	Oleg Kucherenko (CIS)

Flyweight (up to 52kg)

1948	Pietro Lombardi (Ita)
1952	Boris Gurevich (USSR)
1956	Nikolay Solovyov (USSR)
1960	Dumitru Pirvulescu (Rom)
1964	Tsutomu Hanahara (Jap)
1968	Peter Kirov (Bul)
1972	Peter Kirov (Bul)
1976	Vitaliy Konstantinov (USSR)
1980	Vakhtang Blagidze (USSR)
1984	Atsuji Miyahara (Jap)
1988	Jon Ronningen (Nor)
1992	Jon Ronningen (Nor)

Bantamweight (up to 57kg)

1924	Eduard Putsep (Est)
1928	Kurt Leucht (Ger)
1932	Jakob Brendel (Ger)
1936	Màrton Lörincz (Hun)
1948	Kurt Pettersén (Swe)
1952	Imre Hódos (Hun)
1956	Konstantin Vyrupayev (USSR)
1960	Oleg Karaveyev (USSR)
1964	Masamitsu Ichiguchi (Jap)
1968	János Varga (Hun)
1972	Rustem Kazakov (USSR)
1976	Pertti Ukkola (Fin)
1980	Shamil Serikov (USSR)
1984	Pasquale Passarelli (FRG)
1988	Andras Sike (Hun)
1992	An Hau-Bong (SKo)

Featherweight (up to 62kg)

1912	Kaarlo Koskelo (Fin)
1920	Oskari Friman (Fin)
1924	Kalle Antila (Fin)
1928	Voldemar Väli (Est)
1932	Giovanni Gozzi (Ita)
1936	Yasar Erkan (Tur)
1948	Mehmet Oktav (Tur)
1952	Yakov Punkin (USSR)
1956	Rauno Makinen (Fin)
1960	Müzahir Sille (Tur)
1964	Imre Polyák (Hun)
1968	Roman Rurua (USSR)
1972	Gheorghi Markov (Bul)
1976	Kazimierz Lipién (Pol)
1980	Stylianos Migiakis (Gre)
1984	Weon-Kee Kim (SKo)
1988	Kamadar Madjidov (USSR)
1992	Akif Pirim (Tur)

Lightweight (up to 68kg)

1908	Enrico Porro (Ita)
1912	Eemil Väre (Fin)
1920	Eemil Väre (Fin)
1924	Oskari Friman (Fin)
1928	Lajos Keresztes (Hun)
1932	Erik Malmberg (Swe)
1936	Lauri Koskela (Fin)
1948	Gustaf Freij (Swe)
1952	Schazam Safin (USSR)
1956	Kyösti Lehtonen (Fin)
1960	Avtandil Koridze (USSR)
1964	Kazim Ayvaz (Tur)
1968	Munji Mumemura (Jap)
1972	Shamil Khisamutdinov (USSR)
1976	Suren Nalbandyan (USSR)
1980	Stefan Rusu (Rom)
1984	Vlado Lisjak (Yug)
1988	Levon Dzhulfalakyan (USSR)
1992	Attila Repka (Hun)

Welterweight (up to 74kg)

1932	Ivar Johansson (Swe)
1936	Rudolf Svedberg (Swe)
1948	Gösta Andersson (Swe)
1952	Miklós Szelvási (Hun)
1956	Mithat Bayrak (Tur)
1960	Mithat Bayrak (Tur)
1964	Anatoliy Kolesov (USSR)

1968	Rudolf Vesper (GDR)	1960	Tevfik Kis (Tur)
1972	Vitezslav Mácha (Cze)	1964	Boyan Radev (Bul)
1976	Anatoliy Bykov (USSR)	1968	Boyan Radev (Bul)
1980	Ferenc Kocsis (Hun)	1972	Valeriy Rezantsev (USSR)
1984	Jouko Salomaki (Fin)	1976	Valeriy Rezantsev (USSR)
1988	Kim Young-Nam (SKo)	1980	Norbert Növényi (Hun)
1992	Mnatsakan Iskandanan (CIS)	1984	Steven Fraser (USA)
		1988	Atanas Komchev (Bul)
		1992	Maik Bullmann (Ger)

Middleweight (up to 82kg)

1908	Frithiof Märtensson (Fin)
1912	Claes Johansson (Swe)
1920	Carl Westergren (Swe)
1924	Edvard Westerlund (Fin)
1928	Väinö Kokkinen (Fin)
1932	Väinö Kokkinen (Fin)
1936	Ivar Johansson (Swe)
1948	Axel Grönberg (Swe)
1952	Axel Grönberg (Swe)
1956	Givy Kartoziya (USSR)
1960	Dimiter Dobrev (Bul)
1964	Branislav Simic (Yug)
1968	Lothar Metz (GDR)
1972	Csaba Hegedus (Hun)
1976	Momir Petkovic (Yug)
1980	Gennadiy Korban (USSR)
1984	Ion Draica (Rom)
1988	Mikhail Mamiachvili (USSR)
1992	Peter Farkas (Hun)

Heavyweight (up to 100kg)

1896	Carl Schuhmann (Ger)
1908	Richárd Weisz (Hun)
1912	Yrjö Saarela (Fin)
1920	Adolf Lindfors (Fin)
1924	Henri Deglane (Fra)
1928	Rudolf Svensson (Swe)
1932	Carl Westergren (Swe)
1936	Kristjan Paluslu (Est)
1948	Ahmet Kirecci (Tur)
1952	Johannes Kotkas (USSR)
1956	Anatoliy Parfenov (USSR)
1960	Ivan Bogdan (USSR)
1964	István Kozma (Hun)
1968	István Kozma (Hun)
1972	Nicolae Martinescu (Rom)
1976	Nicolay Balboshin (USSR)
1980	Gheorghi Raikov (Bul)
1984	Vasile Andrei (Rom)
1988	Andrzej Wronski (Pol)
1992	Hector Milian (Cub)

Light-heavyweight (up to 90kg)

1908	Verner Weckman (Fin)
1912	*no winner declared*
1920	Claes Johansson (Swe)
1924	Carl Westergren (Swe)
1928	Ibrahim Moustafa (Egy)
1932	Rudolf Svensson (Swe)
1936	Axel Cadier (Swe)
1948	Karl-Eric Nilsson (Swe)
1952	Koelpo Gröndahl (Fin)
1956	Valentin Nikolayev (USSR)

Super-heavyweight (over 100kg)

1972	Anatoliy Roschin (USSR)
1976	Aleksandr Kolchinsky (USSR)
1980	Aleksandr Kolchinsky (USSR)
1984	Jeffrey Blatnick (USA)
1988	Alexandr Karelin (USSR)
1992	Alexandr Karelin (CIS)

YACHTING

ADMIRAL'S CUP

1957	Great Britain	1967	Australia	1977	Great Britain
1959	Great Britain	1969	USA	1979	Australia
1961	USA	1971	Great Britain	1981	Great Britain
1963	Great Britain	1973	West Germany	1983	West Germany
1965	Great Britain	1975	Great Britain	1985	West Germany

1985	West Germany	1993	Germany	1991	France
1987	New Zealand	1985	West Germany	1993	Germany
1989	Great Britain	1987	New Zealand		
1991	France	1989	Great Britain		

BRITISH STEEL 'ROUND THE WORLD' RACE

	Winning skipper/boat
1973/4	Ramon Carlin (Mex) *Sayula II*
1977/8	Cornelius van Rietschoten (Hol) *Flyer*
1981/2	Cornelius van Rietschoten (Hol) *Flyer II*

1985/6	Pierre Fehlmann (Swi) *UBS Switzerland*
1989/90	Peter Blake (NZ) *Steinlager*
1993/4	John Chittenden (UK) *Nuclear Electric*

AMERICA'S CUP

	Winning skipper/boat
1870	Andrew Comstock (USA) *Magic*
1871	Nelson Comstock (USA) *Columbia* / Sam Greenwood (USA) *Sappho*
1876	Josephus Williams (USA) *Madeleine*
1881	Nathaniel Clock (USA) *Mischief*
1885	Aubrey Crocker (USA) *Puritan*
1886	Martin Stone (USA) *Mayflower*
1887	Henry Haff (USA) *Volunteer*
1893	William Hansen (USA) *Vigilant*
1895	Henry Haff (USA) *Defender*
1899	Charlie Barr (USA) *Columbia*
1901	Charlie Barr (USA) *Columbia*
1903	Charlie Barr (USA) *Reliance*
1920	Charles Adams (USA) *Resolute*
1930	Harold Vanderbilt (USA) *Enterprise*
1934	Harold Vanderbilt (USA) *Rainbow*

1937	Harold Vanderbilt (USA) *Ranger*
1958	Briggs Cunningham (USA) *Columbia*
1962	Emil Mosbacher Jr (USA) *Weatherly*
1964	Bob Bavier Jr (USA) *Constellation*
1967	Emil Mosbacher Jr (USA) *Intrepid*
1970	Bill Ficker (USA) *Intrepid*
1974	Ted Hood (USA) *Courageous*
1977	Ted Turner (USA) *Courageous*
1980	Dennis Conner (USA) *Freedom*
1983	John Bertrand (Aus) *Australia II*
1987	Dennis Conner (USA) *Stars & Stripes*
1988	Dennis Conner (USA) *Stars & Stripes*
1992	Bill Koch (USA) *America 3*

JULES VERNE TROPHY

In April 1994 this trophy, for the fastest circumnavigation of the world under sail, was awarded to *ENZA*, a 92ft catamaran, skippered by Britain's Robin Knox-Johnston and New Zealand's Peter Blake. *ENZA*'s voyage lasted 74 days.

OLYMPIC GAMES

Soling

1972	USA	1984	USA
1976	Denmark	1988	East Germany
1980	Denmark	1992	Denmark

Star

1932	Gilbert Gray and Andrew Libano Jnr (USA)
1936	Peter Bischoff and Hans-Joachim Weise (Ger)
1948	Hilary Smart and Paul Smart (USA)
1952	Nicolo Rode and Agostino Straulino (Ita)
1956	Lawrence Low and Herbert Williams (USA)
1960	Timir Pinegin and Fyodor Shukov (USSR)
1964	Cecil Cooke and Durward Knowles (Bah)
1968	Peter Barrett and Lowell North (USA)
1972	John Anderson and David Forbes (Aus)
1980	Valentine Mankin and Aleksandr Muzychenko (USSR)
1984	Bill Buchan and Stephen Erickson (USA)
1988	Michael McIntyre and Bryn Vaile (GB)
1992	Mark Reynolds and Hal Haenel (USA)

Flying Dutchman

1956	John Cropp and Peter Mander (NZ)
1960	Bergvall and Peter Lunde Jur (Nor)
1964	Helmer Pederson and Earle Wells (NZ)
1968	Iain Macdonald-Smith and Rodney Pattisson (GB)
1972	Christopher Davies and Rodney Pattisson (GB)
1976	Eckert Diesch and Jorg Diesch (FRG)
1980	Alejandro Abascal and Miguel Noguer (Spa)
1984	William Carl Buchan and Jonathan McKee (USA)
1988	Christian Gronborg and Jorgen Bojsen-Moeller (Den)
1992	Luis Doresto and Domingo Manrique (Spa)

Tornado

1976	John Osborn and Reg White (GB)
1980	Lars Bjorkstrom and Alexandre Welter (Bra)
1984	Rex Sellers and Christopher Timms (NZ)
1988	Nicholas Henrad and Jean-Yves Le Deroff (Fra)
1992	Yves Leday and Nicolas Henrad (Fra)

Finn

1920	Franciscus Hin and Johannes Hin (Hol)
1920	Francis Richards and T. Hedberg (GB)
1924	Leon Huybrechts (Bel)
1928	Sven Thorell (Swe)
1932	Jacques Lebrun (Fra)
1936	Daniel Kagchelland (Hol)
1948	Paul Elvstrom (Den)
1952	Paul Elvstrom (Den)
1956	Paul Elvstrom (Den)
1960	Paul Elvstrom (Den)
1964	Willi Kuhweide (Ger)
1968	Valentin Mankin (Fra)
1972	Serge Maury (Fra)
1976	Jochen Schumann (Ger)
1980	Esko Rechardt (Fin)
1984	Russell Coutts (NZ)
1988	Jose-Luis Doreste (Spa)
1992	Jose Maria van der Ploeg (Spa)

470 Class

1976	Harro Bode and Frank Hubner (FRG)
1980	Eduardo Pendo and Marcos Soares (Bra)
1984	Jose-Luis Doreste and Roberto Malina (Spa)
1988	Thierry Peponnet and Luc Pillot (Fra)
1992	Jorge Calafar and Francisco Sauchez (Spa)

Boardsailing

1984	Stephen van den Berg (Hol)
1988	Bruce Kendall (NZ)
1992	Franck David (Fra)

Women's 470 Class

1988	Lynne Jewell and Alison Jolly (USA)
1992	Theresa Zabell and Patricia Guerra (Spa)

INDEX

Subject headings are in capitals.